NEWCOMER'S
HANDBOOK®

FOR MOVING TO AND LIVING IN

Chicago

Including Evanston, Oak Park, Schaumburg,
Wheaton, and Naperville

4th Edition

FIRST BOOKS®

6750 SW Franklin
Portland, OR 97223
503-968-6777
www.firstbooks.com

4th edition

Newcomer's Handbook® and First Books® are registered trademarks of First Books.

Contributors: Deborah Bosi, Susie Redfern, Thor Ringler, Danelle Till, Mark Wukas
Series Editor: Bernadette Duperron
Publisher: Jeremy Solomon
Design and composition: Erin Johnson
Maps provided by Jim Miller/fennana design
Transit map courtesy of the Chicago Transit Authority, Map ©2003 Chicago Transit Authority. All rights reserved. Used with permission.

ISBN: 0-912301-53-8
ISSN: 1545-7478

Printed in the USA on recycled paper.

Published by First Books, 6750 SW Franklin Street, Portland, OR 97223-2542, 503-968-6777, www.firstbooks.com.

What readers are saying about Newcomer's Handbooks:

I recently got a copy of your Newcomer's Handbook for Chicago, and wanted to let you know how invaluable it was for my move. I must have consulted it a dozen times a day preparing for my move. It helped me find my way around town, find a place to live, and so many other things. Thanks.

—Mike L.
Chicago, Illinois

Excellent reading (Newcomer's Handbook for San Francisco and the Bay Area) ... balanced and trustworthy. One of the very best guides if you are considering moving/relocation. Way above the usual tourist crap.

—Gunnar E.
Stockholm, Sweden

I was very impressed with the latest edition of the Newcomer's Handbook for Los Angeles. It is well organized, concise and up-to-date. I would recommend this book to anyone considering a move to Los Angeles.

—Jannette L.
Attorney Recruiting Administrator for a large Los Angeles law firm

I recently moved to Atlanta from San Francisco, and LOVE the Newcomer's Handbook for Atlanta. It has been an invaluable resource – it's helped me find everything from a neighborhood in which to live to the local hardware store. I look something up in it everyday, and know I will continue to use it to find things long after I'm no longer a newcomer. And if I ever decide to move again, your book will be the first thing I buy for my next destination.

—Courtney R.
Atlanta, Georgia

In looking to move to the Boston area, a potential employer in that area gave me a copy of the Newcomer's Handbook for Boston. It's a great book that's very comprehensive, outlining good and bad points about each neighborhood in the Boston area. Very helpful in helping me decide where to move.

—no name given (online submit form)

TABLE OF CONTENTS

CONTENTS

CONTENTS

W ELCOME TO CHICAGO—AND CONGRATULATIONS! YOU ARE now living in the best-kept secret in the United States. What's the secret about Chicago? Simply that it is one of the most livable big cities in America. With over 500 parks, 29 miles of gorgeous lakefront, 33 beaches, six golf courses, and tennis courts throughout the city, you are sure to find some way to wile away a summer day. Couple that with Chicago's cultural and ethnic diversity, officially celebrated in dozens of annual festivals, fairs and parades, it's easy to see why so many are happy to call Chicago home. And if the out-of-doors doesn't entice you, Chicago's shopping and cultural opportunities will. From its famous Magnificent Mile to its neighborhood boutiques, suburban malls and designer outlets, Chicago is a shopping addict's nirvana, with enough variety to please the pickiest clothes horse. More interested in Italian opera than Italian shoes? Chicago is the cultural and artistic Goliath of the Midwest, home to the world renowned Lyric Opera of Chicago, the Chicago Symphony Orchestra, the Art Institute of Chicago, Ballet Chicago, the Steppenwolf and Goodman theater companies, the University of Chicago, Columbia College, Northwestern University, and hundreds of art galleries, museums, dance and theater companies, arts organizations and schools, pop music venues, performance art spaces, comedy clubs....

Word is out, though: as the 2000 Census reported, for the first time in decades the city grew, by four percent since 1990, to 2.9 million people (the metro area population weighed-in at an all-time high of 8.4 million). Chicago's varied and deep economy, its cultural diversity, and its beautification and gentrification is even luring former residents who left decades ago. Now, with their suburban nests empty, these ex-Chicagoans are coming back to live where the action is.

So if you have already taken the first step and decided that Chicago is the place for you, many would agree that you have made a great choice. If you have bought this book hoping to find out more about the ins and outs of living in Chicago, read on. We offer you details about city living, descriptions of Chicago neighborhoods and suburbs, house or apartment hunting tips, information on signing leases or finding a real estate agent, and much more.

CHICAGO'S HISTORY

Native Americans called the area around the mouth of the Chicago River "Che-cau-gou," possibly after the strong-smelling wild onions that grew there. In 1673, a Jesuit missionary, Fr. Jacques Marquette, and Louis Jolliet, a Canadian mapmaker and explorer, are thought to have been the first Europeans to come upon the future site of Chicago. Here they encountered three Native American villages with an estimated population of 6,500. The explorers were treated well by the natives: a peace pipe was extended, and when the Frenchmen left six hundred natives escorted them on their way. Their journey took them down the Mississippi River to the mouth of the Arkansas River before they turned back due to reports of hostile Spaniards and natives further south. Marquette and two companions spent the winter of 1674-75 in a shelter on the south branch of the Chicago River at what is now Damen Avenue. A cross at the bottom of the Damen Avenue Bridge marks the site. ·

Chicago's position near an easily portaged moraine, providing access to the Mississippi River on the west, made it a popular transit point with Native Americans and later with European explorers. The famed Chicago Portage National Historic Site is at the head of the I&M Canal National Heritage Corridor in a Cook County Forest Preserve, near 45th Street and Harlem Avenue.

By 1679, another French explorer, Robert de La Salle had built a small outpost in the vicinity of the southwest suburb now known as Palos Hills. Little is known about the Chicago area between 1700 and 1763 when the region passed into the hands of the British after the French and Indian War. It wasn't until after the Revolutionary War, when the new country began to turn its attention westwards, that Chicago was really established. In 1779, Haitian trapper and fur trader Jean Baptiste Pointe du Sable and his Indian wife became the first permanent settlers here, establishing a fur-trading post on the left bank of the Chicago River near the present site of the Equitable Building. In 1804, the federal government completed Fort Dearborn.

Illinois formally joined the Union in 1818. In 1830, the construction of the Illinois-Michigan Canal began, which connected the Chicago River with the Mississippi River. The canal, completed in 1848 the same year as the arrival of the first locomotives, positioned Chicago to become the crossroads of the nation. In 1833 Chicago was incorporated as a town, and as a city in 1837. By 1848, recognizing the need for a centralized marketplace and a way to ensure the timely execution of agricultural orders, 82 merchants joined forces to create one of the world's great financial institutions, the Chicago Board of Trade. The Union Stockyards opened on Chicago's South Side in 1865, organizing the many small meat operations throughout the area. This, coupled with the extensive rail network and the introduction of the refrigerated train car, put Chicago on the map as the nation's meat-packer for nearly 100 years.

Chicago's stupendous growth was temporarily cut short on October 8, 1871, when disaster struck. Starting on Chicago's West Side, the Great Fire destroyed most of the city. By midnight the fire had jumped to the south branch of the Chicago River and raced through the downtown business district and the Near North side before stopping three days later at Clark Street and Belden Avenue, a block south of Fullerton. As the fires dimmed, Chicagoans calculated the damage: 300 dead, 100,000 homeless, the entire central business district destroyed, and property losses of $200 million. Even the thickest safes and vaults could not escape the fire: over $1 million in currency was incinerated at the Custom House and Post Office alone.

EVEN THE THICKEST SAFES AND VAULTS COULD NOT ESCAPE THE FIRE: OVER $1 MILLION IN CURRENCY WAS INCINERATED AT THE CUSTOM HOUSE AND POST OFFICE ALONE.

Chicagoans dug in their heels and set to work to rebuild the more than two thousand acres known as the "Burnt District." Debris from the fire was pushed into the lake, making landfill for what is today much of Chicago's downtown lakefront. Shanties were quickly built on top of the town's ashes, and citizens vowed to rebuild their lost homes and business-es. One doughty businessman, Kerfoot Block, put it best on a sign outside the shack that housed his newly opened real estate office: "All gone but wife, children and energy." Chicago's plight touched the hearts of many Americans as school children, civic organizations and labor organizations from all over the country sent contributions totaling five million dollars.

Out of the rubble emerged one the country's finest architectural movements. Innovative East Coast architects came and rebuilt the city in a new design style that came to be known as the Chicago School. Daniel Burnham, Louis Sullivan, William Holabird, John Welborn Root, and a young Frank Lloyd Wright were instrumental in rebuilding the city in the decades following the Great Fire.

Following the Civil War, Chicago proved to be a popular destination for European immigrants and displaced Americans. Germans, Swedes, and Norwegians joined the already present Irish in making Chicago home. African-Americans, many of whom had abandoned Chicago in the years leading up to the Civil War due to its strict enforcement of the state's fugitive slave laws, returned despite hostilities to their homecoming.

Between 1890 and 1910, waves of immigrants from across Europe contributed to the further growth of the city and added to its cacophony of tongues.

After World War I, in 1919, Prohibition went into effect, and with it came America's failed experiment with sobriety. It was during the Prohibition era, 1919-1933, that Chicago acquired its reputation as the gangster capital of the world. Most of the mob violence was inspired by turf wars over the lucrative trade in bootleg alcohol. The 1929 St. Valentine's Day Massacre, which left seven dead in a North Clark Street garage, stemmed from a conflict between a North Side Irish gang led by Bugs Moran with a South Side Italian gang led by Al Capone. Fortunately for Moran, he wasn't at the garage that morning. He retired from bootlegging shortly thereafter.

The first half of the 20th century saw the arrival of hundreds of thousands of African-Americans from the South, who, like newcomers from across the Atlantic, came to escape political oppression and economic deprivation. The second half of the 20th century brought a new wave of newcomers to Chicago, primarily from Spanish-speaking countries, especially Mexico.

According to the 2000 Census, 37% of the city population is African-American, 32% is white, and 26% is Hispanic. The suburbs are a different, much whiter story. In spite of the city's racial mix, there's no denying that Chicago remains highly segregated, notably by race and economics. Thus the North Side is primarily white and affluent, the West Side is more Hispanic, and the South Side is more African-American and poorer. Unlike years past, however, the city is tolerant and cosmopolitan, with the many diverse communities that live here making one rich and dynamic human tapestry.

CHICAGO'S GEOGRAPHY

While hills are virtually non-existent in the city of Chicago (thanks to a series of glacial lakes that covered the area for several thousand years), its waterways offer a striking natural reminder of the days before concrete. Most of Chicago sits on marshy soil, only a few feet above the water level of Lake Michigan. Just a few miles west of the lake, parallel to what is now Harlem Avenue, is a natural sub-continental drainage divide. To the east of this divide, rivers drained into Lake Michigan and the St. Lawrence River; to the west of the divide, rivers, including the Des Plaines and Illinois, flowed to the Mississippi and onward to the Gulf of Mexico. When the water levels were high, the two water systems were nearly as one. Boats could easily navigate between the two systems without any trouble. When the water levels were low, the area was a dense marshland full of leeches and mosquitoes.

Portaging during late summer required dragging boats through waist high muck. The solution was to dig a canal between the Chicago and Des Plaines rivers. In 1834, soldiers from Fort Dearborn, with the help of Chicago's new Irish and Norwegian immigrants, cut a canal in the sandbar that blocked the mouth of the Chicago River, giving traders direct access to the Chicago River. While the creation of a navigable harbor improved water traffic, an increasing Chicago population along the riverbanks caused major health problems.

As the turn of the century approached, Chicago's port was the busiest in the United States, and the population grew at an unprecedented rate. Although many efforts were made by the city to create a reliable sewage system, it continuously failed to meet the needs of its exploding population. The problem: sewage flowed from the Chicago River into Lake Michigan, which was the source of the city's drinking water. Epidemics of typhoid, cholera and other diseases killed thousands. Eventually the mounting deaths from typhoid created a public health problem so serious that the Legislature was called upon to devise a permanent solution to Chicago's sanitation problems.

In 1892, Sanitary District engineers began to dig what would be called the Chicago Drainage Canal later renamed the Sanitary and Ship Canal. This new canal would run from the southern tip of the south branch of the Chicago River, taking waste away from the lake and towards the Mississippi River via the Des Plaines and Illinois rivers. The Sanitary and Ship Canal would run 28 miles from the tip of the south branch of

> THE SANITARY AND SHIP CANAL MEASURED 25 FEET DEEP, 306 FEET WIDE, LARGER THAN THE SUEZ CANAL IN EGYPT, AND IT REPRESENTED THE LARGEST EARTH MOVING PROJECT IN THE WORLD.

the Chicago River to the town of Lockport. It was designed as a continuous waterway to carry 10,000 cubic feet of water per second. Upon completion, eight years later, the Sanitary and Ship Canal measured 25 feet deep, 306 feet wide, larger than the Suez Canal in Egypt, and it represented the largest earth moving project in the world. Laborers, 8,500 of them, included many African-Americans as well as recently arrived Poles. This project had its critics, and at the end of 1899, the State of Missouri sought an injunction to opening the canal, fearing its use would pollute St. Louis' drinking water. The following month, January 1900, Sanitary District engineers, fearing the termination of their project, secretly detonated the temporary dam that separated the Chicago River from the new canal. The result was the permanent reversal of the Chicago River, the world's first river to flow away from its mouth—still considered one of the seven engineering feats of the world. Ongoing sewage projects in the years to come diverted all sewage and storm overflow into the Sanitary and Ship Canal, virtually eliminating any outflow into the lake. By 1908, these and other measures helped to reduce Chicago's typhoid rate by 91%.

As Chicago continued to expand into suburban areas after WW II, the sewage system began to show signs of strain, especially after rainstorms. By the 1970s, raw sewage was being dispersed directly into local rivers on the average of once every four days. Fearing a repeat of history, the city devised a new plan: the installation of an innovative new "Deep Tunnel System" that would divert and store all overflow storm water and sewage to storage reservoirs until treatment plants could process it. Today, Chicago continues to revise its sanitation techniques, upgrade its plants, and extend its reach. The Chicago Department of Sewers is responsible for more than 4,300 miles of sewer pipe, 230,000 catch basins and 148,000 manholes. The Chicago River, once devoid of wildlife, now has 50 species of fish, and canoes, last seen on the river in 1850, now travel freely.

CHICAGO'S REPUTATION

Although Chicago remains a Daley fiefdom under Richard M. Daley ("da Mayor"), the eldest son of the late machine strongman Mayor Richard J. Daley, Chicagoans showed that they could (at least momentarily) control the ballot box with the election of Jane Byrne, in 1979, and the late Harold Washington in 1983 and 1987. Corruption still occurs in Chicago politics, but today it appears to be more individual in nature. Mayor Daley is adept at holding together broad coalitions of ethnic and political groups, something his predecessors in city hall had no interest in even attempting.

There are some things that the newcomer to Chicago needs to learn right away in order not to be recognized as an out-of-towner. First and foremost, the subway here is the 'L,' which is short for elevated, Chicago's rapid transit system. Even though some lines do go underground, it's still always referred to first as the 'L.'

Next is "the Loop," a portion of Chicago's downtown business and retail district encircled by elevated train tracks. While generally speaking, the Loop is any part of the downtown area south of the Chicago River, specifically, the elevated tracks surround the Loop on Wabash Avenue on the east, Lake Street on the north, Wells Street on the west, and Van Buren Street on the south. The area also is referred to as "downtown," but beware: suburbanites often use the term "downtown" to refer to anything in Chicago. What you will find in the Loop are office towers, terrific modern architecture, and the bustling recently renovated turn-of-the-century, gaslight shopping district on State Street, complete with the venerable Marshall Field's Department store.

"The Magnificent Mile," the stretch of North Michigan Avenue north of the Chicago River to Oak Street, is the city's premier shopping area. It boasts many international retail stores and shopping malls, including Water Tower Place and Chicago Place. If you're a shopper (or just a people watcher), walking here is always a pleasure.

Although the Second City comedy troupe still performs at its Old Town location, Chicago is no longer the second city. Population-wise, it sits third, behind New York and Los Angeles. And O'Hare International Airport continues to jockey with Atlanta's Hartsfield Airport for the title of busiest airport in the world.

Chicago, home of the first skyscraper, has several of the world's tallest buildings. The Sears Tower, located outside the southwest corner of the Loop, was once the tallest; it now shares a disputed title with a Malaysian competitor. The Standard Oil Building, now referred to as the Aon Center, is a white neo-classical building at the north end of Grant Park on Randolph Street, is ranked eighth in the world. The John Hancock Center, at the north end of Michigan Avenue, is the 16th tallest. It was built in the late 1960s, the first of Chicago's great towers.

GETTING AROUND IN CHICAGO

Unlike some large cities in the United States, Chicago offers its residents a variety of transportation options, from bus to subway to commuter rail and automobile.

Our advice: *if possible, take public transportation*. Negotiating the Kennedy, or any of the other major expressways, especially at rush hour, can be a true exercise in patience. The Chicago Transportation Authority's (CTA's) rail transit system, is safe, reliable, and fast. The only negative is that unlike, say the New York City subway system, the 'L' is not comprehensive. Where the 'L' does not reach, buses will be an option, but service can vary depending on location. The 'L' will get you to O'Hare and Midway airports. Whether you are taking the 'L' or the bus, expect a cozy ride during rush hours. If you are doing a suburb-to-city (or reverse) commute, Metra, the commuter railroad, is the way to go. It's reliable, comfortable, and affordable.

If you're wondering whether you'll need a car to live in Chicago, the answer is no, not if you are in Chicago proper. But the suburbs, with a few exceptions such as Evanston and Oak Park, are a different story, created as they were with the automobile in mind. While a car is certainly convenient for some excursions, trains, buses, and taxis are all easily accessible for daily commuting, or for the trip home after a night out. Regular use of Metra, the CTA's 'L' or bus lines, and taxis should cost far less than monthly car payments and auto insurance, not to mention the headache and expense of parking. For more details on getting around Chicago see the **Chicago Address Locator** section and the **Transportation** chapter.

CHICAGOLAND

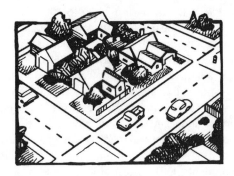

C HICAGO IS DIVIDED, ROUGHLY, INTO THREE PARTS: THE NORTH Side, the West Side, and the South Side. Each of these geographical divisions is a mosaic of neighborhoods divided, at times by ethnicity, other times, by income. (Due to its location on Lake Michigan, Chicago has no official East Side, although parts of southeast Chicago on the Indiana border are referred to as the East Side.)

Do not be overwhelmed by Chicago's size. Take it slowly. There's no need to memorize the whole city. Find your niche, your neighborhood grocery store, coffee shop, bar, 'L' stop, book or music store, and you will begin to have a sense of belonging. A good way to get acquainted with some of Chicago's more historical neighborhoods is to take a guided tour. Check with Chicago Neighborhood Tours, 312-742-1190, www.chgocity tours.com, and Chicago Greeter (free tours led by volunteers), 312-742-1284, www.ci.chi.il.us/CulturalAffairs/Tourism/, for more information.

Like any other big city, Chicago has its share of crime, and no neighborhood is completely safe. But, according to the Chicago Police Department, since 1991 overall crime has continued to decline. If you keep your eyes open and use common sense, you should have no problem getting around safely. There are neighborhoods that would be best for newcomers to avoid, and for that reason we have profiled only those neighborhoods that are most likely to attract new arrivals. Up and coming communities, those in the process of revitalization/gentrification such as Pilsen and Edgewater, have been included. Since the publication of the previous edition of the *Newcomer's Handbook® for Chicago*, areas such as the Kenmore-Winthrop corridor of Edgewater, which were reported to be crime-ridden, have made tremendous improvements.

A word about police protection in Chicago. The city is divided into 25 police districts that serve as neighborhood headquarters for beat and tactical officers. The 25 districts are grouped into four areas. If you need police for an emergency, dial 911. For non-emergencies, dial 311—outside the city, 311 can be accessed by dialing 312-746-6000. The Chicago Police Department web site can help you locate your local police station and provide other information about the city's neighborhoods, crime rates, and other police numbers: www.cityofchicago.org/CAPS.

Chicago has a large immigrant population, and there are neighborhoods where it is possible to imagine you are in a different country. Some of the most notable on the north and northwest sides include an Asian (mainly Vietnamese and Chinese) community centered at the intersection of Argyle, Broadway, and Sheridan roads; a primarily Indian neighborhood with a mix of Jewish, Assyrian, Pakistani, Thai, Russian, Croatian, Syrian, and Nepalese residents, located east of Kedzie and west of Ravenswood along Devon Avenue; and a Korean neighborhood west of the Chicago River and east of the Edens Expressway, between Foster and Montrose avenues. Southwest of the Loop is Pilsen, which is a Hispanic community west of Halsted Street, near 18th Street; and then south of the South Loop neighborhood is where you will find the bustling Chinatown, in the neighborhood of Bridgeport. (Comprehensive listings and descriptions of these and other areas can be found in *Passport's Guide to Ethnic Chicago* by Richard Lindberg; McGraw-Hill Publishers.) Also, Chicago Neighborhood Tours and Chicago Greeter (see above,) offer tours through these and other ethnically or historically noteworthy neighborhoods. Contact them for schedules and meeting places.

This fourth edition of the *Newcomer's Handbook®* for Chicago covers many of Chicago's neighborhoods and outlying communities, with particular emphasis on the areas that are most likely to attract newcomers. In Chicago proper we begin with the downtown neighborhoods, work our way north along the lake, then head west for neighborhoods that are northwest of the Loop, then it's to the South Side, beginning with the South Loop area, and finally the suburbs, beginning with Evanston and going north. Included after the neighborhood profiles are pertinent information such as area codes, zip codes, the nearest post offices, district police stations, local hospitals, public libraries, public schools, community publications (check **Newspapers and Magazines** in the **Getting Settled** chapter for contact information), and community resources. Also listed are the nearest rapid-transit stations and the major bus routes running through the neighborhoods. To get a handle on what you can expect to pay for an apartment, scan the rental classifieds in the newspaper of your choice—many opt for the *Chicago Reader*—or go to the web to find price ranges of some of Chicago's neighborhoods. The priciest neighborhoods are generally north of the Loop: Streeterville, River North, Old Town, Gold Coast, and Lincoln Park. Comparable space and convenient location minus the high rent can be found, at least for now, in the booming South Loop neighborhood, and those looking to buy will find housing prices in the South Loop significantly cheaper than what can be found north of the Loop. The university neighborhoods of Rogers Park, Edgewater, North Center, and Hyde Park continue to offer a good selection of affordable student accommodations. Not so true in the DePaul/Lincoln Park West neighborhood; just west of Lincoln Park, this area is becoming less affordable for the student set. (For more see the **Finding a Place to Live** chapter.)

If you're looking for interesting pictures of Chicago neighborhoods, go to Carla Surratt's engaging web site: www.picturingchicago.com

As far as neighborhood boundaries go, those used in this book are basic guidelines, designed to make learning the city easier for newcomers. Once you get to know Chicago, you can debate and gerrymander neighborhood boundaries at your leisure.

CHICAGO STREET ADDRESS LOCATOR

It is nearly impossible to get lost in Chicago. City surveyors designed much of Chicago on a grid system; just check street signs for area cross streets, and you'll know how far you are from downtown Chicago. The system is planned at eight city blocks to the mile with major streets every half mile. Addresses are divided north and south by Madison Street, and east and west by State Street. The intersection of State and Madison streets is at the heart of the Loop: all north/south running streets are indicated as being either east or west of State street; east/west streets, running parallel to Madison, are indicated as being north or south of Madison. So, if you are standing on the corner of Belmont (3200 North) and Sheffield (1000 West), you are four miles north of Madison and a mile and a half west of State Street.

An exception to this eight-blocks-to-the-mile rule is on the South Side, due to this area being settled early in Chicago's history. Although Roosevelt Road is 1200 South by numbers, it is one mile south of Madison. Cermak Road, which is 2200 South is a mile south of Roosevelt even though it's a 10-block count. The next mile comes at 31st Street, even though it's nine blocks south of Cermak.

All north-south and east-west streets on the North Side have names. On the South Side, north-south streets have names, except in the southeast part of the city where a few have letters; most east-west streets are numbered, although some have both names and numbers, e.g., 22nd Street is also Cermak Road, and 39th Street is Pershing Road. The east-west streets are double-numbered, e.g., West 66th Street and a West 66th Place, to represent half blocks. (See diagram on following page.)

The shaded area represents a full square city block. The distance between West 66th Street and West 66th Place and between Fremont and

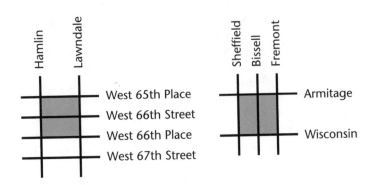

Bissell is considered a half city block. This is an esoteric point, but one that creates a lot of confusion when trying to give directions and tell people how many blocks away something is.

While the city's layout is well designed, it helps to have a good street map handy the first few months. Make sure that the one you buy covers your neighborhood—many parts of the city are ignored by tourist-oriented maps. **The Savvy Traveller**, 310 South Michigan Avenue, or **Rand McNally Map & Travel**: 444 North Michigan Avenue and 150 South Wacker Drive, are good places to shop for maps. You can also find newcomer-oriented maps at **www.firstbooks.com**.

Note: with some rare exceptions (State Street for example), Chicagoans do not refer to their streets and avenues by their complete names, i.e. Addison Street will be referred to only as "Addison." It may take some getting used to if you are from an area that uses the words, avenue, boulevard, or street regularly.

See the **Transportation** chapter for details about area expressways.

COUNTY BASICS

At one time, the Chicago area was made up of Cook, Lake, and DuPage counties. But the explosive growth in neighboring counties has made Chicago rethink area counties that were once thought of as "too far" to be part of the Chicago area. Today, "Chicagoland," as it's often called, encompasses six counties:

- **Cook County**—www.co.cook.il.us; home to Chicago proper as well as many north, northwest, west, and south suburbs. It is the largest county in the area.
- **DuPage County**—www.co.dupage.il.us; within the DuPage County limits are the suburban communities of Schaumburg, Wheaton, Bensenville, Elmhurst, Lombard, Carol Stream and West Chicago. DuPage County is a heavily developed county, with strong retail base,

and a solid highway network. Traffic is heavy in this area with many residents commuting to Chicago on a daily basis.

- **Kane County**—www.co.kane.il.us; famous for its fairgrounds, Kane County is west of DuPage County, placing it among the communities that lie to the far west of Chicago. Within Kane County are Aurora, St. Charles, and Geneva.
- **Lake County**—www.co.lake.il.us; lies inland from Lake Michigan and runs up to the Wisconsin border. Lake County is experiencing tremendous housing development. Communities that lie within Lake County include Barrington, Antioch, Grayslake, Round Beach Lake, Zion, Waukegan, Winthrop Harbor, and North Chicago.
- **McHenry County**—www.co.mchenry.il.us; McHenry communities are far northwest of Chicago. McHenry County borders the western edge of Lake County. Its communities include Woodstock, Crystal Lake, Cary, and Lake in the Hills.
- **Will County**—www.willcountyillinois.com; is southwest of Chicago. It includes the towns of Joliet and Bolingbrook. There is a great deal of available land in this area. Also hosts a small airport (Lewis University Airport), and the Stateville and Joliet Correctional centers.

COOK COUNTY INFORMATION

- **Web Site**: www.co.cook.il.us
- **County Law Enforcement** (Sheriff): www.cookcountysheriff.org
- **Public School Districts**: www.cook.k12.il.us; this site is the Regional Office of Education which oversees the 690 public schools which fall within the Cook County jurisdiction.
- **County State Attorney**: www.statesattorney.org
- **County Information Center**: www.cookcountygov.com
- **Cook County Treasurer**: www2.cookcountytreasurer.com
- **Emergency Hospital**: John H. Stroger, Jr. Hospital of Cook County, 1969 West Ogden Avenue, 312-864-6000

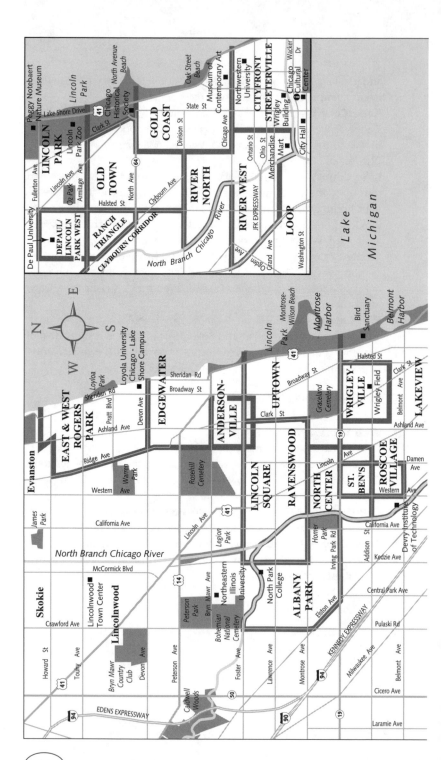

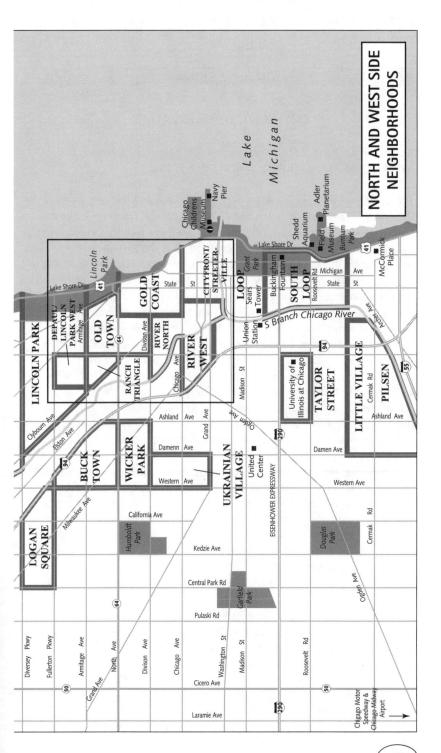

NORTH AND WEST SIDE NEIGHBORHOODS

NORTH SIDE

CITYFRONT/STREETERVILLE

Boundaries: **East**: Lake Michigan; **West**: Michigan Avenue (100E); **North**: Grand Avenue (500N); **South**: Chicago River

The **Cityfront** area lies between Michigan Avenue and the lake, north of the Chicago River, and since the mid 1990s, it has been home to one of the fastest growing commercial and residential areas in Chicago. Dotted with now converted warehouses built originally to serve the Nicholson shipping terminal in the 1920s and '30s, **Cityfront** today is known for its expensive, high-rise apartments, upscale shopping, and fine restaurants. Cityfront is popular with young married and single professionals. You may hear some Chicagoans refer to this area as River East, North Pier, or even the Near North, and some consider it a part of the greater Streeterville area.

At the east end of Grand Avenue is Navy Pier. It was constructed in 1916 as a commercial shipping pier, and renamed in honor of the Navy in 1927. Today, the pier serves as a docking site for large dinner cruise ships, Lake Michigan tour boats, and the occasional naval vessel. Once an abandoned pier, Mayor Daley saw potential in this waterfront site, and spearheaded a full-scale renovation, which was completed in 1995. Navy Pier is now a multi-use complex and one of Chicago's best attractions. The area attracts locals as well as out-of-towners for concerts at the 1,500 seat Skyline Stage, theater performances, rides on the 15-story Ferris wheel, and some go to the Chicago Children's Museum. Also here: an ice rink in the winter, an outdoor beer garden in the summer, the Crystal Gardens, one of the country's largest indoor botanical parks, and an Imax theater.

Just to the north of Navy Pier, is the Milton Lee Olive Park, right on Lake Michigan. It was named after 18-year-old Vietnam War Congressional Medal of Honor winner Milton Lee Olive. Don't let the Jardine Water Filtration plant nearby put you off. Olive Park is a small, quiet area, favored by bicyclists needing a rest, bird watchers, or picnickers looking for a great view. If you are heading to Olive Park from Navy Pier, you will pass Ohio Street Beach, 400 North Lake Shore Drive. Triathletes come here to train and it is popular with area residents. West of Lake Shore Drive is the Family Golf Center, 221 North Columbus Drive, where you can practice your drive or play a quick nine holes with a panoramic view of Lake Michigan. Renting here is expensive.

Streeterville, north of Cityfront, is named for Captain George Wellington "Cap" Streeter, one of Chicago's great eccentrics. This neighborhood was once covered by Lake Michigan. In 1886, Streeter ran his schooner aground on a sandbar near Michigan Avenue. Unable to free his vessel, Streeter made his home on it. He encouraged contractors to deposit their debris there—for a fee. Gradually the landfill turned the lake into approximately 186 new acres and Streeter laid claim to 168 acres of it. After scuffles with police and an extended court battle Streeter was evicted, though he pressed his claim until his death in 1921.

Streeterville is the heart of North Michigan Avenue, Chicago's blue-chip shopping district, which features Water Tower Place (Marshall Field's, Lord & Taylor), 900 North Michigan Avenue (Bloomingdale's, Gucci), as well as Neiman Marcus, Saks Fifth Avenue, Crate & Barrel, and many more upscale retail shops. In addition to being home to fine restaurants, Rush Street bars, clubs, and movie theaters, Streeterville is home to Northwestern University's Chicago campus, which includes its law and medical schools. Nearby is the University of Chicago's Graduate School of Business evening program, and one of the area's premiere hospitals—Northwestern Memorial Hospital. Indeed, you can probably find everything in this upscale neighborhood except a parking place. If you're moving here, and you have a car and intend to keep it, you'll want to find a building with parking or rent space in a lot.

Web Site: www.ci.chi.il.us

Area Code: 312

Zip Codes: 60610, 60611

Post Offices: Fort Dearborn, 540 North Dearborn Street; Ontario Street Station, 227 East Ontario, 800-275-8777

Police District: 18th/East Chicago District (Area 3), 133 West Chicago Avenue, 312-742-5870

Emergency Hospital: Northwestern Memorial Hospital, Superior Street and Fairbanks Court, 312-908-2000, www.nmh.org

Libraries: Chicago Public, Harold Washington Library, 400 South State, 312-747-4300; Newberry Library, 60 West Walton, has a first rate collection of rare books, manuscripts and maps. Open to the public. Research scholars and university students are its most frequent visitors; call first: 312-943-9090.

Parks: www.chicagoparkdistrict.com, 312-742-PLAY; among the dozen area parks included in the 60610 and 60611 zip codes, are Esplanade Park, 401 East River Drive, and Lake Shore Drive Park, 808 North Lake Shore Drive.

Community Publications: *Crain's Chicago Business, Chicago Magazine, Chicago Reader, Chicago Reporter, N'DIGO, New City*

Public Schools: Chicago School District 299, 125 South Clark Street, Chicago, IL 60603, 773-553-1000, www.cps.k12.il.us

Transportation—Rapid Transit: Red Line (stations: Grand, Chicago); Brown Line (station: Chicago)

Transportation—Main Bus Routes: #65 Grand, #66 Chicago, #125 Water Tower Express, #151 Sheridan, #156 LaSalle, #157 Streeterville

RIVER NORTH/RIVER WEST

Boundaries: **North**: Division and Chicago Avenue; **East**: Wabash Avenue and LaSalle Street; **South**: Kinzie Street and the Chicago River; **West**: Kennedy Expressway and the Chicago River

What was once a neighborhood of factories and warehouses has blossomed into Chicago's answer to New York's SoHo. **River North** is a thriving neighborhood of art galleries, trendy restaurants, hotels, and nightclubs. Each Saturday from 10:30 a.m. until noon, local gallery owners conduct free tours. Meet at the Starbucks located at 750 North Franklin Street, no reservations needed. If you are ready for brunch after your tour, there are bistros, traditional diners, and cafes to suit every palate. The River North neighborhood appeals to all the senses. If you are in the mood to be pampered head to toe, you might indulge yourself at a spa, say, Tirra Salon & Spa, 375 West Erie Street, Studio 10, or Tiffani Kim Institute, 310 West Superior Street. Some of the city's top health clubs hail here too: East Bank Club, 500 North Kingbury Street, and The Lakeshore Athletic Club, 441 North Wabash Avenue. Need a personal trainer to keep you on track? Check out Sharper Fitness, 401 West Ontario Street.

The Merchandise Mart, 222 Merchandise Mart, between Wells and Orleans, is an unofficial landmark. Sitting on the north bank of the Chicago River, the Mart was built in 1931 by Marshall Field & Co. At 25 floors high and two city blocks long, it still holds the title as the world's largest commercial building. The Mart is part shopping center, which is open to the public—the first two floors feature 50 retail stores including a few restaurants—and part designer-only showrooms, featuring commercial and residential furnishings, and kitchen and bath wares. (Tours are available to the public on Mondays and Fridays. Call 312-527-7762 for more information.)

Many of the warehouses in the neighborhood have been converted into loft space for offices and apartments. Rents have risen considerably here as they would in any up-and-coming neighborhood, but especially in River North because of its proximity to Michigan Avenue.

River West, sometimes referred to as Illinois Center, is a former industrial/manufacturing zone located west of the Chicago River and east of the Kennedy Expressway. The neighborhood remains a maze of railroad tracks, under- and over-passes, and truncated streets, but there are apartments and condos to be found here. And, if you love chocolate, you may just *have* to live here. The Blommer Chocolate Company, at the corner of Kinzie and

Des Plaines streets, lofts a heavenly aroma skyward, making River West one of the best-smelling neighborhoods in the city.

It wasn't always so. A little more than a hundred years ago the Chicago River was the largest open sewer in the Midwest and emptied, quite logically, into Lake Michigan, the city's source for drinking water. Nowadays the river actually supports aquatic life of the non-microbial sort. The sight of a turtle paddling along in the shadow of the Merchandise Mart is not the kind of urban scene you might expect this close to the Loop, but River North and River West are full of surprises.

Web Site: www.ci.chi.il.us
Area Code: 312
Zip Codes: 60610, 60622
Post Offices: Fort Dearborn, 540 North Dearborn Street; Merchandise Mart, 222 Merchandise Mart Plaza, 800-275-8777
Police District: 18th/East Chicago District (Area 3), 133 West Chicago Avenue, 312-742-5870
Emergency Hospital: Northwestern Memorial Hospital, Superior Street and Fairbanks Court, 312-908-2000, www.nmh.org
Library: Harold Washington Library, 400 South State Street, 312-747-4300, www.chipublib.org
Parks: www.chicagoparkdistrict.com, 312-742-PLAY
Community Publications: *Crain's Chicago Business, Chicago Magazine, Chicago Reader, Chicago Reporter, N'DIGO, New City*
Public Schools: Chicago School District 299, 125 South Clark Street, Chicago, IL 60603, 773-553-1000, www.cps.k12.il.us
Transportation—Rapid Transit: Red Line (stations: Grand, Chicago); Brown Line (stations: Merchandise Mart, Chicago)
Transportation—Main Bus Routes: #8 Halsted, #11 Lincoln, #22 Clark, #36 Broadway, #56 Milwaukee, #65 Grand, #66 Chicago, #156 LaSalle

GOLD COAST

Boundaries: **North**: North Avenue (1660N); **South**: Chicago Avenue; **East**: Lake Michigan; **West**: LaSalle Avenue

The Gold Coast was Chicago's second Millionaires' Row (the first was on the near South Side around 18th Street and Prairie Avenue, where a few old mansions still exist) and remains home to many well-to-do Chicagoans. Although the days when it was the heart of Chicago society have passed, this area retains much of its turn-of-the-century charm and is still synonymous with living the high life. While there are a few single family homes and apartments, most of the remaining brown-, red-, and gray-stone mansions in this two square mile neighborhood have been converted into expensive condominiums. Notably, Astor Street has landmark status and is protected from further development.

Due to the wall of Lake Shore Drive high-rises, the Gold Coast sometimes feels like the bottom of a canyon. Despite this walled-in atmosphere, if you use your imagination you can almost see the gaslights and hear the carriages and horse hooves on the cobblestones. If you happen to live in one of the Lake Shore Drive high-rises, you will enjoy a spectacular view of the lake. If you want a view that includes Lincoln Park, investigate some of the buildings bordering North Avenue.

A landmark along the Clark Street boundary between the Gold Coast and Old Town is Carl Sandburg Village, a combination high-rise and low-rise condominium community constructed in the 1960s. One of the few remaining mansions, and the only one with real grounds, can be found on North Boulevard at the base of Lincoln Park, home to the Archbishop of Chicago. While it's unlikely that you will find an apartment or condo with a lawn on the Gold Coast, you will find that Lincoln Park and the lakeshore are virtually at your doorstep.

The Gold Coast high-rises make for a high density population, but that doesn't keep people from living and living well in this neighborhood; rentals are comparable to the upper end of Streeterville-area prices. Apartments here are mostly in high rises, and many have garage space available for their tenants. The shopper's paradise of North Michigan Avenue is a brisk walk away, and Division Street nightlife is just around the corner. Oak Street beach, dramatically situated at the bend in the lake where Michigan Avenue ends, is a favorite lunch spot and a great escape destination. Again, here as in other downtown neighborhoods, on-street parking is at a premium; owning a car is not recommended, unless you can find and afford garage space.

Web Site: www.ci.chi.il.us
Area Code: 312
Zip Codes: 60610, 60611
Post Office: Fort Dearborn, 540 North Dearborn Street, 800-275-8777
Police District: 18th/East Chicago District (Area 3), 133 West Chicago Avenue, 312-742-5870
Emergency Hospital: Northwestern Memorial Hospital, Superior Street and Fairbanks Court, 312-908-2000
Libraries: Harold Washington Library, 400 South State Street, 312-747-4300; Lincoln Park Library, 1150 West Fullerton Avenue, 312-744-1926; Newberry Library, 60 West Walton, 312-943-9090. Though not technically in the Gold Coast neighborhood, the Near North Branch of

the Chicago Public Library, 310 West Division Street, 312-744-0991, is one of the closest neighborhood branches, www.chipublib.org.

Community Resources: every August is the Gold Coast Art Fair, which attracts dozens of exhibitors from across the country.

Parks: www.chicagoparkdistrict.com, 312-742-PLAY: Lincoln Park, 2045 North Lincoln Park West, 312-742-7726; Lake Shore Park, 808 North Lake Shore Drive, 773-294-4720; Lake Front Trails, which lead to 15 miles of bathing beaches and 18 miles of bike paths along the Lakefront. Oak Street Beach is famous for its volleyball sand courts, beautiful sun worshippers, and inline skaters. Use one of the over or underpasses to cross Lake Shore Drive.

Community Publications: *Crain's Chicago Business, Chicago Magazine, Chicago Reader, Chicago Reporter, N'DIGO, New City*

Public Schools: Chicago School District 299, 125 South Clark Street, Chicago, IL 60603, 773-553-1000, www.cps.k12.il.us

Transportation—Rapid Transit: Red Line (Clark/Division Street station or the Chicago Avenue station)

Transportation—Major Bus Routes: #11 Lincoln, #22 Clark, #36 Broadway, #65 Grand, #66 Chicago, #70 Division, #72 North, #125 Water Tower Express, #135, #136, #145, #146, #147, #151 Sheridan, #156 LaSalle, #157 Streeterville

OLD TOWN

Boundaries: **North**: Armitage Avenue; **South**: Division; **East**: Clark Street; **West**: Halsted Street

Nestled between the Gold Coast and Lincoln Park is Old Town, a neighborhood once made up of German farmers who migrated here in the 1830s. The Great Fire of 1871 leveled the area from the lake to Larrabee Street, leaving only the smoldering shell of St. Michael's Church. Undaunted, Old Town residents rebuilt their neighborhood and church quickly. Wooden structures were built in the workers' cottage style, which featured one and a half story homes set atop a raised basement, until a city ordinance forbade further wooden structures. The larger homes, row houses, and apartment buildings along these narrow tree-lined streets are made of brick, as are the Victorian single-family homes, and the two- and three-flats. The entire neighborhood was designated a landmark by the City of Chicago in 1977.

Old Town is the closest neighborhood to the Loop and North Michigan Avenue that truly has a neighborhood feel to it: small front lawns, old architectural details, and balconies. Single-professionals, and many of the gay community are drawn to its attractiveness and convenience.

Wells Street is Old Town's main commercial street, with many good eateries and interesting shops. You will also find a number of enjoyable restaurants on North Avenue. Many of the stores in Old Town are locally run and operated, adding to the feeling of neighborhood and community here. During the second weekend of June, Old Town hosts the Wells Street Art Festival, (also known as the Old Town Art Fair). The festival, one of the largest neighborhood festivals in Chicago, attracts over 60,000 visitors and participants. Old Town also is known for being home to the legendary improvisational comedy theater, Second City, 1616 North Wells Street, where aspiring John Belushis and Bill Murrays perform nightly for city dwellers and tourists alike. A theater district, including the renowned Steppenwolf Theatre, has taken root on Halsted, just north of North Avenue. Neighborhood bars are friendly and comfortable. Parking gets tougher closer to the lake.

Web Sites: www.ci.chi.il.us, www.oldtowntriangle.com
Area Codes: 773, 312
Zip Code: 60614, 60010
Post Office: Lincoln Park, 2643 North Clark Street, 800-275-8777
Police District: 18th/East Chicago District (Area 3), 133 West Chicago Avenue, 312-742-5870
Emergency Hospitals: Children's Memorial Medical Center, Lincoln Avenue and Fullerton Avenue, 773-880-4000; Lincoln Park Hospital, 550 West Webster Avenue, 773-883-2000
Libraries: Public Library Branch facilities include: Lincoln Park, 1150 West Fullerton Avenue, 312-744-1926/9160; John Merlo, 644 West Belmont Avenue, 60657, 312-744-1139/5553; Conrad Sulzer Regional Library, 4455 North Lincoln Avenue, 312-744-7616, www.chipublib.org
Community Resources: Chicago Historical Society, 1601 North Clark Street, 312-642-4600, www.chicagohistory.org; Old Town Merchants & Residents Association, 1520 North Wells, 312-951-6106; non-profit Chicago Artists' Coalition, 312-670-2060, www.caconline.org; Old Town Triangle Association, 1763 North Park Avenue, 312-337-1938, www.oldtowntriangle.com
Parks: www.chicagoparkdistrict.com, 312-742-PLAY: Oz Park, 601-733 West Webster Avenue
Community Publications: *Crain's Chicago Business, Chicago Magazine, Chicago Reader, Chicago Reporter, N'DIGO, New City, Windy City Times*
Public Schools: Chicago School District 299, 125 South Clark Street, Chicago, IL 60603, 773-553-1000, www.cps.k12.il.us
Transportation—Rapid Transit: Brown Line (station: Sedgwick); Red Line (station: Clark/Division or North/Clybourn for the western edge of the neighborhood)

Transportation—Major Bus Routes: #11 Lincoln, #22 Clark, #36 Broadway, #37 Sedgwick/Ogden, #72 North, #73 Armitage, #135 Wilson/LaSalle express, #151 Sheridan, #156 LaSalle

RANCH TRIANGLE/CLYBOURN CORRIDOR

Boundaries: **North**: Armitage Avenue; **East**: Halsted Street; **South**: North Avenue: **West**: Clybourn and Racine avenues

Heading west, away from Old Town, is the older community known as **RANCH**, and the recently transformed section of Clybourn Avenue. RANCH stands for the neighborhood boundaries of Racine, Armitage, North, Clybourn, and Halsted. The residential area is located east of Clybourn toward the western fringes of Old Town (the spire of St. Michael's Church is a few blocks away). Here you'll find single-family homes, three-flats and larger apartment buildings. Because it's not as close to the lake as some other near north neighborhoods (about a mile away at this point), the RANCH neighborhood was a relative late bloomer in the North Side gentrification tsunami, going through its upscale makeover in the 1990s. During this time, many Victorian-era buildings were either torn town or remodeled to a point beyond recognition. However, in an attempt to slow down the mass modernization of building facades, The RANCH Conservation Association has been working hard to get official recognition for some of the buildings they consider significant to the community. While they still have a long way to go, the group has managed to get some buildings listed as architecturally significant on the Illinois State Historic Resources Survey. As the desirability of the area is increasingly recognized, i.e., its proximity to shopping, public transportation, and the lake, housing prices in the area have risen. Prices for single family homes and condos have been reported to increase in recent years by as much as 30%.

As recently as the 1980s, Clybourn Avenue was the main artery through an industrial work zone. At night and on weekends, when the laborers went home and the trucks and freight cars stopped rolling, it was a no-man's land of railroad crossings, hulking factories, and blowing trash. These days just try to find a parking space on Saturday morning: heavy industry has given way to consumer frenzy. What is referred to as the **Clybourn Corridor** is the area that stretches from Clybourn to the Chicago River, and North Avenue (1600N), to Wrightwood (2600N). Clybourn is home to strip malls, megastores, and loft apartments in buildings that once were factories. Some small retail developments have been added along Clybourn between North and Webster avenues. Highlights at the south end of the Clybourn Corridor are a Best Buy and Sam's Wine and Spirits, which many North-Siders consider the best liquor store in the city—it's certainly one of the biggest. There is also a cluster of outlet stores for major retailers, including a Bed Bath & Beyond, a gourmet supermarket, a Crown Books, and several furniture stores. Further north are the Goose Island Brewery, a microbrewery and restaurant, and the Webster Place cinemas. In short, you could spend your whole weekend shopping this mile-long stretch. While parking lots are provided at many of the stores, road congestion is a big topic of conversation, and a sore point, in this neighborhood.

A few factories remain in the neighborhood, and the community is working to keep them from leaving. If you're tired of shopping but feeling adventurous, you may want to check out the Finkl Steel Company (where Cortland Street crosses the river) for a firsthand glimpse of this neighborhood's industrial heritage. Though there are no official tours, the bay doors on Cortland open into the factory and are frequently left open in the summer to help cool the place down. As you walk or drive by, you may see molten steel being poured.

Web Sites: www.ci.chi.il.us, www.ranchtriangle.org

Area Codes: 773, 312

Zip Code: 60614

Post Office: Lincoln Park, 2643 North Clark Street, 800-275-8777

Police District: 18th/East Chicago District (Area 3), 133 West Chicago Avenue, 312-742-5870

Emergency Hospitals: Children's Memorial Medical Center, Lincoln Avenue and Fullerton Avenue, 773-880-4000; Lincoln Park Hospital, 550 West Webster Avenue, 773-883-2000

Library: Lincoln Park, 1150 West Fullerton Avenue, 312-744-1926, www.chipublib.org

Community Resources: Ranch Triangle Conservation Community Association, www.ranchtriangle.org

Parks: www.chicagoparkdistrict.com, 312-742-PLAY: Clybourn Park, 1755 North Clybourn; New City YMCA, 1515 North Halsted, 312-440-7272, www.ymca.org

Community Publications: *Crain's Chicago Business, Chicago Magazine, Chicago Reader, Chicago Reporter, N'DIGO, New City, Windy City Times*

Public Schools: Chicago School District 299, 125 South Clark Street, Chicago, IL 60603, 773-553-1000, www.cps.k12.il.us

Transportation—Rapid Transit: Red Line (North & Clybourn stations); Brown Line (station: Armitage)

Transportation—Major Bus Routes: #8 Halsted, #73 Armitage, #72 North

LINCOLN PARK

Boundaries: **North**: Diversey Parkway (1800N); **South**: North Avenue (1600N); **East**: Lake Michigan; **West**: Clybourn Avenue

Lincoln Park is at the heart of Chicago's North Side. For many it is a quintessential city neighborhood with everything you could possibly want (except readily available parking and affordable rents). Housing ranges from high rises to two- and three-flat brownstones to cottages. Unfortunately, after more than 30 years of gentrification, there are no real-estate bargains left.

Lincoln Park is lively and serves as the host of many young Chicago families and singles alike; the median age here is 31. You'll find restaurants galore to match any taste and budget; bars and dance clubs run the gamut; and there's little you won't find shopping-wise on Clark Street. The area's most obvious asset is Lincoln Park itself. Designed by Frederick Law Olmstead, designer of New York City's Central Park, this rolling 1,200-plus acre park is the largest of Chicago's 550 parks. The south end of the park has extensive playing fields for soccer and football, and barbecues. In the spring, bird lovers lead walks around the North Pond, seeking out the migratory birds as they gather around the lily pond at Fullerton and North Cannon Drive. There are bike paths, picnic areas, and the lovely Lincoln Park Zoo with free admission, and 20 free tennis courts. In the summer, the zoo hosts a summer concert series. Or you might investigate the nine-week play-series at Theatre on the Lake (Fullerton & Lake Shore Drive). For up to date information about family programs, plays, and live performances available in the park year-round, call the hotline: 312-742-2283.

Lincoln Park is steeped in history. A lone fenced-off mausoleum on LaSalle Drive behind the Historical Society stands as a reminder that the park first served as a city cemetery, holding many victims of the small pox and cholera plagues. (The bodies have long been relocated). The park's old name, Lake Park, was changed in 1886 to honor the assassinated president. A boulder near Clark Street and Wisconsin Street marks the grave of the last survivor of the Boston Tea Party. The Great Fire of 1871 reached its northernmost extent at roughly Clark and Belden. Two blocks south at 2221 North Clark Street, now a lawn, stood the garage where the infamous St. Valentine's Day Massacre took place.

You will find single family homes, condos and rentals in this area. Its popularity is reflected in its prices, but you may find some discounted real estate as you search closer to one of the three elevated train stops in this neighborhood. The train service is another top draw to this neighborhood. With an average three- to six-minute wait between trains during rush hour, Lincoln Park is an ideal location for Loop-area commuters. Drawbacks? Its cost and congestion—both symptoms of its enduring popularity. There isn't a lot of street parking available either. Still, it remains the preferred address for many Chicagoans.

Web Sites: www.ci.chi.il.us; Lincoln Central Association, www.lincolncentral.org; Mid-North Association, 773-296-1721

Area Code: 773, 312

Zip Code: 60614

Post Offices: Lincoln Park, 2643 North Clark Street; Lincoln Park Postal Store, 2405 North Sheffield Avenue, 800-275-8777

Police Districts: South of Fullerton: 18th/East Chicago District (Area 3), 133 West Chicago Avenue, 312-742-5870; north of Fullerton, Lake Michigan to Clark Street: 23rd/Town Hall District (Area 3), 3600 North Halsted Street, 312-744-8320; north of Fullerton, Clark Street west to the Chicago River: 19th/Belmont District, 2452 West Belmont Avenue (Area 3), 312-744-5983

Emergency Hospitals: Children's Memorial Medical Center, Lincoln Avenue and Fullerton Avenue, 773-880-4000; Lincoln Park Hospital, 550 West Webster Avenue, 773-883-2000

Libraries: Lincoln Park, 1150 West Fullerton Avenue, 312-744-1926; John Merlo/Lake View, 644 West Belmont Avenue, 312-744-1139; Eckhart Park Branch, 1371 West Chicago, 312-746-6069, www.chipublib.org

Community Resources: Lincoln Park Chamber of Commerce, 2534 North Lincoln, 773-880-5200; Lincoln Park Conservancy, 773-883-7275; Chicago Ornithological Society, 312-409-9678, www.chicagobirder.org; Peggy Notebaert Nature Museum, 2430 North Cannon Drive, 773-755-5100; Florence G. Heller, JCC, 524 West Melrose, 773-871-6780. Community policing groups (CAPS) meetings are held at St. Josaphat Church, 2245 North Southport, first Wednesday of each month.

Parks: www.chicagoparkdistrict.com, 312-742-PLAY: Lincoln Park Conservatory, 2400 North Stockton Drive

Community Publications: *Crain's Chicago Business, Chicago Magazine, Chicago Parent, Chicago Reader, Chicago Reporter, N'DIGO, New City, Windy City Times*

Public Schools: Chicago School District 299, 125 South Clark Street, Chicago, IL 60603, 773-553-1000, www.cps.k12.il.us

Transportation—Rapid Transit: Red Line (Fullerton station); Brown Line (stations: Armitage, Fullerton, Wellington, Diversey)

Transportation—Major Bus Routes: #8 Halsted, #11 Lincoln, #22 Clark, #36 Broadway, #73 Armitage, #74 Fullerton, #76 Diversey, #151 Sheridan, #156 LaSalle

DEPAUL/LINCOLN PARK WEST

Boundaries: **North**: Fullerton Pkwy (2400N); **South**: Armitage (2000N) to Fullerton; **East**: Halsted Street (800W); **West**: Racine Avenue (1200W)

DePaul University is the anchor for this affluent neighborhood located just to the west of Lincoln Park proper. Founded in 1898 by the Catholic Vincentian Fathers, DePaul University has expanded over the years to accommodate over 20,000 students. The twin towers of St. Vincent's Church, where the school got its start, are still neighborhood landmarks. DePaul's Lincoln Park Campus, which lies south of Fullerton Avenue between Halsted Street and Seminary Avenue, offers a quiet refuge from the buzz of the main thoroughfares. The showpiece of the campus is the $25 million John T. Richardson Library, built in 1992, on Kenmore Avenue.

While the eastern edge of **DePaul** blends seamlessly into the upscale verve of Lincoln Park, as you move westward the neighborhood's character changes. Immediately adjacent to the university the population is younger, which makes for a lively nightlife. Popular options include the nightclubs, restaurants, movie theaters, and bars along Lincoln Avenue. On weekend nights those without a parking permit will find it impossible to park in the vicinity.

West of DePaul, in an area called **Lincoln Park West**, the neighborhood was once firmly working class, home to the blue-collar laborers who worked in the factories along Southport Avenue and the Clybourn Corridor. All that has changed in recent years with the transformation of those old factories into residential lofts and major new construction of luxury homes on former abandoned industrial lots. There have also been plenty of tear downs of older and smaller single family homes to make way for larger apartment buildings and condos. It's quieter in the area west of DePaul but by no means dead; there are many excellent restaurants and corner bars, especially along Webster and Wrightwood avenues.

At its western edge, Lincoln Park West is bounded by Clybourn Avenue and the pace picks up considerably. There's great shopping along Clybourn (see **RANCH Triangle/Clybourn Corridor** profile in this chapter), though best to do by foot, and even grimy Ashland is catching the gentrification bug, with new apartment buildings and former-factory makeovers. Some light industry still exists here. Nevertheless, it seems only a matter of time before the whole neighborhood becomes exclusively residential and service-oriented.

Web Sites: www.ci.chi.il.us; www.Chicago-Scene.com; www.footlights.com
Area Code: 773

Zip Code: 60614

Post Offices: Lincoln Park, 2643 North Clark Street; Lincoln Park Postal Store, 2405 North Sheffield Avenue, 800-275-8777

Police Districts: South of Fullerton: 18th/East Chicago District (Area 3), 133 West Chicago Avenue, 312-742-5870; North of Fullerton: 19th/Belmont District (Area 3), 2452 West Belmont Avenue, 312-744-5983

Emergency Hospitals: Children's Memorial Medical Center, Lincoln Avenue and Fullerton Avenue, 773-880-4000; Lincoln Park Hospital, 550 West Webster Avenue, 773-883-2000; Illinois Masonic Medical Center, 836 West Wellington Avenue, 773-975-1600

Library: Lincoln Park, 1150 West Fullerton Avenue, 312-744-1926, www.chipublib.org

Community Resources: DePaul Community Music, 773-325-7262; DePaul University School of Music Concert Hall, 800 West Belden Avenue, 773-325-7260

Parks: www.chicagoparkdistrict.com, 312-742-PLAY

Community Publications: *Crain's Chicago Business*, *Chicago Magazine*, *Chicago Parent*, *Chicago Reader*, *Chicago Reporter*, *N'DIGO*, *New City*, *Windy City Times*

Public Schools: Chicago School District 299, 125 South Clark Street, Chicago, IL 60603, 773-553-1000, www.cps.k12.il.us

Transportation—Rapid Transit: Red Line (Fullerton station); Brown Line (stations: Armitage, Fullerton, Wellington, Diversey)

Transportation—Major Bus Routes: #8 Halsted, #9 Ashland, #11 Lincoln, #73 Armitage, #74 Fullerton, #76 Diversey

WRIGLEYVILLE/LAKEVIEW

Boundaries: **Wrigleyville**: **North**: Irving Park Road (4000N) **South**: Roscoe Street; **East**: Halsted Street (800W); **West**: Southport Avenue; **Lakeview**: **North**: Irving Park Road (4000N); **South**: Diversey Pkwy (2800N), **East**: Lake Michigan; **West**: Chicago River (includes Lakeview East, Lakeview Central, and West Lakeview)

Wrigleyville, so named for its most famous landmark, Wrigley Field, is located directly north of the DePaul/Lincoln Park West area. It is the neighborhood of choice for many recent college grads because of its proximity to the lake, its relative affordability, and its lively social scene. In fact, Wrigleyville has all of the amenities of Lincoln Park, not to mention its own baseball team, without the higher prices of its well-to-do neighbor to the south.

Wrigleyville/Lakeview is a dynamic part of town and includes a large gay population along Broadway, between Diversey and Addison. Area amenities include antique shops, florists, furniture stores, and coffeehouses dotting the retail areas along Broadway and Halsted Street. The majority of the buildings here are two- and three-story brick or graystone flats, and several buildings in the neighborhood are listed on the National Register of Historic Places. Parking for visitors can be a problem closer to the lake, particularly when the Cubs play day games. Parking without a neighborhood permit is tough, and is strictly enforced on game days. Permits are easily obtained at the 44th Ward police office on Belmont. Selling parking spaces has become a cottage industry for some residents, who will rent their garages to fans not wanting to get blocked-in in the neighborhood parking lots. With the large number of sports bars and restaurants noise can be an issue on weekends and most nights throughout the year. Those seeking quiet and solitude will not find it in Wrigleyville.

Although some single-family homes exist in the Wrigleyville/Lakeview neighborhood, most housing is a mixture of new and turn-of-the-century buildings that were designed for apartment living. The recent restoration of several grand buildings into deluxe condominiums near the corner of Surf Street and Broadway has given the neighborhood an upscale environ and it may take some effort to find lower rental priced apartments in the Wrigleyville area.

For a slightly quieter scene check out the area around Southport Avenue on Lakeview's western edge where you may be able to find some single-family homes on the market. While Southport has seen an explosion of trendy restaurants and bars in recent years, the pedestrian-friendly avenue lacks the party-hearty atmosphere of Clark and Halsted. It is also home to one of Chicago's few remaining old-style movie palaces, the Music Box Theater, 3733 North Southport, 773-871-6604. Films featured here are mainly foreign and independent features, and the beautifully restored interior only adds to the feeling of escapism. Walking south on Southport you'll spot the narrow green spire of St. Alphonsus Redemptorist Church. Look up and you may catch a glimpse of the only residents of West Lakeview who actually get a lakeview—the pigeons.

Web Sites: Southport Neighbors Association,www.southportneighbors. com; www.ci.chi.il.us

Area Code: 773

Zip Codes: 60613, 60657

Post Offices: Lake View, 1343 West Irving Park Road; 3026 North Ashland, 800-275-8777

Police Districts: Lake Michigan to Clark Street: 23rd/Town Hall District (Area 3), 3600 North Halsted Street, 312-744-8320; west of Clark Street to the Chicago River: 19th/Belmont District (Area 3), 2452 West Belmont Avenue, 312-744-5983

Emergency Hospitals: St. Joseph Hospital and Health Care Center, 2900

North Lake Shore Drive, 773-665-3000; Illinois Masonic Medical Center, 836 West Wellington Avenue, 773-975-1600; Thorek Hospital & Medical Center, 850 West Irving Park Road, 773-525-6780

Libraries: John Merlo, 644 West Belmont Avenue, 312-744-1139; Uptown Branch, 929 West Buena Avenue, 312-744-8400, www.chipublib.org

Community Resources: Lakeview Chamber of Commerce, 1609 West Belmont, 773-472-7171; Organization of the NorthEast, www.onechicago.org, 773-769-3232, www.wnkhome.northstarnet.org

Parks: www.chicagoparkdistrict.com, 312-742-PLAY: Gill Park, 825 West Sheridan Road, 312-742-7802

Community Publication: *Chicago Magazine, Chicago Parent, Chicago Reader, Chicago Reporter, N'DIGO, New City, Windy City Times*

Public Schools: Chicago School District 299, 125 South Clark Street, Chicago, IL 60603, 773-553-1000, www.cps.k12.il.us

Transportation—Rapid Transit: Red Line (stations: Belmont, Addison, Sheridan); Brown Line (stations: Wellington, Belmont, Southport)

Transportation—Major Bus Routes: #8 Halsted, #9 Ashland, #11 Lincoln, #22 Clark, #36 Broadway, #76 Diversey, #77 Belmont, #80 Irving Park, #151 Sheridan, #152 Addison, #156 LaSalle

NORTH CENTER/ST. BEN'S/ROSCOE VILLAGE

Boundaries: **North Center**: **North**: Montrose Avenue (4400N); **South**: Addison Street (3600N); **East**: Ravenswood (1800W); **West**: Chicago River; **St. Ben's**: **North**: Irving Park Road (4000N); **South**: Addison Street (3600N); **East**: Damen Avenue (2000W); **West**: Western Avenue (2400W); **Roscoe Village**: **North**: Addison Street (3600N); **South**: Belmont Avenue (3200N); **East**: Damen Avenue (2000W); **West**: Western Avenue (2400W)

One hundred years ago **North Center** was primarily a German/Swedish neighborhood, but the delis, social clubs, and beer halls with singing waiters have all but faded in memory. In the last ten years the eastern edge of North Center, and the Belmont/Lincoln/Ashland intersection in particular, has seen explosive growth. Former department stores, movie palaces, and factories have been tastefully transformed (with original facades intact) into lofts and condos, and delightfully, the diners and bowling alleys remain. This gentrification, though slow in coming, was inevitable once the development in North Center's tonier neighbor, Lakeview/Wrigleyville peaked. This tri-neighborhood area has more breathing space than the heavily populated Lakeview area; and it's quiet but still convenient to public transportation, making it very attractive to young families, and young professionals. Both Roscoe Village and St. Ben's are neighborhoods within the North Center boundaries. (Officially, Roscoe Village, sitting south of North Center, is the western edge of West Lakeview, bound by Addison, Ravenswood, Belmont, and the Chicago River.) **Roscoe Village** is predominately made up of single family homes and converted-condos. Roscoe Street, the main thoroughfare, is where you will find several restaurants, small shops and antique stores. Wander over to Belmont for Roscoe Village's own little antique row, with several shops tucked between Ravenswood and Western to consider. Just north of Roscoe Village is **St. Ben's**. The St. Ben's neighborhood is named after the Catholic Church, St. Benedict's, which has been here for over 100 years, serving and educating what was once a German community. St. Ben's neighborhood is rapidly being developed, with a lot of rehabbing of single-family homes, two flats, as well as apartment buildings, all of which are nestled on clean, tree-lined streets. Homeowners tend to be young professionals, though there are still some long time residents of German ancestry here too.

While it may be true that North Center is not as trendy as Wrigleyville to the east, it is considerably quieter, and in most cases you can even park your car on the street at night without a permit. The 'L' Brown Line runs along the eastern edge of the neighborhood and is the commute of choice for those who work downtown. Lincoln Avenue, North Center's main shopping drag, is a collage of old-world and new-age businesses where chic blends into kitsch and comes out ... unique. And, last but not least, for an old-fashioned Chicago experience—driving way too fast, radio blaring, windows open, straight as an arrow down a pot-holed, neon-drenched street, lined with used-car lots, strip malls, and fast food joints—check out Western Avenue, one of the longest, continuous city streets in the country.

Web Site: www.ci.chi.il.us

Area Code: 773

Zip Codes: 60613, 60618, 60657

Post Offices: Graceland (Postal Finance Station), 3024 North Ashland Avenue; Graceland Annex, 3635 North Lincoln Avenue; Lakeview, 1343 West Irving Park Road, 800-275-8777

Police District: 19th/Belmont District (Area 3), 2542 West Belmont Avenue, 312-744-5983

Emergency Hospitals: Illinois Masonic Medical Center, 836 West Wellington Avenue, 773-975-1600

Libraries: Hamlin Park, 2205 West Belmont Avenue, 312-744-0166; Conrad Sulzer Regional Library, 4455 North Lincoln Avenue, 312-744-7616, Uptown Branch, 929 West Buena Avenue, 312-744-8400, www.chipublib.org

Community Resources: Roscoe Village Chamber of Commerce, 2200 West Roscoe, 773-327-5123

Parks: www.chicagoparkdistrict.com, 312-742-PLAY: Challenger Park, 1100 West Irving Park Road; Filbert Park, 1822 West Larchmont; Weiboldt Park, 1747 West Nelson Street

Community Publications: *Chicago Magazine, Chicago Parent, Chicago Reader, Chicago Reporter, N'DIGO, New City, Windy City Times*

Public Schools: Chicago School District 299, 125 South Clark Street, Chicago, IL 60603, 773-553-1000, www.cps.k12.il.us

Transportation—Rapid Transit: Brown Line (stations: Paulina, Addison, Irving Park)

Transportation—Major Bus Routes: #9 Ashland, #11 Lincoln, #49 Western, #50 Damen, #76 Diversey, #77 Belmont, #80 Irving Park, #152 Addison

---

RAVENSWOOD/LINCOLN SQUARE

Boundaries: **North**: Foster Avenue (5200N); **South**: Montrose Avenue (4400N); **East**: Clark Street; **West**: Chicago River

The **Ravenswood** neighborhood, located directly north of North Center, was named for Ravenswood Avenue, which runs alongside the Chicago and North Western Railway (C&NW). The neighborhood became popular in the 1860s when the C&NW opened a station at Wilson Avenue and then really grew during the 1880s and '90s when streetcar lines reached the area. While the official name of the community is Lincoln Square, and that is how most realtors and city officials will refer to this area, most Chicago residents think of Ravenswood as the larger community, and Lincoln Square as a neighborhood within the Ravenswood area.

Ravenswood is a family neighborhood filled with wonderful vintage buildings and multi-unit apartment complexes—an area where renovation and rehabilitation have taken precedence over raze and ruin. The East Ravenswood Historic District (bounded by Lawrence Avenue/Irving Park Road/Ravenswood Street), one of Chicago's first planned communities, has been placed on the National Register of Historic Places. Today you'll find carefully rehabbed Victorian homes and two- and three-flat brick buildings. Many apartments in Ravenswood have been converted into condos, and many older homes, prized for their oversized lots, have been sold as teardowns. As with much of Chicago's neighborhoods, young professionals have discovered the area and are thought to be the driving force behind the real estate boom here. Ravenswood gained some national attention in recent years as one of the sections of Chicago that was plagued by an infestation of the Asian long-horned beetle.

Right across the street from the neighborhood's southwest corner is one of Chicago's best-known funerary landmarks, Graceland Cemetery. Here you can marvel (or wince) at the sumptuous sepulchers of former captains of industry, such as Pullman, Potter, and Getty. Ravenswood is a quiet, family-oriented part of town, and while the neighborhood lacks the restaurants and nightlife of nearby Wrigleyville and Andersonville, it's conveniently close to them.

Lincoln Square (boundaries: Ainslie Street, Eastwood Avenue, Bell Avenue, Rockwell Street), is an old German neighborhood that grew during the late 19th century, and which still retains its European flair. In the newly renovated two-block long Lincoln Square Mall, you will find plenty of German shops, restaurants and outdoor cafes, which lend authenticity to its theme of "A Touch of Europe." Meier's Deli, on Lincoln Avenue, is definitely worth a visit for its homemade German cheeses, sausages, and fine chocolates. However, the neighborhood is not homogeneous by any means. Amidst the cafes in the strip between Lincoln and Lawrence there is a row of Greek restaurants that lend a distinctly Mediterranean flavor as well as several nearby Korean, Mexican, and Baltic establishments, which reflect this neighborhood's truly international make-up. Come to the mall on Tuesday mornings for the open-air farmers' market. In the summer it's the Auto Show, the Sidewalk Arts & Crafts show, the Folk & Roots Festival, the German-American Fest, and the Lincoln Square Applefest. The number of community activities and local merchants—there are approximately 1,000 small and medium-sized local businesses in the Lincoln Square neighborhood—is a testament to the community's diversity and vitality.

This neighborhood also offers a collection of tasteful public art which includes, murals, copper fountains, German maypoles and statues, peppered with wonderful examples of Chicago Style architecture, as featured in the wood-frame Victorians, graystone mansions, and single family bungalows. One of the most beautiful and best examples of 1920s architecture is the Museum of Decorative Arts, located at 4611 North Lincoln Avenue. Once the home and music store of William Krause, this building is Louis Sullivan's last work, the same architect who was responsible for many Chicago landmarks including the Carson Pirie Scott building on State Street. The Museum sells a wide variety of decorative art and objects from the Victorian, Art Deco, Art Nouveau, and Arts and Crafts movement-era. Directly across the street is the flickering marquee of the Davis Theater, www.davistheater.com, which shows first-run Hollywood movies and independent films. South of the Davis are the digs of the popular and long-lived Old Town School of Folk Music. Conrad Sulzer Regional Library, located on the corner of Lincoln and Sunnyside, is another example of the area's outstanding architecture. Sulzer is one of the largest neighborhood library branches in the city, housing more than 250,000 books. It was designed by Hammond, Beeby and Babka, the architects who designed the Harold Washington Library in the Loop.

Web Sites: www.ci.chi.il.us, www.lincolnsquare.org
Area Code: 773
Zip Codes: 60625, 60640
Post Offices: Ravenswood, 2522 West Lawrence Avenue; Lakeview, 1343 West Irving Park Road; Uptown, 4850 North Broadway, 800-275-8777
Police District: 19th/Belmont District (Area 3), 2452 West Belmont Avenue, 312-744-5983
Emergency Hospitals: Methodist Hospital, 5025 North Paulina Street, 773-271-9040; Swedish Covenant Hospital, 5145 North California Avenue, 773-878-8200
Library: Conrad Sulzer, 4455 North Lincoln Avenue, 312-744-7616, www.chipublib.org
Community Resources: Old Town School of Folk Music, 4544 North Lincoln Avenue, 773-728-6000, www.oldtownschool.org; Jane Addams Resource Corp., 4432 North Ravenswood Avenue, 773-728-9769; Lincoln Square Chamber of Commerce, 773-728-3890, www.lincoln square.org; Organization of the Northeast (ONE), 1329 West Wilson, 773-769-3232
Parks: www.chicagoparkdistrict.com, 312-742-PLAY: Clarendon Community Center, 4501 North Clarendon Avenue; Welles Park, 2333 West Sunnyside Avenue; Winnemac Park, 5100 North Leavitt Avenue
Community Publications: *Chicago Magazine, Chicago Parent, Chicago Reader, Chicago Reporter, N'DIGO, New City, Windy City Times*
Public Schools: Chicago School District 299, 125 South Clark Street, Chicago, IL 60603, 773-553-1000, www.cps.k12.il.us
Transportation—Rapid Transit: Brown Line (stations: Irving Park, Montrose, Damen, Western); Metra/Union Pacific North Line (station: Ravenswood)
Transportation—Major Bus Routes: #11 Lincoln, #22 Clark, #49 Western, #50 Damen, #78 Montrose, #80 Irving Park, #81 Lawrence, #92 Foster

EDGEWATER

Boundaries: **North**: Devon Avenue; **South**: Foster Avenue; **East**: Lake Michigan; **West**: Ravenswood Avenue

Moving diagonally east from Ravenswood toward Lake Michigan is the Edgewater neighborhood. Between World War I and World War II, Edgewater was synonymous with elegance. This was when the Edgewater

Beach Hotel was *the* north shore spot for fine dining and dancing. But times changed, and this community, originally designed for Chicago's elite, fell into decline. The Edgewater Hotel was torn down in 1969, along with many other fine, lakeshore mansions that surrounded it. One survivor is the 19-story, flamingo pink cooperative, which houses the Edgewater Beach Apartments. While the majority of housing in Edgewater is in the form of apartments and condos, especially along the lakefront, if you walk inland a few blocks you will find parts of Edgewater that still include large houses now being rehabbed by a new generation of homeowners.

Edgewater's more recent history is a wonderful example of community spirit. The area has experienced a remarkable turnaround over the past two decades. At one time, sixteen boarded-up buildings marred the Kenmore-Winthrop corridor, and the commercial strip along Bryn Mawr Avenue contained grimy storefronts, rundown residential hotels, and abandoned buildings. Gang infestation was driving the neighborhood into rapid decay. But the community was given a second chance in 1995, when a section of Bryn Mawr Avenue, from Broadway to Lake Michigan, was declared a historic district. That led the way for tax breaks, and a renewed interest in the area by commercial developers. Ridge Avenue was another blighted area in the 1990s; buildings owned by absentee landlords attracted criminal activity and threatened the core of the neighborhood. The Edgewater Community Council led the way for several of those buildings to transfer ownership, and another 72-unit building to be renovated. Just recently, another section of Edgewater was added to the National Register of Historic Places: **Lakewood Balmoral**, a 12- square-block area stretching from Broadway to Glenwood, and Foster to Bryn Mawr. The community's efforts have paid off with the crime rate in Edgewater consistently decreasing over the past several years. Today, Edgewater is a multicultural mix of Chicagoans, who have brought to the neighborhood a variety of restaurants—from Ethiopian to Asian to Bosnian. There are several large supermarkets here, as well as interesting community theater.

At its northern edge is Loyola University, and many students live in the surrounding area. Also here: home-based businesses owners, retirees, and a large number of families of Hispanic, Asian, and Russian decent. And, according to the 2000 Census, Edgewater has the largest community of gay couples in Chicago, many of whom live in Andersonville, Edgewater's little Scandinavian enclave in its southwest corner (see next profile). With its convenient location, easy access to Lake Shore Drive, major bus routes running through it, and an active community council, this area will likely become the next great neighborhood in north Chicago. While real estate prices here are still affordable for many middle-income families and population growth over the next few years is expected to be slow, the prices for homes, brick flats, and condos are steadily rising.

The vast park and its accompanying bike path that follows the beach side of Lake Shore Drive come to an end at Edgewater's southeast corner. The family-friendly beaches here at Hollywood, Ardmore, and Foster avenues are beautiful and offer excellent views of the shoreline to the north. On clear days you can make out the lakeshore campus of Northwestern University in Evanston. Looking eastward, out across the lake, you will spot a squat, cylindrical shape that hovers about two miles off the shoreline. Don't be misled by locals who may try to convince you that it is (1) a giant floating storage tank for industrial waste, (2) a casino, or (3) the new Bears stadium. It's actually a water intake crib, one of three (if you look south you can see the others) that provides the city with its fresh water.

Web Sites: www.ci.chi.il.us; Edgewater Triangle Neighborhood Association, www.andersonville.org

Area Code: 773

Zip Codes: 60640, 60660

Post Offices: Rogers Park, 1723 West Devon Avenue; Uptown, 4850 North Broadway, 800-275-8777

Police Districts: South of Peterson Avenue: 20th/Foster Avenue District (Area 3), 5400 North Lincoln Avenue, 312-744-8330; north of Peterson Avenue: 24th/Rogers Park District (Area 3), 6464 North Clark Street, 312-744-5907

Emergency Hospitals: Weiss Memorial Hospital, 4646 North Marine Drive, 773-878-8700

Library: Edgewater, 1210 West Elmdale Avenue, 312-744-0718, www.chipublib.org

Community Resources: Edgewater Chamber of Commerce, 1210 North Thorndale, 773-561-6000, www.edgewater.org; Music Theatre Workshop (MTW), 7359 North Greenview, 773-973-7266; Organization of the NorthEast, www.onechicago.org, 773-769-3232; Edgewater Development Corporation, 773-506-4016; Edgewater Historical Society, 773-561-0893

Parks: www.chicagoparkdistrict.com, 312-742-PLAY: Berger Park, 6205-47 North Sheridan Road; Broadway Armory Park, 5917 North Broadway Street; Foster Beach, Foster Avenue and Lake Michigan; Lane Beach & Park, 5915 North Sheridan Road, (Loyola)

Community Publications: *Chicago Magazine, Chicago Parent, Chicago Reader, Chicago Reporter, N'DIGO, New City, Windy City Times*

Public Schools: Chicago School District 299, 125 South Clark Street, Chicago, IL 60603, 773-553-1000, www.cps.k12.il.us

Transportation—Rapid Transit: Red Line (stations: Berwyn, Bryn Mawr, Thorndale, Granville)

Transportation—Major Bus Routes: #22 Clark, #36 Broadway, #50
Damen, #84 Peterson, #92 Foster, #136 Sheridan/LaSalle Express, #147
Outer Drive Express, #151 Sheridan, #155 Devon

ANDERSONVILLE

Boundaries: **North**: Bryn Mawr (5600N); **South**: Foster (5200N); **East**:
Clark Street; **West**: Ravenswood Avenue (1800W)

Who needs Wisconsin or Minnesota? If you're looking for Scandinavian history and heritage, you can find it here. Andersonville, located in a half
square mile in the southwest corner of Edgewater, is an old Swedish neighborhood, first settled in the mid-19th century and planted with cherry
orchards. Although most of the Swedes are long gone, Andersonville
retains some of its ethnic flavor in its neighborhood bakeries, gift shops,
and, of course, the Swedish American Museum at 5211 North Clark Street,
773-728-8111. The neighborhood has evolved into an ethnic mosaic easily
seen by the restaurants, bakeries, and produce stands, along Clark Street,
ranging from the Swedish to Persian, Asian to Mexican, and beyond.

Housing in this neighborhood consists primarily of attractive, large single family homes and stylish three-flats. While it is less expensive than the
better-known areas to the south, Andersonville is no longer the delightful
bargain it once was. For those without a car, there is one drawback to living
here: no easy access to the 'L.' Yet somehow, each June, nearly 40,000 people find their way to Andersonville's Midsommarfest, for two days of eating, dancing, and music.

Clark Street is Andersonville's commercial strip; it's full of antiques,
books, jewelry, toys, chocolates, and restaurants, with several of the stores
and restaurants owned and operated by local residents, many of them
women. A large gay and lesbian population thrives in Andersonville, and
many businesses, such as video rental stores, bookstores and restaurants
are owned by and cater to this crowd. One of the better-known bookstores, Women and Children First, has a large collection of feminist/lesbian
material, and is known for its author signings. North of Catalpa Avenue,
you will find a large commercial area catering to the neighborhood's
Hispanic community. Two of the city's best bakeries are located in
Andersonville. For freshly baked pita bread and scrumptious spinach pies,
check out the Middle Eastern Bakery on Foster Avenue between Clark and
Ashland. Finally, for your own sake, do not buy a coffeecake from the
Swedish Bakery at 5348 North Clark Street, 773-561-8919! You will devour
the whole thing and wind up guilt-ridden, covered with crumbs, and completely satisfied. On second thought . . .

Web Sites: www.ci.chi.il.us; Edgewater Triangle Neighborhood Association, www.andersonville.org

Area Code: 773

Zip Code: 60640

Post Office: Uptown, 4850 North Broadway, 800-275-8777

Police District: 20th/Foster Avenue District (Area 3), 5400 North Lincoln Avenue, 312-744-8330

Emergency Hospitals: Methodist Hospital, 5025 North Paulina Street, 773-271-9040; Weiss Memorial Hospital, 4646 North Marine Drive, 773-878-8700

Library: Edgewater, 1210 West Elmdale Avenue, 312-744-0718, www.chipublib.org

Community Resources: Andersonville Chamber of Commerce, 1478 West Catalpa, 773-728-2995; Edgewater Development Corporation, 773-506-4016; Edgewater Historical Society, 773-561-0893; East Andersonville Residents' Council, 773-275-2228

Parks: www. chicagoparkdistrict.com, 312-742-PLAY

Community Publications: *Chicago Magazine, Chicago Parent, Chicago Reader, Chicago Reporter, N'DIGO, New City, Windy City Times*

Public Schools: Chicago School District 299, 125 South Clark Street, Chicago, IL 60603, 773-553-1000, www.cps.k12.il.us

Transportation—Rapid Transit: Red Line (station: Berwyn)

Transportation—Major Bus Routes: #22 Clark, #50 Damen, #92 Foster, #36 Broadway

---

EAST AND WEST ROGERS PARK

Boundaries: **North**: city limits with Evanston; **South**: Devon Avenue; **East**: Lake Michigan; **West**: Ridge Avenue

Just north of Edgewater, Rogers Park is Chicago's northernmost neighborhood, located on Lake Michigan. Originally a village along the old post road (Clark Street) to Green Bay, Wisconsin, and a suburb of Evanston, it was annexed by the City of Chicago in 1893. Rogers Park is perhaps Chicago's most culturally diverse community. According to 2000 Census figures, over 80 languages are spoken in this community. It is a mix of people of European Mexican, Asian, Hispanic, Caribbean, African, and Middle Eastern descent, among others, and there is a large number of Orthodox Jews.

Rogers Park has enjoyed an alliance of proactive and civic-minded residents ever since 1952 when neighbors organized to prevent private developers from building high rise apartments along the beachfront. Today, Rogers Park still attracts people who want the feeling of suburbia, but the convenience of living within the city limits. Rogers Park has a tradition of offering a wide range of affordable housing—a feature that has caused it to suffer from negligent landlords, transients, and the crime that is often associated with it. Community groups continue to work hard to remove slumlords, and the criminals and prostitutes who live in their buildings by working closely with local officials. Though the area still needs vigilant residents to keep the crime rate at bay, the result has been a reduction of crime throughout Rogers Park. Meanwhile, the oversized apartments, the vintage fixtures of the old Victorian buildings, the beckoning beaches, and the affordable rents, continue to lure many Chicagoans—some from Lakeview and Lincoln Park.

The majority of housing in Rogers Park is rental housing, but many—estimates range from 10% to 30%—have been converted into condominiums. **East Rogers Park**, a neighborhood filled with low-rise apartment buildings, and two- and three-flat houses, offers truly affordable living close to Lake Michigan. You'll find a string of Asian and Mexican restaurants along Howard Avenue, but the lack of retail stores and restaurants continues to be a sore point for many area residents. Recent additions include a 16-acre Gateway Center, which includes a Dominick's supermarket. In the summer, residents relax in the lovely green environs of Loyola Park or at one of eight beaches that extend south from Evanston like pearls on a string. The Heartland Café, located at 7000 North Glenwood, is still going strong, offering mostly vegetarian fare, outdoors or in, as well as poetry, live music, and even its own newspaper, *The Heartland Journal*, focusing on community issues. With its large student population, the neighborhood's counter-cultural legacy is in some way continually being reborn. In addition, it is estimated that Rogers Park has the largest population of artists living in the city. Late spring, when college students from nearby Loyola and Northwestern University (in Evanston) head home for the summer, is the best time to find an apartment

West Rogers Park, i.e., west of Ridge Avenue, is a bit more suburban-like, with fewer apartment buildings and more single family homes. You'll find well-kept bungalows and apartment buildings. This area is a haven for newly arrived immigrants. Devon Avenue, which runs along its southern edge, is the main shopping strip. Here are stores selling every conceivable foodstuff—Indian, Syrian, Pakistani, and Kosher—and restaurants to please every palate. If you're looking for a truly diverse neighborhood or just looking for a great, inexpensive meal, West Rogers Park is the place to go.

Web Sites: www.ci.chi.il.us; Rogers Park Community Council,www.rogers park.org
Area Code: 773
Zip Codes: 60626, 60645, 60059, 60660

Post Office: Rogers Park, 1723 West Devon Avenue, 800-275-8777

Police District: 24th/Rogers Park District (Area 3), 6464 North Clark Street, 312-744-5907

Emergency Hospitals: St. Francis Hospital of Evanston, 355 Ridge Avenue, Evanston, 847-316-4000

Library: Edgewater, 1210 West Elmdale Avenue, 312-744-0718, www.chipublib.org

Community Resources: Rogers Park Community Council, 773-338-7722; Seniors Initiative Program, 773-338-7722; Organization of the NorthEast, www.onechicago.org, 773-769-3232; Community Awareness & Pride Program, 773-338-7722; Loyola University Crown Center Gallery, 1001 West Loyola Avenue, 773-508-3811; North Lakeside Cultural Center, 6219 North Sheridan Road, 773-743-4477

Parks & Beaches: www.chicagoparkdistrict.com; 312-742-PLAY (see **Greenspace and Beaches** for a list of Rogers Park's street-end beaches).

Community Publications: *Chicago Magazine, Chicago Parent, Chicago Reader, Chicago Reporter, The Heartland Journal, N'DIGO, New City, Windy City Times*

Public Schools: Chicago School District 299, 125 South Clark Street, Chicago, IL 60603, 773-553-1000, www.cps.k12.il.us

Transportation—Rapid Transit: Red Line (stations: Loyola, Morse, Jarvis, Howard); Metra/Union Pacific North Line (station: Rogers Park)

Transportation—Major Bus Routes: #22 Clark, #49B North Western, #50 Damen, #93 North California, #96 Lunt, #147 Outer Drive Express, #151 Sheridan, #155 Devon

WEST SIDE

ALBANY PARK

Boundaries: **North**: Chicago River; **South**: Irving Park Road and Elston Avenue; **East**: Chicago River; **West**: Elston Avenue and Pulaski Road

Leaving the lakeshore, Albany Park is directly west of Ravenswood and is another example of Chicago's amazing diversity. With a foreign born population of nearly 50%, and with more than 70 languages spoken in this community, it's easy to walk down the streets here on a hot summer night and be convinced that you're in another country. But which one? When it comes to food, the questions can get overwhelming, especially on an empty stomach. Kimchee? Falafel? Fajita? Paht Thai? Happily, the answers are all equally delicious.

Albany Park, once a large Jewish community, is often referred to as Koreatown, best known now for its concentration of Korean restaurants, retail shops, and grocery stores along Lawrence Avenue. In fact the mile-long section of Lawrence between the river and Pulaski Road has been given the honorary name of Seoul Drive. While nearly 40% of the stores here are Korean owned, if you veer off towards Kedzie, between Lawrence and Wilson avenues, you'll find the neighborhood's Middle Eastern identity, with its bakeries, bookstores, and restaurants. There is also a large Hispanic and Caucasian community in Albany Park. The Lawrence Avenue strip is always busy, especially on the weekends, and traffic frequently slows to a crawl. But don't let the hustle and bustle of the avenues mislead you; veer down a side street and you will understand the practical and quiet reasons why people choose to live here: two- and three-story brick flats and single-family homes on tree-lined streets, friendly neighbors, and easy access to markets and local eating establishments. Public Transportation is good. The northbound 'L' Brown Line meets land in Albany Park after crossing the Chicago River. The resulting street-level crossings, with flashing red lights, warning bells, and barriers, give the southeast corner of the neighborhood the feel of a small town. This area is also bounded, and very much defined, by the river; along it you will find quiet streets, abundant greenery, and plenty of attractive single family-homes and apartments. Westward, the neighborhood recovers its big city edge but remains quiet and residential. Easy access to the Kennedy and Edens expressways are also perks. It should be noted that Albany Park is poorer than neighboring Lincoln Square and parts of it are rough, particularly the area north of Lawrence and east of Kedzie avenues. Many of the apartment buildings here were built in the 1920s and while many offer five, six- and seven-room apartments, this is not a gentrified area—not yet anyway. For new construction, you might look toward Ainslie Street, where new three-story homes have been built.

Albany Park's ethnic diversity is not surprising. It has always been known as a stepping-stone neighborhood, a place where generations of immigrants have cut their teeth on the New World before moving on to the suburbs. What is surprising is that the natives haven't discovered it.

Web Sites: www.ci.chi.il.us, www.albanyparkcommunitycenter.org
Area Code: 773
Zip Codes: 60018, 60625, 60630, 60646
Post Offices: Kedzie-Grace, 3750 North Kedzie Avenue; Ravenswood, 2522 West Lawrence Avenue, 800-275-8777
Police District: 17th/Albany Park District (Area 5), 4461 North Pulaski Road, 312-744-8346

Emergency Hospitals: Methodist Hospital, 5025 North Paulina Street, 773-271-9040; Ravenswood Hospital, 4550 North Winchester Avenue, 773-878-4300; Swedish Covenant Hospital, 5145 North California Avenue, 773-878-8200

Libraries: Albany Park Branch, 5150 North Kimball, 312-744-1933; Mayfair, 4400 West Lawrence Avenue, 312-744-1254, www.chipublib.org

Community Resources: Albany Park Theatre Project, 773-866-0875; Albany Park Community Center, 3403 West Lawrence, 773-583-5111

Parks: www.chicagoparkdistrict.com, 312-742-PLAY: Buffalo Park 4501 North California Avenue; Ravenswood Manor Park, 4604-46 North Manor Avenue; Ronan Park, 2900 West Lawrence Avenue

Community Publications: *Albany Park Community Center Newsletter*, www.albanyparkcommunitycenter.org, *Chicago Magazine, Chicago Parent, Chicago Reader, Chicago Reporter, N'DIGO, New City, Windy City Times*

Public Schools: Chicago School District 299, 125 South Clark Street, Chicago, IL 60603, 773-553-1000, www.cps.k12.il.us

Transportation—Rapid Transit: Brown Line (stations: Francisco, Kedzie, Kimball)

Transportation—Major Bus Routes: #53 Pulaski, #78 Montrose, #81 Lawrence, #82 Kimball/Homan, #93 North California

LOGAN SQUARE (WEST TOWN)

Boundaries: **North**: Diversey Pkwy (2800N); **South**; Fullerton Pkwy (2400N); **East**: Western Avenue (2400W)/Kennedy Expressway; **West**: Central Park Avenue (3600W)

South of Albany Park but still in the northern neighborhoods of Chicago is West Town, or as it is more commonly known, Logan Square. Virtually the center of the northwest side of Chicago, it is the city's fifth largest neighborhood. It is known for its European-style, tree-lined boulevards, its central square, and architectural variety. Also here, a substantial number of multi-family dwellings, including two-flats and apartment buildings. In the center of Logan Square stands a 68-foot tall pink marble column topped with an eagle, which commemorates the 100th anniversary of Illinois' entry into the Union. Architecturally speaking this is a delightful neighborhood. A number of homes here, many of them now restored, are of the Art Nouveau, Prairie, Renaissance Revival, and Gothic styles of architecture. Purists beware however, many homes are a compilation of styles—architecturally inspired creations rather than formally designed. Because most of the mansions in the Logan Square area were not converted into rooming houses or low rent apartments as in many other Chicago neighborhoods, you'll find many unique characteristics, including original stained glass and carved woodwork, still intact. In 1985, the boulevards of Logan Square were included on the National Register of Historic Places. For a closer look at these beautiful homes, check out the neighborhood Historic Housewalk, which takes place each September.

The Logan Square community is an economically and ethnically mixed neighborhood; many residents are of Hispanic and Eastern European, particularly Polish, descent. A recent *Wall Street Journal* article reported that there are 800,000 people of Polish descent in Chicago—many of whom can be found in and around the Logan Square community. The housing here is close to 70% multi-family, much of it in the form of two-flat brick buildings. Crime in Logan Square has been a concern, however an active community alliance has been instrumental in tempering the crime rate. Community groups are vocal and cooperate with the police to actively reduce criminal activity, including loitering and littering. But there are still problems and there are areas newcomers may want to avoid including Armitage Avenue west of Western Avenue. Recently there has been an increased interest in this neighborhood by more affluent Chicagoans, especially in the townhouses around Logan Boulevard, Palmer Square, and Fullerton and Kedzie avenues. Many of those coming here to make their homes were raised in this neighborhood, then moved to the suburbs, and are now returning to their roots. As is often the case, as the economic mix continues to improve, crime lessens.

You won't find many coffeeshops or trendy boutiques in Logan Square, there are lower rents here compared to its easterly neighbors and it is conveniently located for commuters: the Kennedy Expressway cuts through its northeastern corner, and the 'L' Blue Line runs parallel to Milwaukee Avenue. Elston and Milwaukee avenues are Logan Square's two main commercial streets. Milwaukee is lined with popular thrift stores, fruit markets, and Mexican restaurants, and the Logan Theater shows second-run Hollywood films for a song ($3 at press time). For a real time warp, don't miss the local landmark: Margie's Candies (at the southwest corner of Western and Armitage avenues). An honest to goodness ice cream parlor, Margie's has been dishing out homemade ice cream and fudge sauce for over seventy-five years.

Web Site: www.ci.chi.il.us
Area Code: 773
Zip Code: 60647
Post Office: Logan Square, 2339 North California Avenue, 800-275-8777
Police District: 14th/Shakespeare District (Area 5), 2150 North California Avenue, 312-744-8290

Emergency Hospitals: St. Elizabeth's Hospital, 1431 North Claremont Avenue, 773-278-2000; Norwegian American Hospital, 1044 North Francisco Avenue, 773-292-8200

Library: Logan Square, 3255 West Altgeld Street, 312-744-5295; West Town, 1701 North Milwaukee Avenue, 312-744-1473

Community Resources: Fullerton Avenue Chamber of Commerce, 3561 West Fullerton, 773-489-3222, www.fullertonave.org; Near Northwest Arts Council, 773-278-7677, www.nnwac.org; Logan Square Neighborhood Association, 2840 North Milwaukee Avenue, 773-384-4370; Logan Square Boys & Girls Club, 3228 West Palmer Avenue, 773-342-8800, www.bgcc.org

Parks: www.chicagoparkdistrict.com, 312-742-PLAY, Holstein Park (with pool facilities), 2200 North Oakley; Senior Citizens Park, 2238 North Oakley; Erhler Park, 2230 West Cortland; Churchill Field Park (dog friendly areas), 1825 North Damen Avenue; Walsh Park (dog friendly area), 1722 North Ashland

Community Publications: *Chicago Magazine, Chicago Parent, Chicago Reader, Chicago Reporter, N'DIGO, New City*

Public Schools: Chicago School District 299, 125 South Clark Street, Chicago, IL 60603, 773-553-1000, www.cps.k12.il.us

Transportation—Rapid Transit: Blue Line (stations: Western, California, Logan Square)

Transportation—Major Bus Routes: #49 Western, #52 Kedzie/California, #56 Milwaukee, #73 Armitage, #74 Fullerton, #76 Diversey, #82 Kimball/Homan

WICKER PARK AND BUCKTOWN

Boundaries: **Bucktown**: **North**: Fullerton Avenue (2400N); **South**: North Avenue (1600N); **East**: Kennedy Expressway/Ashland Avenue (1600W); **West**: Western Avenue (2400W); **Wicker Park**: **North**: North Avenue (1600N); **South**: Division Avenue (1200N); **East**: Ashland Avenue (1600W); **West**: Western Avenue (2400W)

Southeast of Logan Square is the Wicker Park/Bucktown community, which is blessed with gorgeous and once forgotten Queen Anne and Italianate mansions. In the late 1980s and 1990s Wicker Park became a "slacker haven" and music hub. It is now considered one of the hippest neighborhoods in Chicago. Rapid gentrification and the opening of new clubs, boutiques, and restaurants are causing many residents who came to the area for its bohemian atmosphere, inexpensive rents, and racial mix to reconsider their living options. Rents have risen with property values, making bargains much harder to come by.

Historically, Wicker Park and Bucktown were bastions of European immigration, with Germans holding sway in Wicker Park and Poles in Bucktown. Wicker Park is named for the small park in the middle of the neighborhood; Bucktown got its name because its poorer immigrants kept goats in their backyards. Median incomes have jumped substantially in both neighborhoods, particularly in Bucktown, which now boasts some of the highest rents in Chicago, although apartments are still a better deal here compared to the Gold Coast or Lincoln Park. Some community leaders have criticized area landlords for increasing the street-level rents for retail shops in order to keep the second floor rents affordable for the community's artists—good news for those in the arts! In fact, the neighborhood is very proud of its artistic residents: Wicker Park claims it is the largest working artist community in the nation; and Bucktown promotes the creative elements of its neighborhood by hosting the annual Bucktown Art-Fest. This 20-year-old neighborhood tradition draws over 30,000 art lovers to the area each August.

The boundary between Wicker Park and Bucktown is the elevated Soo Line railroad track, with Wicker Park to the north and Bucktown to the south. Beyond that, it's difficult to distinguish one neighborhood from the other. But you may notice that Wicker Park has more period homes, including turn-of-the-century mansions, while Bucktown is characterized by its cottage-style homes and coach houses. Both Wicker Park and Bucktown fell on hard times during the flight to the suburbs after World War II. The area was further splintered by the building of I-55 in the 1950s. Latinos filled the post-war void and today remain the area's largest ethnic group—although that's changing as gentrification creeps north and west. New single-family homes are available on the 2300 block of West Wabansia, in the southwest corner of Bucktown. This 33-unit development offers four-bedroom, 2 1/2 bath units with between 3,000 and 4,600 square feet of space. While the price tag for these units (base price was almost $600,000 in 2002) is below what you might find in the heart of Chicago, it is still beyond the scope of many long-term residents. Throughout Chicago, new construction is being targeted to empty nesters, upscale families, or single professionals. Often, the introduction of these new residents has energized many communities, and in some cases, incoming residents have worked with long-term residents, galvanizing efforts to improve neighborhood living conditions. In Bucktown, for example, cooperation between the community and the local police department contributed to over 600 prostitution arrests in one year.

In recent years, Wicker Park/Bucktown has become a favorite destination for chic and savvy diners; the intersection of Damen, Milwaukee, and

North avenues are a kind of gastronomical hub. Many of the restaurants are French, but you will also find Mexican, Costa Rican, Asian, Chilean, and Italian as well. Valet and permit parking have also arrived and vehicular mayhem reigns, especially on the weekends. But take care, a short walk north of this intersection the area turns grittier.

Web Sites: Bucktown Community Organization, www.bucktown.org; http://groups.msn.com/ChicagoBucktownPublicSquare; West Town Chamber of Commerce, www.westownchamber.org; Chicago Bucktown North-Hermitage-Paulina-Wabansia Block Club: http://groups.msn.com/ChicagoBucktownNorthHermitagePaulinaWab ansiaBlockClub, http://groups.msn.com/ChicagoBucktownNews

Area Codes: 312 and 773

Zip Codes: 60614, 60622, 60647

Post Offices: Wicker Park, 1635 West Division Street; Logan Square, 2339 North California Avenue, 800-275-8777

Police District: 14th/Shakespeare District (Area 5), 2150 North California Avenue, 312-744-8290

Emergency Hospitals: St. Elizabeth's Hospital, 1431 North Claremont Avenue, 773-278-2000; St. Mary of Nazareth Hospital Center, 2233 West Division Street, 312-770-2000

Libraries: Eckhart Park, 1373 West Chicago Avenue, 312-746-6069; West Town, 1701 North Milwaukee Avenue, 312-744-1473

Community Resources: Wicker Park & Bucktown Chamber of Commerce, 1608 North Milwaukee Avenue, 773-384-2672, www.wickerparkbuck town.com; Wicker Park Garden Club, 773-278-9075, www.mywicker park.org; Wicker Park Advisory Council, 1425 North Damen, 312-742-7553, www.mywickerpark.org; CAPS, 773-781-5991; Bucktown Community Organization, www.bucktown.org, 312-409-4003; Polish Museum of America, 984 North Milwaukee Avenue, 773-384-3352

Parks: www.chicagoparkdistrict.com, 312-742-PLAY, Clemente Park, 2334 West Division; Bickerdike Square Park, 1461 West Ohio; Commercial Park, 1845 West Rice; Eckhart Park, 1330 West Chicago; Humboldt Park, 1400 West Sacramento; Pulaski Park, 1419 West Blackhawk; Wicker Park, 1425 North Damen; Holstein Park (pool facilities), 2200 North Oakley Avenue; Senior Citizens Memorial Park, 2238 North Oakley Avenue; Erhler Park, 2230 West Cortland; Churchill Field Park (dog friendly), 1825 North Damen; Walsh Park (dog friendly), 1722 North Ashland

Community Publications: www.wickerparkbucktown.com/news, *Chicago Magazine, Chicago Parent, Chicago Reader, Chicago Reporter, N'DIGO, New City, Windy City Times*

Public Schools: Chicago School District 299, 125 South Clark Street, Chicago, IL 60603, 773-553-1000, www.cps.k12.il.us

Transportation—Rapid Transit: Blue Line (stations: Division, Damen, Western, California)

Transportation—Major Bus Routes: #9 Ashland, #49 Western, #50 Damen, #56 Milwaukee, #70 Division, #72 North, #73 Armitage, #74 Fullerton.

UKRAINIAN VILLAGE

Boundaries: **North**: Division Street (1200N); **South**: Grand Avenue (500N); **East**: Damen Avenue (2000W); **West**: Western Avenue (2400W)

The name says it all: mostly Ukrainian immigrants who came to Chicago at the turn of the 20th century settled this west side neighborhood, located southwest of Wicker Park. Unlike other ethnic enclaves in Chicago, the Ukrainian stamp remains on this quiet neighborhood with its onion-domed churches and signs lettered in Cyrillic. The Holy Trinity Orthodox Cathedral, 1121 North Leavitt Street, designed by famed Chicago architect Louis Sullivan, was granted landmark status in 1979, and is well worth a visit. Also check the Ukrainian National Museum, 721 North Oakley Blvd. The area bordered by Haddon Avenue on the north, Cortez Street on the south, Damen Avenue on the east, and Leavitt Avenue on the west, was granted preliminary landmark status in 2002. Approximately one-third of the brick flats in this area were completed by 1906 and were built by William de Kerfoot's construction company. De Kerfoot was also instrumental in rebuilding Chicago after the Great Fire of 1871.

The rapidly growing eastern section of the neighborhood (from Damen to Ashland) has attracted large numbers of Hispanic families as well as artists and students seeking bargains. There are, however, still descendants of the Eastern Europeans who founded the area. Live here and you may find yourself living next door to the adult children and grandchildren of a building's original inhabitants.

Architecturally, the neighborhood has everything, from mansions on Hoyne, to graystone flats, to workers' cottages. Many of these buildings retain their original, ornate designs and details that attract rehabbers and do-it-yourselfers. Housing prices are generally lower here than in Wicker Park, though recent interest in this community has raised prices. According to the 2000 Census, median home values here increased 176% during the 1990s, the steepest increase in the city. Local community groups have pressed for more affordable housing and some builders have responded with reasonably priced two flats.

Division Street forms the border between Wicker Park and the Ukranian Village; along this section of Division, you will find Greek, Italian, and Japanese restaurants, as well as resale shops, grocery stores, and video stores.

On Western and Chicago avenues, you will find Polish restaurants, bakeries, Italian delis, French, and even a vegetarian restaurant. All told, you will find the Ukranian Village is a rich mix of old-world traditions and modern sensibilities.

Web Site: www.ci.chi.il.us

Area Code: 312

Zip Codes: 60612, 60622

Post Offices: Wicker Park, 1635 West Division Street; Midwest, 2419 West Monroe, 800-275-8777

Police District: 13th/Wood District (Area 4), 937 North Wood Street, 312-746-8350

Emergency Hospitals: St. Elizabeth's Hospital, 1431 North Claremont Avenue, 773-278-2000; St. Mary of Nazareth Hospital Center, 2233 West Division Street, 312-770-2000; Rush-Presbyterian St. Luke's Medical Center, 1653 West Congress Parkway, 312-942-5000

Libraries: Eckhart Park, 1371 West Chicago Avenue, 312-746-6069; West Town, 1701 North Milwaukee Avenue, 312-744-1473

Community Resources: West Town Chamber of Commerce, www.west townchamber.org; Ukrainian Village Preservation Group, 773-486-3891; Ukrainian National Museum, 721 North Oakley Blvd., 312-421-8020

Parks: www.chicagoparkdistrict.com, 312-742-PLAY, Clemente Park, 2334 West Division Street; Commercial Park, 1845 West Rice Street; Dean Park, 1344 North Dean Street; Dogwood Park, 2732 North Polk Street; Eckhart Park, 1330 West Chicago Avenue; Humboldt Park, 1400 North Sacramento; Pulaski Park, 1419 West Blackhawk Street; Sain Park, 2453 West Monroe; Western Park, 902 North Western; Wicker Park, 1425 North Damen

Community Publications: *Chicago Magazine, Chicago Parent, Chicago Reader, Chicago Reporter, N'DIGO, New City*

Public Schools: Chicago School District 299, 125 South Clark Street, Chicago, IL 60603, 773-553-1000, www.cps.k12.il.us

Transportation—Rapid Transit: Blue Line (enter and exit at Damen)

Transportation—Major Bus Routes: #9 Ashland, #49 Western, #50 Damen, #65 Grand, #66 Chicago, #70 Division

TAYLOR STREET/UNIVERSITY OF ILLINOIS–CHICAGO

Boundaries: **North**: Harrison Street (600S); **South**: Roosevelt Road (1200S); **East**: Halsted Street (800W); **West**: Ashland Avenue (1600W)

Heading south from the Ukranian Village is an area of Chicago that is generally referred to as the Near West Side. It includes several neighborhoods, such as **Little Italy**, **University Village**, and the **Jackson Boulevard Historic District**. The Little Italy area is the oldest continuously Italian neighborhood in Chicago. Now only a small enclave, this neighborhood has suffered severe demolition of its pre-World War II row houses and brick flats. Initially, demolition was to make way for the 560-acre University of Illinois Medical District and a 305-acre West Side Medical Center, now one of the world's largest concentrations of medical facilities. The area was reduced again to make room for the Eisenhower Expressway, and then again, for the university's Circle Campus. These demolitions dispersed the tight-knit Italian community to neighborhoods as far west as Harlem Avenue, and on into the neighboring Melrose Park, Chicago Heights, and Blue Island communities. While these areas went on to form strong Italian communities, in Chicago, it is Taylor Street that is synonymous with "Little Italy."

As the university continues to grow (what once was a commuter college now has dormitories), the neighborhood loses a little more of its ethnic color. The strip of Italian restaurants on Taylor Street and Vernon Park Place are a fine example of what the entire area once looked like. Recently there has been a revived interest in the area, and building renovation is taking place in the Taylor Street neighborhood; most of the construction consists of new townhomes to accommodate the medical personnel who want to live close to the cluster of large hospitals in the area.

UIC is in the midst of a large southward expansion of its campus, which is good news for construction companies and students—but neighbors to the south are wary. Given the college's track record of swallowing up low-income neighborhoods, they have good reason. But this time it seems community interests have been given some consideration, especially in the area of preserving the old Maxwell Street Market, a popular open-air marketplace. At the former site of the market there are plans to build a community of over 900 townhomes and condominiums with a wide range of pricing. The university envisions a development that will create a new community here, not merely academic residences. The University Village Marketplace, as it is being called, includes 12 new buildings as well as the rehabbing of eight old buildings on Halsted and Maxwell streets, making them available for retail shops, restaurants, and offices. A system of public parks will run through the area as well.

Web Site: www.ci.chi.il.us
Area Code: 312
Zip Code: 60607
Post Office: Main Post Office, 433 West Harrison Street, 800-275-8777
Police District: 12th/Monroe District (Area 4), 100 South Racine Avenue, 312-746-8396

Emergency Hospitals: John H. Stroger Jr. Hospital of Cook County, 1901 West Harrison, 312-864-6000; Rush-Presbyterian St. Luke's Hospital, 1653 West Congress Parkway, 312-942-5000; University of Illinois Hospital and Clinics, 1740 West Taylor Street, 312-996-9634

Library: Roosevelt, 1055 West Roosevelt Road, 312-746-5656

Parks: www.chicagoparkdistrict.com, 312-742-PLAY, Arrigo Park, 801 South Loomis Street; Garibaldi Park, 1520 West Polk; Miller Playlot, 848 South Miller; Sheridan Park, 910 South Aberdeen Street; Union Park, 1501 West Randolph Street

Community Publications: *Chicago Magazine, Chicago Parent, Chicago Reader, Chicago Reporter, N'DIGO, New City*

Public Schools: Chicago School District 299, 125 South Clark Street, Chicago, IL 60603, 773-553-1000, www.cps.k12.il.us

Transportation—Rapid Transit: Blue Line (stations: U of I/Halsted, Racine, Polk, Medical Center)

Transportation—Major Bus Routes: #8 Halsted, #9 Ashland, #12 Roosevelt, #37 Sedgwick/Ogden, #50 Racine, #60 Blue Island

PILSEN/LITTLE VILLAGE

Boundaries: **North**: 16th Street; **South**: South Branch of Chicago River; **East**: Canal Street; **West**: Damen Avenue

In recent decades it's been a familiar story: a poor neighborhood with attractive but run-down housing stock is "discovered" by budding creative types, who gradually rehab the area and who are then in turn replaced by well-heeled newcomers with higher economic means. For better or for worse, Pilsen is the latest of these discoveries. Conveniently located south of the University of Illinois Chicago campus and in close proximity to the Loop, public transit, and three expressways, its turn around was inevitable, though this is scarce comfort to many families who now find themselves unable to afford living here.

Also known as the **Lower West Side**, in the 1920s immigrant Czechs dubbed it Pilsen after the city of the same name in the former Czechoslovakia. Germans, Czechs, Poles, Bohemians, and Lithuanians originally settled it, and for many years it was an industrial neighborhood whose inhabitants worked in the factories, lumberyards, and docks along the Chicago River and the Sanitary and Ship Canal. Beginning in the 1950s, Mexicans and Puerto-Ricans began arriving—and today it has the highest percentage of Latino residents (close to 90%) of any Chicago neighborhood. In fact, it is one of the largest Mexican communities in the United

States. The median age of a Pilsen resident is 18; more than a third of the neighborhood's children live below the poverty line.

While many area residents are poor, there are many positive developments brewing in Pilsen. Eighteenth Street, the main east-west artery through the neighborhood, with its restaurants aplenty, and bars, ice cream shops, and bakeries galore, is hopping at all hours. Blue Island and Ashland avenues cut across 18th Street, and is where you'll find small grocery stores and taquerias. The creative types head to the area called **Pilsen East**, the unofficial artists' community clustered mainly around 18th, 19th, and Halsted streets. A one-time commercial district where stores and factories have become artists' studios, you can find ample living/work space (well over 1,000 square feet) for less than $1,000 a month. (Note: tenants are usually responsible for gas and electric bills.) During the last weekend of September, the artists who live in the buildings along 18th and 19th streets open up their studios to the public. Don't overlook the courtyards between buildings—there are exhibits set up there too. Also in the neighborhood, the Mexican Fine Arts Center Museum (MFACM), 1852 West 19th Street, is the largest Latino or Mexican art institute in the nation and has an excellent gift shop. Pilsen leads the way in public art. You will be hard pressed to find another Chicago community that has so many examples of artistic expression displayed throughout its streets. From 16th Street to the Chicago River east and south, then west to Western Avenue, are vibrant murals painted on public spaces. There are even some along the 18th Street station of the Blue Line.

Given the background of most area residents it's no surprise there are plenty of celebrations revolving around Mexican culture. On the last weekend of July, make plans to attend the Fiesta del Sol for live music, games, rides and food. Each spring the Mexican Fine Arts Museum hosts the Del Corazon Performing Arts Festival, and the Sor Juana Festival in the fall. Then through October and early November, experience the Dia de los Muertos, the Day of the Dead festival. If you enjoy parades you won't want to miss the Cinco de Mayo parade on the first Sunday in May. The parade travels up Cermack Road and ends with a festival in Douglas Park.

While Pilsen has its charms, it is like many other poor areas in the nation—the crime rate is high, especially property crime, and there is gang violence. Caution should be exercised when considering living in this neighborhood. Visit and see for yourself.

Web Site: www.ci.chi.il.us
Area Code: 312
Zip Codes: 60608, 60616
Post Office: Pilsen, 1859 South Ashland Avenue; Twenty-second, 2035 South State, 800-275-8777

Police District: 12th/Monroe District (Area 4), 100 South Racine Avenue, 312-746-8396

Emergency Hospitals: John H. Stroger Jr. Hospital of Cook County, 1901 West Harrison, 312-864-6000; Mercy Hospital and Medical Center, 2525 South Michigan Avenue, 312-567-2000; Rush-Presbyterian St. Luke's Medical Center, 1653 West Congress Parkway, 312-942-5000; University of Illinois Hospital and Clinics, 1740 West Taylor Street, 312-996-9634

Library: Lozano, 1805 South Loomis Street, 312-746-4329

Community Resources: Early Outreach Hispanic Math/Science Initiative, 1101 West Taylor Street, 312-996-0979; WRTE 90.5 FM Radio (youth operated community radio station), 312-455-9455; MFACM, 1852 West 19th Street, 312-738-1503, www.mfacmchicago.org

Community Publications: *Chicago Magazine, Chicago Parent, Chicago Reader, Chicago Reporter, N'DIGO, New City*

Public Schools: Chicago School District 299, 125 South Clark Street, Chicago, IL 60603, 773-553-1000, www.cps.k12.il.us

Transportation—Rapid Transit: Blue Line (stations: 18th, Hoyne)

Transportation—Major Bus Routes: #8 Halsted, #9 Ashland, #18 16th-18th, #21 Cermak, #50 Damen, #60 Blue Island

SOUTH SIDE

SOUTH LOOP

Boundaries: **North**: Jackson Boulevard; **South**: 16th Street; **East**: Lake Shore Drive; **West**: Chicago River

DEARBORN PARK/PRINTERS ROW/RIVER CITY/CENTRAL STATION

The South Loop has been developing steadily since the early 1980s and continues to enjoy a construction boom. Most recently, and most exciting is the Lake Shore Drive Improvement Project. In 1997, the city moved Lake Shore Drive's northbound lanes west of Soldier Field and the Field Museum. That created ten acres of parkland along the shore, which was finished with elegant landscaping and bike and footpaths. Neighborhoods to the west of Lake Shore Drive are connected to the park and to CTA's Blue Line stop by newly constructed bridges and walkways. If you work in the Loop and want to live close to the office, few locations are more convenient or as architecturally attractive as those in the South Loop.

Renewed interest in the South Loop is great news for an area that was once labeled a slum. At the turn of the 20th century, grand mansions sat on

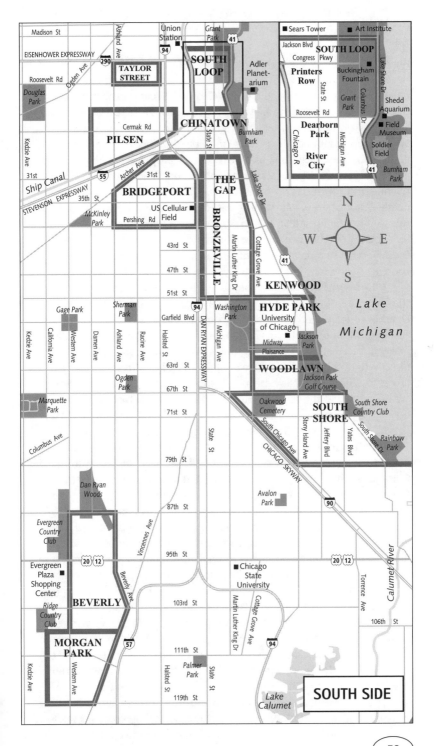

Prairie Avenue, but the wealthy left these grand residences behind and headed north to the newer environs of the Gold Coast and North Shore neighborhoods. Eventually, the Illinois Central Railroad too abandoned the tracks and rail yard, and the area became a no-man's land. Desolate, unsafe, and minimally populated, the area remained that way for years. Today the South Loop consists of three established neighborhoods: Dearborn Park, Printers Row, and River City, as well as other nearby developments, including the largest, the Central Station neighborhood, which is east of Michigan Avenue and south of Roosevelt Road. While the support services most neighborhoods enjoy—grocery stores, dry cleaners, drug stores, and the like—are slowly filtering in, the South Loop does have a neighborhood feel to it and is poised to become one of the most desirable locations to live in the city. What's more, at least for the time being, home prices in the South Loop are significantly less than what you can find in the Near North Side.

Dearborn Park is a townhouse/rentals/condominium development that has been in the making for well over 20 years. The dream that Dearborn Park would some day become a reality survived through the administrations of six mayors and innumerable political stalemates. But a reality it became. Built on land formerly owned by several railroads, it lies directly south of the Loop between State and Clark streets, south of Polk Street to 15th Street. New, beautiful, and expensive single-family homes are being built to the south of Dearborn Park's original high-rise and town house development. Dearborn Park II, as it is called, at 14th and State streets, contains single family homes, row houses, and town homes.

Printers Row, a condominium and rental area in buildings that once housed printing firms, is located just south of the Loop, steps away from the Chicago Board of Trade, and centrally located to several colleges, including Columbia College, Roosevelt University, and John Marshall Law School. Despite its urban surrounds, the area has a definite neighborhood feel to it. The intimate Dearborn Park is a friendly place, with bike paths, leafy trees, and young families. Restaurants, bars, and bookstores abound, and every June the neighborhood hosts one of the largest outdoor book fairs in the country. Five blocks, in the 500 to 700 blocks of South Dearborn, are tented to make way for the 70,000 people that attend this fair each year (see **Literary Life** in the **Cultural Life** chapter for more information).

A little further south, **River City**, 312-431-2800, www.rivercityrentals.com, an apartments-only complex, boasts outstanding views of the Loop and has docking facilities for 70 boats on the south branch of the Chicago River. Developed in the mid-1980s, River City is a city within a city, containing a health club, restaurants, and other amenities.

The largest of the planned communities downtown, **Central Station**, 312-663-5750, www.centralstationsouthloop.com, sits west of Soldier Field. Among those who live in the 80-acre mixed-use project is

Mayor Richard M. Daley and his family, who moved from their longtime South Side home in the Bridgeport neighborhood. This development, with its proximity to the lovely Museum Campus—the green spaces, trails, and parks surrounding Shedd Aquarium, the Field Museum, and the Adler Planetarium—is popular with area residents and tourists alike. In addition to the residential properties, when finished Central Station will contain 3,500 hotel rooms, over seven million square feet of office space, one million square feet of retail space, and three million square feet of building space for medical, trade, exhibition, cultural, and educational use. Among the many residential developments in Central Station, **Burnham Station** at 15th and Clark streets has condominiums and row houses ready to go; **Prairie District Homes** at 18th Street and Prairie Avenue offers town-homes and tower residences, and a new pedestrian bridge to Soldier Field; and **Museum Park** (www.museumpark.com) is a posh development, complete with a clubhouse, swimming pool and fitness center.

Area amenities include two grocery chains, a Dominick's at Canal and Roosevelt, and a Jewel at Roosevelt and State, and new restaurants and art galleries.

Web Sites: www.ci.chi.il.us, Historic Printers Row Neighbors, www.hprn.org, www.rivercityrentals.com, www.friendsofdown-town.org, www.centralstation.org

Area Code: 312

Zip Codes: 60604, 60605, 60606, 60607

Post Offices: Main Post Office, Cardiss Collins Postal Store, 433 West Harrison Street, 312-983-8182, open 24/7 (except for postal holidays and every third Saturday p.m./Sunday a.m. for an audit); Loop Station, 211 South Clark Street; 22nd Street, 2035 South State Street, 800-275-8777

Police District: 1st/Central District (Area 1), 1718 South State Street, 312-745-4290

Emergency Hospitals: University of Illinois Hospital and Clinics, 1740 West Taylor Street, 312-996-7000; Mercy Hospital and Medical Center, 2525 South Michigan Avenue, 312-567-2000

Libraries: Harold Washington Library, 400 South State Street, 312-747-4300, www.chipublib.org

Community Resources: Historic Printers Row Neighbors, 312-409-1700, www.hprn.org; Near South Planning Board, 1727 South Indiana, 312-987-1980; Sherwood Conservatory of Music, 1312 South Michigan Avenue, 312-427-6267

Parks: www.chicagoparkdistrict.com, 312-742-PLAY, Dearborn Park, 865 South Terrace Park; Burnham Park, 424 East McFetridge Drive; Coliseum Park, 1466 South Wabash Avenue; Indigo Bird Park, 1240 South Plymouth Court; Roosevelt Park, 62 West Roosevelt Road

Community Publications: *Columbia Chronicle Newspaper*, 312-344-7253, *Chicago Daily Defender*, *Chicago Journal*, *Chicago Magazine*, *Chicago Parent*, *Chicago Reader*, *Chicago Reporter*, *Crain's Chicago Business*, *N'DIGO*, *New City*

Public Schools: Chicago School District 299, 125 South Clark Street, Chicago, IL 60603, 773-553-1000, www.cps.k12.il.us

Transportation—Rapid Transit: Red Line (stations: Jackson, Harrison, Roosevelt); Brown Line (station: Van Buren & LaSalle); Green Line (station: Adams-Wabash); Blue Line (stations: Jackson, LaSalle); Orange Line (stations: Roosevelt, Library)

Transportation—Main Bus Routes: #3 King Drive, #4 Cottage Grove, #11, #12 Roosevelt, #22 Clark, #24 Wentworth, #29 State, #36 Broadway, #62 Archer

THE GAP/BRONZEVILLE/DOUGLAS

Boundaries: **North**: 26th Street; **South**: 47th Street; **East**: Cottage Grove; **West**: Federal Street

Bronzeville is the nickname this South Side neighborhood acquired in the 1930s and '40s, and includes the adjoining Gap and Douglas neighborhoods. **The Gap** is a near South Side neighborhood that is a mixture of high-rise developments, including South Commons located at 2845 South Indiana Avenue, and original Victorian gray- and brown-stone flats. This area, between 25th and 36th streets, earned its name years ago when it literally was the gap between Chinatown to the north and De LaSalle High School to the south. (Some residents have adopted a new moniker for a part of the neighborhood that is undergoing extensive development: "South Gap," which refers to the area south to Pershing Road, between Giles and Prairie streets.)

Today there is renewed interest in **Bronzeville's** residential properties, including rehabbing landmark homes, as well as the creation of new luxury townhomes. Good news in an area of subsidized housing complexes, criminal activity, and high jobless rates. While many of the earlier Victorian and graystone homes are gone, some highly altered versions of the first buildings still exist facing the Groveland Park. Groveland Park, which lies between 33rd and 35th streets near Lake Michigan, is a remnant of Senator Stephen A. Douglas' landholdings in the area. (Douglas ran against Abraham Lincoln for president in 1860.)

In the 1870s, the Bronzeville area was an upper-class neighborhood of mostly white residents. After the Great Fire of 1871, many German Jews who lost their homes in the fire relocated to Bronzeville. They along with many of the already established residents helped create the historic landmarks you see today: street after street of Victorian row houses, some designed by Louis Sullivan and later, by Frank Lloyd Wright. Between the 1870s and the early 1900s, Bronzeville continued to thrive as a wealthy commercial and residential area. One of the country's first African-American surgeons, Daniel Hale Williams, established Provident Hospital in the area, in 1891. It was one of only a handful of interracial institutions.

In the first half of the 20th century, the neighborhood saw a lot of change: apartment buildings were added by the 1900s, and the area moved from being a wealthy enclave to a working class residential area with some light industry. The western portion of **Douglas** was settled by Italian immigrants and southern Blacks, both looking for work and a better life. Racial tensions in the area resulted in the Race Riot of 1919 on the 29th Street Beach, signaling the beginning of the exodus of white residents; by 1924, the Douglas neighborhood was predominately black. By the 1940s, Bronzeville was the heart and soul of the African-American community of Chicago. The area surrounding 47th Street was known as the "Harlem of Chicago." As Bronzeville's popularity increased, so did demand for housing. Single-family homes were altered to create apartments, and by 1950, the solution was to tear down houses to make way for the much publicized and even then much criticized public housing developments. These included the Robert Taylor Homes, Stateway Gardens, and the Ida B. Wells projects. What followed was an absolute downturn of any remaining community vitality: crime rose dramatically, industry moved out, and buildings were left vacant. Between 1950-1990, the area lost nearly two-thirds of its population.

Today, Bronzeville is making a strong comeback as professionals, many of them African-American, are picking up the run-down graystones at bargain-basement prices and rehabbing them to their former glory. Chicago instituted the African-American Showcase of Homes to encourage residents to rebuild Bronzeville. The City of Chicago donated the land and the African-American Home Builders Association donated two million dollars to assist local builders to create market-rate homes on South St. Lawrence Avenue.

Driving south on Dr. Martin Luther King Jr. Drive, the contrast between old and new is remarkable. From 26th Street to 35th street, the new developments tower overhead, but they are surrounded by large open spaces. South of 35th you feel like you've stepped back a hundred years. The houses are spectacular, with intricate stonework and wrought iron fences, a perfect complement to this wide, tree-lined boulevard.

A word of caution, this neighborhood is still edgy in terms of safety and is best suited for those comfortable with urban environs.

Web Sites: www.bronzevilleonline.com, www.ci.chi.il.us
Area Codes: 312 and 773

Zip Codes: 60616, 60653

Post Offices: Twenty-second Street, 2035 South State Street; Hyde Park, 4601 South Cottage Grove Avenue, 800-275-8777

Police Districts: North of 35th Street and east of Cottage Grove Avenue: 21st/Prairie District (Area 1), 300 East 29th Street, 312-747-8340; south of 35th Street and west of Cottage Grove: 2nd/Wentworth District (Area 1), 5101 South Wentworth Avenue, 312-747-8366

Emergency Hospitals: Mercy Hospital and Medical Center, 2525 South Michigan Avenue, 312-567-2000; Michael Reese Hospital & Medical Center, 2929 South Ellis Avenue, 312-791-2000

Library: King, 3436 South King Drive, 312-747-7543; Chicago Bee Branch, 3647 South State Street, 312-747-6872, www.chipublib.org

Community Resources: Chicago Urban League Development Corp., 4510 South Michigan Avenue, 773-285-1500; Wabash Avenue YMCA, 3763 South Wabash, 773-285-0020; Community Policing, 312-747-2930

Parks: www.chicagoparkdistrict.com, 312-742-PLAY, Groveland Park, 35th Street/Cottage Grove Drive: site of Senator Stephen Douglas' tomb; Victory Monument, 31st Street/King Drive (starting point for the annual Bud Billiken Parade); Walk of Fame/King Drive (series of bronze plaques honoring neighborhood's celebrities); Monument to the Great Northern Migration, 25th Street/King Drive

Community Publications: *Chicago Daily Defender, Chicago Journal, Chicago Magazine, Chicago Parent, Chicago Reader, Chicago Reporter, Hyde Park Herald, N'DIGO*

Public Schools: Chicago School District 299, 125 South Clark Street, Chicago, IL 60603, 773-553-1000, www.cps.k12.il.us

Transportation—Rapid Transit: Green Line (stations: 35, Bronzeville, IIT); Metra/Electric Line (station: 27th Street)

Transportation—Major Bus Routes: #1 Indiana/Hyde Park, #3 King Drive, #4 Cottage Grove, #35 35th Street, #39 Pershing

---

BRIDGEPORT/CHINATOWN

Boundaries: **North**: Archer Avenue; **South**: Pershing Road (3900S); **East**: Dan Ryan Expressway; **West**: Ashland Avenue (1600W)

West of The Gap is **Bridgeport**; a fine old Chicago neighborhood which encompasses the area around the new US Cellular Field (formerly Comiskey Park), home of the Chicago White Sox. Bridgeport is filled with bungalows, two- and three-flats, and a few churches built in the 1800s. While real-estate prices have risen dramatically here in this middle-income neighborhood well away from the lake, as much as 35% in some areas, you can still find a single-family home in Bridgeport for less than $200,000—still affordable for many first-time home buyers. Rentals too are a good deal.

Bridgeport has been an established community for over 160 years. First here were Lithuanian, Italian, Polish, and Irish immigrants who moved in to work on the Illinois & Michigan Canal. Bridgeport has since served as the breeding ground for five Chicago mayors, and is perhaps best known as the one-time home of both Mayor Daleys.

Bridgeport is a world unto itself, a residential island surrounded by factories, railroad tracks, and the Stevenson Expressway. The world-famous Chicago stockyards lie just south of here, which inspired the material for Upton Sinclair's classic exposé of the meat-packing industry, *The Jungle*. These days, though it remains a bit insular (it's not unusual for residents to live within a few doors of the house where they grew up), names on Bridgeport mailboxes have been changing as a new wave of immigrants make this family-friendly neighborhood their own. In addition to the established Chinese population, Bridgeport's newest immigrant residents, those of Mexican descent, are pumping new life into the once declining retail strip on Halsted Street. Move here, and along with the remaining Lithuanian and Italian restaurants, you will also find Asian grocery stores, myriad discount variety stores, Mexican restaurants, and other businesses catering to the local ethnic enclaves. While most street parking is zoned residential (meaning you must have a sticker in order to be legally parked), there is metered parking available along Halsted, 31st, and 35th streets.

New housing is being erected in the vicinity of the ball park, and developers have targeted other areas too, such as the Old Glue section of Bridgeport, where new housing developments in the bungalow style, and one- and two-story buildings blend in with the existing styles. Improvements in the quality of the Chicago River have made it an attractive feature to homeowners along its banks. There are several housing developments, in various stages of completion, being built along the west bank of the river, and along Bubble Creek, a tributary of the river's south branch.

Bridgeport includes Chicago's eight-block **Chinatown**, bounded by Cermak Road, Wentworth, and 26th Street. According to a recent *Chicago Tribune* article, revitalization is also happening in this often-overlooked part of the city. Development geared toward residential life, including a new community center and the building of single-family homes, townhomes, and condominiums, is meeting the needs of would-be homeowners, many of whom are long-time residents of Chinatown. Located just south of the South Loop area, and with housing prices going for far less, Chinatown is a good prospect for many.

Strategically located, with easy access to downtown Chicago and industry, Bridgeport/Chinatown continues to attract many to its borders.

Web Site: www.ci.chi.il.us

Area Codes: 312 and 773

Zip Codes: 60608, 60609, 60616

Post Office: Stockyards, 4101 South Halsted Street, 800-275-8777

Police District: 9th/Deering District (Area 3), 3501 South Lowe Avenue, 312-747-8227

Emergency Hospitals: Mercy Hospital and Medical Center, 2525 South Michigan Avenue, 312-567-2000; Michael Reese Hospital & Medical Center, 2929 South Ellis Avenue, 312-791-2000

Library: Daley Branch, 3400 South Halsted Street, 312-747-8990, www.chipublib.org

Community Resources: Chicago Chinatown Chamber of Commerce, 2169B South China Place, 312-326-5320

Parks: www.chicagoparkdistrict.com, 312-742-PLAY, Armour Square Park, 3309 South Shields Avenue; Donvan Park, 3620 South Lituanica Avenue; McKeon Park, 3548 South Wallace Street

Public Schools: Chicago School District 299, 125 South Clark Street, Chicago, IL 60603, 773-553-1000, www.cps.k12.il.us

Community Publications: *Chicago Daily Defender, Chicago Journal, Chicago Magazine, Chicago Parent, Chicago Reader, Chicago Reporter, Hyde Park Herald, N'DIGO*

Transportation—Rapid Transit: Red Line (stations: Sox/35th); Orange Line (Halsted, Ashland stops)

Transportation—Major Bus Routes: #8 Halsted, #35 35th Street, #39 Pershing, #44 Wallace/Racine, #62 Archer

HYDE PARK/KENWOOD

Boundaries: **North**: 47th Street; **South**: 60th Street; **East**: Lake Michigan; **West**: Cottage Grove Avenue

Thanks to the University of Chicago, **Hyde Park** is a bastion of cosmopolitan culture, which makes it something of an anomaly on the otherwise unpolished South Side. Although the area is surrounded by poor neighborhoods, Hyde Park prides itself on being one of the few racially integrated neighborhoods in Chicago. Established in 1925 when this area was one of wealth and prestige, the University's continued presence in this area known for its racial tensions and impoverished, crime-ridden neighborhoods may be helping to create safer surrounding neighborhoods. Slowly but surely, neighborhoods to the north, south, and west are improving. In terms of immediate safety for those living in Hyde Park proper, the neighborhood is patrolled by the Chicago Police and by the University of Chicago Police

Force, once the second largest force in the state of Illinois. With such diligence, it is no wonder that crime statistics show Hyde Park to have a relatively low crime rate, however, it is never wise to wander late at night alone. (Hyde Park residents should check the university's web site, www.chicagolife.uchicago.edu, for the wide range of transportation services available around the campus grounds and housing facilities. There is even an on-call late night van service.)

In 1893, Hyde Park was the site of the World Columbian Exposition, celebrating the 400th anniversary of the discovery of America. The reconstructed Museum of Science and Industry, 5700 South Lake Shore Drive, is the only surviving building from that enormous event. If you stop by at the Museum, don't forget to visit the lovely Osaka Gardens, between the east and west lagoons; it's a Chicago designated landmark. In addition, the neighborhood is filled with architectural jewels, including Frank Lloyd Wright's famous Robie House at 5757 South Woodlawn Avenue, the Rockefeller Memorial Chapel, located at 1156 East 59th Avenue, and the University's Oriental Institute, 1155 East 58th Street—home to a vast collection of Egyptian, Persian, and Sumerian antiquities. If you decide to make Hyde Park your home, you will quickly become acquainted with yet another landmark area, the large expanse right on Lake Michigan, called Promonotory Point (5491 South Shore Drive)—popular with area residents, university students, and faculty alike.

Grand old high-rise apartment buildings line the lakefront, and away from the lake the neighborhood is chock-a-block with low-rise apartments, many of which have become condominiums. While single-family homes in Hyde Park are expensive (rivaling the Gold Coast and Lincoln Park areas), townhouses and condominiums are more in line with the price of new construction in other middle class areas of the South Side. As befits an area with one of the country's leading universities, there are several first-rate book stores on South Hyde Park Boulevard, and between 53rd and 59th streets, particularly The Seminary Co-op, 5757 South University, and Powell's, 1501 East 57th Street.

With all of the university activity going on in Hyde Park, it is easy to overlook the quiet elegance of Hyde Park's northerly neighbor, **Kenwood**. The last ten years has seen the development of new townhouses that are well below the price of the Hyde Park homes. New businesses have also been developing on 47th Street. Kenwood is worth looking into if you like quiet shaded streets, and easy university access. More than half of the university's faculty live between Hyde Park and Kenwood, in what locals call **South Kenwood**: between 51st and 47th streets, running east to Lake Michigan, and west to Cottage Grove Avenue. It's a small neighborhood with old estates on large lots.

As mentioned earlier, violent crime is not overly common in the Hyde Park-South Kenwood community, but it does happen. (See the **Getting Settled** chapter for more on personal safety issues.) The good news: in this neighborhood in 2000, violent crime was the lowest recorded since 1975, when the South East Chicago Commission first began collecting data.

Web Sites: www.ci.chi.il.us, www.uchicago.edu, www.hydepark.org
Area Code: 773
Zip Codes: 60615, 60637
Post Offices: Hyde Park, 4601 South Cottage Grove Avenue; Station U, 956 East 58th Street; Jackson Park Post Office, 700 East 61st Street; Lake Park Station, 1526 East 55th Street, 800-275-8777
Police District: 21st/Prairie District (Area 1), 300 East 29th Street, 312-747-8340
Emergency Hospitals: The University of Chicago Hospitals, 5841 South Maryland Avenue, 773-702-1000
Library: Blackstone, 4904 South Lake Park Avenue, 312-747-0511, wwwchipublib.org
Community Resources: Hyde Park Art Center, 5307 South Hyde Park Boulevard, 773-324-5520; Southeast Chicago Commission, 773-324-6926; Oriental Institute, 1155 East 58th Street, 773-702-1845; Museum of Science & Industry, 57th Street and Lake Shore Drive, 773-684-1414; DuSable Museum of African-American History, 740 East 56th Place, 773-947-0600
Local Annual Events: 57th Street Art Fair (June); Boulevard Lakefront Tour, (www.chibikefed.org, June bike tour); 53rd Street Parade (4th of July); Chicago Half Marathon (September); World Music Festival, www.ci.chi.il.us/WorldMusic; UofC Annual Folk Festival of Traditional Music (February); Rockefeller Chapel Events, www.rockefeller.uchicago.edu; University of Chicago Presents, a classical music series, www.chicagopresents.uchicago.edu
Parks: www.chicagoparkdistrict.com, 312-742-PLAY, Bixler Park, 5651 South Kenwood Avenue; Butternut Park, 5324 South Woodlawn Avenue; Dyett Recreation Center, 513 East 51 Street; Elm Park 5215 South Woodlawn Avenue; Nichols Park, 1300 East 55th Street; Promontory Point, 5491 South Shore Drive; Spruce Park, 5337 South Blackstone Avenue; Stout Park, 5446 South Greenwood Avenue; Midway Plaisance Park, East 59th Street/Stony Island and South Cottage Grove avenues
Community Publications: *Chicago Daily Defender, Chicago Daily Law Bulletin, Chicago Journal, Chicago Magazine, Chicago Maroon, Chicago Parent, Chicago Reader, Chicago Reporter, Hyde Park Herald, N'DIGO*

Public Schools: Chicago School District 299, 125 South Clark Street, Chicago, IL 60603, 773-553-1000, www.cps.k12.il.us

Transportation—Rapid Transit: Metra/Electric Line (stations: 47th Street, 51st Street, 55th Street, 59th Street, Hyde Park, South Shore, Kenwood); CTA trains: Red Line (stations: Garfield Boulevard, 63rd at State Street)

Transportation—Major Bus Routes: #1 Indiana/Hyde Park, #2 Hyde Park Express, #4 Cottage Grove, #6 Jeffery Express, #28 Stony Island, #47 47th Street, #51 51st Street, #55 Garfield

Note: U of C students can ride CTA bus routes #170, 171, and 172 for free when they present their student IDs.

WOODLAWN

Boundaries: **North**: 60th Street; **South**: 67th Street; **East**: Lake Michigan; **West**: Cottage Grove Avenue

Woodlawn is a largely African-American neighborhood (99% according to 2000 Census reports) just south of Hyde Park. The revitalization of this neighborhood has been slow, but bit by bit the neighborhood has improved, becoming an established community of choice. Revitalization here has been made possible by independent initiatives led by several organizations including The Woodlawn Organization (TWO), which was established in the 1960s, the University of Chicago, private investors, and groups like WECAN (Woodlawn East Community And Neighbors), and Woodlawn Preservation Investment Coprproation (WPIC). WECAN works to renovate the area's low-income flats, rebuilding them into affordable, attractive apartments for families or singles. Columbia Pointe, a joint effort of Woodlawn's community revitalization organizations, is a housing development program. It has finished phase one of 34 units of new, moderately priced single-family homes. Phase two will include some multi-family housing. Other developments in the area include new upscale homes being built on 63rd Street, from Ingleside to Kimbark avenues. All of this is welcome news in a community that was once plagued with gangs and deteriorating housing. As a result of these efforts, professionals, working-class families, and staff and students from the University of Chicago have begun to relocate here. Additionally, the openings of two banks within the past few years, (branches of the Cole Taylor Bank and First Chicago banks) have helped to attract businesses, and several areas of the neighborhood have been voted "dry" to curb the illegal sale of liquor to minors, and to help remove loitering and other illegal activities.

Woodlawn is within walking distance of Jackson Park, a neighborhood favorite with its beach, harbor, and lagoons. Washington Park is to the west, and the colossal Museum of Science and Industry is nearby as well. Woodlawn residents enjoy the proximity to Hyde Park's retail district, although several small grocery stores have served the neighborhood for over 50 years.

While the area has improved, safety is definitely a concern in Woodlawn, especially in the west end. Be sure to visit at different points of the day to ascertain your comfort level before deciding to move here.

Web Site: www.ch.chi.il.us

Area Code: 773

Zip Code: 60637

Post Office: Jackson Park Post Office, 700 East 61st Street, 800-275-8777

Police District: Third District (Area 2), 7040 South Cottage Grove Avenue, 312-747-8201

Emergency Hospitals: The University of Chicago Hospitals, 5841 South Maryland Avenue, 773-702-1000

Library: Bessie Coleman, 731 East 63rd Street, 312-747-7770, www. chipublib.org

Community Resources: Woodlawn Development Associates, 773-667-8456; The Woodlawn Organization, 773-288-5840, a community development program, which includes property management and human services; WECAN, 773-288-3000; Columbia Pointe Housing, 773-684-7122; DuSable Museum of African-American History, 740 East 56th Place, 773-947-0600

Parks: www.chicagoparkdistrict.com, 312-742-PLAY, Jackson Park, 6401 South Stony Island Avenue; Midway Plaisance Park, East 59th Street/Stony Island and South Cottage Grove avenues

Community Publications: *Chicago Daily Defender, Chicago Journal, Chicago Magazine, Chicago Maroon, Chicago Parent, Chicago Reader, Chicago Reporter, Hyde Park Herald, N'DIGO*

Public Schools: Chicago School District 299, 125 South Clark Street, Chicago, IL 60603, 773-553-1000, www.cps.k12.il.us

Transportation—Rapid Transit: Green Line (station: Cottage Grove); Metra/Electric Line (stations: 59th Street, 63rd Street)

Transportation—Major Bus Routes: #4 Cottage Grove, #28 Stony Island, #59 59th to 61st Street, #63 63rd Street

SOUTH SHORE

Boundaries: **North**: 67th Street; **South**: 79th Street; **East**: Lake Michigan; **West**: South Chicago Avenue

South of Woodlawn is the South Shore neighborhood. Extending from the base of Jackson Park to 79th Street, South Shore is a study in contrasts. Many working professionals live along the park, attracted by the ease of the commute downtown via South Shore and Lake Shore drives (20 minutes to the Loop) and affordable housing. Artists live here too, attracted by inexpensive rents and local theater companies.

In this neighborhood where the population is predominantly African-American, the divisions are based on economics rather than race. While South Shore has the most subsidized housing units in the city, immediately south of Jackson Park the apartments and high rises are well maintained. Head further south along South Shore Drive and the buildings tend to be more run down. Away from the lake there are blighted areas, but again these are balanced by immaculate middle- and upper middle-class residential streets.

Jackson Park, at the neighborhood's northern edge, is a beautiful lakeshore park with inland lagoons and a golf course. There is an extensive lakefront bike path that starts at Soldier Field and ends at 71st Street. To the south of the park is the landmark South Shore Cultural Center. Built as an elite country club in 1906, it was acquired by the Chicago Park District in the 1970s. It offers daily classes in the performing arts, as well as a full schedule of concerts, lectures, and plays. The South Shore is home to the annual Jazz Fest, which happens each July, and the annual Gospel Fest in August. (Call 312-747-2536 or go to www.chicagoparkdistrict.com, for more information.) A short walk away is BAGIT, Black Art Group International Art Gallery. If you are interested in historical architecture, then take a walk through the **Jackson Park Highlands**, an area bounded by Jeffrey Boulevard, Cregier Avenue, 67th to 71st streets, where you will find no less than 278 historically significant homes, some of which are listed in the National Register of Historic Places.

At the south end of the neighborhood and at the lakefront is where you will find restaurants and entertainment. The New Regal Theatre, 1645 East 79th Street, hosts live comedy showcases, children's theater, as well as some touring productions. Originally built in the 1920s and called the Avalon, the theater was remodeled at the cost of $4.5 million by the local community. It was renamed the New Regal Theatre as a salute to the original Regal Theatre that hosted many of the great African-American entertainers of the 20th century.

Web Site: www.ci.chi.il.us

Area Code: 773

Zip Code: 60649

Post Office: South Shore, 2207 East 57th Street, 800-275-8777

Police District: 3rd/Grand Crossing District (Area 2), 7040 South Cottage Grove Avenue, 312-747-8201

Emergency Hospitals: Jackson Park Hospital, 7531 South Stony Island Avenue, 773-947-7500; St. Bernard Hospital, 64th Street and Dan Ryan Expressway, 773-962-3900; South Shore Hospital, 8012 South Crandon Avenue, 773-768-0810

Library: South Shore, 2505 East 73rd Street, 312-747-5281

Community Resources: South Central Community Services, 773-483-0900; South Shore Country Club, 7059 South Shore Drive, 312-747-6250 (call 312-245-0909 for a tee time); Du Sable Museum of African-American History, 740 East 56th Place, 773-947-0600

Parks: www.chicagoparkdistrict.com, 312-742-PLAY, Jackson Park, 6401 South Stony Island Avenue

Community Publications: *Chicago Daily Defender, Chicago Journal, Chicago Magazine, Chicago Maroon, Chicago Parent, Chicago Reader, Chicago Reporter, Hyde Park Herald, N'DIGO*

Public Schools: Chicago School District 299, 125 South Clark Street, Chicago, IL 60603, 773-553-1000, www.cps.k12.il.us

Transportation—Rapid Transit: Metra/Electric South Chicago Branch Line (stations: 75th Street, Stony Island, Bryn Mawr, South Shore, Windsor Park, Cheltenham); since there is no CTA station servicing South Shore directly, commuters can take a bus to the 63rd Street/Red Line station (6300S/200W), where they can board a CTA train to the Loop. Also available, the South Shore/South Bend Railroad

Transportation—Major Bus Routes: #6 Jeffery Local, #22, #27 South Deering, #28 Stony Island, #67 67th-69th-91st, #71 71st, #75 74th-75th, #79 79th

---

BEVERLY/MORGAN PARK

Boundaries: **Beverly**: **North**: 87th Street; **South**: 107th Street; **East**: Beverly Avenue; **West**: Western Avenue; **Morgan Park**: **North**: 107th Street; **South**: 119th Street; **East**: Vincennes Avenue; **West**: California Avenue

The Gold Coast of the South Side, **Beverly** is one of the most affluent neighborhoods in Chicago. Huge old mansions, including a Frank Lloyd Wright, line the top of Longwood Drive (which was the edge of Lake

Michigan about 10,000 years ago, and is one of the highest points geographically in Chicago). The proper name of this community is Beverly Hills, but you will find that most locals refer this southwest neighborhood simply as Beverly. The most exclusive section, **North Beverly**, between 89th Street and 94th Street, features many large, Revival-style houses built in the 1920s and '30s on hilly lots. In fact, Beverly has one of the largest historic districts in the country, with more than 3,000 buildings registered. The first homes in the area date from the mid-19th century, before Beverly was incorporated into Chicago. Although once predominantly Irish-Catholic, the neighborhood is integrating successfully and remains a stable and desirable place to live. The average homeowners are young to middle-aged professionals, many with children, seeking an alternative to life in downtown Chicago. Apartment seekers should note that Beverly is primarily a neighborhood of single-family residences, though there are a handful of apartment buildings. There is very little turnover in the single-family housing market, where the median price for a single family home in 2001 was $229,000.

Morgan Park, nestled in the southeast corner of Beverly Hills, is a predominately African-American community. Here too, the neighborhood is comprised of young, professional families and there is a similar variety of architecture along well-kept streets. Home prices are a bit lower compared to Beverly but still maintain a strong market value, and there are more apartments to be had, including some vintage Tudor buildings that have been converted into studios and condominiums.

The commercial district, 111th to 115th streets and Western Avenue, was targeted as a Chicago redevelopment area for the two communities. The investment has attracted new businesses to the area. Through various agencies and organizations, the Beverly Arts Center was able to raise the $10 million it needed to build a new and larger center, replacing its 30+ year-old facility. In September 2002, the 40,000 square foot Arts Center reopened to the public, featuring a 420-seat theater, performance and rehearsal space, classrooms, a gift shop, gourmet café, and a landscaped courtyard for seasonal performances. The Arts Center is open year round and offers a wide range of programs, such as workshops, community outreach programs, and artist-in-residence programs.

Web Site: www.ci.chi.il.us, www.ridgehistoricalsociety.org
Area Code: 773
Zip Codes: 60620, 60643, 60655
Post Office: Morgan Park, 1805 West Monterey Avenue, 800-275-8777
Police District: 22nd/Morgan Park District (Area 2), 1830 West Monterey Avenue, 312-747-6381

Emergency Hospitals: Little Company of Mary Hospital, 2800 West 95th Street; Evergreen Park, 708-422-6200; Roseland Community Hospital, 45 West 111th Street, 773-995-3000

Library: Beverly, 2121 West 95th Street, 312-747-9673; Walker Branch, 11071 South Hoyne, 312-747-1920; Woodson Regional, 9525 South Halsted Street, 312-747-6900; Mount Greenwood, 11010 South Kedzie Avenue, 312-747-2805, www.chipublib.org

Community Resources: Edna White Community Garden, 111th Street & Homewood Avenue; Ridge Historical Society, 10621 South Seeley Avenue, 773-881-1675, www.ridgehistoricalsociety.org; Beverly Area Planning Association, 10233 South Wood Street, 773-233-3100; Beverly Arts Center, 2407 West 111th Street, 773-445-3838

Parks: www.chicagoparkdistrict.com, 312-742-PLAY, Ridge Park, 9625 South Longwood Drive; Ridge Park Wetlands, 9516 South Wood Street

Community Publications: *Beverly Review, Daily Southtown, Chicago Daily Defender, Chicago Heights Star, Chicago Journal, Chicago Magazine, Chicago Maroon, Chicago Parent, Chicago Reporter, N'DIGO, Ridge Historical Society Newsletter, Suburban Focus Magazine, The Villager*

Public Schools: Chicago School District 299, 125 South Clark Street, Chicago, IL 60603, 773-553-1000, www.cps.k12.il.us

Transportation—Rapid Transit: Metra/Rock Island Suburban Line (91st Street; 95th Street; 99th Street; 103rd Street; 107th Street, 111th Street; 115th Street; 119th Street)

Transportation—Major Bus Routes: #49A South Western, #49 Western, #87 87th Street, #95 95th Street, #112 Vincennes/111th, #111 Pullman/111th to 115th, #119 Michigan/119th

NORTH AND NORTHWEST SUBURBS

EVANSTON

If city life is where it's at, why would anyone move to the suburbs? Well if the 'burb is Evanston, it's not hard to understand. Evanston's environs, its physical beauty, both man-made and natural, leave a lasting impression. Here you can live on a wide, tree-lined street, walk to the lakeshore at dusk for an evening stroll, or easily pop over to a cafe in Evanston's thriving downtown. All this while being only 14 miles from downtown Chicago. With its history, culture, natural beauty, academic offerings, wide range of ethnic dining, and lively entertainment, Evanston is the perfect suburb.

Census 2000 results reported an Evanston population of 74,000, and city planners predict a population of almost 80,000 by 2004. Area residents come from all walks of life—from high-tech developers to home-based entrepreneurs, from medical researchers, to graduate students, and university professors to stay-at-home moms. While predominately white, many nationalities are represented here, including a substantial African-American population. It's a thriving community with a well-developed shopping district, lakefront parks and, last but certainly not least, the renowned Northwestern University. The extensive network of biking paths, running trails, 65 public parks, and beaches along the shoreline are additional assets. Lovely, turn of the century mansions, lining either side of Sheridan Road will take your breath away. In fact, Evanston has three neighborhood districts listed on the National Register of Historic Places. A recent study by Runzheimer International reported the average price for a 2,200-square foot house (eight rooms) in Evanston was close to $500,000. Although the lakeshore area is often the only part of Evanston that many people see, it should be noted that not all of the neighborhoods are as spectacular, and some are affordable.

Evanston's downtown shopping area, around Central Street is a mix of chain stores, cafes, modest ethnic restaurants, bookstores, and small businesses with ample, inexpensive parking. The nearby Church Street/ Davis/Sherman area is in the midst of a remarkable revitalization effort, producing a great deal of excitement in an area of town that had been bypassed by developers. Church Street has been transformed from a no-man's land near the train tracks, to a trendy, upbeat part of downtown, with an 18-screen movie theater, luxury condos, a 178-room Hilton Inn, and a Wolfgang Puck restaurant. Throughout Evanston, you will be relieved by the lack of panhandlers in shopping areas. In 1994, the city enacted an innovative initiative urging residents not to give money to beggars. Instead, businesses contribute to a separate program that provides food and clothing to those in need.

A bustling office park near Northwestern University has brought more business to the community and the quick Purple Line Express commuter train offers direct transportation to and from the Loop during rush hours. Board the Purple Line Express at any of the following 'L' stations: Central Street, Davis Street and Main Street. The Metra commuter train (same stations as for the 'L') will make a trip to downtown Chicago in 25 minutes. Most streets are biker-friendly, and if you work in Evanston you can easily commute via bicycle to and from your office.

As home to a large university, Evanston enjoys the benefits that hosting such an institution brings. There are a variety of cultural events, festivals and fairs, most featured during the warm weather months. The public schools enjoy a solid reputation and childcare options are numerous. Students looking for housing should contact the Northwestern University Student Housing Office at 847-491-7564 (312-503-8514 Chicago campus), or go online to www.northwestern.edu/housing for more information.

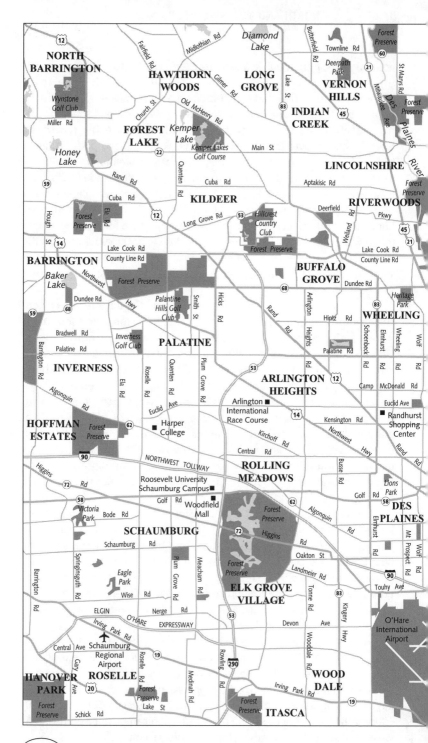

NORTH AND NORTHWEST SUBURBS

Web Sites: www.evanstonillinois.net, www.cityofevanston.org
Area Code: 847
Zip Codes: 60201, 60202, 60603, 60204, 60608, 60609
Post Offices: Main Post Office, 1101 Davis Street; South Station Branch, 701 Main Street; North Station Branch, 1929 Central Street, 800-275-8777
Police: Evanston Police Department, 1454 Elmwood Street, 847-866-5000
Emergency Hospitals: Evanston Hospital, 2650 Ridge Avenue, Evanston, 847-570-2000; St. Francis Hospital of Evanston, 355 Ridge Avenue, Evanston, 847-316-4000
Libraries: Evanston Public Library, 1703 Orrington (entrance on Church Street), 847-866-0300; North Branch Public Library, 2026 Central, 847-866-0330; South Branch Public Library, 949 Chicago Avenue, 847-866-0333
Community Resources: Civic Center, 2100 Ridge Avenue, 847-328-2100; Evanston Chamber of Commerce, One Rotary Center, 1560 Sherman Avenue, 847-328-1500; Evanston Historical Society, 225 Greenwood, 847-475-3410; for community workshops, classes, and festivals, go to www.evanston.lib.il.us/community/arts.
Parks: 847-866-2900 www.cityofevanston.org, Eugune Beck Park, east of the canal/Lyons to Emerson Street; Burnham Shores, lakefront between Dempster/Commit; Butler Park, east of canal/Emerson to Bridge Street; Centennial, lakefront/Church Street to University Place; Dawes, lakefront/Dempster to Church Street; Elliot, lakefront/Hamilton to Lee Street; Garden, lakefront/north of Sheridan Square; Ladd Arboretum, southeast of McCormick/Emerson to Grant Street; Lighthouse Landing, 2603 Sheridan Road; Lomar, south of Mulford Street/Wesley Avenue; **Beaches**: Lighthouse Beach, Central Road/Sheridan Road; Clark Street Beach, Clark Street/Sheridan Road; Dempster/Greenwood Street Beach, Greenwood Street/Lakefront; Lee Street Beach, Lee/Lake Shore Boulevard; South Boulevard Beach, South Boulevard/Lakefront
Community Publications: *Courier News*, *Daily Herald* (Chicago suburban edition), *Evanston Review*, *North Shore Magazine*, *Reader's Guide to Arts and Entertainment*
Public Schools: **Evanston School District 65** (elementary), 1500 McDaniel Avenue, 847-859-8000, www.d65.k12.il.us; **High School**: Evanston Township High, 1600 Dodge Avenue, 847-424-7000, www.eths.k12.il.us
Transportation—Rapid Transit: Purple Line (stations: South Boulevard, Main, Dempster, Davis, Foster, Noyes, Central); Metra/Union Pacific North Line (stations: Main, Evanston, and Central)
Transportation—Major CTA Bus Routes: #97: Skokie (Evanston & Skokie), #215 Howard, #97 Oakton, #250 Dempster, #208 Church,

#210 Lincoln Avenue, #212 Golf, #202 Main/Emerson, #213 Green Bay Road, #201 Central/Sherman, #203 Ridge, #204 Dodge, #290 Touhy Avenue. Evanston has several dozen buses traveling throughout the Chicagoland area, including shuttle buses to shopping malls and Metra train stations. To find the bus service you need, please check www.pacebus.com or call 847-364-7223.

SKOKIE

Three miles west of the lake is Skokie, Evanston's western neighbor. A village of 63,000, it was incorporated almost 100 years ago. In 1940, the name was changed from Niles Center to Skokie, which is a Potawatomis word for swamp. An agricultural and greenhouse center for years, its early settlers emigrated here from Germany, Switzerland and Luxembourg in the 1830s. Known as a western settlement in the early part of the 20th century, film studios once used the village's unpretentious main street to film cowboy movies. After World War II, large numbers of Jewish refugees settled in Skokie, and to this day there is a substantial Orthodox/Hasidic Jewish population. More recently, immigrants from Korea, Malaysia, India, and Russia are calling Skokie home.

Much of the village consists of single-family homes, most of which are owner occupied, although there are some condominiums and apartment buildings scattered throughout. Rentals make up about 25% of the housing market. Typical family homes here are brick bungalows from the 1940s and, like Evanston, can be pricey. The community has done a good job of combining family programs and an interest in the arts. Skokie's North Shore Center for the Performing Arts is home to the Northlight Theatre, Centre East Theatre, an active youth theater, and The Skokie Valley Symphony Orchestra. The park district boasts of a nine-hole golf course, an ice skating rink, and almost 200 acres of parkland and swimming pools. The Skokie Historical Society organizes tours and publishes a chronicle of the village's early days. Topics include the history of the circa-1887 fire station (now a museum) and other buildings included on the National Registry. The Chamber of Commerce is active in community celebrations, sponsoring the widely regarded North Shore Arts Festival, sidewalk sales, the Festival of Cultures, Fourth of July parade, and many others. The Fine Arts Promenade, held each September in the Old Orchard Shopping Mall, is another noteworthy fair. Skokie's industrial base is mainly light industry, with firms such as Bell & Howell, Rand McNally, and G.D. Searle in the area.

Skokie has established itself as a suburban shopper's paradise. There are small malls, such as Village Crossing Center, and Fashion Square Center, strip malls in downtown Skokie, and shops, ethnic grocery stores, and bakeries along Dempster Street. The recently revamped outdoor Old Orchard Mall makes the community the eighth largest retail center in the state.

Web Sites: www.skokienet.org, www.skokiechamber.org, www.skokie.org
Area Code: 847
Zip Codes: 60076, 60077
Post Office: 4950 Madison Street, 800-275-8777
Police: Skokie Police Department, 8350 Laramie Avenue, 847-982-5910
Emergency Hospitals: Rush North Shore Medical Center, 9600 Gross Point Road, 847-677-9600; St. Francis Health Center, 7126 Lincoln Avenue, Lincolnwood, 847-675-2273; Lutheran General, 847-423-5154
Library: Skokie Public Library, 5215 Oakton Street, 847-673-7774
Community Resources: Chamber of Commerce, 5002-5006 Oakton Street, 847-673-0240; Village of Skokie, 847-673-0500, www.skokie.org; Skokie's North Shore Center for the Performing Arts/Centre East, www.centreeast.org, 847-673-6300; Skokie Historical Society, www.skokiehistory.info, 847-673-1888
Parks: www.skokieparkdistrict.org: indoor ice rink, water playground, 43 parks, 40 tennis courts
Community Publications: *Courier News*, *Daily Herald* (Chicago suburban edition), *North Shore Magazine*, *Reader's Guide to Arts and Entertainment*, *Skokie Review*
Public Schools: Skokie School District 68, 9440 Kenton Avenue, Skokie, 847-676-9000, www.sd68.k12.il.us; Skokie School District 69, 5050 Madison Street, 847-675-7666, www.skokie69.k12.il.us; Skokie School District 73-5, 8000 East Prairie Road, 847-673-1220, www.skokie735.k12.il.us
Transportation—Metra, (Park Ridge Station); CTA Rapid Transit: Yellow Line (Skokie station)
Transportation—Major PACE Bus Routes: #97 (Skokie station)
By Car: I-90, I-94; local main roads: Dempster, Skokie, Touhy

WILMETTE

The lakeshore Village of Wilmette, just north of Evanston, is a relatively affluent suburb (median family income is nearly $82,000 a year) of approximately 28,000 residents. Bordering the lake, it is a community best known for its tree-lined streets and large, expensive homes, and one of the finest school districts in the country. Besides the expansive, impeccably manicured lawns and homes, one way to tell that you have passed from Evanston into Wilmette is by the brick streets, which Wilmette residents have fought to keep over the years. The village is run by a president and board of trustees, employing 210 full-time employees (including a village nurse). They can be reached at 847-251-2700.

Wilmette's prosperous homogeneity gives it a crime rate less than half that of many of Chicago's North Side communities. Located only 16 miles north of the Loop, residents have an easy weekday commute by Metra. Known as the place where many Evanston residents move when they have outgrown a first home, much of Wilmette's real estate prices reflect its exclusivity (2003 median home value according to *Money* magazine was $502,000). Wilmette's neighboring suburbs of Kenilworth, Winnetka, and Glencoe (see next profile) are even more well to do. In addition to the lovely homes in Wilmette, there is a wide range of amenities: two public and two private golf courses, an extensive park system, one of the longest beach fronts in the area, and beautiful Wilmette Harbor from which residents can launch their sail boats. Also in Wilmette, a public outdoor pool, an indoor arena for the performing arts, and two indoor ice-skating rinks.

Wilmette is the home of Bahá'í Temple, a gleaming nine-sided white-domed building which is situated on Sheridan Road across from Lake Michigan. This beautiful (and incongruous on the suburban North Shore) sight is worth stopping for, even if you're just passing through. (See **Places of Worship** for more information.)

Web Site: www.wilmette.com
Area Code: 847
Zip Code: 60091
Post Office: 1241 Central Avenue, 800-275-8777
Police: Wilmette Police Department, 710 Ridge Road, 847-256-1200
Emergency Hospitals: Evanston Hospital, 2650 Ridge Avenue, Evanston, 847-570-2000; Rush North Shore Medical Center, 9600 Gross Point Road, Skokie, 847-677-9600; Glenbrook Hospital, 2100 Pfingsten Road, Glenview, 847-657-5800; St. Francis Hospital, 355 Ridge Avenue, Evanston, 847-492-4000
Library: Wilmette Public Library, 1242 Wilmette Avenue, 847-256-5025
Community Resources: Village of Wilmette, 1200 Wilmette Avenue, 847-251-2700; Wilmette Golf Course, 3900 Fairway Drive, 847-256-9646; Starlight Theatre at Gillson Park, 847-256-9656; Chamber of Commerce, 1150 Wilmette Avenue, 847-251-3800
Parks: www.wilmettepark.org, 847-256-6100, Centennial Recreation Complex, 2300 Old Glenview Road, 847-256-9686; Gillson Park, Lake Street and Sheridan Road, 847-256-9656; Avoca Park, Iroquois Avenue/Ramona Road; Bateman Park, Sheridan Road/Michigan Avenue; Green Bay Bike Trail, Shorewood Park/Wilmette/Kenilworth border.

Community Publications: *Courier News, Daily Herald* (Chicago suburban edition), *North Shore Magazine, Reader's Guide to Arts and Entertainment, Wilmette Life, Winnetka Talk*

Public Schools: Wilmette School District 39, 615 Locust Road Wilmette, 847-256-2450, http://wilmette.newtrier.k12.il.us; www.nttc.org

Transportation—Rapid Transit: Purple Line (Linden Street station); Metra/Union Pacific North Line (Wilmette station)

By Car: I-94 (30 minutes to the Loop)

KENILWORTH/WINNETKA/GLENCOE

Some might label **Kenilworth**, a community 17 miles north of Chicago's Loop, a hamlet instead of a town since its borders barely comprise a square mile, and its population is a mere 2,500. Kenilworth is slightly older than its neighbors, and richer too; regularly ranked as one of the wealthiest communities in the country. Unlike many other suburbs, Kenilworth was a planned community. Streets run at northeast and southwest angles, so that sunlight reaches every window in every house at some point in the day. The homes are understated mansions in a mix of styles that appear to blend seamlessly: English Tudor, Classical Revival, Contemporary, and Georgian styles. There is a feeling of old money about this town, similar perhaps to Newport, Rhode Island. Everything is within walking distance, including the commuter train and the shopping area along Green Bay Road. Like its neighbor Wilmette, Kenilworth boasts a good school district, and shares the New Trier Township High School with Evanston.

Head a bit north to get to **Winnetka**, another hamlet-like sized town (population 12,000). Winnetka is an upscale, young to middle-aged family community (average resident age 39, average household income about $160,000), with a lot of perks: excellent schools, a comprehensive park district that offers residents golfing, ice skating, sailing, and boating lessons. It has four beaches (including a dog-friendly beach), tennis courts, and despite its small size, Winnetka offers one of the largest hockey club programs in the state.

Last in the trio is **Glencoe**, 21 miles north of the Loop and home to about 8,400. This village is the most northern of the three communities, built on the bluffs of Lake Michigan. It's a bit roomier than Winnetka and Kenilworth: 3.8 square miles—room enough for the nine Frank Lloyd Wright homes, and the nearly 100 homes that are listed as architecturally significant with the town's Historic Preservation Commission. Homes here are expensive, especially those on the lakeside of town. With a bit of luck, you might find a home in or around the business district that is below the half million-dollar mark. Despite all appearances, this is not just another wealthy suburb. Call it the Berkeley of Chicago's North Shore, Glencoe has no police or fire department, instead, public safety officers carry out those functions, and it was the first community in Illinois to establish a council-manager form of government.

The location of Glencoe makes it accessible to several of Chicago's outdoor delights: the Chicago Botanic Garden is just outside its borders, and three golf courses (one public, two private) are close by. On the western boundary of Glencoe lies Skokie Lagoons, with bike paths that meander past 300 acres of woods and water ending at the Botanic Garden. All this just 35 minutes from the Loop.

Web Sites: www.glencoevillage.org, www.villageofwinnetka.org

Area Codes: 847, 224

Zip Codes: 60043, 60022, 60093

Police: Winnetka Police, 410 Green Bay Road, 847-501-6034

Emergency Hospitals: Evanston Hospital, 2650 Ridge Avenue, Evanston, 847-570-2000; Rush North Shore Medical Center, 9600 Gross Pointe Road, Skokie, 847-677-9600; Highland Park Hospital, 718 Glenview Avenue, Highland Park, 847-432-8000; Glenbrook Hospital, 2100 Pfingsten Road, Glenview, 847-657-5800

Library: Glencoe Public Library, 847-835-5056; Winnetka Public Library, 768 Oak Street, 847-446-7220, www.wpld.alibrary.com

Post Office: Glencoe Post Office: 800-275-8777

Community Resources: Writer's Theatre/Glencoe, 664 Vernon Avenue, 847-242-6000; Chicago Botanic Garden, 847-835-8208, www.chicagobotanic.org

Parks: Glencoe Park District, 999 Green Bay Road, 847-835-3030, www.glencoeparkdistrict.com; Winnetka Park District, 540 Hibbard Road, 847-501-2040, www.winpark.org

Community Publications: *Courier News, Daily Herald* (Chicago suburban edition), *Glencoe News, North Shore Magazine, Reader's Guide to Arts and Entertainment, Winnetka Talk*

Public Schools: Kenilworth School District 38, 542 Abbotsford Road, 847-256-5006, www.kenilworth.k12.il.us; Glencoe School District 35, 620 Greenwood Avenue, 847-835-7800, www.glencoe.k12.il.us; Winnetka Public School District 36, 1235 Oak Street, 847-446-9400, www.winnetka.k12.il.us

Transportation: Metra: Chicago/Kenosha Suburban Service (Glencoe station); Metra Union/Pacific North line (Kenilworth station) (32 minute commute); PACE Suburban Bus Service, www.pace.com

HIGHLAND PARK

North of Glencoe on Lake Michigan and 26 miles north of downtown Chicago, lies Highland Park. As one of Chicago's fringe suburbs, it is unique in that it offers residents a variety of single and multi-family housing. Styles range from the Chicago Bungalow-style, to Frank Lloyd Wright designs. Thirty-two homes and sites in Highland Park are listed on the National Register of Historic Places. It is a well-to-do community. In 2000, Highland Park Village demographics suggested its median home value was close to $400,000, and the median family income was $158,000.

Much to the delight of area residents and Chicagoans alike, Highland Park is home to the Ravinia Festival and summer host to the Chicago Symphony Orchestra. Ravinia, offers a summer-long series of open-air concerts (ranging from classical to folk and jazz) with much of the seating on the lawn. People bring blankets and elaborate picnics and dine al fresco to the music of Bach or Broadway—it's all very refined and very fun. The community has an active and rich repertoire of its own for creative outlets. Some of these include the Highland Park String Orchestra, Pilgrim Chamber Players, Opera, Theater, and an annual arts journal called *East on Central*. Though the trip to downtown Chicago is approximately 30 minutes long via the commuter train, Highland Park's 32,000 residents find plenty to do in town. The 44 parks here cover 600 acres and offer fishing, boating, ice-skating, hockey, water sports, an 18-hole golf course, and an extensive park district program.

Web Site: www.cityhpil.com

Area Code: 847

Zip Code: 60035

Post Office: 833 Central Avenue; 582 Roger Williams Avenue, 800-275-8777

Police: 1677 Old Deerfield Road, 847-432-7730

Emergency Hospitals: Highland Park Hospital, 718 Glenview Avenue, Highland Park, 847-432-8000

Library: Highland Park Library 494 Laurel Avenue, 847-432-0216, www.hplibrary.org

Community Resources: Chamber of Commerce, 508 Central Avenue, 847-432-0284; City of Highland Park, 1707 St. Johns, 847-432-0800; Suburban Fine Arts Center, 1957 Sheridan Road, 847-432-1888, www.sfaconline.com; Sunset Valley Golf Course, 1390 Sunset Road, 847-432-7140; North Shore Yacht Club, 847-432-9800; Ravinia Festival, 200 Ravinia Park Road (north of Lake Cook Road, right off of Greenbay Road), 847-266-5100, www.ravinia.org

Parks: Highland Park Park District, 636 Ridge Road, 847-831-3810, www.pdhp.org: Hidden Creek Aqua Park, 1220 Frederickson Place, 847-433-3170; Centennial Ice Arena, 3100 Trailway, 847-432-4790; **Beaches**: Park Avenue Beach, Park Avenue/Lake Michigan; Moraine Beach (dog friendly with permit), 2501 Sheridan Road; Rosewood Beach, 883 Sheridan Road

Community Publications: *Courier News, Highland Park News, Highland Park Newsletter*, www.cityhpil.com, *Highland Park Conservation Society Newsletter*, www.highlandpark.org, *Reader's Guide to Arts and Entertainment*

Public Schools: District 113: 847-926-9327, www.d113.lake.k12.il.us; District 112: 847-681-6700, www.nssd112.k12.il.us; Special Education: 847-831-5100

Transportation: Metra Union/Pacific North Line/Highland Park (Highland Park Station); Metra Deerfield/Milwaukee North Line; local bus service provided by PACE buses. For schedule information go to www.pacebus.com or call 847-364-8183.

By Car: I-94, US-41

DEERFIELD

Southwest of Highland Park, next to the Tri-State Tollway in Lake County, is the Village of Deerfield (population 19,000). According to the village, in 2000 the average selling price for a home was about $347,000, and there are a variety of smaller less expensive homes available. Deerfield offers plenty of family-friendly features including an extensive system of parks and recreational facilities, and an excellent public school system. The majority of residents are homeowners, and the median household income is close to $90,000. While Deerfield offers easy access to Chicago by car or train—it is only 21 miles north of downtown—there are a number of large companies that call Deerfield home, including Baxter International, Dade Behring, and Walgreens, offering employment to many residents.

Deerfield is close to the Chicago Botanic Garden and the North Branch Bicycle Trail (see **Greenspaces and Beaches** for more information on both). It's also close to the famous Ravinia Park, which is located in the neighboring suburb of Highland Park (see above).

On a more raucous note, professional basketball fans may be interested to know that the Berto Center, the Chicago Bulls' practice facility, is in Deerfield, and the village is home to several players and coaches. With three malls within limits and an easy drive to five other malls, including Gurnee Mills and Hawthorne Center, shopping here is a breeze. The Deerfield Park District manages over 21 parks and playgrounds, as well as two swimming pools, and every type of playing field or sports facility you can imagine.

Web Site: www.deerfield-il.org

Area Code: 847, 224

Zip Code: 60015

Post Office: 707 Osterman Avenue, 800-275-8777

Police: 850 North Waukegan Road, 847-945-8636

Emergency Hospital: Highland Park Hospital, 718 Glenview Avenue, Highland Park, 847-432-8000

Library: Deerfield Public Library, 920 North Waukegan Road, 847-945-3311, TDD 847-945-3372

Community Resources: Village of Deerfield, 847-945-5000, www.deerfield-il.org; Deerfield Chamber of Commerce, 850 Waukegan Road, 847-945-4660; Historic Village & Society, Deerfield/Kipling Roads, 847-948-0680; **Shopping**: Deerfield Center, southeast corner Waukegan/Deerfield Road; Deerfield Square, southwest corner Waukegan/Deerfield Road; Caldwell Corners, northeast corner Lake Cook Road/Waukegan Road

Community Publications: *Courier News, Daily Herald* (Chicago suburban edition), *Deerfield Review, North Shore Magazine, Reader's Guide to Arts and Entertainment*

Public Schools: Deerfield School District 109, 517 Deerfield Road, 847-945-1844, www.dps109.org

Transportation: Metra/Milwaukee District North Line (Lake Cook or Deerfield station, 30 minute commute via express train to downtown Chicago); local bus service is provided by PACE buses, includes shuttle buses to some Metra stations. www.pacebus.com

By Car: I-41/94, I-294; major roads are Deerfield and Waukegan roads

NORTHBROOK

The Village of Northbrook, with a population just over 33,000 and a median age of about 50, is a much sought after community. Incorporated in 1901 as Shermerville, it is located twenty-five miles northwest of downtown Chicago. Northbrook is commuter-friendly (a 40-minute Metra ride to downtown Chicago from the Northbrook station), and offers instant access to both the Edens Expressway (I-94) and the Tri-State Tollway (I-294). A popular place with families, the neighborhoods are quiet and the Northbrook Park District offers tennis courts, two swimming pools, a golf course, indoor ice arenas, and even a velodrome. The local schools have a reputation for excellence. Single-family homes account for more than 75% of the housing stock; median price for homes in 2000: $364,000.

Northbrook's most prominent architectural landmark is probably Northbrook Court. The first of Chicago's luxury malls, it is home to Lord & Taylor, Neiman Marcus, I. Magnin, and other blue-chip retailers. For more down-to-earth shopping, the area has expanded their retail base to include Home Depot, Borders Books, Barnes & Noble, and a string of smaller shops, and chain stores.

Northbrook offers a lot to its residents. The good news is that, even if you can't afford to live here, you can shop here.

Web Sites: www.northbrook.il.us, www.northbrookchamber.org

Area Codes: 847, 224

Zip Codes: 60025, 60062, 60093

Post Offices: Main Post Office, 2460 Dundee Road; Downtown Station, 1157 Church Street, 800-275-8777

Police: 1225 Cedar Lane, 847-564-2060

Emergency Hospitals: Highland Park Hospital, 718 Glenview Avenue, Highland Park, 847-432-8000; Glenbrook Hospital, 2100 Pfingsten Road, Glenview, 847-657-5800; Evanston Hospital, 2650 Ridge Avenue, Evanston, 847-570-2000

Library: Northbrook Public Library, 1201 Cedar Lane, 847-272-6224, http://nbpl.nsn.org

Community Resources: Northbrook Theatre, 3323 Walters Avenue, 847-291-2367; North Suburban YMCA, 2705 Techny Road, 847-272-7250; Chicago Botanic Garden, www.chicagobotanic.org, 847-835-8208

Parks: Northbrook Park District, 545 Academy Drive, 847-291-2980, www.nbparks.org, Countryside Park, Walter Circle/Oakwood Road; Indian Ridge Park, 3323 Walters Avenue; Oakland Park, Berglund Place/Midway Road; Village Green, Shermer Road/Walters Avenue; West Park, 1720 Pfingsten Road; Wescott Park, Farnsworth Lane/Western Avenue; Williamsburg Square Park, 200 Lee Road

Community Publications: *Daily Herald* (Chicago suburban edition), *North Shore Magazine*, *Northbrook Star*, *Reader's Guide to Arts and Entertainment*

Public Schools: Northbrook School District 27, 1250 Sanders Road, 847-498-2610, www.northbrook27.k12.il.us; Northbrook School District 28, 1475 Maple Avenue, 847-498-7900, www.district28.k12.il.us; Northbrook-Glenview School District 30, 2374 Shermer Road, Northbrook, 847-498-4190, www.district30.k12.il.us; high school: Glenbrook North, 2300 Shermer Road, 847-272-6400

Transportation: Metra/Milwaukee District North Line (Northbrook station)

By Car: I-94, I-294; major local roads: Dundee Road, Milwaukee Avenue, and Waukegan Road

ARLINGTON HEIGHTS

One of the most successful mergers of small town cozy comforts with big city amenities can be found in Arlington Heights. Located 27 miles north-west of downtown Chicago, Arlington Heights is a vibrant community with a long history. Established in 1850, Dunton, as it was first known, was incorporated and renamed Arlington Heights in 1887. Today it is home to about 76,000 and is unique among Chicago's suburban communities as it provides approximately 50,000 local jobs. Its busy downtown area is a mixed-use environment, which includes apartment living, townhouses, and single-family homes. It is a walker's delight with small shops and free parking. Strong local-merchant loyalty keeps locally owned cafes, profes-sional services, and boutiques thriving in the downtown area. The city's central business district includes 7,000-square feet of restaurant space, 22,000-square feet of retail space, and 35,000-square feet of office space. Obviously many area residents make their living right here. But for those who need to head to the city, you can board a Metra train for a 45-minute ride to downtown Chicago; newly renovated train platforms are centrally located in downtown Arlington Heights. Light industry is located on the north and south sides of town.

Two area-attractions dominate Arlington Heights: the 325-acre Arlington Park Racetrack (see **Sports and Recreation**) and the 300-seat Metropolis Performing Arts Centre, located in the central business district. In addition to theater arts workshops, children's theater, and professional live theater, the Arts Centre provides a home-away-from-home to the Second City comedy troupe. And the Boiler Room is an 88-seat basement jazz supper club.

Arlington Heights is a carefully planned city and, unlike many rural-styled suburban towns, it features sidewalks and streetlights. A recently completed 10-year city plan included the upgrade of the storm sewer sys-tem, and the five-acre man-made Lake Arlington, which has a boathouse, boat rentals, a small sandy beach, and a bike/walk path around the lake's perimeter. A former landfill was transformed into the nine-hole Nickol Knoll Golf Course. Also, Arlington Heights boasts its own cable network station and a state-of-the-art library facility—weekend used-book sales, which are held several times a year, are well attended. Housing options are varied in Arlington Heights. While the average single family home costs approxi-mately $380,000 (according to Monstermoving.com), there are three fed-erally subsidized housing complexes offering seniors and low-income families affordable housing. A shared housing program matches the elderly with low-income families, providing seniors with a viable option to living alone. The Single Family Rehabilitation Loan program offers zero percent loans to low-to-moderate income homeowners. Empty nesters and commuting couples are attracted to the chic new townhouses and loft-style apartments located near the Arts Centre, as well as the larger-scaled apartment houses located within walking distance of the train station. In addition to the variety of housing and stable business community, area residents benefit greatly from the local park system. There are 58 parks in Arlington Heights, several include indoor or outdoor swimming pools. Residents and neighboring folks alike enjoy a wealth of year round activities and special events sponsored by the park district.

Web Site: www.vah.com

Area Code: 847

Zip Code: 60004, 60005, and 60006

Post Office: 909 West Euclid Avenue, 800-275-8777

Police: 33 South Arlington Heights Road, 847-368-5300; enhanced system allows callers to use 911 for all emergency and non-emergency calls.

Emergency Hospitals: Northwest Community Hospital, 800 West Central, 847-618-1000; Holy Family Hospital, 100 North River Road, Des Plaines, 847-297-1800

Library: Arlington Heights Memorial Library, 500 North Dunton, 847-392-0100

Community Resources: Arlington Heights Teen Center, 847-577-5394; Chamber of Commerce, 180 North Arlington Heights Road, 847-253-1703; Village of Arlington Heights, 33 South Arlington Heights Road, 847-368-5000

Parks: Arlington Heights Park District, 410 North Arlington Heights Road, 847-577-3000, www.ahpd.org

Community Publications: *Arlington Heights Post, Courier News, Daily Herald* (Chicago suburban edition), *Reader's Guide to Arts and Entertainment, Suburban Focus*

Public Schools: Arlington Heights School District 25, 1200 South Dunton Avenue, 847-758-4900, www.ahsd25.n-cook.k12.il.us

Transportation: Metra Train: 312-322-6777 (Arlington Heights and Arlington Park stations, 45 minutes to downtown on express train). Local bus service provided by PACE Buses: 847-364-8130, www.pacebus.com.

By Car: I-3, I-290, I-90; local major roads: US-12/Rand Road, US-14/Northwest Highway, US-58/Golf Road

SCHAUMBURG

The Village of Schaumburg, one of seven municipalities in Schaumburg Township, is 29 miles northwest of Chicago's downtown. An old community—settlers first began arriving in the 1830s—it grew slowly and steadily. By 1886 Schaumburg hosted a school, a church, a couple of stores, and a dozen homes. In 1956, with a population of just 130, the Village of Schaumburg was incorporated. Area population boomed from there, to about 19,000 in 1970 and to over twice that by 1976. Today there are more than 75,000 residents in Schaumburg. While some commute daily to Chicago, this is not primarily a bedroom community. Motorola is headquartered here, and IBM, Zurich-American Insurance, and Cellular One have offices in Schaumburg as well, bringing in commuters from across the Northwest Chicago region. Area centers of light industry and warehousing add to the diversity and health of Schaumburg's local economy. Also a draw is the shopping: it is home to Woodfield Shopping Mall, one of the largest enclosed shopping malls in the US, an Ikea, and the recently developed Town Square (at Roselle and Schaumburg roads). Designed as an indoor/outdoor center, Town Square offers shopping, dining, and entertainment. Just east of Town Square across Roselle Road, is the Schaumburg Prairie Center for the Arts, www.prairiecenter.org, 847-895-3600, a performance space for local and visiting theater productions, professional musical acts, and comedy and dance troupes. Each Christmas season the center puts on the Nutcracker and each spring a ballet recital.

Most of the housing in Schaumburg has been built since 1970, and is a mix of a few scattered farm houses, 1960s tract homes, 1970s split-levels and ranches, and contemporary homes in newer developments. Because of a lack of available land, new development has slowed; most building is going on to the west of town. Teardowns of older homes to make way for new housing is becoming more common. Upscale townhomes in the $400,000 range can be found near Town Square. More affordable multifamily housing is also available in Schaumburg, particularly in the northwest corner, off Roselle and Golf roads.

Schaumburg is a pleasant place to live, and is particularly popular with families. The Schaumburg Parks Department offers recreation centers, an aquatic center, the Volkening Farm, and two golf courses. The farmers' market, held in the Town Square on the south side of the Athenaeum, runs from mid-June to mid-October, Fridays, 7 a.m. to 1 p.m. Fruits, vegetables, baked goods, and specialty items, as well as entertainment are all part of the offerings. Call 847-923-3855 for more information.

One pleasant and unusual feature of owning a home in Schaumburg: there is no municipal property tax. Municipal services are funded by sales tax revenue, hotel/motel taxes, and license and user fees. As the village web site proudly proclaims: "Careful planning and sound investment policies by past and present village leaders have ensured the financial health of the community, as well as its no municipal property tax status." Interstates

90 and 290 intersect at Schaumburg's northeast corner, allowing easy access to nearby communities including Hoffman Estates, Palatine, Rolling Meadows, and Arlington Heights to the north. Drive time to O'Hare Airport is about 20 minutes; to the Loop about 45. (FYI, Village of Schaumburg vehicle stickers are required; call the Vehicle Sticker Hotline for details, 847-923-4541.) The Metra station is at 2000 South Springinsguth Road.

Web Sites: www.ci.schaumburg.il.us, www.schaumburgtownship.org
Area Code: 847
Zip Codes: 60159, 60168, 60173, 60179, 60192-60196
Post Office: Schaumburg, 450 West Schaumburg Road, 800-275-8777
Police: 1000 West Schaumburg Road, 847-882-3586
Emergency Hospital: Northwest Community Hospital, 800 West Central Road, Arlington Heights, 847-618-1000, www.nch.org; St. Alexius Medical Center, 1555 North Barrington Road, Hoffman Estates, 847-843-2000, www.stalexius.org; Alexian Brothers Medical Center, 800 West Biesterfield Road, Elk Grove Village, 847-437-5500, www.alexian.org
Library: Schaumburg Township District Library, 130 South Roselle Road, Schaumburg, 847-985-4000, www.stdl.org
Community Resources: Village of Schaumburg, 101 Schaumburg Court, 847-895-4500, www.ci.schaumburg.il.us; Township of Schaumburg, 25 Illinois Blvd., Hoffman Estates, 847-884-0030, TTY 847-884-1560; Schaumburg Prairie Center for the Arts, 847-895-3600, www.prairiecenter.org; Roosevelt University, Schaumburg Campus, 1400 North Roosevelt Blvd., 847-619-7300, www.roosevelt.edu/schaumburg; Schaumburg Regional Airport, 905 West Irving Park Road, 847-895-0315; Chamber of Commerce, 847-517-7110, www.nsaci.org; SeptemberFest, www.septemberfest.org
Parks: Schaumburg Parks Department, 847-985-2115, 847-490-7020 (programs), www.parkfun.com; Family Aquatic Center, 505 North Springinsguth Road, 847-490-2505; Walnut Greens Golf Course (nine holes) 847-490-7878; Schaumburg Golf Club (27 holes), 847-885-9000; Alfred Campanelli YMCA, 300 West Wise Road, 847-891-9622
Community Publications: *Daily Herald* (Chicago suburban edition), *Reader's Guide to Arts and Entertainment, Schaumburg Review*
Public Schools: Schaumburg School District 54, 524 East Schaumburg Road, 847-885-6700, www.sd54.k12.il.us; Township High School District 211, 1750 Roselle Road, Palatine, 847-755-6600, www.d211.org
Transportation: Schaumburg Metra Station, 847-895-9260
By Car: I-90 (45 minutes to the Loop)

DES PLAINES

East of Schaumburg and about 17 miles northwest of the city, is the Village of Des Plaines (pronounced with the "s" sounds), maybe best known as the birthplace of McDonald's. In fact, one of the village's biggest attractions is the McDonald's Original Restaurant and Museum. Founded in 1835, the Village of Des Plaines was named for its location along the river of the same name. Before the construction of O'Hare International Airport it consisted mostly of truck farms and factories. Today, Des Plaines is a thriving middle-class town of about 50,000. Residents needing to make the daily commute into the city do so via the Metra/Union Pacific Rail (about a 45-minute trip to the Loop) or by the Tri-State Tollway. Des Plaines has 37 parks, including the expansive 73-acre Lake Park, which offers boating, a golf course, and spacious picnic spots. Other facilities include bike trails and a large family aquatic center. Teeming shopping centers and malls, the world's largest non-residential YMCA, and excellent schools add to this very suburban community. The town is home to several Fortune 500 companies. Its industrial and commercial base allows the residents to enjoy a variety of services with a low property tax base. Although rental properties are somewhat limited, apartments are affordable—expect to pay in the $1,000 range for a basic two-bedroom unit.

In 2000, the town began a revitalization project for the downtown area. Along with a new state-of-the-art library, and several new retail shops and condos, local businesses took part in a Façade Rehabilitation Program that included replacement of signage, lighting, and restoration of original architectural features. Additional improvements, such as a parking deck for commuters and shoppers, a health club, and additional landscaping are in the works.

Web Site: www.desplaines.org
Area Code: 847
Zip Codes: 60016, 60017, 60018, and 60019
Post Office: 1000 East Oakton Street, 800-275-8777
Police: Des Plaines Police Department, 1420 Miner Street, 847-391-5400
Emergency Hospitals: Holy Family Hospital, 100 North River Road, Des Plaines, 847-297-1800; Advocate Medical Lutheran General, 1775 West Dempster Street, Park Ridge, 847-723-5154
Library: Des Plaines Public Library, 841 Graceland Avenue, 847-827-5551
Community Resources: Des Plaines Chamber of Commerce, 1401 Oakton Street, 847-824-4200; Village of Des Plaines, 1420 Miner Street, 847-391-5300, www.desplaines.org; YMCA (Lattof Y), 300 East Northwest Highway, 847-296-3376, www.lattofymca.org

Parks: Des Plaines Park District, 847-391-5700, www.desplaines.org: Community Center, 515 East Thacker Street, Des Plaines, 847-391-5711

Community Publications: *Des Plaines Journal, Des Plaines Times, Reader's Guide to Arts and Entertainment*

Public Schools: District #62, 777 Algonquin Road, 847-824-1136, www.d62.org

Transportation—Rapid Transit: Metra/Union Pacific Northwest Line (stations: Des Plaines, Minor and Lee Streets, and Cumberland, Golf Road and Northwest Highway). Local bus service is provided by PACE, for schedule information go to www.pacebus.com or call 847-364-7223.

ROSEMONT

South of Des Plaines, and only five minutes from O'Hare International Airport, the small (population 4,200) Village of Rosemont was initially established as an industrial park, offering support to the airport and nearby office parks. While only 25% of the village is zoned for residential housing, there is a variety of townhouses, and apartments to choose from, including a senior citizen housing complex.

The same mayor, Donald E. Stephens, has been in office since the village incorporated in 1956, when the place consisted of little more than truck farms (where vegetables were grown and then driven into the city) and several sparsely populated subdivisions. When O'Hare International Airport was built, both the Northwest Tollway and the Tri-State Tollway soon followed, making the village a convenient stop-off and eventually a convention destination. Not surprisingly, many of the residents work in one of the office parks, at the Convention Center or in the nearby restaurants, area hotels, or retail shops. Advance Transformer and Galileo International are also major area employers. In 1976, a former factory was converted into the Rosemont Convention Center, the tenth-largest meeting space in the country. In addition, the Rosemont Horizon indoor stadium regularly hosts the Ringling Brothers and Barnum & Bailey Circus, DePaul University basketball and the Chicago Wolves, an International Hockey League team.

Web Sites: www.rosemontchamber.com; www.rosemont.com

Area Code: 847

Zip Codes: 60018, 60019

Post Office: Rosemont Post Office, 6153 Gage Street (drop-off only, no phone).

Police: Rosemont Public Safety, 9501 West Devon Avenue, 847-823-1134

Emergency Hospitals: Holy Family Medical Center, 100 North River Road, Des Plaines, 847-297-1800; Rush North Shore Medical Center, 9600

Gross Pointe Road, Skokie, 847-677-9600; Advocate Medical Lutheran General, 1775 West Dempster Street, Park Ridge, 847-723-5154

Library: Des Plaines Public Library, 841 Graceland Avenue, 847-827-5551

Parks: Rosemont Park District, 6140 North Scott Street, 847-823-6685

Community Publications: *Daily Herald* (Chicago suburban edition), *Des Plaines Times, Reader's Guide to Arts and Entertainment, Rosemont Journal*

Public Schools: Rosemont School District 78, 6101 Ruby Street, 847-825-0144

Transportation—Rapid Transit: Blue Line (Rosemont or River Road station); Metra trains (Park Ridge or Franklin Park stations); local bus service provided by PACE buses, www.pacebus.com.

By Car: I-90, I-294; major local roads: Route 72/Higgins Road, US 45/Manheim Avenue, and Touhy Avenue

ADDITIONAL NORTH/NORTHWEST SUBURBS

Bannockburn: www.d113.lake.k12.il.us
Barrington: www.ci.barrington.il.us
Buffalo Grove: www.vbg.org
Elk Grove Village: www.elkgrove.org
Glenview: www.glenview.il.us
Hoffman Estates: www.hoffmanestates.com
Morton Grove: www.mortongroveil.org
Mount Prospect: www.mountprospect.org
Palatine: www.palatine.il.us
Park Ridge: www.park-ridge.il.us
Prospect Heights: http://phkhome.northstarnet.org
Rolling Meadows: www.ci.rolling-meadows.il.us
Roselle: www.roselle.il.us
Wheeling: www.vi.wheeling.il.us

WEST SUBURBS

OAK PARK

One of Oak Park's famous sons, Ernest Hemingway, is said to have described this western suburb as a community of wide lawns and narrow minds. The wide lawns (and avenues) remain, but the narrow minds do not. Oak Park today is a vibrant community whose progressive policies in the mid-20th century provided for controlled integration rather than the white flight that plagued other suburbs. It was also the first municipality in

Illinois to offer same-sex domestic partner benefits to city employees. The village is filled with architectural landmarks, including Frank Lloyd Wright's long-time home and studio at 951 Chicago Avenue, as well as his Unity Temple, 875 Lake Street, and many residences designed by the master.

Directly west of the city, Oak Park is divided by the Eisenhower Expressway. (You'll notice that the ramps at Austin and Harlem enter and exit on the left; residents didn't want Oak Park cut up any more than necessary.) Generally, the area south of the expressway is more affordable. If you want to live close to Chicago, but not in it, Oak Park is a good choice. It's convenient for those needing to commute to Chicago: two CTA train lines run through the community, Metra's Oak Park station is at Harlem/Marion streets, and the Eisenhower Expressway is immediately accessible. The downtown is quaint, with a small town feel to it, and there are several good shopping areas throughout the village. Many of the streets are beautiful, lined with huge oak and maple trees, and the homes are generally large and rambling brick dwellings—very attractive and well-kept. According to 2000 Census statistics, the median home value in Oak Park was $273,000.

If you do decide to live here, parking can be a problem, especially if you have guests. Residents may not park on the streets between 2:30 a.m. and 6 a.m. Visitors can park on the street, but only if you notify the Oak Park Police and give them the car's license plate number. As a new resident, you will receive a 30-day pass from the parking office to park on the street. After that, you'll need to buy a sticker and park overnight in village lots. For more information, call the Oak Park Village parking department at 708-383-6400, ext. 236.

Web Site: http://vil.oak-park.il.us
Area Code: 708
Zip Codes: 60301, 60302, 60304
Post Offices: Main Station, 901 Lake Street; South Station, 917 South Oak Park Avenue, 800-275-8777
Police: Oak Park Police, One Village Hall Plaza (Lombard and Madison), 708-386-3800
Emergency Hospitals: Rush Oak Park Hospital, 1653 West Congress Parkway, 708-383-9300; West Suburban Hospital, 3 Erie Court (Erie Street at Austin Boulevard), Oak Park, 708-383-6200, www.westsub.com
Libraries: Oak Park Main Library, 834 Lake Street, 708-383-8200; Dole Branch, 255 Augusta Boulevard, 708-386-9032; Maze Branch, 845 South Gunderson, 708-386-4751, www.oppl.org
Community Resources: Village of Oak Park, 123 Madison Street, 708-383-6400, www.oak-park.il.us; Frank Lloyd Wright Home & Studio, 951 Chicago Avenue, 708-848-1978; Unity Temple Restoration Foundation, 875 Lake Street, 708-383-8873; Unity Temple Unitarian

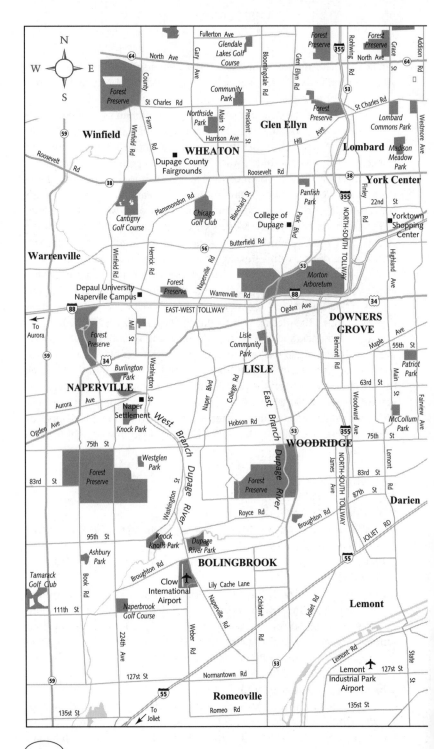

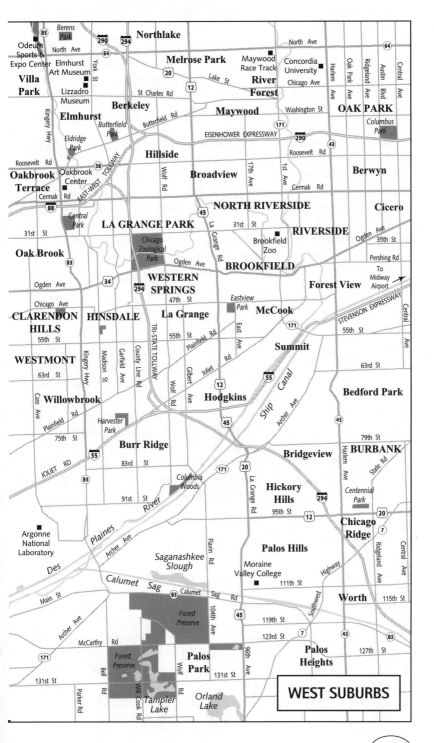

WEST SUBURBS

Universalist Congregation, 708-848-6225, www.unitytemple.org; Historical Society of Oak Park and River Forest, 217 Home Avenue, 708-848-6755; Oak Park YMCA, 708-383-5200, www.opymca.org

Parks: Oak Park Parks District, 218 West Madison Street, 708-383-0002, www.oakparkparks.com

Community Publications: *Oak Park Journal, Oak Leaves, Reader's Guide to Arts and Entertainment*

Public Schools: School District 97 (elementary), 970 Madison Street, 708-524-3000, www.op97.org; Oak Park & River Forest School District 200 (high schools), 201 North Scoville Avenue, Oak Park, 708-383-0700, http://oprfhs.org

Public Transportation—Rapid Transit: Green Line (Austin; Ridgeland; Oak Park; Harlem); Blue Line (Austin; Oak Park; Harlem; Forest Park); Metra/Union Pacific West Line (Oak Park Station.)

BROOKFIELD

Follow Ogden Avenue about thirteen miles west of the Loop to the modest community of Brookfield. Incorporated in 1893 it has approximately 19,000 residents. This solidly middle-class community, where the median home values hover around $150,000 and about 25% of its residents are renters, enjoys quiet environs, a low crime rate, and a good network of solid schools. Though there are more than a dozen Fortune 1000 companies within a 10-mile radius of Brookfield, the world class Brookfield Zoo, 8400 West 31st Street, 708-485-2200, is the community's major in-town employer. A marvelous claim to fame, the zoo organizes a wide range of family activities on its premises, from travel lectures to celebrating National Pig Day.

Web Site: www.brookfield-il.org
Area Code: 708
Zip Code: 60513
Post Office: 3731 Prairie Avenue, 800-275-8777
Police: 8820 Brookfield Avenue, 708-485-8131
Emergency Hospitals: LaGrange Memorial Hospital, 5101 South Willow Springs Road, LaGrange, 708-352-1200; Riveredge Hospital, 8311 West Roosevelt Road, Forest Park, 708-771-7000; MacNeal Hospital, 3249 South Oak Park Avenue, Berwyn, 708-783-9100
Library: Brookfield Library, Grand Boulevard/Lincoln Avenue, 708-485-6917, www.brookfield.lib.il.us
Community Resources: Village of Brookfield, 8820 Brookfield Avenue, 708-485-7344; Chamber of Commerce, 3724 Grand Boulevard, 708-485-1434

Parks: Brookfield Park District: 708-485-7344
Community Publications: *Daily Herald* (Chicago suburban edition), *Reader's Guide to Arts and Entertainment, Suburban Life*
Public Schools: Brookfield School District 95, 3524 Maple Avenue, Brookfield, 708-485-0606, www.d95.w-cook.k12.il.us
Transportation: Metra Burlington Northern Line (Congress Parkway, Brookfield, Hollywood), for information call: 312-322-6777; CTA/Blue Line, (Cumberland Station); local bus service is provided by PACE buses, for schedule check web site: www.pacebus.com or call, 847-364-PACE.
By Car: I-80, I-55, I-290, I-294

DOWNERS GROVE

Continue west on Ogden from Brookfield, past LaGrange Park, Hinsdale, and Clarendon, and you come to Downers Grove. Incorporated in 1873, Downers Grove is one of DuPage County's more vibrant communities. Only 23 miles west of Chicago's Loop, Downers Grove is experiencing an economic boom, due in part to its carefully planned expansion projects. Over the past several years, this community of 51,000 has upgraded its downtown infrastructure to encourage more retail investments and downtown living. In addition to landscape and streetscape enhancements, a 40-unit condo development and additional parking spaces have been added to improve the downtown's appearance and livability. Quickly these efforts have paid off by generating new sales tax revenues, helping to keep property taxes among the lowest in the county. Headquartered here are FTD, Spiegel, Butterball, and Service Master. Downers Grove's job growth rate has been above average, and the local economy is supported by incomes above the national average (mean household income estimated at $81,000 by the village in 2002). Though the community has a well-established history, the residents here tend to be on the younger side, and much of the housing is dedicated to family living, with homes ranging from first-time buyer's price tags, to custom-built luxury homes. The median home value as of 2002 was $187,000.

The Downers Grove Parks District maintains 48 public parks located on 600 acres of land, 17 tennis courts, several community pools, walking trails, and baseball fields.

Web Site: www.vil.downers-grove.il.us
Area Code: 630
Zip Code: 60516
Post Office: 920 Curtiss Street, 800-275-8777
Police: 825 Burlington Avenue, 630-434-5600

Emergency Hospital: Advocates Good Samaritan Hospital, 3815 Highland Avenue, 630-275-5900

Library: Downers Grove Library, 1050 Curtiss Street, 630-960-1200, www.downersgrovelibrary.org

Community Resources: Village Hall, 801 Burlington, 630-434-5500; Illinois Prairie Path, www.ipp.org; YMCA, 711 59th Street, 630-968-8400; Downers Grove Chamber of Commerce, 1015 Curtiss Street, 630-968-4050

Parks: Downers Grove Park District, 2455 Warrenville Avenue, 630-963-1304

Community Publications: *Downers Grove Reporter, Reader's Guide to Arts and Entertainment*

Public Schools: Downers Grove School District 58 (elementary and middle school), 1860 63rd Street, 630-719-5800, www.dg58.dupage.k12.il.us; Community High School District 99, 6301 Springside Avenue, 630-795-7100, www.csd99.k12.il.us

Transportation: Metra/Burlington Northern express (Downers Grove station) to Union Station, 27 minutes; from Fairview Avenue Station to Union Station, 34 minutes.

By Car: I-294, I-355, I-88, I-55 (approximately 45 minutes to downtown Chicago).

WHEATON

Northwest of Downers Grove lies Wheaton. In the mid-1830s, two brothers, Jesse and Warren Wheaton, with Erastus Gary settled in what was to become the City of Wheaton. In 1890, the village was officially incorporated as a city, which grew steadily until it became the DuPage County seat, a position it still holds today. Wheaton is located five miles northeast of Naperville and 23 miles west of Chicago. With a population of 55,000, Wheaton is a middle- to upper-income community, with many professionals calling it home. In 2003, Monstermoving.com listed the median home value at $330,000. Rentals make up about 25% of the housing market. There are close to 40 churches and 20 public schools here, and the park facilities are generous, featuring 40 public tennis courts and four public golf courses. Definitely a family focused community.

In an effort to attract and retain local business, the city has given the downtown area a face-lift, which included refurbishing historic storefronts and cobblestone streets, installing new traffic systems, and replacing awnings. The results were so successful that *Midwest Living Magazine* featured the downtown area in its March/April 2002 issue. There are dozens of small boutiques, cafes, wine shops, and day spas to visit. The Downtown Wheaton Association is very active in organizing community events.

Wheaton is home to the highly respected Wheaton College, which also houses the Billy Graham Museum, documenting evangelism in the US. The Catigny Gardens, the 500+ acres of wooded lands and gardens that was once home to Colonel McCormick, publisher of the *Chicago Tribune*, is now a public garden. Outdoor concerts are performed here during the summer months.

While there are several large employers in Wheaton, including NICOR, Tellabs, Molex, and the Hub Group, the two biggest employers are county government and the local school districts.

Web Site: www.wheaton.il.us

Area Code: 630

Zip Code: 60187, 60189

Post Office: 122 North Wheaton Avenue, 800-275-8777

Police: 900 West Liberty Drive, 630-260-2161

Emergency Hospitals: Central DuPage Hospital, 25 North Winfield Road, Winfield, 630-682-1600; Elmhurst Memorial Hospital, 200 Berteau Avenue, Elmhurst, 630-833-1400

Library: Wheaton Public Library, 225 North Cross Street, 630-668-1374, www.wheaton.lib.il.us/library

Community Resources: City Office: 630-260-2000, www.wheaton.il.us; Wheaton Chamber of Commerce, 128 East Wesley Street, 630-668-6464; Illinois Prairie Path, www.ipp.org; Catigny, One South 151 Winfield Road, 630-668-6151; Arrowhead Golf Club, 630-653-5800, www.wheatonparkdistrict.org

Parks: Wheaton Park District, 666 South Main Street, 630-665-4710, www.wheatonparkdistrict.org

Community Publications: *Reader's Guide to Arts and Entertainment*, *Wheaton Sun*, *Beacon News*, *Wheaton City Newsletter*, www.wheaton.il.us

Public Schools: Wheaton/Warrenville Community School District 200, 130 West Park Avenue, Wheaton, 630-682-2000; Community School District 89, 789 Sheehan Avenue, Glen Ellyn, 630-469-8900, www.ccsd.89.org

Transportation: travel time to downtown via Metra (2 station stops in town) is 40 minutes; local bus service provided by PACE buses. For schedule information, visit www.pacebus.com or call 888-405-2061.

By Car: I-290, I-294, I-355, I-88; major local roads: Roosevelt Road, Routes 56, 64, 53

NAPERVILLE

South of Wheaton lies Naperville, which, with its 135,000+ residents, is the fourth largest city in Illinois. It is known as a main stop on the Illinois High

Tech Corridor, an area where many companies specializing in high technology have set down roots. Naperville has consistently ranked high in the nation as a good place to start a business, raise a family, or retire. In addition to a low crime rate, solid educational system (there are 34 public schools currently, with plans to construct more), and one of the finest libraries in the country, Naperville provides its residents with a wealth of services. As the oldest city in DuPage County, Naperville has carefully preserved many of its historical sites. The Naperville Settlement, located at 523 South Webster Street, is a museum village, complete with costumed workers who demonstrate what life was like during the 1800s. There are many private homes with historic or architectural significance in Naperville, including some Frank Lloyd Wright homes. More than 150 sites dating from 1830 to 1920 are located in Naperville and are listed on the National Register of Historic Places.

While there are many features of interest in Naperville, two stand out in particular. The 72 bronze bell Millennium Carillon, located in the Bell Tower, one-quarter mile west of Washington Street on Aurora Avenue, is one of only four in the world spanning six full octaves. The bells are heard several times a day automatically, and in the summer visiting musicians are invited to play the bells. Also in Naperville, the award-winning Riverwalk, created by Naperville residents in celebration of its 150th birthday. It consists of a brick paved path that winds along the DuPage River through downtown Naperville. It features fountains, covered bridges, a sled hill, a gazebo, amphitheater, shaded seating areas, and paddleboat rides. Maintained by the park district, it's open year-round, from dawn until midnight. For a Riverwalk map, call 630-848-5000.

There are several shopping options for residents. The downtown area offers boutiques, antique stores and a variety of small shops and restaurants. For more serious shopping, residents take to the road and head for the Fox Valley Mall on Route 59 and Aurora Avenue. All along Route 59 from 111th Street to Diehl Road, shoppers will find a number of outdoor malls and stores.

Web Site: www.naperville.il.us, www.naperville.net
Area Code: 630
Zip Code: 60563, 60564, 60540, 60566
Post Office: 5 South Washington Street (downtown); main office: 1750 West Ogden Avenue, 800-275-8777
Police: 1350 Aurora Avenue, 630-420-6666 (non-emergency)
Emergency Hospital: Edward Hospital, 801 South Washington Street, 630-527-3000, www.edward.org
Library: 200 West Jefferson Street, 630-961-4100, www.naperville-lib.org
Community Resources: City of Naperville: 400 South Eagle Street, 630-420-6111; Chamber of Commerce, 131 West Jefferson Avenue, 630-355-

4141, www.naperville.net; DuPage Children's Museum, 301 North Washington Street, 630-637-8000; Heritage YMCA, 630-420-6275

Parks: Naperville Park District, 320 West Jackson Avenue, 630-848-5000, www.napervilleparks.org; Centennial Beach; DuPage River Trails, Burr Oak Park to 115th Street; Fox Valley Park District, www.foxvalley parkdistrict.org; Morton Arboretum, 4100 Route 53, Lisle, 630-968-0074; Riverwalk, 630-848-5000

Community Publications: *Naperville Sun, Reader's Guide to Arts and Entertainment*

Public Schools: Naperville C.U. School District 203, 203 West Hillside Avenue, 630-420-6300, www.ncusd203.org; Indian Prairie School District 204, 780 Shoreline Drive, Aurora, 630-375-3000, www.ipsd.org

Transportation: MetraBurlington Northern Line (2 station stops in town); Amtrak for points west of Aurora (www.amtrak.com, 800-USA-RAIL); local service and Dial-a-Ride service provided by PACE, see www.pacebus.com for schedule or call 888-405-2061.

By Car: I-88, I-355; local main roads: Naper Boulevard, Washington Street, Ogden Avenue.

BOLINGBROOOK

South of Naperville and thirty miles southwest of Chicago's downtown area, is Bolingbrook (population 65,000). Once made up of farm fields of Will and DuPage counties, it wasn't incorporated until 1965. Three-quarters of its residents are homeowners, but there is a good market for multi-family units and apartments here as well. Housing values in Bolingbrook haven't appreciated as much as in other fringe suburbs in the Chicagoland area; Census 2000 results put Bolingbrook's median home value at 142,000. Housing starts are still very strong in this community, as are the number of business start-ups. Good news for first time home-buyers and middle income families. Increasing sales tax revenues from new businesses are helping to keep property taxes down. In fact property taxes have declined steadily since 1990. According to local realtors, Bolingbrook is a growing, middle-income, and racially integrated community.

In this community made up of a lot of young families you'd be correct to expect a lot of play space. Bolingbrook offers a variety of sports and recreation facilities, including two-fitness centers, an indoor and outdoor aquatic center, and more than 30 neighborhood parks. Area shopping is good too. The Michigan grocery giant Meijer selected Bolingbrook for its first Chicagoland stores: 755 East Boughton Road, 630-783-5300, and 225 North Naperville Road, 630-679-6506. And there are plans to build a new regional shopping center on Bolingbrook's east side, which will be the first new mall in the Chicagoland area in 20 years.

Web Site: www.bolingbrook.com
Area Code: 630
Zip Code: 60440
Post Office: 105 Canterbury Lane, 800-275-8777
Police: 375 West Briarcliff, 630-226-0600
Emergency Hospitals: Bolingbrook Medical Center, 400 Medical Center Drive, 630-226-8100; Edward Healthcare Center, 130 North Weber Road, Bolingbrook, 630-646-5770
Library: 300 West Briarcliff Road, 630-759-2102
Community Resources: Village of Bolingbrook, 375 West Briarcliff, 630-226-8400; Bolingbrook Performing Arts Center, 375 West Briarcliff Road, 630-226-8400; Bolingbrook Chamber of Commerce, 375 West Briarcliff Road, 630-226-8420; Bolingbrook Golf Course, 2001 Rodeo Drive, 630-771-9400; Bolingbrook Community Television, 375 West Briarcliff Road, 630-226-8425
Parks, Park District, 201 Recreation Drive, 630-739-0272, www.boling brookparks.org
Community Publications: *Beacon News, Bolingbrook Sun, Bolingbrook Reporter, Reader's Guide to Arts and Entertainment*
Public Schools: 815-886-2700 (administration), www.vvsd.org
Transportation: Metra Burlington/Northern Line, (two station stops in town); local bus service provided by PACE buses, call 847-364-7223 for more information. Amtrak information: 800-USA-RAIL.
By Car: I-355, I-80 (extension under construction), I-55, I-294

ADDITIONAL WESTERN SUBURBS

Clarendon Hills: Village Hall, 630-323-3500, www.clarendon-hills.il.us
Hinsdale: Village Hall, 630-789-7000, http://vil.hinsdale.il.us
LaGrange Park: 708-354-0225, www.lagrangepark.org
Lisle: Village Hall: 630-271-4100, www.vil.lisle.il.us
North Riverside: Village Hall, 708-447-4211, www.northriverside.info
Riverside: Village Hall, 708-447-2700, www.riverside-illinois.com
Western Springs: Village Hall, 708-246-1800, www.wsprings.com
Westmont: Village Hall, 630-829-4400, www.westmont.il.us
Woodridge: Village Hall, 630-719-4706, www.vil.woodridge.il.us

SOUTH SUBURBS

BURBANK

North and west of Chicago's Beverly Hills neighborhood and 15 miles southwest of the Loop in Cook County, is the town of Burbank. Incorporated in 1970, Burbank is a relatively new community, and today has nearly 28,000 residents. It is a safe, middle-class neighborhood where new housing construction is the rule rather than the exception. While there are some rental apartments, single family homes predominate, many in residential developments. Home values are just slightly above the national average, and Burbank's tax base remains one of the lowest in the southwest Chicagoland area, making it a good deal for many first time home buyers. The town supports a dozen parks, one community pool, and two volunteer fire departments. Burbank is home to some large-scale employers, and several of *Fortune's* Top 1000 have offices here, including McDonald's, Sara Lee, Abbott Laboratories, Baxter International, Walgreen, and the Aon Corporation. Burbank is just a few miles from St. Xavier University and Trinity Christian College. A straight shot up Cicero Avenue to Midway Airport offers easy access for those needing to fly. Travel time to downtown Chicago via the Metra train is approximately 35 minutes.

Web Site: www.geocities.com/burbank_illinois/
Area Code: 708
Zip Code: 60459
Post Office: Stickney, 5635 State Road, 800-275-8777
Burbank Police Department: 708-924-7300
Emergency Hospitals: Little Company of Mary Hospital, 2800 West 95th Street, Evergreen Park, 708-422-6200, St. Francis Hospital and Health Center, 12935 South Gregory Street, Blue Island, 708-597-2000
Library: Prairie Trails Public Library, 8449 South Moody Avenue, 708-430-3688, www.prairietrailslibrary.org
Community Resources: City of Burbank, 708-599-5500, 6530 West 79th Street; Stickney Township, 5635 State Road, 708-424-9200; Senior Center, 708-636-8850
Parks: Burbank Park District, 8050 South Newcastle, 708-599-2070; Pool and Recreation Center, 85th Street and State Road, 708-430-8688
Community Publications: *Daily Southtown, Southwest Courier, Southwest News Herald, The Star, Suburban Life*
Public Schools: elementary: Burbank, District 111, 7600 South Central, 708-496-0500; high school: Reavis/District 220, 6034 West 77th Street, Burbank 708-599-7200; www.burbank.k12.il.us

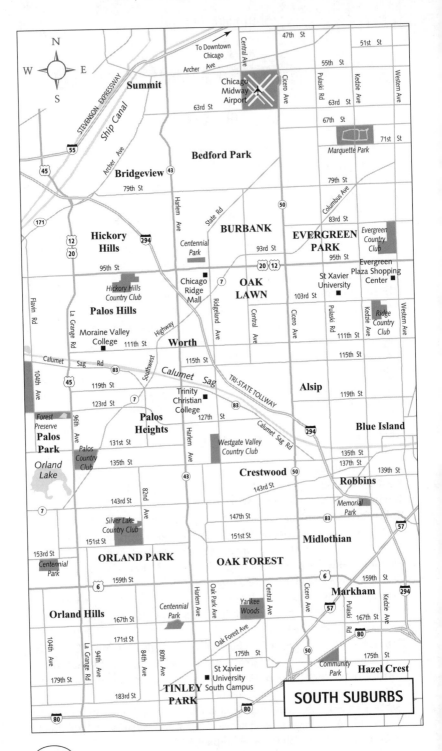

SOUTH SUBURBS

Public Transportation: PACE: Norfolk & Western Line; Amtrak (in Summit); RTA & Orange Line
By Car: I-294, I-57

EVERGREEN PARK

Flush against the west side of Beverly and 17 miles southwest of the Loop is Evergreen Park, (median age 39 according to last Census), middle-income community. From a town with 500 residents in 1893, to 21,000+ residents today, Evergreen Park continues to grow at a leisurely pace. There is no industry to speak of and its main employers are the numerous health centers and hospitals, as well as a variety of service-oriented businesses. But what Evergreen Park is perhaps best known for is the Evergreen Shopping Plaza, one of the first regional malls in the country, as well as the Drury Lane Theatre on West 95th Street, a popular dinner theater, offering Broadway productions with nationally recognized performers.

The majority of residents are homeowners, and Evergreen's wide range of housing prices attracts both first time buyers as well as those further up the corporate ladder. (The village web site lists area housing in the affordable range of $80,000 to $275,000.) Homes in Evergreen are predominately the single-family type, but come in a variety of styles: Victorians, bungalows, Cape Cods, and Georgians. Some condos and apartment units are available as well. It's a well-kept community, with tree-lined streets, good schools, and good services.

Web Sites: http://everythingep.com, www.evergreenpark-ill.com
Area Code: 708
Zip Code: 60805
Post Office: Evergreen Post Office, 9359 South Kedzie Avenue, 800-275-8777
Police: Evergreen Park Police Department, 9420 South Kedzie Avenue, 708-422-2142
Emergency Hospitals: Advocate Christ Medical Center and Hope Children's Hospital, 4440 West 95th Street Oak Lawn, 708-425-8000; Little Company of Mary Hospital, 2800 West 95th Street, Evergreen Park, 708-422-6200; Palos Community Hospital, 12251 South 80th Avenue, Palos Heights, 708-923-4000; St. Francis Hospital and Health Center, 12935 South Gregory Street, Blue Island, 708-597-2000
Library: Evergreen Park Public Library, 9400 South Troy, 708-422-8522, www.evergreenparklibrary.org
Community Resources: Village Hall, 708-422-1551, www.evergreen park-ill.com; Office of Citizens Newsletter, 708-422-8776; Drury Lane Theatre, 2500 West 95th Street, 708-422-0404, www.drurylane.com

Parks: Evergreen Park Recreation District, 708-229-3374; Hamilton Maher Community Center, 3450 West 97th Street, 708-229-3373; Youth Center, 3450 West 97th Street, 708-229-3377; Ice Rink, 8900 South Kedzie, 708-606-7093

Community Publications: *Daily Southtown, Evergreen Park Courier, Suburban Life, Southwest Courier, Southwest News Herald, The Star*

Public Schools: Evergreen Park School District 124 (elementary), 708-423-0950; Evergreen Park Community High School District 231, 708-424-7400; www.d124.s-cook.k12.il.us

Public Transportation: METRA/Rock Island/Beverly Line; Orland Park Suburban Service; PACE Route 835, Bus #381

By Car: I-294, I-94, I-57

OAK LAWN

Directly west of Evergreen Park is Oak Lawn. This small-to-medium sized, middle-income community is home to about 57,000. Despite its small size, it provides a wide range of services to its residents: public parks, recreational sites, 24 tennis courts, nature trails, three outdoor swimming pools, and a golf course all spread throughout a 300 acre area. Shopping opportunities abound, with 1,200 merchants established in area malls and individual stores in the downtown business area.

Oak Lawn has no industrial center; the source of its commercial viability is its service sector. There are two large hotels in the area, the Oak Lawn Hilton Hotel & Conference Center, 9333 South Cicero, and the Holiday Inn of Oak Lawn, 4140 West 95th Street. With Oak Lawn being only 15 miles southwest of the Loop, the hotels attract business conferences throughout the year.

Housing styles here range from colonials to ranch style homes, with many at the first-home-buyer price-range. If you are looking for a newly built home, Oak Lawn has at least 13 new developments to choose from. Several subdivisions are in the final stages of construction or have been completed since 2000.

Web Site: www.villageofoaklawn.com
Area Code: 708
Zip Codes: 60453, 60415
Post Office: 9249 South Cicero, 800-275-8777
Oak Lawn Police: 708-422-8292
Emergency Hospitals: Advocate Christ Medical Center and Hope Children's Hospital, 4440 West 95th Street, 708-425-8000, Oak Lawn
Library: Oak Lawn Library, 9427 Raymond Avenue, 708-422-4990

Community Resources: Oak Lawn Chamber of Commerce, 708-424-8300; Village Hall, 708-636-4400; farmers' market, 57th Street/Cook, beginning each June through the summer season. Summer concerts on the Village Green.

Parks: Oak Lawn Park District, 708-857-2200, www.olparks.com

Community Publications: *Daily Southtown, Suburban Life, Southwest Courier, Southwest News Herald, The Star*

Public Schools: Oak Lawn-Hometown School District 123, 4201 West 93rd Street, 708-423-0150, www.d123.s-cook.k12.il.us; Oak Lawn Community High School District 229, 9400 SW Hwy, Oak Lawn, 708-424-5200, www.olchs.org

Public Transportation: CTA bus service: #52A, #53A Pulaski; RTA PACE Buses: Norfolk-Western Line

By Car: I-80, I-90, I-94, I-295, I-55, I-57

OAK FOREST

Further south of Oak Lawn is Oak Forest, a small community (population 28,000) tucked in the southwest corner of Cook County. The overwhelming majority of residents are homeowners (about 80%), many with families. Area homes are reasonably priced, despite a recent eight percent jump in market value. Taxes are also low. With big employers right here in their own back yard, Oak Forest residents don't have to commute to the Loop for employment. Companies such as Corn Products International, Tellabs, The ServiceMaster Company, and Molex all have facilities nearby. In addition, there are two areas in town set aside for industrial development, the Harlem Avenue Business Center, and the Corporate Center of Oak Forest. Those who do need to head north to Chicago will find their Kennedy/Dan Ryan expressway trip will take about 40 minutes.

There are 19 public parks located in Oak Forest and the park district runs a health and fitness center. For the serious golfer, there's the George W. Dunne National Golf Course, one of the best public courses in the country; for the less serious player, there's a public mini-golf course as well.

Web Site: www.oak-forest.org
Area Code: 708
Zip Code: 60452
Post Office: 15811 Central Avenue, 800-275-8777
Police: 15440 South Central Avenue, 708-687-1376
Emergency Hospital: Oak Forest Hospital, 159th Street & Cicero Avenue, 708-687-7200

Library: Acorn (district) Public Library, 15624 South Central Avenue, 708-687-3700

Community Resources: City Hall, 15440 South Central Avenue, 708-687-4050; Oak Forest Chamber of Commerce, 708-687-4600; Tweeter Music Theater, 708-614-1550, www.tweetercenterchicago.com; De Paul University Oak Forest Campus, 16333 South Kilbourn Avenue, 708-633-9091; **Shopping**: Calumet City Mall, Orland Park Mall

Community Publications: *Daily Southtown, Suburban Life, Southwest Courier, Southwest News Herald, The Star*

Public Schools: Arbor Park District 145, 708-687-8040 (elementary), www.arbor.s-cook.k12.il.us; Bremen High School District 228, 708-389-1175, www.bhsd228.s-cook.k12.il.us, also check Tinley Park below.

Public Transportation: Amtrak and Metra Rock Island Line, both at the 159th Street/Cicero Station in Oak Forest.

By Car: I-57, I-80, I-294

ORLAND PARK

Upscale, business friendly, quality-of-life focused, and family oriented, that's Orland Park in a nutshell. Incorporated in 1892, this community, located 25-30 miles southwest of downtown Chicago, has witnessed planned and controlled growth over the past decade and shows no sign of slowing down. From its present population of close to 52,000 residents, Census experts anticipate the town will top 70,000 by the year 2010. It's no mystery why with its low crime rate, attractive amenities, 25 tennis courts, 46 baseball fields, 39 basketball courts, 23 soccer fields, 48 well-equipped parks, an aquatic center, hiking and biking trails, and 21 public golf courses in the area. The government of Orland Park has been actively encouraging more diverse businesses to its borders, especially upscale retail, light industrial businesses, and high-tech and research facilities. The village has a 10,000 square foot civic center available for conferences, weddings, and other events. Additionally, two large regional shopping centers, Orland Square Mall and Orland Park Place, serve the Chicago Southland—shoppers come from as far as Kankakee and from Indiana. The town's largest employer is the corporate headquarters of telecommunications firm, Andrews Corporation, followed by School District 135.

Web Site: www.orland-park.il.us
Area Code: 708
Zip Code: 60462
Post Office: 9500 West 144th Place, 800-275-8777
Police: 14600 Ravinia Avenue, 708-349-4111

Emergency Hospital: Palos Community Hospital, 12251 South 80th Avenue, Palos Heights, 708-923-4000

Library: Orland Park Library, 14760 Park Lane, 708-349-8138, www.orlandparklibrary.org

Community Resources: Village Hall, 708-403-6100, www.orland-park.il.us; Orland Park Chamber of Commerce, 708-349-2972

Parks: Orland Park Recreation & Park District, 708-403-7275, www.orland-park.il.us; Centennial Park Aquatics Center, 15600 West Avenue, 708-349-4386

Community Publications: *Daily Southtown, Suburban Life, Southwest Courier, Southwest News Herald, The Regional, The Star*

Public Schools: Orland Park School District 135, 15100 South 94th Avenue, 708-349-5700, www.orland135.org

Public Transportation: METRA/Rock Island/Southwest Service; Norfolk Southern (3 days/week)

By Car: I-80, I-57, I-294, I-355 (extension planned)

TINLEY PARK

It's the tale of two counties—Cook and Will. Tinley Park, divided by the I-80 Development Corridor, sits mostly in the southwest corner of Cook County, but it is Tinley Park's section of Will County that is a blessing to this community. The lower tax base of Will County is very attractive to local businesses, and is one of the features that the local government uses to bring more business to the community. And, a solid foundation for area businesses creates a low tax base for residents. Tinley Park is experiencing a steady growth rate, much like its Orland Park neighbor to the north. Affordable single-family homes are being built on land that was once set aside for farms. Young and growing families are those most attracted to Tinley Park, but since Tinley Park issues as many multi-family building permits as it does single family homes, there are many condos and townhouses available as well. This is unusual in a Chicago fringe community where typically the overwhelming choice is single-family homes—good news for empty nesters, young singles, childless couples, and seniors who are looking for living space without a high price tag.

Hiking trails, a water park, an 18-hole public golf course, and the famous New World Theater (now renamed Tweeter Center—the largest outdoor performance facility in North America) are among some of the niceties available in the area.

Web Sites: www.tinelynet.org; www.tinleypark.org
Area Code: 708
Zip Code: 60477

Post Office: 7230 West 171st Street, 800-275-8777

Police: 708-444-5300

Emergency Hospitals: St. James Hospital, Olympia Fields Campus, 20201 South Crawford Avenue, Olympia Fields, 708-747-4000; Advocate South Suburban Hospital, 17800 South Kedzie Avenue, Hazel Crest, 708-799-8000

Library: 17107 South 71st Avenue, 708-532-0160

Community Resources: Village of Tinley Park, 16250 South Oak Park Avenue, 708-444-5000; Tinley Park Chamber of Commerce, 708-532-5700; New World Theatre, 19100 South Ridgeland Avenue, 708-614-1550

Parks: Park District, 8125 West 171st Street, 708-532-8698

Community Publications: *Daily Southtown, Suburban Life, Southwest Courier, Southwest News Herald, Tinley Park Star*

Public Schools: C.C. School District 146 (elementary), 708-614-4500, www.ccsd146.k12.il.us; Kirby School District 140 (elementary), 708-532-6462, www.ksd140.org; Bremen High School District 228, 708-389-1175, www.bhsd228.s-cook.k12.il.us (also see Oak Forest and Orland Park).

Public Transportation: METRA/Rock Island/Beverly Line (80th Avenue station); CTA at North Racine

By Car: I-80, Route 43, Route 45

ADDITIONAL SOUTH SIDE COMMUNITIES

Check www.villageprofile.com for more information about the following communities:

- **Chicago Ridge**
- **Burbank**
- **Blue Island**
- **Bridgeview**
- **Calumet Park**
- **Summit**
- **University Park**
- **Park Forest**, www.villageofparkforest.com

I F YOU'RE COMING TO CHICAGO FROM A SMALLER TOWN, FINDING A place to live here may feel overwhelming; those from another large metropolis will probably find Chicago's housing market easier to manuever. Where's the ideal place to live in the Chicago area? That depends on what you want, of course, but for many, the perfect place is attractive, clean, spacious, affordable, conveniently located to work and public transportation, in a safe area, perhaps close to the lake, with spectacular views, central air, ample on-street parking, and if it's a rental, one that allows pets. Sound impossible? It's not, of course, if you have enough money ... but knowing what is most important to you, before you begin your search will save time and reduce stress.

In Illinois there is no upper limit on how much rent a landlord can charge for a rental property. That, combined with the area's high incomes, the transformation of Chicago into a cultural powerhouse, and the continued gentrification and beautification of the downtown, means many formerly affordable neighborhoods are now filled with the wealthier than average, often over-55 former suburbanites, who own not rent. So, if you want to live near Oprah in the Gold Coast and be able to walk from your apartment to shop on the Magnificent Mile, brace yourself for sticker shock. But don't despair! Chicago is a large and varied city and the rental market in particular is softer and more renter friendly now than it was in the 1990s. You *can* find a great, affordable apartment if you are willing to do a bit of digging, particularly outside the most popular neighborhoods. It will require some research and exploring—which can be interesting and is important if you want to get to know your new city.

Unless you're fabulously wealthy, cost will probably be a major consideration. Try the following web sites for **average rental prices** in various neighborhoods (note: the neighborhood names and boundaries do not always correspond with the names and boundaries in this book):

www.theapartmentsource.com or www.apartmentpeople.com or www.chicagoapartmentsforrent.com.

Whether you are looking for an apartment to rent or a place to buy, here are some issues to keep in mind when exploring your targeted neighborhood:

- **Airport noise**; if you are considering living in the suburbs, you will want to know if your potential new home is in a landing or takeoff route of one of the major airlines. Here's where an experienced real estate broker may be of assistance. Airport noise is no small matter, it can make a big difference in the quality of your television/cell phone reception, outdoor entertaining, the resale value of your home, and the likelihood of getting a good night's sleep. The good news is that overall airport noise complaints have dropped significantly since 1998 with the introduction of quieter aircraft and permanent noise monitoring. But with a proposed third airport in the south and new runways for O'Hare also being discussed, it will remain an important issue for years to come. Contact the O'Hare Noise Commission at 773-686-3198 or www.oharenoise.org for more information.

- **Flooding**; much of the Chicago area was once swamp and some suburbs are situated on flood plains, so a big thunderstorm may mean a mini-lake in your backyard or worse, your basement. This can also affect your insurance coverage. Try to stay away from flood-prone areas, no matter how much of a bargain the house may seem. If you're considering a "garden" apartment, be aware that if the storm sewers back up, and they do in the heaviest downpours, you may find yourself bailing to save yourself from a rush of brown water. These types of mini-floods can occur very quickly, often at night in tandem with a thunderstorm; fortunately, they seem to disappear almost as fast as they come.

- **Bugs**: termites, carpenter ants, long-horned beetles, cockroaches—find out the specifics on such pests in your neighborhood and in your building, and whether they have been or can be eradicated from the place you are considering. (See **Helpful Services** for more on area pests.) Roaches, for example, sometimes infest one building while another, right next door, may be roach free.

- **Turnover**; are you considering a neighborhood where residents move out regularly after a few years, or is it a stable community? If you have school-aged children, this may be of particular interest to you.

- Can you get a **sense of community** in the neighborhood or building you are visiting? Neighborhood types vary greatly but some are specifically bedroom-commuter suburbs, young singles areas, retiree havens, or neighborhoods made up of mostly young families—which is right for you?

- **Traffic**; during rush-hour commutes, when major thoroughfares are crowded, many drivers use residential streets as shortcuts. Some neighborhoods have speed bumps, frequent stop signs, and one-way streets to discourage commuters, still many streets that are tranquil on weekends turn into speedways come Monday mornings.

- **Highway noise** can also be a problem depending on how close you are to the road. The best way to find out about noise problems in a prospective neighborhood is to visit several times, at different times of day. Also, if you are moving within the city limits, be aware that if you live right next to the 'L,' vibrations from the train can be a nuisance—a lot depends on the building, however. Remember, being close to an 'L' stop makes getting around the city much easier!

APARTMENT HUNTING

Take a breath and tell yourself you don't expect to find a new pad in one day, otherwise you may end of with something that isn't right for you. Ideally you should give yourself at least a week to find your first apartment here.

DIRECT ACTION

If you're the do-it-yourself kind of person, the **classifieds**, either print or online, are still probably the best way to find a place to live in Chicago. **Word of mouth referrals** and **pavement pounding** are among the next best direct methods to finding a future pad in the Windy City. Old school and hometown connections can be helpful in choosing a neighborhood and a home. As soon as you know you're moving to Chicago, you may want to contact friends or family who have moved here, or who know someone here, and ask them to keep their eyes and ears open. Also, check with your **college alumni office** for help with finding housing here. If you know of a building you'd like to live in, call the rental office, management company or condo association and simply ask about upcoming vacancies. Other tactics include looking for posted rental notices on coffee shop, grocery store, and laundromat bulletin boards, and on vacant apartment windows in the neighborhoods that attract you. If you are a university student, contact your **student services office** for tips about where to look and which areas of town to avoid. For example, Loyola University Chicago has useful housing information on its web site (www.luc.edu) as does Chicago Kent College of Law (www.kentlaw.edu) and you don't need to be a student to read their web pages. If you are enrolled at the University of Chicago as a graduate student, you can take advantage of their student housing program. Go to http://reo.uchicago.edu where you can view vacancies. The UofC student government, also lists Hyde Park rental information at http://apartments.uchicago.edu/realtors, and you can find even more (Hyde Park mostly) housing possibilities at the UofC "marketplace" web site: http://marketplace.uchicago.edu. Northwestern University has a similar program for graduate students and a program for students who will be living on campus with spouses or families: contact the Northwestern University Student Housing Office at 847-491-7564, 312-503-8514 (Chicago campus), or go online to www.northwestern.edu/housing for more information.

Is your job bringing you to the Chicago area? If so, be sure to ask about any **relocation assistance** your employer might provide. Benefits vary but many organizations provide temporary housing and assistance finding permanent housing.

If perusing classifieds and pavement pounding is too much work for you, or if your time is limited, you may do better to go to a **Rental Agent** (see below).

CLASSIFIED ADVERTISEMENTS

Reading the newspaper classifieds is the most common way to begin searching for an apartment. They will also give you a good sense of the market. Most rental ads are placed in the Sunday newspapers, which are available on Saturday at convenience stores, some of the larger supermarkets, and newsstands. If weren't able to buy a copy of the Sunday paper, you can always go to the local library. Also, many newspaper classifieds are online:

- **Chicago Reader**: this free weekly paper has a good rentals real estate section. The online version's housing section is updated every Tuesday by about 7 p.m., www.chireader.com.
- **Chicago Sun-Times**: available at newsstands, drugstores, and convenience stores throughout Chicago. The *Sun Times* contains rental and real estate classifieds. The online section is a bit more cumbersome to navigate than the *Tribune's*, but there are tons of listings—go to www.suntimes.com/classifieds/homes/rentals.
- **Chicago Tribune**: get the Sunday edition, which has the most comprehensive rental and real estate listings for Chicago and surrounding communities. Rentals are divided into apartments and houses in the rental section, and further subdivided by location. Houses for sale are listed in the "Home/Real Estate" section, also organized by location. Online, homes for sale appear in the www.chicagotribune.com/homes section; likewise, apartment listings appear in the www.chicagotribune.com/apartments section. You can also use the *Tribune's* links to find a roommate, obtain a free credit report, learn more about renter's insurance, read their neighborhood profiles, and many other moving related topics.
- **New City**, entertainment-oriented free weekly and competitor to the *Reader*, has some rental classifieds. Available at bars, restaurants and convenience stores and online at www.newcitychicago.com.

To find housing in Chicago's **surrounding communities**, check out the classified ads in these major newspapers:

- Access the following suburban newspapers online at www.suburbanchicagonews.com: *Naperville Sun, Beacon News, Courier News*.
- *Daily Herald*, www.dailyherald.com, a good resource for the five-county area.
- *Daily Southtown*, www.dailysouthtown.com

RENTAL AGENTS/APARTMENT SEARCH FIRMS/ONLINE RESOURCES

One way to find an apartment, particularly if your time is limited, is to use an apartment search firm. When speaking to an apartment search firm agent, be specific about your needs and budget. Also, find out if there is a fee. Some services charge to view their listings, others get their revenue from the property owners. Here are a few to get you started. The local ones tend to favor the North Side, where most of them are located. For more check the Yellow Pages or go online and look for "Apartments & Home Rentals," or "Apartment Agency Referral Services." Note: rental agents typically favor units in larger buildings and this is especially true with the national services. You'll probably have to find that charming floor-through in a two-flat on your own.

LOCAL APARTMENT SEARCH FIRMS

- **The Apartment Connection**, www.theaptconnection.com, 1000 West Diversey, Chicago, 60614, 773-525-3888 or 800-546-7800 (Chicago only)
- **Apartments and Homeseekers**, 5354 North Broadway, Chicago 60640, 773-784-9100, www.aptandhomeseekers.com
- **The Apartment People**, 3121 North Broadway, 800-447-3684 or 773-248-8800, www.apartmentpeople.com
- **Chicago Apartments and Condos**, 3534 North Broadway, Chicago 60657, 773-525-3900, www.homes-condos.com
- **The Chicago Apartment Exchange**, 700 North Carpenter, Chicago 60622, 312-951-6000, www.chicagoaptexchange.com
- **Chicago Apartments for Rent**, 2440 North Lakeview, Chicago 60614, 888-284-1437, www.chicagoapartmentsforrent.com
- **Chicago Apartment Finders**, 906 West Belmont Avenue, Chicago 60657, 773-883-8800, www.chicagoapartmentfinders.com
- **The Chicago Apartment Source**, 2638 North Halsted, Chicago, 773-404-9900, www.theapartmentsource.com

NATIONAL APARTMENT SEARCH FIRMS

- **www.apartments.com**, national online apartment search service/guides based in Chicago
- **www.apartments-in-chicago.com**
- **www.chicago-apartments.org**
- **www.homestore.com**
- **www.relocationcentral.com**; national agency with Chicago office at 21 West Elm Street, 312-255-9920, as well as three offices in the suburbs (Oak Brook, Naperville and Schaumburg)
- **www.rent.com**
- **www.rentwave.com**

If you are interested in renting in a high-rise, there's a web site just for you: www.highriseliving.com. Locally, **The Habitat Company** is worth investigating. One of the largest residential property managers in Chicago, their big buildings include Cityfront Place and Huron Plaza. They also manage over 3,000 condos in the Chicago area. Their headquarters are located at 350 West Hubbard Street, Chicago, IL 60610, 312-527-5400, and you can find them on the web at www.habitat.com.

The Anti-Cruelty Society (SPCA of Illinois) offers information on **pet-friendly apartments**. Call 312-644-8338 or visit their web site at www.anticruelty.org and click on "Pet Friendly Apartment List."

ROOMMATES AND SUBLETS

If you're single and moving here on your own, perhaps you'd like to share an apartment—it's more economical, and renting a room in a house can be a great way to meet people. Sometimes a group will get together and find a home, though more often one or two people will rent a house and then seek roommates through advertising, word-of-mouth referrals, or a roommate referral service. There is a brisk market for summer sublets, particularly near colleges and universities. Or, with luck and connections, you might even find a house sitting position.

Some find roommates through the bulletin boards in college and universities, in cafes, and in bookstores. You can find listings in the major newspapers above, as well on as their web sites, under "Housing to Share" and "Rooms for Rent."

If you don't want to do the work yourself, contact **Simply Roommates and Sublets**, www.simplyroommates.com, 2438 North Clark Street, 773-755-4400. They charge $75 for 90 days of roommate searching.

The following web sites appear to offer **roommate finding/matching**; they may also offer online dating:

- **www.chicagoroommate.com**
- **www.easyroommate.com**
- **www.metroroommates.com**

Keep in mind that with roommates come issues: cleaning, guests, smoking/drinking/drugs, the kitchen, pets, rent … things to think about and discuss frankly before you agree to join forces in rental real estate. Also, it's always a good idea to ask for (and check) references—personal, and professional—and you should have your references ready too.

Sublets are another option. University neighborhoods, such as Evanston, Hyde Park, around DePaul University, and the area around Northwestern University's downtown campus are good bets for summer vacancies. Check with the university or walk around the neighborhood and look for sublet postings on bulletin boards in coffee shops, supermarkets, and bookstores.

On the web you may find listings at the following sites:

- **www.collegesublease.com**
- **www.simplyroommates.com** (see information above).
- **www.sublet.com**

CHECKING IT OUT

It's two months into your lease and suddenly, the cozy budget bachelor pad you found is feeling a little claustrophobic; to make matters worse the neighbors argue all night long, the water pressure is dismal and there's a smell coming from under the floor that you can't (and don't want to) put your finger on. To avoid this scenario we suggest you view prospective apartments knowing what's crucial for you and that you inspect to make sure the apartment's beauty is not just skin deep. A little forethought and advance scrutiny could save you a huge headache later on. Specifically, you may want to look for the following:

- Are the kitchen appliances clean and in working order? Do the stove's burners work? How about the oven? Is there enough counter and shelf space?
- Do the windows open, close, and lock? Do the bedroom windows open onto a noisy or potentially dangerous area? Is there an air-conditioning unit or central air?
- Are there enough closets and is there enough storage space? Any basement storage for renters?
- Are there enough electrical outlets for your needs? Do the outlets work?
- Does the toilet flush properly?
- What about laundry facilities? Are they in the building or nearby? Is the area well lit?

- Outside, do you feel comfortable? Will you feel safe here at night? Is there secured parking? Is there an extra fee for parking? How far is public transportation and shopping?
- Are you responsible for paying gas, water, and/or electricity? (This varies from the tenant paying any combination or none at all.)
- If you are looking at a "garden apartment" are there bars on the windows? Any signs of water damage or flooding?
- If it smells as if it has just been sprayed for bugs that may be a sign that the building has a problem.
- Is there a smoke detector in the apartment?
- Turn on the faucets; check the water pressure. Water pressure throughout Chicago is low; if the building is old, you might only get a trickle. Can you imagine washing your hair? Taking a long shower? If not, and those things are important to you, move on.

Ed Sacks' *Savvy Renter's Kit* contains a thorough renter's checklist for those interested in augmenting theirs.

If it all passes muster, be prepared to stake your claim without delay!

STAKING A CLAIM

While the market is softer now than it has been in years past, it's still true that the early bird gets the worm. This is particularly true for the most desirable apartments. Take along your checkbook, photo ID, a cell phone, and references (personal and professional) so you can be ready. Generally, a landlord will do a credit check and possibly contact your references. Once that is done and the landlord is satisfied that you are good tenant material, you can expect to sign a lease and provide a security deposit. Normally, the security deposit is equal to one month's rent.

LANDLORD/TENANT RIGHTS AND RESPONSIBILITIES

A lease is a legally binding contract that outlines the landlord's responsibilities as well as your obligations as a tenant. It goes without saying that you should read your lease carefully before signing it.

The lease should state your name and address as well as the name and address of the landlord. It should state the first and last dates of your contracted occupancy, the monthly rent figure, and when and where it is to be paid. Look for language that may be added to the contract concerning pets or guests, for example. Remember that you don't have to sign the lease immediately. You have the right to examine it and return it at a mutually agreed-upon time. Illinois law doesn't require that you have a written lease, but it is in your best interest to have one. Without a written lease the land-lord can evict you without cause.

Quite often, you will be moving into your new apartment on the heels of the previous tenant, leaving no time for a proper inspection of the unit accompanied with your landlord. If you notice problems such as beat-up cabinets, chipped tiles or a damaged floor, make note of them and have the landlord write these conditions into your lease so you are not held liable when moving out. It's a good idea to have your landlord visit and verify the damage as soon as possible or you can provide photographs to be attached to the lease. (Be sure to provide the landlord with copies of the photos as soon as possible.)

Landlords typically ask for one to two months' rent as security deposit to protect them from damages after a tenant moves out. If you leave your apartment in good condition, you are entitled to a refund of your security deposit within 45 days. If your landlord dawdles in returning your security deposit you can file a claim in pro se court (where you don't need a lawyer to represent you) for up to double the amount of your deposit. If you live in a building with more than six units, Illinois requires the landlord to pay interest on your security deposit.

Chicago's **Residential Landlord and Tenant Ordinance**, which was enacted in 1986 and amended in 1991, applies to tenants who live in all-rental units with written or oral leases, and to tenants of single family residences and condominiums. It does not apply to tenants living in owner-occupied buildings containing six units or less. The ordinance spells out the contractual obligations between landlord and tenant. You can pick up a copy of the ordinance at the **Chicago Department of Housing**, 318 South Michigan Avenue, 312-747-1655, or you can buy a copy at the Office of the City Clerk, Room 107, 121 North LaSalle Street, 312-744-6861. For more information about your rights, contact the **Chicago Rent Rights Hotline** at 312-742-7368.

Among their obligations, landlords must supply adequate heat from September 15 to June 1 (68° during the day and 63° at night), hot water, plumbing, security, extermination of pests, and perform general mainte-nance. Your landlord may keep a key to your apartment and can enter only after giving you proper notice and if there is a specific need for the entry or in the event of an emergency. If your landlord is not meeting these con-tractual requirements your first recourse is to call and discuss the problem with him or her. If your request about heat or hot water is not met within a reasonable amount of time, you can call the **City's Heat Hotline** at 312-744-5000. If that doesn't resolve the problem, you have the option of reducing your rent as outlined under the Tenants' Rights Ordinance (see above). If a repair is at issue, you can have the repair made yourself, and deduct those costs from future rental payments. Before you bring in a handyman to work on your apartment, you may want to consult a lawyer or a tenant's rights organization. While your complaint may be valid and your understanding of the Tenant's Ordinance clear, having repairs done on your own can be an expensive decision. If the repairs are not made by licensed repairmen (plumbers for example), and your repairman inadvertently causes structural damage in an attempt to make your repairs ... well you can see how sticky this situation can get. In addition, the Illinois Tenant's Union warns tenants that while there is a legal way to reduce your rent for failure to make repairs, if you don't follow proper procedure your landlord can start eviction proceedings against you for failure to pay the rent.

Organizations that may be helpful in disputes with a landlord or provide more detailed information about your rights as a tenant include:

- **Chicago Department of Housing**, 318 South Michigan Avenue, 312-747-1655, www.cityofchicaog.org/housing
- **Chicago Urban League**, 4510 South Michigan Avenue, 773-285-5800
- **Housing Resource Center**, 4429 North Clifton, 773-769-1555, (low income and senior housing)
- **Illinois Tenants Union**, 4616 North Drake Avenue, 773-478-1133, www.tenant.org
- **Lawyers Committee for Better Housing** (Edgewater and Rogers Park), 407 South Dearborn Street, 312-347-7600
- **Legal Assistance Foundation of Chicago**, 312-341-1070
- **Metropolitan Tenants Organization**, 773-292-4988, www.tenants-right.org
- **Landlord and Tenant Fact Sheet** from the Office of the Attorney General, www.ag.state.il.us
- **Rogers Park Community Action Network (RPCAN)**, 1545 West Morse, 773-973-7888

If your lease is set to expire and you plan on moving out, you should inform your landlord of your plans. In the event you must **break your lease**, you are required to give your landlord one month's written notice of your intent to vacate. Close to moving day, take pictures of your apartment to verify its condition and ask your landlord to meet you before moving to examine the apartment together. The ideal scenario to is to have your landlord sign a statement indicating that you have left the apartment in good condition, return the keys directly to him/her and on time, and that you notified him/her of your plans to move in a timely fashion. Short of that, mail him/her the keys prior to the last day of your lease, keeping a copy of the attached letter which states you are leaving the apartment at the appointed time, and in good condition. If you break your lease, your landlord can charge a subletting fee to cover the cost of finding a new tenant for the apartment. If a new tenant cannot be found who will rent the apartment at the same rate you were charged, you will be liable for the balance for the remainder of the lease. It might be a good idea to find a new tenant on your own to save on these expenses—although the new tenant will need to be approved by the landlord. If your landlord does find a new tenant to take your place, it is illegal for him/her to charge you for the remainder of your lease.

A landlord may not refuse to rent or lease an apartment or house to potential tenants or have different rental terms on the basis of race, religion, national origin, ancestry, sex and marital status, or disability. Under the Federal Fair Housing Act, it is illegal to discriminate against families with children when leasing a rental unit. Complaints about discrimination may be filed with the **Illinois Department of Human Rights**, 312-814-6200.

To complain of discrimination in the suburbs, call, **HUD** at 800-669-9777 or **South Suburban Housing Center**, 708-957-4674. In Chicago, contact the **Leadership Council for Metropolitan Open Communities**, 312-341-5678, TTY 800-927-9275, www.lcmoc.org.

RENT CONTROL

Neither the City of Chicago nor the State of Illinois impose rent control. That means your landlord can charge whatever the market will bear. If you are renting on a month-to-month basis, your landlord can legally raise your rent by any amount, as long as you are given 30 days' notice. If you have a fixed-term lease, your rent can only be raised when the lease expires.

RENTER'S/HOMEOWNER'S INSURANCE

You've moved into your new place, and the last boxes have been cleared away. Look around and ask yourself, "How much would it cost to start over if everything I see was destroyed by fire?" Probably more than you think. Imagine having to replace your clothing, furniture, computer, and other accumulations of a lifetime. The bill might be enormous.

With renter's insurance, typically you are protected against fire, hail, lightning, explosion, aircraft, smoke, vandalism, theft, building collapse, frozen plumbing, defective appliances, and sudden electrical damage. Renter's/Homeowner's insurance also may cover personal liability as well as damage done (by you) to the property of others. Be sure to shop around as insurance rates vary considerably and, when deciding on a policy, consider replacement cost coverage rather than a cash value policy. It's worth the (usually) modest extra premium.

Before looking in the phone book or contacting your own insurance company, you might want to call the **Illinois Department of Insurance** at 312-814-2427, www.ins.state.il.us. They keep track of all major insurance companies' "complaint ratios" (number of complaints filed per year to dollars paid out each year). Tell them that you're interested in the ratios for homeowner's or renter's insurance, though ratios for other types of insurance are also available. If the company that insures your car has a clean record, you might want to consult with them. Many companies offer a discount if you purchase more than one type of coverage with them.

You can purchase renter's/homeowner's insurance through almost any insurance agency or company. Try the Yellow Pages for an agency near you. Web sites worth investigating as you search for renter's insurance are www.quotesmith.com, which offers quotes from over 300 insurance companies. It is linked to www.insure.com, which offers an extensive Q&A section about insurance in general. QuickenInsurance, www.insuremarket.com and www.insweb.com also offer online insurance hunting. Insurance Finder at www.insurancefinder.com can help you find insurance companies in the Chicago area.

HOUSE, CONDO, AND CO-OP HUNTING/BUYING

Ah, yes, the American dream of a white picket fence, grassy front lawn, and a wide front porch on which to wile away the day. As you might have expected Chicago didn't escape the residential real estate craze that struck the country. With the demand for owner occupied housing seemingly insatiable, housing starts and sales of existing properties skyrocketed over the past decade. Even with the collapse of the late-century financial bubble and the downturn of the economy, Chicagoans kept right on buying and building.

According to the city, Chicago has more owner-occupied housing than any other metropolitan area in the United States. This fact is all the more remarkable given the sustained rise of real-estate prices in the last couple of decades. According to *Chicago Magazine*, top neighborhoods for real estate appreciation in the 1990s included the usual suspects: Lincoln Park, DePaul, Lakeview, Wicker Park, Bucktown, and Wrigleyville. The condo conversion tide has swept across ever more of the North Side and West Loop to include Ravenswood, Lincoln Square, North Central, and Andersonville. Many of the city neighborhoods profiled in this book have led the charge, with annual eight- to twelve-percent increases in appreciation. But, if you think that you need to make a large down payment and have an income in the six figures, you are in for a nice surprise. With interest rates low, and lenders willing to lend, you don't need a huge income or a large sum of cash to join the American dream club.

That said, buying a house or condo is no small undertaking. With time and effort, though, you will be rewarded. To get a sense of the market, read the "Real Estate" section of Sunday's *Chicago Tribune*. Most weeks, the

Tribune features a chart showing, by zip code, the number of homes sold and the median price of home sales in the past year; current mortgage rates at area lenders, and a weekly profile of a Chicago neighborhood.

When figuring how much money you'll need, be aware that in addition to the purchase price there is title insurance, the inspection, land survey, recording tax, mortgage origination, and usually some real estate transfer tax ("stamp tax"); in Chicago the buyer is responsible for this levy and it's set at $3.75 for every $500 of the home's purchase price. So, for a $300,000 townhouse, you'll owe the city an additional $2,250. Then there's the property tax payment and homeowner's insurance premiums you'll be required to place in an escrow account. In all, expect to pay five to eight percent more than the purchase price. Assuming you are not paying cash but seeking a mortgage, you can usually borrow up to three or four times your annual income. Be prepared for a thorough examination of your credit history, finances, and employment status. The required down payment varies with the loan program for which you are eligible. Lenders are required to give you a good-faith estimate of closing costs.

Fannie Mae, www.fanniemae.com, 202-752-7000, and the **US Department of Housing and Urban Development**, www.hud.gov, are terrific resources for information on home buying and government assistance.

Most people wanting to buy a house (or condo or co-op) enlist the services of a real estate broker—a buyer's agent who knows the market and the neighborhood. You might also want a real estate lawyer to make sure the sales contract is in order, to guide you through the latest available tax credits, and perhaps help you with any special hurdles involved in buying a home that is, or could be, declared historic. And you might benefit from the services of a mortgage broker—a financial specialist who is supposed to help you get the best possible mortgage (see the end of the chapter for mortgage resources). Lenders suggest that you "pre-qualify" for a loan so that when you do find a place you like, you can make a swift, credible offer. Before talking to a lender, contact one or more of the three major credit bureaus listed below to make sure your credit history is accurate and up to date. You will need to provide your name, address, previous address, and social security number with your request. Contact each company for specific instructions, or visit www.icreditreport.com, for online access to all three. You can obtain a free report if you've been denied credit within the last 30 days; otherwise, you may be charged up to $8.

The major **credit bureaus** are:

- **Experian** (formerly TRW), P.O. Box 2104, Allen, TX 75002-2104, 888-397-3742
- **TransUnion**, P.O. Box 390, Springfield, PA 19064-0390, 800-916-8800
- **Equifax**, P.O. Box 105873, Atlanta, GA 30348, 800-685-1111

Before a home sale can be completed, a termite inspection is mandatory, and most prospective homeowners will hire a building engineer to make a thorough inspection of the structure, heating and cooling systems, plumbing, roof, and major appliances, if any. Should an inspector's report find that major repairs will be likely within a few years, you may be able to negotiate a reduction in the purchase price—or you might decide to keep looking.

If you're **purchasing a condo**, you are buying a unit in a building with multiple units. Each one is the owner's to live in, rent, or sell. Annual or monthly condo fees cover the expenses of a condo association, which takes care of the building and grounds, laundry room, parking lots or garages, swimming pool, and any other shared amenities. Condo fees can be steep, and when looking at prospective units, it's not enough to have the annual fee quoted. Check past records to find out how often the fees have been raised, by how much and if there were any special assessments. You will also want a lawyer, or a real estate agent specializing in condos, to examine the condominium's prospectus and financial statement, so you don't buy into a financially unstable property.

If you're in the market for a condominium, and you think you might want to rent out your unit in the future, keep in mind that condominium associations might have restrictions in place on renting out units. The association even has the power to limit renting out a unit even if there is no specific ban on it in the association bylaws. As the *Sun-Times* reported, "renters have become such a problem that the associations are starting to declare them persona non grata." More broadly, if you're the kind of person who likes to be left alone or has trouble getting along in a group with strict rules, a condominium or co-op could be a nightmare. If such possible limitations are not an issue, then take the plunge.

Questions to ask about a co-op or condo:

- What percentage of the units are owner-occupied?
- How much are the association dues and projected assessments?
- What are the rules and regulations?
- Who manages the property?
- Have there been any lawsuits involving the association in the past five years?

These and many other issues are covered in the "Condominium/Townhome Guide," published by Re/Max Real Estate, 800-878-8404. The guide provides information about different styles of housing, associations, and comprehensive checklists to use to evaluate developments.

Upon signing a standard purchase agreement, the seller is required to disclose only certain problems and environmental hazards like lead paint. It is wise to protect yourself by having a professional roof/mechanical systems inspection before purchase. Professional residential inspectors can be found in the Yellow Pages under "Home and Building Inspection" or ask your realtor for a recommendation. There is a free pamphlet available from the **American Society of Home Inspectors**, 800-743-ASHI or www.ashi.com; ask for document #1029.

Chicago is one of the few places in the country where you will find housing cooperatives for sale. **Co-ops** as they are commonly known, are most popular in New York City, and in Chicago are found mainly in the tonier downtown and lakefront neighborhoods and can sell from $150,000 to over two million dollars for a 1920s-era co-op building facing Oak Street Beach near Michigan Avenue. Affordable cooperative units can be found in communities like Hyde Park and South Shore on the South Side or on the North Side in Lakeview, Uptown, Edgewater, and Rogers Park.

The cooperative structure is fairly simple, with co-ops consisting of membership shares in a corporation that owns a residential building. While condominiums offer outright ownership of a particular unit plus a share of the common area, buying a housing cooperative entitles you to a share of the value of the building, not a particular unit. However, just as in a condominium development, the cooperative's members elect a board of directors, and they typically have financial responsibility for the cooperative corporation. Housing cooperatives function best through a form of participatory democracy that encourages owners to get involved by serving on the board and committees, which reduces the costs of operating the cooperative. Those who wish to sell their cooperative share earn interest and equity on their initial investment and can also pass along improvements that they have made to their cooperative unit to the future buyer. You can also deduct your pro-rata share of your mortgage interest on your taxes, just like a single-family home or condominium. Moreover, these are no longer the days when prospective buyers had to self-finance their cooperative unit, with banks in Chicago (such as the National Cooperative Bank at 202-336-7700) willing to offer financing.

For more information:

- **Chicago Mutual Housing Network**, 2418 West Bloomingdale, 773-278-9210, www.chicagomutual.org
- **National Association of Housing Cooperatives**, www.coop-housing.org

BUYING STRATEGIES

If you're ready to jump on the owner bandwagon, you might want to consider the following strategies. As with apartment hunting, perhaps the simplest way to look for a place to buy is to walk or drive around the neighborhood you're interested in and look for "For Sale" signs. At the same time start scanning the classifieds. Both the *Chicago Tribune* and the *Sun-Times* have extensive real estate sections. The *Tribune* also offers an online database of residential properties for sale at its web site, as well as a weekly "Your Place" section in Friday's paper. Then there's the tried-and-true method: enlist the services of a real estate agent or broker. Ask around for a recommendation or look in the Yellow Pages under "Real Estate." If you are computer savvy and want to narrow down the search on your own, most real estate companies now have web sites, often great ones. Here you can check out the available homes through photos, floor-plans, community information, and organize your search along whatever line suits you.

For starters, check out the following sites, or ask your real estate agent for the web address of his or her company:

- **Baird & Warner**, www.bairdwarner.com (local)
- **Koenig & Strey**, www.koenig-strey.com (local)
- **Rubloff Residential Properties**, www.rubloff.com (local)
- **Coldwell Banker**, www.coldwellbanker.com
- **The Prudential**, www.prudential.com
- **www.homestore.com**
- **http://houseandhome.msn.com**
- **www.homeGain.com**
- **www.homes.com**
- **National Association of Realtors**, www.realtor.com
- **www.realtylocator.com**

REAL ESTATE BROKERS

There is no substitute for the advice of an experienced, local real estate broker. Brokers are highly trained, tested, licensed professionals who keep a close eye on the neighborhoods they serve. A good broker knows the average SAT scores at the local high school, the crime rate in the local police precinct, how many minutes it takes to drive to the highway, and—most important—the trends in property values right down to a given block. A good broker will interview you in detail about your needs and desires as they relate to buying a place to live. Are you planning to have more children? Do you like to garden? Do you hate to drive to work? The more of such information you share with your broker, the better he or she can match you with a home.

So how do you find a broker who knows the neighborhood where you want to live? Most real estate agencies claim to serve the entire Chicago area, and indeed, most agencies can offer some assistance with any home on the market. However, an agency is best qualified to show you homes in the neighborhood where it is located—where their geographic expertise is greatest. In the absence of a personal recommendation, try the Yellow

Pages or go online to **www.realtor.com** for real estate brokers serving the neighborhoods or cities you select.

FOR SALE BY OWNER

If you are familiar with your targeted neighborhood, are an experienced homeowner and/or would like to eliminate the not insignificant cost of the middleman (the real estate broker), you can look for For Sale By Owner ("fsbo") properties. Even if you have a real estate broker, you may consider such properties, especially since your realtor may not. Web sites specializing in home listings by owners include:

- **www.4SaleByOwner.com**
- **www.HomesByOwner.com**
- **www.owners.com**

ADDITIONAL ONLINE RESOURCES—BUYING A HOME

Another good resource if you are looking in the northernmost Illinois counties is the National Association of Realtors' **Multiple Listing Service of Northern Illinois**. They claim to list over half of the houses for sale in the northern counties. Try them at www.realtor.com/chicago.

The following web sites offer a variety of services including listings of homes nationwide, and information about moving, mortgages, real estate agents, neighborhoods, home improvement, and more:

- **Bankrate.com**, www.bankrate.com, as its name suggests, everything about mortgages and interest rates.
- **Freddie Mac**, www.freddiemac.com, provides information on low-cost loans, a home inspection kit, and tips to help avoid unfair lending practices.
- **iOwn**, www.iown.com, by Citibank, claims to provide the best mortgage deals online, plus information about buying and selling a home, relocating and a nifty "most recent home sales" feature searchable by zip code.
- **The Mortgage Professor**, www.mtgprofessor.com, demystifies and clarifies the confusing and often expensive world of mortgage brokers, helpfully written by an emeritus Wharton professor who answers questions(!), useful calculators.
- **www.quickenmortgage.com**, from the people who brought you Quicken.
- **www.scorecard.org**, learn about pollution and toxic waste in a prospective neighborhood *before* you buy there; includes useful and eye-opening zip code searchable database.

PRINTED RESOURCES—BUYING A HOME

Five books that we found useful:

- *100 Questions Every First Time Homebuyer Should Ask: With Answers from Top Brokers From Around the Country*, 2nd edition (Times Books) by Ilyce R.Glink
- *The 106 Common Mistakes Homebuyers Make (And How to Avoid Them)*, 3rd edition (Wiley) by Gary W. Eldred
- *The Co-Op Bible: Everything You Need to Know About Co-Ops and Condos: Getting In, Staying In, Surviving, Thriving*, (Griffin) by Sylvia Shapiro
- *Opening the Door to a Home of Your Own*, a free pamphlet by the Fannie Mae Foundation, 800-834-3377
- *Your New House: the Alert Consumer's Guide to Buying and Building a Quality New Home*; (Windsor Peak) by Alan and Denise Fields

BEFORE YOU CAN START YOUR NEW LIFE IN CHICAGO, YOU AND your worldly possessions have to get here. How difficult that will be depends on how much stuff you've accumulated, how much money you're willing or able to spend on the move, and from where you are coming. A word of advice to packrats: the less stuff you move, the easier and cheaper your move will be!

Most leases in Chicago start either May 1 or October 1, which makes the last weekends in April and September a time of chaos in certain neighborhoods. Those **moving within the city** should be aware that during these busy times Chicago truck-rental companies rent trucks in three four-hour shifts—from 8 a.m. to noon, noon to 4 p.m., and 4 p.m. to 8 p.m. If you're moving locally, be sure to reserve a truck early (at least four weeks in advance) to ensure availability.

TRUCK RENTALS

The first question you need to answer: am I going to move myself or will I have someone else do it for me? If you're used to doing everything yourself, you can rent a vehicle, load it up, and head for the open road. Look in the Yellow Pages under "Truck Rental" and call around and compare; also ask about any specials. Below we list four national truck rental firms and their toll-free numbers and web sites. For the best information, you should call a local office. Note: most truck rental companies now offer "one-way" rentals (don't forget to ask whether they have a drop-off/return location in or near your destination) as well as packing accessories and storage facilities. Of course, these extras are not free and if you're cost conscious you may want to scavenge boxes in advance of your move and make sure you have a place to store your belongings upon arrival (see **Storage** below). Also, if you're planning on moving during the peak moving months (May through September) call well in advance of when you think you'll need the vehicle. A month at least.

Once you're on the road, keep in mind that your rental truck may be a tempting target for thieves. If you must park it overnight or for an extended period (more than a couple of hours), try to find a safe place, preferably somewhere well-lit and easily observable by you, and do your best not leave anything of particular value in the cab.

- **Budget**, 800-428-7825, www.budget.com
- **Penske**, 800-222-0277, www.penske.com
- **Ryder**, 800-467-9337, www.ryder.com (now a Budget company, still operating under the Ryder name)
- **U-haul**, 800-468-4285, www.uhaul.com

Not sure if you want to drive the truck yourself? Commercial freight carriers, such as **ABF**, 800-355-1696, www.upack.com, offer an in-between service: they deliver a 28-foot trailer to your home, you pack and load as much of it as you need, and they drive the vehicle to your destination (often with some other freight filling up the empty space). Keep in mind though, if you have to share truck space with another customer you may arrive far in advance of your boxes—or bed. Try to estimate your needs beforehand and ask for a date when you can expect your boxes to arrive. You can get an online estimate from some shippers, so you can compare rates. If you aren't moving an entire house and can't estimate how much truck space you will need, keep in mind this general guideline: two to three furnished rooms equal a 15-foot truck. Four to five rooms, a 20-foot truck.

MOVERS

INTERSTATE

First, the good news: moving can be affordable and problem-free. The bad news: if you're hiring a mover, the chances of it being so are much less.

Probably the best way to find a mover is through a **personal recommendation**. Absent a friend or relative who can point you to a trusted moving company, you can turn to what surveys show is the most popular method of finding a mover: the **Yellow Pages**. Then there's the **internet**; just type in "movers" on a search engine and you'll be directed to hundreds of more or less helpful moving-related sites.

In the past, *Consumer Reports*, www.consumerreports.org, has published useful information on moving. You might ask a local realtor, who may be able to steer you towards a good mover, or at least tell you which ones to avoid. Members of the **AAA** can call their local office and receive discounted rates and service through their Consumer Relocation Service.

But beware! Since 1995, when the Interstate Commerce Commission was eliminated by the federal government, the interstate moving business has degenerated into a wild and virtually unregulated industry with thousands of unhappy, ripped-off customers annually. (There are so many reports of unscrupulous carriers that we no longer list movers in this book.) Since states do not have the authority to regulate interstate movers and since the federal government won't, you are pretty much on your own when it comes to finding an honest, hassle-free interstate mover. That's why we can't emphasize enough the importance of carefully researching and choosing who will move you.

To aid you in your search for an honest and hassle-free **interstate mover**, we offer a few general recommendations.

First, get the names of a half-dozen movers and check to make sure they are licensed by the US Department of Transportation's Federal Motor Carrier Safety Administration (FMCSA). Call 888-368-7238 or 202-358-7000 or go online to www.fmcsa.dot.gov. If the companies you're considering are federally licensed, your next step should be to check with the Better Business Bureau, www.bbb.org, in the state where the moving company is licensed as well as with that state's Attorney General and Consumer Protection office. Assuming there is no negative information, you can move on to the next step: asking for references. Particularly important are references from customers who did moves similar to yours. If a moving company is unable or unwilling to provide references or tells you that they can't give out names because their customers are all in the federal Witness Protection Program, eliminate them from your list. Unscrupulous movers have even been known to give phony references who will falsely sing the mover's praises—so talk to more than one reference and ask questions. If something feels fishy, it probably is. One way to learn more about a prospective mover: ask them if they have a local office (they should) and then walk in and check it out.

Once you have at least three movers you feel reasonably comfortable with, it's time to ask for price quotes (always free). Best is a binding "not-to-exceed" quote, of course in writing. This will require an on-site visual inspection of what you are shipping. If you have *any* doubts about a prospective mover, drop them from your list before you invite a stranger into your home to catalog your belongings.

Additional moving recommendations:
- If someone recommends a mover to you, get names (the salesperson or estimator, the drivers, the loaders). To paraphrase the NRA, moving companies don't move people, people do. Likewise, if someone tells you they had a bad moving experience, note the name of the company and try to avoid it.

- Remember that price, while important, isn't everything, especially when you're entrusting all of your worldly possessions to strangers.
- Ask about the other end—subcontracting increases the chances that something could go wrong.
- In general, ask questions, and if you're concerned about something, ask for an explanation in writing. If you change your mind about a mover after you've signed on the dotted line, write them a letter explaining that you've changed your mind and that you won't be using their services. Better safe than sorry.
- Ask about insurance, the "basic" 60 cents per pound industry standard coverage is not enough. If you have homeowner's or renter's insurance, check to see if it will cover your belongings during transit. If not, ask your insurer if you can add that coverage for your move. Otherwise, consider purchasing "full replacement" or "full value" coverage from the carrier for the estimated value of your shipment. Though it's the most expensive type of coverage offered, it's probably worth it. Trucks get into accidents, they catch fire, they get stolen—if such insurance seems pricey to you, ask about a $250 or $500 deductible. This can reduce your cost substantially while still giving you much better protection in case of a catastrophic loss.
- Before a move takes place, ask your mover to give you a copy of "Your Rights and Responsibilities When You Move," which provides detailed information about your rights and what you can expect from your moving company. Ask for it as soon as you decide on a mover.
- Whatever you do, do not mislead a salesperson/estimator about how much and what you are moving. And make sure you tell a prospective mover about how far they'll have to transport your stuff to and from the truck as well as any stairs, driveways, obstacles or difficult vegetation, long paths or sidewalks, etc. The clearer you are with your mover, the better he or she will be able to serve you.
- Think about packing. If you plan to pack yourself, you can save some money, but if something is damaged because of your packing, you may not be able to file a claim for it. On the other hand, if you hire the mover to do the packing, they may not treat your belongings as well as you will. They will certainly do it faster, that's for sure. Depending on the size of your move and whether or not you are packing yourself, you may need a lot of boxes, tape and packing material. Mover boxes, while not cheap, are usually sturdy and the right size. Sometimes a mover will give a customer free used boxes. It doesn't hurt to ask. Also, don't wait to pack until the last minute. If you're doing the packing, give yourself at least a week to do the job, two or more is better.
- You should transport all irreplaceable items such as jewelry, photographs or key work documents. Do not put them in the moving van!

For less precious items that you do not want to put in the moving truck, consider sending them via the US Postal Service or UPS.

- Ask your mover what is not permitted in the truck: usually anything flammable or combustible, as well as certain types of valuables.
- Although movers will put numbered labels on your possessions, you should make a numbered list of every box and item that is going in the truck. Detail box contents and photograph anything of particular value. Once the truck arrives on the other end, you can check off every piece and know for sure what did (or did not) make it. In case of claims, this list can be invaluable. Even after the move, keep the list; it can be surprisingly useful.
- Movers are required to issue you a "bill of lading"; do not hire a mover who does not use them.
- Consider keeping a log of every expense you incur for your move, i.e., phone calls, trips to Chicago, etc. In many instances, the IRS allows you to claim these types of expenses on your income taxes. (See **Taxes** below.)
- Be aware that during the busy season (May through September), demand can exceed supply and moving may be more difficult and more expensive than during the rest of the year. If you must relocate during the peak moving months, call and book service well in advance of when you plan on moving. A month at least. If you can reserve service way in advance, say four to six months early, you may be able to lock in a lower winter rate for your summer move.
- Listen to what the movers say; they are professionals and can give you expert advice about packing and preparing. Also, be ready for the truck on both ends—don't make them wait. Not only will it irritate your movers, but it may cost you. Understand, too, that things can happen on the road that are beyond a carrier's control (weather, accidents, etc.) and your belongings may not get to you at the time or on the day promised.
- Treat your movers well, especially the ones loading your stuff on and off the truck. Offer to buy them lunch, and tip them if they do a good job.
- Before moving pets, attach a tag to your pet's collar with your new address and phone number in case your furry friend accidentally wanders off in the confusion of moving. Of course, never plan on moving a pet inside a moving van.
- Be prepared to pay the full moving bill upon delivery. Cash or bank/cashier's check may be required. Some carriers will take VISA and MasterCard but it is a good idea to get it in writing that you will be permitted to pay with a credit card since the delivering driver may not be aware of this and may demand cash. Unless you routinely keep thousands of greenbacks on you, you could have a problem getting your stuff off the truck.

INTRASTATE AND LOCAL MOVES

All moves within Illinois are regulated by the Illinois Commerce Commission (ICC) and all movers operating within the state of Illinois are required to have an active license issued by the ICC. Contact them at 217-782-6448, www.icc.state.il.us, for information on a prospective mover.

For moves within Illinois, ones that are less than 35 miles are designated **local moves**, ones greater than 35 miles are designated **intrastate moves**.

In Illinois, local moves are charged on an hourly basis, intrastate move prices are regulated by the state and are calculated based on the weight of the shipment, distance, and additional services, if any.

To find a local or intrastate mover, follow many of the same guidelines (above) as with an interstate move. After you've verified that a prospective mover is currently licensed to operate in Illinois (www.icc.state.il.us/hg/householdgoods.aspx), you can call the **Illinois Attorney General Consumer Fraud Bureau** at 800-243-0618 to find out if the company you're considering has a complaint history. Another good idea is to contact the **Illinois Mover's and Warehousemen's Association (IMAWA)**, to see if a mover is a member. The IMAWA is a professional organization whose members must be licensed movers, hold the appropriate insurance minimums, and works with the government agencies that oversee this industry. You can reach the IMAWA for a membership list or other information by calling 217-585-2470 or by visiting their web site at www.imawa.com. Another industry group that you can check with: the **American Moving and Storage Association**, 703-683-7410, www.moving.org.

STORAGE

If your new pad is too small for all of your belongings or if you need a temporary place to store your stuff while you find a new home, self-storage may be the answer. Most units are clean, secure, insured, and inexpensive, and you can rent anything from a locker to your own mini-warehouse. You may need to bring your own padlock, and be prepared to pay first and last month's rent up front. Many will offer special deals to entice you, such as second month free. Probably the easiest way to find storage is to look in the Yellow Pages under "Storage—Self Service" "Storage—Household & Commercial," or "Movers & Full Service Storage." Online, go to a search engine and type in "Storage, Household." Your mover may also offer storage and while this may be easier than moving it into storage yourself, it may also be much more expensive.

A recent wrinkle in the self-storage business: "containerized storage." This means the storage company will drop off a (large) storage bin at your house, you fill it up, and they return with a truck and cart it off to their storage facility.

Keep in mind that demand for storage surges in the prime moving months (May through September) ... so try not to wait till the last minute to rent storage. Also, if you don't care about convenience, your cheapest storage options may be out in the boonies. You just have to figure out how to get your stuff there and back. Things to keep in mind when considering a storage facility:

- When do I have access?
- Do my belongings need heat and/or AC? If so, ask if the facility is "climate controlled."
- What about security and insurance?
- Will I feel safe visiting the facility?
- Are there carts or hand trucks for moving in and out?
- What are the payment options?

Finally, a word of warning: unless you no longer want your stored belongings, pay your storage bill and pay it on time. Storage companies may auction the contents of delinquent customers' lockers.

STORAGE FACILITIES

Listing here does *not* imply endorsement by First Books. For more options check the Yellow Pages.

- **The Cache**, 3800 North Sheffield Avenue, 773-248-5005
- **Chicago Lock Stock & Storage**, 2001 North Elston Avenue, 773-227-2448
- **East Bank Self-Storage and Truck Rental**, 429 West Ohio Street, 312-644-2000
- **Public Storage** has more than 50 storage facilities in the Chicago metropolitan area. Check the Yellow Pages or call 800-447-8673, www.publicstorage.com
- **Shurgard**, 800-947-8673, www.shurgard.com
- **Strongbox** has two Chicago locations: 1516 North Orleans Street, 312-787-2800; 1650 West Irving Park Road, 773-248-6800.
- **U-Haul Self-Storage** has storage facilities throughout the Chicago area. In Chicago, check 1200 West Fullerton Avenue, 773-935-0620 or 4055 North Broadway, 773-871-7155.

CHILDREN

Studies show that moving, especially frequent moving, can be hard on children. According to an American Medical Association study, children who move often are more likely to suffer from such problems as depression, worthlessness and aggression. Often their academic performance suffers as well. Aside from not moving more than is necessary, there are a few things you can do to help your children through this stressful time:

- Talk about the move with your kids. Be honest but positive. Listen to their concerns. To the extent possible, involve them in the process.
- Make sure the child has his or her favorite possessions with them on the trip; don't pack "blanky" in the moving van.
- Make sure you have some social life planned on the other end. Your child may feel lonely in your new home and such activities can ease the transition.
- Keep in touch with family and loved ones as much as possible. Photos and phone calls are important ways of maintaining links to the important people you have left behind.
- If your children are school age, take the time to introduce them to their new school as soon as possible, preferably before they start the new school year. In this way, they can dispel any unfounded fears and apprehensions they have about the next school. And finally, try to involve yourself in their new school and in their academic life.

For children ages 6-11, *The Moving Book: A Kids' Survival Guide* by Gabriel Davis is a wonderful gift. Other titles include: *Alexander, Who's Not (Do You Hear Me? I Mean It!) Going to Move* by Judith Viorst; *Goodbye/Hello* by Barbara Hazen, *The Leaving Morning* by Angela Johnson; and the *Little Monster's Moving Day* by Mercer Mayer.

For older children, try: *Amber Brown is Not a Crayon* by Paula Danziger; the *Kid in the Red Jacket* by Barbara Park; *Hold Fast to Dreams* by Andrea Davis Pinkney; *Flip Flop Girl* by Katherine Paterson and *My Fabulous New Life* by Sheila Greenwald.

For general guidance, read *Smart Moves: Your Guide through the Emotional Maze of Relocation* by Nadia Jensen, Audrey McCollum and Stuart Copans (Smith & Krauss).

Visit firstbooks.com to order any of the above resources.

TAXES

If your move is work-related, some or all of your moving expenses may be tax-deductible—so you may want to keep those receipts. Though eligibility varies, depending for example, on whether you have a job or are self-employed, generally, the cost of moving yourself, your family, and your belongings is tax deductible, even if you don't itemize. The criteria: in order to take the deduction your move must be employment-related, your new job must be more than 50 miles away from your current residence, and you must be here for at least 39 weeks during the first 12 months after your arrival. If you take the deduction and then fail to meet the requirements, you will have to pay the IRS back, unless you were laid off through no fault of your own or transferred again by your employer. It's probably a good idea to consult a tax expert regarding IRS rules related to moving. However, if you're a confident soul, get a copy of IRS Form 3903 (www.irs.gov) and do it yourself!

ADDITIONAL RELOCATION AND MOVING INFORMATION

- **www.erc.org**, the Employee Relocation Council, a professional organization, offers members specialized reports on the relocation and moving industries.
- **www.firstbooks.com**, relocation resources and information on moving to Atlanta, Boston, Chicago, Los Angeles, Minneapolis-St. Paul, New York City, Seattle, San Francisco and the Bay Area, Washington, D.C., as well as London, England.
- **www.homestore.com**, realty listings, moving tips, and more.
- *How to Move Handbook* by Clyde and Shari Steiner, an excellent resource.
- **www.usps.com**, relocation information from the United States Postal Service.

TO EASE YOUR FINANCIAL TRANSITION TO YOUR NEW CITY, HERE IS some information about personal savings and checking accounts, credit cards, and taxes.

BANK ACCOUNTS & SERVICES

As soon as you find a place to hang your hat, you will want to find a home for your money. For major deposits, shop around for the best interest rates, but for routine checking and savings, you'll probably be more interested in fees and services. Check with your employer to find out if direct deposit is an option.

Also consider a **credit union**, which may be your best banking option. Credit unions generally offer affordable banking/financial service packages to their members, and higher interest rates on savings and checking accounts. Look into whether your place of business or professional organization offers a credit union membership. Some credit unions will accept applicants beyond their original membership base; that is, you may not have to be an employee of a specific organization or labor union in order to join. **Credit Union National Association** can help you find a credit union in your area. Visit their web site at www.cuna.org.

With all the mergers and acquisitions in the banking industry it's possible that your old bank has a branch in your new neighborhood. All major banks offer a variety of checking accounts to fit a variety of personal banking habits. And most offer internet access with options to check your balance, transfer money from different accounts, and pay bills. If you write a lot of checks and keep a low average balance, you will want to pay attention to per-check fees and service charges that kick in when your balance drops below a certain minimum. If you only use your checking account to pay your monthly bills, you might want an interest bearing checking account with some fees instead of a non-interest bearing free checking account. Be sure to ask about ATM fees—at your own bank's automated teller machines and at network ATMs owned by other banks. Also, inquire about the average and maximum time between a deposit and the availability of funds.

All major banks also offer money market accounts and certificates of deposit, with terms and interest rates displayed in the lobby or the window, as well as regular passbook savings accounts.

Many prefer the service of a small community bank, of which there are many in the Chicagoland area. Others prefer a large institution, which will have many branches throughout the city or nation for that matter. Here are some of the **largest banks in the Chicago area**:

- **Citibank**, 800-446-5331, www.citibank.com
- **Cole Taylor Bank**, 708-857-4379, www.ctbnk.com
- **First American Bank**, 847-952-3700, www.firstambank.com
- **LaSalle Bank FSB**, 866-904-7222, www.lasallebanks.com

CHECKING/SAVINGS ACCOUNTS

Obtain an application at the bank of your choice. Two references are often required, usually the name of your current or previous bank, and that of your employer—together with two signed pieces of identification: a driver's license, state ID card, credit card, or student ID with photo are all acceptable. It's also a good idea to bring checks along from your previous checking account. If your checking account was in good standing at your previous institution, the new bank will often begin your new checks at a higher number. Some account plans require a minimum start-up deposit, some don't. Your account can be opened immediately. You will be given some temporary checks but checks printed with your name and address won't be issued until your signature is verified. Some firms arrange for employees to open accounts at their own banks, which facilitates the process and may be fee-free; check with your benefits officer.

The best advice when choosing a bank is to shop around and compare services and fees. You might be able to do some of that online while you are still in your former hometown. If you are moving to Chicago due to work relocation, your human resource representative might be able to give you some suggestions for banks within your work neighborhood. Some banks allow you 15 checks per month before they begin charging a per check fee, others allow unlimited checking and charge only a monthly service fee. Area banks lure customers with special offers, such as a special window for business clients, or fee-free checking accounts (read the fine print: some banks may require only a $500 minimum balance, others much more; and many charge fees for other things). "Free" checking is also being offered to customers. With such an account, you can generally expect no monthly fees, no minimum balance, internet access to your account, and unlimited use of your checking account. However, these accounts often do not earn interest. The more traditional interest bearing accounts will often eliminate service charges as long as a minimum daily balance is maintained or if you link your account to a money market account, certificate of deposit, or savings account.

It's a good idea to ask if the bank will charge you to use an ATM other than theirs or to use a teller—different banks have different fee policies.

Whichever bank you finally select, nearly all come with an ATM/ debit card.

CREDIT CARDS

While it seems hard to imagine living without that little plastic pass in your wallet, too many of us are on very intimate terms with our credit card. It is said that the average American owns seven credit cards! If you would like to join the masses, contact the following credit and charge card companies, or just look in your mail box ... an offer is bound to show up soon.

- **American Express**, 800-528-4800, www.americanexpress.com; once famous for issuing charge cards that must be paid off every month, American Express now offers nearly two dozen different cards, including credit cards and airline affinity cards that accumulate frequent-flyer miles. With the exception of a student card, all Amex cards have minimum income requirements, and all but the Optima True Grace Card charge annual fees.

- **Diner's Club**, 800-234-6377, www.dinersclub.com; with annual fees and income requirements, the Diner's Club card is accepted mainly in travel and hospitality circles; cardholders have access to special amenities at most major airports.

- **Discover/Novus**, 800-347-2683, www.discovercard.com; Discover cards and affiliated Novus/Private Issue cards offer an annual rebate based on the amount you charge, and some plans let you accumulate credit at various hotels or retail chains.

- **VISA**, www.visa.com, **MasterCard**, www.mastercard.com; almost all banks issue VISA and MasterCard credit cards, but so do airlines, long distance companies, magazines, car manufacturers, professional associations, charities, and retailers. Competition is fierce not just for interest rates or low fees, but for fringe benefits—from airline mileage to shopper's discounts—so it pays to shop around, especially if you don't pay off your balance every month. Many will offer low introductory rates, no annual fees, and no transfer balance fees. And like American Express, these credit card companies offer more than one kind of card. Check their web sites to find out the particulars. Most purchases made with these cards are automatically insured against loss or damage.

- **Department stores**: most department stores and other major national retailers issue charge cards, sometimes with lines of credit. Usually these accounts are issued automatically and instantly if you already have a VISA or MasterCard account. While the perks may include advance notice of sales, access to special services, and cardholder discounts, be aware that credit cards in this category are usually offered with some of the highest rates around.

For a handy way to compare rates and to learn more about credit cards, visit **bankrate.com**. **Cardweb.com** is an online directory of credit cards; search or browse by interest rates, fees, special offers, or affinity features such as frequent-flyer miles or charity donations based on the amount you charge. The same information can be retrieved by phone at 800-344-7714. And finally, you can visit the personal finance section of **epinions.com** for customer reviews of specific institutions' credit cards.

BANKING AND CREDIT RESOURCES

For a list of articles about trends in banking, and links to the Federal Trade Commission and other consumer protection agencies, visit the **National Institute for Consumer Education's** web site at www.nice.emich.edu. To look up current interest rates on deposits, go to www.rate.net or www.bankrate.com.

If you're buying a car or boat, renovating your new fixer-upper, or sending the kids to college, you can still shop for loans the old-fashioned way, using the Yellow Pages and the financial section of the newspaper, but the internet can make the job a lot easier. Online loan calculators let you experiment with different payment plans. There are several loan calculators on **bankrate.com** but you can look at other sites as well:

- **www.myfico.com**
- **www.411-loans.com**
- **Eloan**, www.eloan.com
- **Financial Power Tools**, http://financialpowertools.com
- **Women's Financial Network**, www.wfn.com
- **The Motley Fool**, www.fool.com; an excellent place to learn about money, investing and banking. They offer online seminars, well-written articles, and an active discussion board.

Obtain copies of your credit report from the three major credit bureaus at **www.icreditreport.com**. Avoid ordering your credit report more than once a year, though—frequent requests could adversely affect your credit rating.

TAXES

FEDERAL

Federal (and state) **Income Tax** forms are available at many libraries or post offices, but don't wait until April 14—indeed, such places may run out of the more common forms by early March and may not have any of the more esoteric forms at all. You can also **download tax forms** at www.irs.gov, order them by mail at 800-829-3676, or have them faxed to you by calling 703-368-9694.

Don't be afraid to call the IRS and ask for help. You may be placed on hold for a long time, but you will get your questions answered by a real person. A variety of recordings regarding general tax questions is available at the **IRS Tele Tax Information Line**, 800-829-4477. Of course, there are plenty of accountants listed in the Yellow Pages. Go to "Tax Return Preparation" for dozens of firms, including the giants: H&R Block, www.hrblock.com, and Jackson Hewitt, www.jacksonhewitt.com.

Federal forms may be obtained in the lobby of the **Federal Building**, 230 South Dearborn Street, 17th floor, or at some local post offices and libraries. Call 800-829-1040, TDD 800-829-4059, to obtain literature as well as answers to specific questions. The **Internal Revenue Service** office, 230 South Dearborn, 312-566-4912, is open from 8:30 a.m. to 4:30 p.m. and provides assistance and answers to specific questions regarding the mysteries of calculating your Federal income tax.

STATE OF ILLINOIS

As with federal tax forms, most of the filing materials you'll need are available at your local library or government office: the **State of Illinois Building**, 100 West Randolph Street, in the lobby or at the Federal Building (see above), or call 800-356-3602 or 312-814-5232. You can also download a number of tax forms from the state's web site, www.iltax.com, or you can file your state taxes electronically. For information about state income taxes, state forms, or filing online, contact the Illinois Department of Revenue toll free at 800-732-8866 or visit their web site. The basic form is the IL-1040—the Illinois Individual Income Tax Return. For individuals, the state income tax rate is three percent of your federal taxable income.

CITY OF CHICAGO

For questions about Chicago taxes, contact the **Chicago Department of Revenue**, 312-747-4747, or check the links online at www.cityofchicago.org. The City of Chicago **Comptroller's Office** can be reached at 312-744-7100.

PROPERTY AND SALES TAX

In Chicago the sales tax rate is 8.75% (five percent for the state, two percent for the city, one percent for the RTA, and .75% for Cook County). Sales tax in DuPage County is 6.75%; 6.5% for Kane, Lake, McHenry, and Will counties.

LUXURY TAX

Historically, according to the AAA-Chicago Motor Club, Chicago area gasoline prices range 20 to 30 cents higher than the national average. Here's why: in addition to the national 18.4 cents motor fuel tax, the State of Illinois charges a 6.25-cents per gallon gasoline sales tax, a 1.1 cents Illinois leaking underground fuel storage tax, and a 19-cents Illinois motor fuel tax, It is one of only seven states that has a fuel sales tax. In addition to the state and federal taxes, Cook County charges a six cents per gallon motor fuel tax. And if you decide to gas up within the city limits, be prepared to pay, in addition to all those levies, an additional five cents per gallon motor fuel tax as well as a one percent sales tax to the City of Chicago for your motoring pleasure. DuPage County collects a four cents per gallon motor fuel tax and a .25% sales tax. Kane County levies a two cents per gallon motor fuel tax.

In Chicago, beer and wine purchases have a city, county, and excise tax applied to them. The state applies a tax to cigarettes—18% of the wholesale price. Surcharges on luxury items, liquor, cigarettes, and gasoline, vary from community to community.

ONLINE FILING AND ASSISTANCE

Filing your taxes online can save you time, especially if you already keep your personal financial records using software such as Turbo Tax, Quicken, or Quickbooks. Visit www.irs.gov/elec_svs for details, including a list of companies that make tax software.

If your taxable income is below a certain amount and you are not self-employed, you may be eligible to file your federal taxes by touch-tone phone—visit www.irs.gov or call 800-829-1040 for more details. If you have filed and have been waiting more than four weeks for your return, contact the IRS at 800-829-4477, for an update on your status. If you need help with a tax problem or are suffering some hardship due to the tax law, you can contact the **Taxpayer Advocate Service**, an independent agency within the IRS designed to help taxpayers resolve tax problems: www.irs.gov/advocate.

The **Arkansas Society of Public Accountants** has a useful list on their web site of a variety of state, federal, and independent agencies having to do with tax revenue. Visit www.arspa.org for more information. For a peek at the extensive online database of **IRS revenue rulings** since 1954, visit www.taxlinks.com, and for questions regarding **individual taxes**, go to www.irs.gov/individuals.

STARTING OR MOVING A BUSINESS

Starting a new business is exciting, and the City of Chicago is rooting for your success. Resources to consider include **Mayor Daley's Business Express**, 312-744-CITY, the city's liaison to the business community. Check here for loan programs, job training, infrastructure specifics, and a host of other solutions to issues faced by business owners. Contact this office (and ask for the mayor), you will be assigned an account manager. Be sure to ask about the *Business Resource Guide*, which discusses how to do business with the city, the bid process, permits, city services and more. It also provides a listing of other agencies that assist business owners in Chicago. The Business Express department is a division of the Department of Planning and Development, located at 121 LaSalle Street, Room 1003. The Illinois State agency **First Stop Business Information Center**, 800-252-2923, www.illinoisbiz.biz, is a referral agency which can direct you to the organizations you will need to contact for forms, licenses, funding, etc. It's a good first step for learning about what you need to do as an Illinois business owner. The State of Illinois also has a site with additional information, www.illinois.gov/businesscenter. Your business may be required to register with the Illinois Department of Revenue; for general information call 800-732-8866 or 312-814-5232 or visit www.revenue.state.il.us where you can register with the state and receive a provisional Federal Employer Identification Number (FEIN) in one online session. Finally, you can also check the **US Small Business Administration Home Page** at www.sba.gov.

NOW THAT YOU'VE FOUND YOUR PLACE, SIGNED ALL THE PAPER-work and are preparing to move in, it's time to get settled. Setting up your utilities and telephone service, registering to vote, getting a library card and driver's license, registering your vehicle, finding a doctor . . . it's all here, and more.

UTILITIES

GAS

If you have an all-electric apartment, skip this section. If you live in the City of Chicago and use gas to heat or cook, call **Peoples Gas** (a subsidiary of **Peoples Energy**) at 312-240-7000 or 866-556-6001 to request service, or sign up at www.peoplesenergy.com. Customer service representatives are available 24 hours Monday-Friday; Saturday, 7 a.m. to 3 p.m. Peoples Gas offers several billing options: automatic withdrawal from your checking account, budget billing, credit card options, or payment via the internet. If you have gas heat, you will be paying a considerably larger bill in winter than in summer. This may seem only logical, but the winter bills can be staggering, especially if you live in an older and/or drafty apartment or bungalow. (In the summer, it's the electric bill that will send you reeling, if you own an air conditioner.) For gas emergencies, call 866-556-6002. **North Shore Gas**, also a subsidiary utility of Peoples Energy Service, serves residents in northern Cook and Lake counties. You can reach them by dialing 866-556-6004, or go to www.peoplesenergy.com; emergencies dial 866-556-6005. To choose a natural gas supplier other than Peoples Gas or North Shore, go to www.peoplesenergy.com or call Peoples Energy and ask about their "Choices for You" program. Outside Chicago, **NICOR**, 888-642-6748, www.nicor.com, serves most of the northern third of Illinois, and is one of the nation's largest gas distributors. It offers a monthly budget billing plan, which varies depending on the size of your apartment. (During the warmer months, your payments build up credit for the more expensive winter months. At the end of a year's service, you will pay the balance of what you owe or receive credit for your next year or next apartment if there are excess funds remaining. If you are leaving town, NICOR will reimburse you for the amount.) Some of the south suburbs such as Olympia Fields, are serviced by **Northern Illinois Gas**, www.nicor.com, a NICOR subsidiary headquartered in Naperville. You can reach them at 800-942-6100.

If you are looking for ways to **reduce your gas bill**, the Energy Information Administration suggests the following:

- Request a home energy audit before the heating season begins; your utility company can send a representative to ensure that all your appliances and space-heating equipment is operating efficiently.
- Make sure your home and hot water heater is properly insulated.
- Reduce the temperature settings on your thermostat when you are not at home.

ELECTRICITY

Commonwealth Edison, commonly referred to as **ComEd** (parent company Exelon), is the electric company for the entire Chicagoland area. It is also the largest nuclear utility in the nation. For electrical service, call Monday-Friday 7 a.m. to 10 p.m., Saturday 7 a.m. to 5 p.m., 800-334-7661, or go to www.exeloncorp.com.

Electric rates have been relatively stable in Illinois for the past few years due to a state cap on pricing. However, that law is set to expire in 2004, when deregulation will take effect. In May 2002, all ComEd residential customers were able to select the electric supplier of their choice, though ComEd continues to *deliver* the electricity. If you wish to use a supplier other than ComEd, call ComEd for a list of certified suppliers at 800-334-7661, or visit their PowerPath web site at www.comedpowerpath.com. You can also view a list of suppliers at the Illinois Commerce Commission's web site, www.icc.state.il.us.

ComEd offers convenient payment centers, a light bulb service, and energy audits of your home, at your request. In addition, ComEd gives you a $10 credit per month during the summer if you allow them to install a control switch on your air-conditioner. Call 800-986-0070 for more information.

TELEPHONE SERVICE

Whether you are calling across town or around the world, in Chicago your connection starts with **SBC** (Southwestern Bell Communications), www.sbc.com (previously Ameritech). To order service, call 800-244-4444. Most apartments in Chicago have phone jacks; just call SBC to request service and then plug in your phones. The installation fee is about $45 for home customers. If your apartment does not have phone jacks, SBC will install them but it will cost you. SBC offers various phone usage options such as Call Waiting, Mover's Voice Mail, Speed Calling, Call Forwarding/Screening, and Voice Mail. Your service representative will explain these options to you when you establish service; they are also detailed in the front of the White Pages phone book. When you call SBC you will be asked to name your **preferred long-distance carrier**. The biggies are:

- **AT&T**, 800-222-0300, www.att.com
- **GTC Telecom**, 800-486-4030, www.gtctelecom.com
- **IDT**, 800-CALL-IDT, www.idt.com
- **MCI-WorldCom**, 800-444-3333, www.mci.com
- **SBC**, 800-244-4444
- **Sprint**, 800-877-7746, www.sprint.com
- **Utility.com**, www.utility.com
- **Verizon**, 800-343-2092, www.verizon.com
- **Working Assets**, 877-255-9253, www.workingforchange.com

If you want to compare long distance pricing, go to **SmartPrice** at www.smartprice.com or call 877-550-5317, Monday-Friday 7 a.m. to 7 p.m. CST. You will be asked questions regarding your phone usage, your area code and the first three digits of your phone number, they will then provide a free instant analysis of the carriers available in your area. Or contact **Telecommunications Research and Action Center**, (**TRAC**) a consumer organization that publishes charts comparing plans and prices: www.trac.org, 202-263-2950.

When you leave your apartment, call SBC, 800-244-4444, to disconnect service and re-establish it at your new place. There is no charge to disconnect service.

Bundled telecommunications: digital phone, cable, and computer service is available from RCN, Comcast, and Wide Open West. See below under **Cable Television** for contact information.

If you have a problem with your carrier, the City of Chicago would like you to report it to its **Department of Consumer Services**. Download a complaint form from their web site, www.ci.chi.il.us/ConsumerServices/telephonecomplaints. The city will not only review your complaint, it will forward it to the **ICC**, which regulates the state's public utilities. If you need to speak to someone at Chicago's Department of Consumer Services, call 312-744-4006. Or contact the State Attorney General's Office, www.ag.state.il.us, 800-386-5438 (consumer hotline).

Phone solicitations can be curbed by going to the government's **do not call registry**, www.donotcall.gov, and registering your phone number—or call 800-382-1222, TTY 866-290-4236.

AREA CODES

With the ever-increasing number of cell phones, pagers, phone and fax lines, Chicago, like the rest of the country, is grappling with the issue of area codes. In the late 1990s, the city was divided into two area codes (the old 312 and the new 773) which created confusion for natives and new-comers alike. The borders of the 312 (central Chicago) area code were North Avenue, Western Avenue, and 35th Street. If you lived south, east, and north of these streets your area code was 312; if you didn't, yours was 773. If only life were so simple. The truth is, the border between the two zones has never been very clear and is getting fuzzier all the time. If you live near the border, you could be in either one. An area code overlay may confuse this even more. In Chicago, it has been proposed that area code 872 will overlay the existing 312 and 773 area codes; 464 will overlay the existing 708 area code; and 331 will overlay area code 630. What this means for you is, depending on where you live, in addition to the older 708, 312, 630, and 773 area codes, newly assigned phones, cell phones, or pager numbers may receive one of three new codes: 464, 872, or 331. The overlay area code 224 has already been added to the 847 region (Chicago's north and northwest suburbs). Where an overlay is in place, callers must dial 11 digits (1 + area code + 7-digit phone number), no matter which area code is being dialed. You may still dial 9-1-1 for emergencies. (See the map of **Chicago Zip Codes & Area Codes** at the back of the book.)

Finally, if you feel frustrated with SBC, a company that serves nearly one-third of the nation, know you are not alone. Contact the **Illinois Commerce Commission** Consumer Services Division, www.icc.state.il.us, 800-524-0795, TTY 800-858-9277, or your Congressional representative with complaints, and join the **Citizen's Utility Board** (**CUB**), www.citizensutilityboard.com, 800-669-5556, in their effort to open and improve local telephone service.

DIRECTORY ASSISTANCE

In today's web-oriented world, directory assistance does not have to cost a lot of money. An online Yellow Pages is available from **Qwest**, www.qwestdex.com, (as of this printing, SBC does not offer an online Yellow Pages), and numerous sites are dedicated to providing telephone listings and web sites. Google's "rphonebook" and "bphonebook" are great. Others include:

- **www.anywho.com** (includes searches for toll-free numbers)
- **Verizon's Super Pages**, www.bigbook.com

- **www.people.yahoo.com**
- **www.switchboard.com**
- **www.whowhere.lycos.com**
- **www.worldpages.com**
- **www.infospace.com**

If you are feeling lazy and dial 411 for directory assistance, keep in mind each call costs .75 cents for local assistance, more if you are asking for nationwide directory help.

CELL PHONES
Here are some of the city's major cellular service providers. Check the Yellow Pages for a provider in your neighborhood.
- **AT&T Wireless Service**, 800-204-7639 (several authorized dealers in Chicagoland area)
- **Sprint PCS**, 312-372-3002 (several locations within Chicago and neighboring area)
- **VoiceStream**, 312-944-9221 (several locations within Chicago and neighboring area)
- **PrimeCo.**, 800-801-2100 312-630-9365 (several locations within Chicago and neighboring area)
- **T-Mobile**, 800-937-8997 (2 locations: Orland Park, Chicago Ridge)
- **Verizon Wireless**, 312-464-1390 (several locations within Chicago and neighboring area)
- **US Cellular**, 888-289-8722

If you are considering a cell phone purchase, find out as much as possible before signing a contract. Better yet, try to find a service that does not require a long-term contract. And be sure to determine whether the cell phone you want to purchase is only operable if you subscribe to a particular service plan. If your phone has a simlock—which prevents you from using your phone with another service provider—go elsewhere. The Better Business Bureau, www.bbb.org, has a page on their web site dedicated to complaints regarding cell phone service providers. TRAC is another good source for more information about cell phone service providers (see above under **Telephone Service**).

ONLINE SERVICE PROVIDERS

Here is a listing of the major local online service providers. Non-national providers are often less expensive, sometimes costing less than half of what the biggies charge—good for those wanting e-mail and internet access sans the bells and whistles.

- **America Online**, 800-827-6364, www.aol.com
- **AT&T**, 800-222-0300, www.consumer.att.com
- **Earthlink**, www.earthlink.net, 800-511-2041
- **MSN8**, 866-523-MSN8, www.msn.com
- **NetZero One**, 877-701-1001, www.net011.net
- **SBC**/**Yahoo**, 800-776-3449, www.sbc.com
- **Verizon Online DSL**, 888-649-9500

WATER

Unless you're a homeowner, you won't be paying for water. If you are living in an older home, you may not have a water meter, in which case, Chicago's **Department of Water Management** will send you a bill semi-annually, based on standard assessments of your property and the home's interior fixtures. If you want to set up service or have questions about your water bill call 312-747-9090. You can also visit the city's web site for more information, www.cityofchicago.org/WaterManagement.

Whether you're paying for it or not, the water here may surprise you, especially if you're moving from an area where the water source is less compromised. In Chicago and many suburbs, tap water comes from Lake Michigan, and while it ends up perfectly safe to drink (after extensive filtering and treatment), the taste can take some getting used to. The water is considered moderately hard, but you will be the best judge of that, and the water is fluoridated.

If you live in a community that depends on well water as their drinking supply, you may notice sediments, a rusty color or other hard minerals. Some will change the color of your white enamel bathtubs and washing machines. Most authorities will tell you there is no cause for alarm; simply run your water until the color and sediments are gone. But if you want the facts, contact your Illinois **Source Water and Assessment Program** (**SWAP**) coordinator at 217-785-4787 or go to www.epa.state.il.us. As part of the state's EPA, SWAP monitors and assesses well water.

Whether you drink lake or well water, you will notice a whitish film on some of your glasses and pots after filling them with water or while they are drying. That is calcium carbonate, courtesy of mother nature. It's harmless, if not attractive, and can be removed with ordinary white vinegar. For drinking water, many opt for bottled water, but over time it's more expensive than even the priciest filters. Water filter pitchers and faucet attachments are available at most hardware and department stores, which will remove the most offensive element—the chlorine taste—but have only a modest impact on other pollutants. If you're concerned, you can buy more expensive filters, which attach directly to the water line. Or you can have bottled water delivered to your home from suppliers like Culligan. Some of the larger supermarkets, such as Jewel, offer drinking water from a coin machine; you supply your own jug. It should be stressed that Chicago water meets or exceeds both the EPA's and the Illinois Pollution Control Board's standards for water purity. And, believe it or not, Chicago water is better than much of the groundwater in the area. Interestingly, 40% of the water that is pumped out of the lake is sold to neighboring suburbs. For more, go to the EPA's site, www.epa.gov, and read their guidelines on microbiological contaminants. Or call the **Safe Drinking Water Hotline**, 800-426-4791.

CONSUMER COMPLAINTS—UTILITIES

If you have problems with any utility company (gas, electric, water, phone, or cable TV) and the service provide does not handle it to your satisfaction, don't hesitate to call the Consumer Services Division of the **Illinois Commerce Commission** at 800-524-0795, TTY 800-858-9277 or go to www.icc.state.il.us. While they are required to take your complaint; how helpful they are can be another matter.

Another group that looks out for consumer's interests in Chicago is the **Citizens Utility Board** (**CUB**), 208 South LaSalle, Suite 1760, Chicago, IL 60604, 800-669-5556, www.citizensutilityboard.org. CUB is a consumer watchdog organization, which, among other things, monitors utility rate hikes. Over the years, they have successfully lobbied for lower rate increases, and even won rate reductions and refunds for Illinois utility customers.

GARBAGE AND RECYCLING

In Chicago, the Department of Streets & Sanitation is in charge of all residential garbage pick-up and disposal. The city defines residential garbage as waste from a single-family home or a unit with four or fewer separate units. No need to call to set up service, just use the alleyway dumpster or city provided cans. Each ward in Chicago has a superintendent responsible for coordinating local area garbage pickups, snow removal, and other services. Visit the Department of Streets and Sanitation's web page to locate your ward and its superintendent, www.cityofchicago.org/StreetsAndSan/Sanitation/WardOffices. If you do not have a trashcan, call the Department of Environment at 311 (312-744-5000) to request one.

In the suburbs sanitation service varies by community. Ask your neighbors or call your city hall for details. Trash haulers can be found in the Yellow Pages under "Garbage & Rubbish Removal." Waste Management serves a large number of outlying communities. Call them at 708-422-2225, or check their web site, www.wastemanagement.com.

Chicago's Blue Bag recycling program began in 1995. The concept is quite simple. Recyclables are divided into three categories: clean containers (plastic, aluminum, steel, or glass); clean wastepaper (newspapers, magazines, junk mail, phone books, paper); and yard waste. Recyclables from each category are put into three separate blue garbage bags. When the bags are full, place them in your city-supplied trashcan or dumpster. Blue bags are available at most grocery stores and hardware stores in different sizes. Call the Blue Bag Hotline, 312-BLUE-BAG, if you have any questions.

From the beginning, the Blue Bag program was criticized by environmentalists for being ineffective, labor intensive, and voluntary. In many other cities, the sorting of recyclables is more thorough but the citizens do it themselves and separate recycling trucks pick it up. By combining recyclable collection with the regular weekly garbage pickup, Chicago saved the expense of buying new trucks. The city is hoping that the initial drawbacks of the program—low participation rates and high labor costs—will be offset in the future by higher participation rates. While the jury is still out about how effective this campaign has been, to date, the city has recovered enough paper to save over 17 million trees! **Waste Management (WMI)** runs the city's four recycling centers: they own and market the recyclables recovered from the Blue Bags. You can take a virtual tour of the recycling process at www.cityofchicago.org/Environment/BlueBag. If you would prefer to see this tour in action, call 312-744-1614 to schedule an appointment.

For those who still want to sort the old-fashioned way—saving recyclables (glass, metal, paper and plastics), and carting them to a recycling site or truck—the **Resource Center** runs two independent recycling centers, including one in Lincoln Park in the parking lot of the 7-Eleven (on the northwest corner of Sheffield, Wrightwood, and Lincoln avenues). They can also give you information on other recycle/reuse programs throughout the city. Call them at 773-821-1351. **Uptown Recycling**, 773-769-5579, also runs an independent drop-off center at 4753 North Broadway.

In some of the suburban areas, Waste Management is the primary pick-up provider for garbage and recyclables. Once you move into your home, you will be provided with a list of acceptable items to be recycled. Though it varies slightly from suburb to suburb, generally you can expect a bin for glass and plastics (those with a stamped recyclable symbol) and a second bin for newspapers. Bins are provided by Waste Management. Yard waste is generally handled by the township. You can obtain special recyclable stickers for your yard waste cans from your local city hall.

Never dispose of motor oil or hazardous liquids via your storm drains.

DRIVER'S LICENSES, AUTOMOBILE REGISTRATION, AND ILLINOIS STATE IDS

CHICAGO VEHICLE STICKERS—CITY STICKERS

Chicago residents with vehicles must have a **Chicago vehicle sticker** (often referred to as a city sticker) attached to the inside windshield of their cars. Think of it as a yearly usage fee for the privilege of parking on city streets. Not everyone living in the suburbs will escape this little urban pocket squeezer, as many of the 'burbs require them too. Rates in the suburbs vary, and the suburban city halls usually offer a discount if you purchase your sticker more than 30 days before the due date. Check with your municipality for details. In Chicago, the cost is $75 (expect to pay an additional $3 to $5 service charge if you use a non-city outlet). Purchase vehicle stickers at City Hall, 121 North LaSalle, 312-744-6861, at most currency exchange offices, or one of the Department of Revenue Payment Centers: 2550 West Addison Street, 800 North Kedzie, 2006 East 95th Street. You can also purchase your vehicle sticker at the City Clerk's Satellite Office, 5301 South Cicero Avenue, Suite 106; at the State of Illinois Building, 100 Randolph Street, lower level; the DMV building at 5401 North Elston Avenue; or the Bureau of Parking Enforcement, Lane Plaza, 2550 West Addison Street. To do it online, go to www.chicity clerk.com. They are valid from July 1st to June 30th of the following year. If you buy your vehicle sticker more than 30 days after the renewal date, an additional $30 fee will be assessed. The ticket price for not having a sticker is $60. (Since the city has access to the Illinois Secretary of State's records, it's easy for a meter reader to enter a plate number on a computer and see if you should have a sticker.) **Note**: if you are new to Chicago, you do not need to wait for your new Illinois license plates in order to purchase a vehicle sticker. Simply bring proof of your new Chicago address to any city clerk facility and purchase your vehicle sticker. For more information call 312-744-6861 or go to www.chicityclerk.com.

DRIVER'S LICENSE AND STATE IDENTIFICATION CARD

Residents of Illinois who own and operate a vehicle must have an Illinois driver's license and Illinois license plates. The grace period to obtain an Illinois license is 90 days. Until then, you are allowed to drive in the state under the driver's license of your former home state. **Illinois driver's licenses** are obtained through the **Illinois Secretary of State**, www.sos.state.il.us. There are 130 facilities located in the Chicagoland area. Contact the Secretary of State's Chicago Information Office at

312-793-1010. They can assist you in finding the closest DMV office, or you can do it yourself at www.cyberdriveillinois.com.

If you do not have an Illinois state driver's license, you'll need your current, out-of-state driver's license, a social security card, and proof of birth: a birth certificate, valid passport, alien registration card, or a military ID card; and proof of your new address—a utility bill, or voters registration card will do. There are several other forms that are acceptable—visit the DMV web site, www.sos.state.il.us, to view all your options. You will be asked to take a written test based on Illinois *Rules of the Road,* and an eye test. If you need to brush up on your rules you can contact the Illinois Secretary of State's Chicago Information Office at 312-793-1010 for a helpful driver's rule book, or download it from www.cyberdriveillinois.com (it's big, 104 pages). The fee for an Illinois driver's license is $10, and it is valid for five years. You may also be asked to take a road test. There is no fee for the road test. If you don't drive but need a **photo identification**, you can get an Illinois identification card through the Illinois Secretary of State and at many of the Motor Vehicle offices. The fee for the state ID is $4 and is valid for four years.

FINES AND TICKETS

Should you be so unfortunate as to receive a ticket for a moving violation or illegal parking in Chicago, you'll need to become acquainted with Chicago's **Traffic Court**. The downtown court is at 50 West Washington. To determine which court office will handle your case, call the Traffic Court's automated information line for Cook County: 312-603-2000. (If you are ticketed outside of Cook County, check with that municipality for court information.) If you receive a ticket for a moving violation, you must either pay the ticket or contest it within seven days. If you contest the ticket, you will be assigned a court date. Be aware that in Illinois you must **post bond** when you receive a moving violation citation. If you do not have a spare $75 in cash or a bail bond card (available through many automobile clubs such as AAA or Allstate) the officer will take your license until you post bond or pay your fine. This can be a huge inconvenience, but you will get a receipt that can be used as a temporary substitute, so it's not the end of the world. If you decide to pay your ticket, you can do so by mail, online at www.cityofchicago.org, or at one of the city's payment facilities. Call 312-603-2000 for payment center addresses. You can also pay at City Hall, 121 North LaSalle, Room 107. If you have any questions about a parking violation, contact the city's **Parking and Compliance Violation Center** at 312-744-PARK (7275). (For more on parking in Chicago see below.)

Go to the **Chicago Bar Association's** web site, www.chicagobar.org, for more information about traffic citations in Cook County or if you need to hire an attorney. Their lawyer referral service line is 312-554-2001.

LICENSE PLATES AND VEHICLE REGISTRATION

New residents have 30 days after bringing their vehicle to Illinois in which to apply for an Illinois title and to have it registered. Bring proof of identification, address, the odometer reading, name and address of any party that has a lien on the vehicle, date your vehicle was purchased, make, model, year, body type, vehicle identification number (VIN), and either the copy of the out of state title or bill of sale. (If you have recently purchased a vehicle and it is not yet registered in any state, you will need to fill out the proper tax forms, pay applicable taxes, and attach them to your application when you mail it to the Illinois Secretary of State's Office. Contact the Department of Revenue for more information, 800-732-8866.) If you have a **disability** and need special plates, you will need to bring in proof of disability or military disability proof. You will also need to provide liability insurance records, and if the car is more than three years old, proof of vehicle inspection certification (see below).

Illinois license plates can be purchased at any office of the Illinois Secretary of State or at neighborhood currency exchanges. The price of plates varies, ranging from $78 to $134, depending on your car ($38 for a motorcycle). Vanity plates cost more. Title fees are $65 for an automobile and $30 for an all terrain vehicle or motorcycle. If you have any questions concerning the registration process, call the Secretary of State's **Vehicle Titles Division** at 217-782-6306.

You can bring your car registration application in to any Secretary of State Driver Service facility. Go to www.cyberdriveillinois.com for a list of facility addresses. Call the Secretary of State's Chicago Information Office at 312-793-1010 with any questions (none of the following Illinois Secretary of State offices accept incoming phone calls):

- **State of Illinois Building**, 100 West Randolph Street
- **North**, 5401 North Elston Avenue
- **South**, 9901 South King Drive

For those moving to Illinois with a **leased vehicle**, there's a bit more work involved to register it with the state. Bring your car's lease, power of attorney from the leasing company, and registration information to the Secretary of State's office (see above), where you will not only pay for normal registration, but will also file an RUT25 form for use tax on the vehicle. If you paid tax on the vehicle in another state you must bring proof of this as well. Call the **Illinois Department of Revenue** at 800-732-8866 with any questions.

EMISSIONS TEST

The State of Illinois requires all gasoline-powered cars and light trucks (diesel-powered vehicles are exempt) to undergo a biannual (once every two years) **auto emissions test** starting in the fourth model year. If you have purchased a vehicle that has an expired emissions test, you will be required to have it re-tested as soon as you receive your new registration. Drivers will receive notification in the mail. The testing takes about 10 minutes—tops. Your notice will provide a list of the nearest emission test centers, but you can take your vehicle to any authorized facility. Look for signs around town. An official notification of the test results will come in the mail in a few weeks. If you have any questions regarding the testing, you can contact the **emissions hotline** at 847-758-3400.

AUTOMOBILE INSURANCE REQUIREMENTS

If you own a registered car in the state of Illinois, the law states you must have auto insurance. Liability insurance of $20,000 per person, $40,000 per accident for bodily injury and $15,000 for property damage is the minimum coverage required. However, the Insurance Information Institute, www.iii.org, recommends that you carry $100,000 for bodily injury per person and $300,000 per accident. Typically this additional coverage will cost you about $200 to $300 more per year. You must also carry uninsured/underinsured motorists insurance, which protects you in the event you are hit by a driver who has no insurance or who is carrying less insurance than what will be needed to pay for the damages. For more information visit their web site or contact their offices at 212-346-5500.

A few notes on **state driving laws**: Illinois has a mandatory seat belt law, and an officer can legally stop your car for non-compliance. The fine for not using a seat belt in the front seat is $25. Children under four need to be seated in a child safety seat. (If you need some tips on how to properly install a **child safety seat**, visit www.safekids.org.) In Illinois, the legal definition of **driving while intoxicated (DWI)** is a blood alcohol limit of 0.08. If you are stopped for suspected intoxication, and you are found to have a blood alcohol level above the legal limit or if you refuse to take the BAC test, it is grounds for on the spot driving license revocation or suspension. You are also forbidden to have any unsealed containers of alcohol in the passenger compartments.

CONSUMER PROTECTION—AUTOMOBILES

Just bought a shiny new lemon? According to Illinois law, if your new car has a "nonconformity that both substantially impairs the use, market value or safety of the vehicle and is not repairable by the dealer or manufacturer in at least four attempts for the same repair" or is "out of service for a total of 30 or more business days" you may be able to receive a replacement vehicle or the manufacturer may be required to buy your car back from you. All of this depends, of course, on the specifics of your case. You must have purchased the vehicle new within the past 12 months, and you should keep records of all receipts related to the vehicle's purchase, problems, and repairs, otherwise making a case that you got a lemon will be more difficult. To find out more, call the Illinois Attorney General at 800-386-5483 or visit the state web site: www.ag.state.il.us.

PARKING

PARKING GARAGES AND LOTS

Parking downtown on a daily basis is prohibitively expensive. A "bargain" day rate can run about $22—and you usually have to get to the lot by 7 a.m. to enjoy that deal. But if you find that you must bring your car downtown occasionally here are a few tips to keep the cost down. As a general rule, the further away from State Street, the kinder the fee. If you try the parking lots east of the Ogilvie Transportation Center, where the Metra trains turn in for their final stop from the suburbs, you can find reasonable parking—$8 to $12. A good deal unless your appointment is across town.

If you plan to spend an evening downtown, say at the opera or theater, you can simply drive around and spot signs that offer "deals" for customers pulling in after 6 p.m. If you are dining along Michigan Avenue, consider parking in the 900 North building, where for a minimum purchase in one of the stores within the building you can have your parking ticket validated.

If you plan on being downtown on a daily basis, consider a monthly pass with CTA or Metra. See the **Transportation** chapter for more details.

RESIDENTIAL PARKING PERMITS

In most neighborhoods, residential parking permits are not valid without a current Chicago Vehicle Sticker. Streets designated R1-R5 are zoned for residential parking permits. The zoning status signifies that more than 33% of the cars parked on a given block, do not belong to residents of the area. This type of zoning is usually bestowed in neighborhoods where parking is an issue, such as Wrigleyville, where Chicago Cubs night games turn the neighborhood into a parking nightmare. If you're not sure whether your neighborhood requires a parking permit, you can call your ward office or, easier still, walk down the block and look for parking regulation signs. You can't miss them. If your neighborhood is zoned for residential parking permits, you can obtain an application from the **City Clerk's Permit Sales Unit**, 312-744-5346, or go to www.chicityclerk.com/residential_parking/. Bring your proof of residence (lease, mortgage book, utility bill) and proof of Chicago Vehicle Sticker (receipt from sticker). At this time you can also purchase packs of one day guest permit parking stickers; three dollars for a pack of 15. Purchase a residential parking permit at several locations:

- City Clerk's Satellite Office, 5301 South Cicero (Room 106)
- City Clerk's Office (Room 106) in City Hall, 121 North LaSalle Street
- Secretary of State Office, 5401 North Elston Avenue
- Secretary of State Office, 9901 South Martin Luther King Jr. Drive

Residential Parking Permits can also be obtained by mail; go to www.chicityclerk.com to download the application. Mail the application to City Clerk, 121 North La Salle, Room 107, Chicago, 60602. The fee is $17.50 and the permit expires each year on June 30th.

PARKING TICKETS

Parking fines range from $25 to $120 depending on the offense. If you want to fight the parking ticket, it's the same procedure as a moving violation: mail back the envelope after marking an "X" in the box requesting a hearing. The city will send a card telling you when and where to go for your hearing. Or you can contest the ticket by mail, writing your reasons why you feel the ticket was unwarranted. The city will respond, informing you whether or not you will have to pay the ticket. (Go to www.city ofchicago.org to pay the ticket online or see **Fines and Tickets** above for a list of payment centers.) For a list of outstanding violations, call 312-744-7275 or go to www.cityofchicago.org.

Parking enforcement in Chicago varies depending upon location. In order to save on-street parking places for residents, permit parking (see previous section) is the rage in many popular neighborhoods. Lincoln Park, DePaul/Lincoln Park West and Wrigleyville/Lakeview are particularly hard places to find a space without a permit, and tow trucks cruise through these areas with cruel regularity.

If you find your car has been towed, call the **Police Department Auto Pound HQ**, 312-744-4444, to find out where your vehicle was taken. To retrieve your wheels, you must pay a $150 towing fee (for cars up to 8,000 pounds), plus a $10 per day holding fee for the first five days; $35 daily after five days. Cars weighing over 8,000 pounds pay $60 for the first five days, $100 daily thereafter. You must pay cash or use VISA or MasterCard; personal checks are not allowed.

If your car was **booted** for unpaid parking violations, you must pay a $60 booting fee and the balance of any unpaid parking tickets within 24 hours after the booting. The city is serious about collecting fines—three unpaid tickets can get your car booted, and even towed. Then you will be required to pay not only the $60 booting fee, but also the $150 towing fee, plus $10 per day for storage for the first five days; $35 thereafter.

Also, be aware that Illinois requires a license plate on both the front end and back end of your car. Failure to comply can result in a $25 fine. A broken windshield will get you the same. Both fines can be issued at the same time your expired parking meter citation is being written.

STOLEN CARS

If it turns out your car has been stolen rather than towed, the police will need your license and city vehicle sticker numbers, the car's year, make, model, and color as well as the vehicle identification number. You also should mark your sound system, radar detector, car phone, and other accessories with your driver's license number. You can borrow an engraving pen through your local police district's Operation Identification program. The pound at 650 West 83rd Street is generally reserved for vehicles involved in a crime.

VOTER REGISTRATION

The old Chicago slogan, "vote early and often," is a reminder of days gone by when elections here were fast and loose and election results were rigged. Today, Chicago elections are honest.

To be eligible to vote in Chicago, you must be a resident of the precinct for 30 days, be 18 years of age by election day, and be a US citizen. You can register to vote anytime during the year, up until 28 days before an election. Register when applying for services at driver's license facilities, the Departments of Public Aid, Public Health, Mental Health & Developmental Disabilities, or Rehabilitation Services; or go to the Board of Elections office, 69 West Washington, #600 and #800, 312-269-7936, your county clerk's office, city hall, or village or township offices. You need two pieces of identification; one must have your current address. If you register at the Board of Elections office, you can also request an absentee ballot or change your voter's registration there.

Close to election time, voter registration drives are held throughout the city. In many cases, you will be able to register with a volunteer in less than five minutes. If you are moving to any of the nearby counties, you can call your county for more information or go to www.voterinfonet.com to find your polling place and to read about the candidates:

- **Suburban Cook County**, 312-603-0906, TDD 312-603-0902
- **DuPage County**, 630-682-7440
- **Kane County**, 630-232-5990
- **Lake County**, 847-360-3610
- **McHenry County**, 815-334-4242

Political campaigns make for exciting times in Chicago. Here are some places for those who want to take a more active role:

- **Chicago Board of Elections**, 312-269-7900, www.chicagoelections.com
- **Democratic Party of Cook County**, 30 North LaSalle Street, Suite 2432, 312-263-0575, www.ildems.org.
- **Republican Party of Cook County**, 32 West Randolph, 312-977-1467, www.ilgop.org
- **Reform Party**, 1255 North Sandburg Terrace, Chicago, 312-266-7431, www.reformpartyillinois.com
- **League of Women Voters**, 332 South Michigan Avenue, Suite 1142, 312-939-5935, www.lwv.org
- **Illinois Green Party** (HQ in Urbana, IL), www.ilgreenparty.org
- **Illinois State Board of Elections**, 312-814-6440, www.elections.state.il.us
- **Libertarian Party**, 847-459-9246, www.il.lp.org

PASSPORTS

You can apply for a passport at the **US State Department** office in the Federal Building, 230 South Dearborn Street, Room 380. There is a suburban satellite office in the **Arlington Heights Post Office**, located at 909 West Euclid Avenue. To make a quick search for the passport facility nearest you, go to http://iafdb.travel.state.gov. The Bureau of Consular Affairs, which is the agency that oversees the issuing of passports, no longer accepts calls with routine passport questions. You can call the **National Passport Information Center** at 900-225-5674 (the charge is $.55 per minute for automated information and $1.50 per minute for operator assistance). Or go to www.travel.state.gov for free. Bring two standard passport photos taken within the last six months, a picture ID, and proof of US citizenship, such as a previous US passport, certified birth certificate, naturalization certificate or certificate of citizenship. The cost is $85 for a new passport and $55 to renew a passport less than 12 years old. The standard turnaround time for a new passport is 25 days, but it can take longer; an expedited three-day passport can be requested for an additional $60 fee. You can download an application (form DSP-11) with instructions from the Bureau of Consular Affairs web site at www.travel.state.gov, or go to the State

Department's forms site at http://travel.state.gov/get_forms and download the application from there. Need more information? Go to the Federal Citizens Information Center, at www.pueblo.gsa.gov/call/travel. This site is very user friendly.

Passports are valid for 10 years for those 16 and older; five years for children 15 and under.

LIBRARIES

If you are a resident of the city of Chicago, you can apply for a Chicago Public Library card at any **Chicago Public Library**, www.chipublib.org. It's simple, fast and free. In addition to the Chicago Public Library's **Harold Washington Library**, the city's beautiful main library at 400 South State Street, 312-747-4300, there are many neighborhood branches throughout the city (check the **Neighborhood Profiles**), as well as university and independent libraries, many of which are open to the public. (See **Literary Life** in the **Cultural Life** chapter for more details.)

BROADCAST AND PRINT MEDIA

TELEVISION STATIONS

Provided you have a good antenna and you don't live in a basement or in a high-rise, you should be able to receive the following network and local independent stations without cable service:

- Channel 2 WBBM (CBS)
- Channel 5 WMAQ (NBC)
- Channel 7 WLS (ABC)
- Channel 9 WGN (Tribune)
- Channel 11 WTTW (Public Broadcasting System)
- Channel 20 WYCC (Public Broadcasting System affiliated with Chicago City Colleges)
- Channel 23 WFBT
- Channel 26 WCIU (Independent)
- Channel 32 WFLD (Fox)
- Channel 38 WCPX (Pax)
- Channel 44 WSNS (Tel)
- Channel 50 WPWR (UPN)
- Channel 62 WJYS (Independent)
- Channel 66 WGBO (Uni)

Daily program listings are printed in both the *Chicago Sun-Times* and the *Chicago Tribune* and their weekly TV magazines, as well as in *TV Guide*.

CABLE TELEVISION

Chicago is divided into five areas for cable service, which is provided by three cable television companies: **Comcast**, 866-594-1234 and 773-736-1800, www.comcast.com; **RCN**, 888-790-2121, www.rcn.com; and **Wide Open West**, 866-496-9669, www.wideopenwest.com. Each company offers basic cable service with the premium channels available for an extra fee; there are slight differences in channels and programming.

To find out which cable area you are in or if you have an issue with your cable service provider, call the **City of Chicago Cable Communications Administration, Information and Complaints**, 312-744-4052.

RADIO STATIONS

If you can't make it through the day without morning talk radio, National Public Radio, or your favorite shock jock, here are Chicago's radio stations and their programming:

FM
- 88.1 WCRX dance music
- 89.3 WNUR Northwestern University Radio
- 90.1 WMBI Christian
- 91.5 WBEZ National Public Radio by day (NPR); jazz at night
- 93.1 WXRT progressive rock, folk, blues, and reggae
- 93.5 WLIT light rock
- 93.9 WLIT adult contemporary
- 94.7 WZZN alternative rock
- 95.5 WNUA jazz and new age
- 96.3 WBBM top 40
- 97.1 WNIB classical
- 97.9 WLUP adult rock
- 98.7 WFMT classical
- 99.5 WUSN country
- 100.3 WNND adult contemporary
- 101.1 WKQX alternative rock
- 101.9 WTMX adult contemporary
- 102.7 WVAZ adult, urban contemporary
- 103.5 WKSC top 40
- 103.9 WXRD classic rock
- 104.3 WJMK oldies (50s, 60s, early 70s)
- 105.1 WOJO Spanish contemporary
- 105.9 WCKG talk

- 106.3 WYCA gospel
- 106.7 WYLL Christian
- 107.5 WGCI urban contemporary
- 107.9 WLEY Spanish regional

AM

- 560 WIND Spanish contemporary
- 670 WSCR News, White Sox, Bulls games
- 720 WGN Talk, Cubs games
- 780 WBBM News
- 850 WAIT Talk from Crystal Lake
- 890 WLS Talk radio
- 930 WAUR religious talk
- 1000 WMVP sports
- 1110 WMBI Christian
- 1160 WYLL Christian talk
- 1240 WSBC foreign language variety
- 1390 WGCI gospel
- 1450 WVON ethnic, religious
- 1530 WJJG news, talk
- 1570 WBEE jazz, blues and gospel
- 1600 WCGO oldies

NEWSPAPERS AND MAGAZINES

Whether your interest is in theater, poetry readings, or trendy restaurants, there is probably a local (and often free) publication to suit you. And since Chicago is one of the few remaining cities with competing daily newspapers, the *Chicago Sun-Times, Daily Herald, The Daily Southtown,* and the *Chicago Tribune*, news coverage is sharp, ground-breaking (the local television news stations regularly pick up stories from the dailies) and thorough. For in-depth regional news and business, *Crain's Chicago Business* is regarded as one of the best weeklies in the country. Alternative papers such as the *Chicago Reader* and *New City* are feature-driven, as is the monthly *Chicago Magazine*. Other publications dedicated to business, legal matters, entertainment or other: *Chicago Computer Guide, Chicago Daily Law Bulletin, Chicago Educator, Chicago Reporter,* and *Chicago Parent*. There are also various student and independent magazines available in area coffeehouses and record stores, although it is best to stick with the *Reader* or *New City* for dependable movie, club, or theater listings. Two local papers which cover news and events with an emphasis on Chicago's African-American community are *N'DIGO*, (a free weekly paper with listings, reviews, editorials, and feature articles), and the *Chicago Daily Defender* (covering local and national news). In addition, there are over 45 community newspapers (not including suburban communities), that cover neighborhood happenings. They are generally weeklies. Check at your local convenience store or drugstore store for a copy.

Corner newsstands are scattered throughout the city and offer a good selection of some of the most popular newspapers and magazines. For the ultimate selection, try Chicago City Newsstand, 4018 North Cicero, 773-545-7377 in Chicago and at 860 Chicago Avenue/Main Street in Evanston, 847-425-8900, www.citynewsstand.com.

- **Chicago Daily Defender**, 2400 South Michigan Avenue, 60616, 312-225-2400
- **Chicago Daily Law Bulletin**, oldest daily courts newspaper in the country, 312-644-7800, www.lawbulletin.com
- **Chicago Educator**, Chicago Public Schools Communications Office, 125 South Clark Street, Chicago, 773-553-1620; published during the school year. Available through the schools.
- **Chicago Journal**, weekly news publication covering, south, near, and west Loop, 141 South Oak Park Avenue, Oak Park, 312-243-2696
- **Chicago Magazine**, 500 North Dearborn Street, 60610, 312-222-8999 or 800-999-0879, www.chicagomagazine.com
- **Chicago Parent**, 141 South Oak Park, Oak Park, 708-386-5555, www.chicagoparent.com; award winning free monthly, found in many libraries.
- **Chicago Reader**, 11 East Illinois Street, 312-828-0350, www.chireader.com; free weekly, comes out on Thursdays. Available in shops, restaurants, clubs all over the North Side and selected South Side areas. In the suburbs look for the **Reader's Guide to Arts and Entertainment**.
- **Chicago Reporter**, 332 South Michigan Avenue, 312-427-4830, www.chicagoreporter.com; publication devoted to the issues of race and poverty
- **Chicago Sun-Times**, 401 North Wabash Avenue, 60611, 312-321-3000 or 800-945-5000, www.suntimes.com; Red Streak at www.redstreak.com
- **Chicago Tribune**, 435 North Michigan Avenue, 60611, 312-222-3232 or 800-TRIBUNE; electronic edition, www.chicagotribune.com; the Red Eye, www.redeyechicago.com
- **Crain's Chicago Business**, 740 North Rush Street, 60611, 312-649-5411, www.chicagobusiness.com; daily local business news.
- **Hyde Park Herald**, Chicago's oldest community newspaper, serving Hyde Park, Oakland, and Kenwood, 5240 South Harper Avenue, Chicago, 773-643-8533, www.hpherald.com.
- **Inside Publications**, 4710 North Lincoln Avenue, 773-878-7333, www.insideonline.com, weekly news coverage of Chicago's North Side:

Loop, Lincoln Park, Gold Coast, Lakeview, Lincoln Square, Uptown, Andersonville.

- **N'DIGO**, 401 North Wabash Avenue, Suite 534, 60611, 312-822-0202; free African-American weekly, available in shops and restaurants throughout Chicago.
- **New City**, 770 North Halsted Street, Suite 208, 60622, 312-243-8786, www.newcitychicago.com; free entertainment weekly, comes out on Thursday. Available in Chicago shops, restaurants, and clubs.
- **Windy City Times**, 1115 West Belmont, Chicago, 773-871-7610, www.windycitymediagroup.com; gay and lesbian focus.

Suburban publications include:

- **Chicago Heights Star**, 708-802-8000, www.starnewspapers.com: southwest suburbs
- **Chicago Suburban Newspapers**, www.chicagosuburbannews.com: **Beacon News**, 630-844-5844, western suburbs; **Bolingbrook Reporter**, 630-969-0885; **Courier News**, 847-888-7800, north and northwest suburbs; **News Sun**: Bolingbrook, Naperville, Wheaton, Glen Ellyn, 847-336-7220; **Herald News**, 815-729-6161, Will and Grundy counties; **Naperville Reporter**, 630-969-0885; **Suburban Life**, 708-352-9852, Dupage County and central and east Cook County; **Downers Grove Reporter**, 708-352-9852
- **Daily Herald**, 155 East Algonquin Road, Arlington Heights, 847-427-4333, www.dailyherald.com
- **Daily Southtown**, 6901 West 159th Street, Tinley Park, 708-633-6777, www.dailysouthtown.com; covers Chicago's south suburbs.
- **Des Plaines Journal**, www.journal-topics.com/dp
- **Lakeland Newspapers**, 30 South Whitney Street, Grayslake; serving 11 Lake County communities, www.lpnews.com/ln, 847-245-7500
- **Lombardian/Villa Park Review**, 116 South Main Street, Lombard, 630-627-7010
- **Northshore Magazine**, 847-486-0600, www.northshoremag.com; covers Chicago's north shore communities.
- **Oak Park Journal Newspaper**, www.oakparkjournal.com
- **Pioneer Press**, www.pioneerlocal.com: **Evanston Review, Skokie Review, Lincolnwood Review**, 847-866-6501; **Highland Park News, Deerfield Review**, 847-599-6900; **Glencoe News, Northbrook Star, Wilmette Life, Winnetka Talk**, 847-486-9200; **Arlington Heights Post, Schaumburg Review**, 847-797-5100; **Oak Leaves**, Oak Park, 708-383-3200; **Des Plaines Times**, 847-696-3133
- **Rosemont Journal**, www.journal-topics.com/ro
- **Southwest News Herald**, 773-476-4800, www.southwestnewsherald.com; south and southwest suburbs including Burbank and Oak Lawn.

- **The Star**, www.starnewspapers.com; covers south and southwest suburbs.
- **Suburban Focus Magazine**, 630-910-7989, www.SuburbanFocus.com; free monthly publication. A leisure magazine covering the west and southwest suburbs of Chicago.

FINDING A PHYSICIAN

Some of the country's best hospitals are in the Chicago area, and include many university-affiliated teaching hospitals as well as first rate specialty clinics. Certainly good news for those needing a specialist. If you just need a family health care provider you should have no trouble finding a good doctor. Usually recommendations from a co-worker or friend are the best way to go when looking for a doctor, although you should check with your medical plan's list of preferred providers. For those less fortunate, area clinics are available. County Health boards are good sources of information about area health clinics for low income/uninsured patients. Here are a few of the **Chicagoland county health boards**: Lake County Board of Health, 847-377-8000; Chicago Department of Public Health, 312-747-9884; Kane County Health Department, 630-208-3801; DuPage County Health Department, 630-682-7400.

Nearly all of the university hospitals have a physician referral line. The **American Medical Association**, www.ama-assn.org, also has a doctor locator service. Following is a list of some **physician referral services** for the Chicagoland area:

- www.chicagodrs.com
- www.alsa.org—for those with Lou Gehrig's disease
- www.thebody.com/hivco/chicagor—for those with HIV
- www.uchospitals.edu, for the University of Chicago Hospital's referral service

For general health questions, the Mayo Clinic, www.mayohealth.org, and the federal government's www.healthfinder.gov, are good resources. To determine if a doctor is board certified in a specialty area you can go to the American Board of Medical Specialties at www.certifieddoctor.org, 800-776-2378, or to HealthGrades, www.healthgrades.com. HealthGrades rates 600,000 physicians and 5,000 hospitals. If you have a complaint about a local physician contact the Illinois Department of Professional Regulation at 312-814-4560 or 312-814-4500.

PET LAWS AND SERVICES

If you're going to keep a dog in Chicago, he or she will need a rabies vaccination and dogs need a license. The former are available from any vet; they will also give you a vaccination tag to put on your dog's collar. Dog licenses are available at the **City Clerk's Office**, 121 North La Salle Street, 312-744-6875 (satellite office: 5301 South Cicero Avenue, Suite 106, 312-745-1100), but you will need proof of a rabies vaccination to get one. Dog licenses cost $5 if your dog is neutered, $10 otherwise (for seniors: $2.50 neutered, $45 unneutered). The licenses are valid for one year. Birds and snakes do not require a license—but horses do! Check with the City Clerk's office for pricing. If Fido is lost and captured by Animal Control, it will cost you $28 to redeem him—if he is licensed; it's $40 for an impounded unlicensed stray. (The cat redemption fee is $28, plus rabies shots if you cannot prove the animal has been properly vaccinated.) Chicago has a leash law and a waste removal (scoop the poop) law so bring a bag or some newspaper when you are out for your daily stroll. Violating any of the above ordinances can bring fines of up to $200.

Dogs are not allowed on Chicago's beaches. Despite this, you will find a multitude of frolicking slap-happy, water loving dogs on the beach in the early mornings. During the day, check out Belmont Harbor just north of Belmont Avenue; there's a small spit of a beach there called Doggie Beach, which on the weekends is more dog than beach. If you don't live near the lake and want companionship for your pup, just wake up early and walk on over to the nearest neighborhood park. All over the city, parks are transformed into early morning doggie play groups. Just remember to pick up the poop! Don't panic if you don't have the time to walk your dog every day, there are plenty of dog-walking services. Just look in the Yellow Pages under "Pet Exercising Services." Check the **Greenspace and Beaches** chapter for more on dog-friendly parks.

In the suburbs, many of the larger pet store chains offer low cost veterinary services several times a year, including inexpensive vaccinations for dogs, cats, and ferrets. Call your local chain and ask about their clinic services. If you lose your cat or dog, first contact your local police district. Then make sure you talk to neighbors, postal carriers or sanitation workers for leads. Also check out the Lost/Found ads in your local newspaper and put up signs with photos in the neighborhood. In Chicago, pets are impounded in three main locations:

- **Animal Control Center**, 312-744-5000 (will keep lost pets for seven days, then they are placed in the adoption pavilion).
- **Animal Welfare League**, 773-667-0088
- **The Anti-Cruelty Society**, 510 North LaSalle, 312-644-8338, www.anticruelty.org; private, non-profit humane society. Their web site offers a host of information about owning pets in Chicago and the suburbs, from downloading license application forms to municipal regulations for pet owners to checking fees.
- **Tree House** (cats only), 773-784-5488

You can also log on to www.chicagolostpets.org for an extensive list of animal rescue organizations in the Chicagoland area. In the suburbs check with your local animal control for information on animal impounds.

Many who want to adopt a pet head to the **City of Chicago's Commission on Animal Care and Control**, 2741 South Western Avenue, 312-747-1406. Or you can do the initial research in the comfort of you own home through their online catalogue that is updated biweekly, www.petfinder.org/shelters. A dog or cat, spayed or neutered, licensed with all necessary shots, and an AVID Microchip for identification, will cost you $65. You will even get a pet carrier in which to take your new pet home. All rabbits are spayed or neutered and the $25 fee includes some educational tips on care and a rabbit carrier. The **Anti-Cruelty Society**, 510 North LaSalle Street, 312-644-8338, www.anticruelty.org; also offers an adoption service for abandoned pets. The fee is a flat $50 for cats or dogs and includes the necessary shots, a free collar, an ID chip, but not spaying or neutering (though these services are available for an additional fee).

FINDING A VETERINARIAN

If you are moving to Chicago with a pet in tow, you'll want to track down a vet at some point. There are several ways to go about choosing one. Start by asking your friendly neighborhood pet owners or check with your local pet store for a referral. Online, you can go to www.chicagopets.net/clinics animal, which has an extensive list of suburban animal hospitals for you to investigate; in Chicago try http://thecityofchicago.org/veterinarian.

If you are looking for pet insurance two national organizations offer medical coverage for pets: Veterinary Pet Insurance, 800-872-7387 and Pet Assure, a Pet HMO, 888-789-7387. Also, most PetSmart stores are affiliated with a clinic that offers pet health insurance. Contact the store nearest you for details.

Finally, be an advocate of the humane treatment of dogs by reporting any incident of dog fighting that you are aware of. It's illegal in all 50 states, and dog fighting is a felony in Illinois. If you suspect there is a dog fighting event being staged in your area, dial 311. To report one in progress, call 911.

SAFETY AND CRIME

Like all big American cities, Chicago has its share of crime. However, it has seen its crime rate drop in the past decade (since 1991, violent crime in Chicago is down 28%). According to the annual Illinois State Police Report for 2002, Illinois and Chicago reported a decrease in major crimes for the seventh year in a row! There was however, an increase in crime in 58 of the

129 towns that make up suburban Cook County. The remaining 71 communities reported stable rates, decreases or, as in the example of two communities (Palos Park and Golf), no violent crime at all. Despite the recent rise in violent crime in some suburban communities, the average crime rate in Cook County is lower than the crime rate reported in Chicago: 37.2 crimes per 1,000 residents in the suburbs, vs. 68.6 crimes per 1,000 reported in Chicago. That said, there are a few common sense things that a newcomer to the Windy City, especially a newcomer to urban life, should keep in mind:

- Trust your intuition. If something doesn't feel right, go with it. Healthy survival instincts are a good thing.
- When outside, keep your eyes and ears open. Always remaining alert and aware of your surroundings is key to personal safety.
- Don't let a stranger get in your car and don't get in a car with a stranger. Studies show that once you are in a vehicle with a would-be criminal, your chances of survival go way down.
- Don't move into a neighborhood that makes you uncomfortable. Before you take an apartment, you should walk around the neighborhood at different times of the day and evening to see what the area is like.
- Make sure your apartment or home is safe from potential intruders. That means, for example, that if you are on a ground floor or in a garden apartment, you should probably have sturdy bars on your windows. Err on the side of caution when assessing your risk.
- On the 'L,' try to sit in a car with other people.
- Resist the temptation to travel alone or at night through a neighborhood with which you are unfamiliar. Also resist taking shortcuts through alleyways that are unfamiliar.
- If something does happen to you, whether you are in your home or car or on the street, remember that most incidences of crime do not result in loss of life. However, if you feel your life may be in danger, run, scream, fight, whatever it takes, to save your life. In life-threatening situations, being passive may not be the best response.
- Report crime immediately. Whether it's happening to you or not, call 911 when you know of any crime in progress. Note, for non-emergency police questions, call 311 "Chicago's other help line," they can tell you the location of your nearest District or Area police headquarters.

If you are interested in finding out more about a specific neighborhood, go to www.chicago-neighborhoods.net/crime_stats.php. There you will find the latest statistics of reported crimes divided into districts. It is a good source of information because it tells you what kind of crime—vandalism, burglary, rape, murder, etc—is going on in different areas. As mentioned earlier in the book, you can and should try to become acquainted with your neighborhood CAPS (Chicago's Alternative Policing Strategy) organization. Another good source is the Chicago Police Department's web site, www.cityofchicago.org/police. Dial in to learn more about citizen policing (CAPS), neighborhood crime maps, and view a list of scheduled neighborhood meetings.

To file a complaint against an officer, see **Police Complaints** at the end of the next chapter.

OKAY, YOU HAVE GONE DOWN YOUR CHECKLIST: PLACE TO LIVE (check); utility accounts established (check); bank accounts set up (check). Now it's time to fine tune that list. What about house-cleaning services, a place to repair the car, pest control, and mail service? All that and more follows. (Inclusion of a company or organization does not imply endorsement by First Books. Be sure you check references of a company or service before hiring, particularly if they will be coming into your house.)

DOMESTIC SERVICES

HOUSECLEANING SERVICES

You may be a star at your office, or like to boast about your skills in the kitchen, but if you lead a busy life, you may not be able to get to all the messes that come your way. If you are looking for a house cleaning service check with your neighbors or co-workers, the Yellow Pages (under "House Cleaning"), or contact one of the following.

- **Dazzle Cleaning Service**, 773-594-0799
- **Maid to Order**, 312-939-6490
- **Merry Maids**, toll-free, 866-251-8948
- **Polish Cleaning Service**, 773-589-2429

DIAPER SERVICES

If you want an old-fashioned cloth diaper service, good luck. Try the Yellow Pages and/or call **Bottoms Up Wash Diaper Service** in Waukegan, 847-336-0040.

DRY CLEANING DELIVERY

You will be hard pressed to find a suburban dry cleaner that picks up and delivers your laundry and dry cleaning to your door, but it is possible in Chicago. Another option worth exploring if you are afraid you are going to get caught with no clean shirts in the closet is to check with your office's services. Many large corporations, especially those located in the suburbs, have dry cleaners on site. You can drop your dry cleaning off in the morning before getting into the elevator and pick it up on your way home.

- **Bennett Cleaners**, 773-768-9010
- **Griffin Cleaners**, 773-723-8832
- **Press This Cleaners & Laundry**, 773-283-5654

PEST CONTROL

Chicago gained nationwide attention in 1998 with the arrival of the Chinese long-horned beetle. Arriving as stowaways in wooden packing crates, these voracious insects spread through neighborhood maple trees so quickly the City of Chicago was forced to cut down 1,400 trees in order to contain the beetle. All crates from China are now either heated before arrival to the United States to kill any infestation, or they must be made with chemically treated wood. While the Department of Agriculture has been diligent and worked quickly to control the problem, there were still sightings of an occasional beetle as late as July 2002. If you see any signs of a long horned beetle infestation in your area, call the Asian long-horned beetle hotline at 800-641-3934 immediately.

The first cases of West Nile virus hit Chicago in 2001 and the city sprung into action, but by 2002, 100 of the state's 102 counties reported infected birds, horses, and mosquitoes. By the end of 2002, Illinois led the nation with more than 800 human cases of this mosquito-borne illness and 63 deaths. The Public Health Department has been active in trying to eliminate mosquito breeding grounds in and around the Chicagoland area through spraying insecticides, surveillance, and testing of mosquitoes and animals indicating infection. Mild cases of West Nile virus include a slight fever and headache. More acute cases include other symptoms such as high fever, body aches, convulsions, tremors, and in the most severe cases, paralysis and death. If you find a dead animal you suspect has been infected with West Nile virus, contact your county health department: Cook County Health Department, 708-492-2010.

Whether it's bugs, weeds, invading deer, or Canadian geese, if your space is being infringed upon, you may need some outside help. You can search the Yellow Pages under "Exterminators" or try one of the following web sites for more information about pest control:

- **www.doityourself.com**; information on controlling pests in lawns, homes, and garden, including a section on Japanese beetles and deer.
- **www.epa.gov**; the EPA's Pesticide Program has suggestions on how to control pests without the use of chemical pesticides.
- **www.victorpest.com**, the web site of Woodstream Corporation's Victor brand of "least toxic" pest controls. Offers poison-free products as well as useful information about the habits of roaches, fleas, flies, ants, mosquitoes, rats, and mice.

MAIL

JUNK MAIL

Junk mail will surely follow you to your new locale. In order to curtail this kind of unwanted mail we suggest you send a written note, including name and address, asking to be purged from the Direct Marketing Association's list (Direct Marketing Association's Mail Preference Service, P.O. Box 9008, Farmingdale, NY 11735). Some catalogue companies will need to be contacted directly with a purge request. For junk e-mail, you may also go to their web site, www.dmaconsumers.org/opoutform, and request an opt-out service for your e-mail address. The service will accept three non-business e-mail addresses at a time. This might reduce the amount of e-mail you receive from national e-mail lists. Another option is to call the "opt-out" line at 888-567-8688, and request that the main credit bureaus not release your name and address to interested marketing companies. (**Curb phone solicitations** by going to the government's do not call registry, www.donotcall.gov, and registering your phone number—or call 800-382-1222, TTY 866-290-4236.)

MAIL DELIVERY/SERVICE

Maybe you've heard, maybe you haven't: Chicago has a terrible reputation when it comes to delivering mail. In the past, thousands of undelivered pieces of mail were discovered in the apartments and houses of carriers and in garbage dumpsters. A federal task force resulted in important management changes, and service has improved (though cynics point out it hardly could have gotten worse). At times you will find letters mailed in the city take longer to arrive in a neighboring town than to travel to the East Coast! If you experience a problem with your postal service, we suggest you contact the **USPS Office of Consumer Affairs** by calling 800-275-8777. Also use this number for postal rates, services, and zip codes, or check their web site at www.usps.com. If a chat with the Consumer Affairs Office at the post office doesn't resolve your problem, contact your congress person; he/she may be able to help.

If you're in between addresses but still need a place to get your mail, there are dozens of businesses that will rent you a mail-box, have your mail forwarded, and accept packages for you. You can use the ones listed below to help you start your search, or check with your local post office.

- **C& L One Stop Postal and Parcel Service**, 1448 East 52nd Street, 773-667-9088
- **Mail Center of Chicago**, 28 East Jackson, 312-922-1788
- **Mailbox Plus**, 2154 West Addison Street, 773-477-5600
- **UPS Stores** (formerly **Mail Boxes, Etc.**): 60 East Chestnut, 312-787-7277; 910 West Van Buren Street, 312-226-3333; 4514 North Lincoln Avenue, 776-784-4487. Check the Yellow Pages for more listings.

For walk-in post office customers, the old USPS "central facility" downtown has been replaced by the **Cardiss Collins Postal Store**, 433 West Harrison Street, 312-983-8182, open 24/7 (except for postal holidays and every third Saturday p.m./Sunday a.m. for an audit). Other US postal facilities include:

- **Haymarket**, 168 North Clinton Street, 312-906-8557; open weekdays: 8 a.m. to 5 p.m.
- **Nancy B**. **Jefferson**, Midwest Station, 116 South Western Avenue, 312-243-2560; open weekdays, 8 a.m. to 5 p.m., Saturday 8 a.m. to 1 p.m.
- **Pilsen**, 1859 South Ashland Avenue, 312-733-4750; open weekdays, weekdays, 8 a.m. to 5 p.m., Saturday 8 a.m. to 1 p.m.
- **Wacker Drive Postal Store**, Sears Tower, 233 South Wacker Drive, lower level one, 312-876-1024; open weekdays, 7:30 a.m. to 5 p.m.

For zip code information, see the **Chicago Zip Codes & Area Codes map** at the back of this book or go to www.usps.com.

SHIPPING SERVICES

For conventional packages, the nationwide parcel services are all familiar names:

- **Airborne Express**, 800-247-2676, www.airborne.com
- **DHL Worldwide Express**, 800-225-5345, www.dhl-usa.com
- **FedEx**, 800-463-3339, www.fedex.com (for ground, express or air freight information)
- **Mail-Sort** (Northbrook), 847-291-4900

- **Packaging Store**, 312-751-1640, www.ilpackagingstore.com
- **Pitney Bowes**, 800-811-1920
- **United Parcel Service**, 800-742-5877, www.ups.com
- **US Postal Service Express Mail**, www.usps.com

AUTOMOBILES

REPAIR

Finding a mechanic you can trust is often a difficult process. The best way to find a shop is to ask around for a referral—co-workers, neighbors, friends. Short of a personal endorsement, you can try a dealer; generally they are reliable and have the right equipment to fix your type of car, though they are usually more expensive than a general repair shop. Contact the Better Business Bureau of Chicago and Northern Illinois, 312-832-0500, about a prospective garage to see if any complaints have been filed against it.

On the lighter side of automobile ownership tune in to "Car Talk" on Saturdays, at 9 a.m., on 91.5 WBEZ FM radio, National Public Radio.

POTHOLES AND WINTERIZING YOUR CAR

Freezing winters followed by spring thaws and the addition of continual heavy truck traffic wreak havoc on area streets. While you will spot repair crews at nearly every block, the process of patching potholes is an on-going battle. If your car has sustained damage due to the potholes on Chicago's city streets, you may be eligible for some reimbursement from the city for repairs. If you think you have a case, take photographs, get at least two estimates for the repair work, and file a report with the City Clerk's office. Download the report form from www.chicityclerk.com/claims.

In general, you should make sure your car's suspension and tires are in good shape, and around Halloween you should also "winterize" your vehicle. This involves checking and replacing all fluids including antifreeze and making sure the car's heater is in good condition. The *Chicago Sun-Times* publishes a guide to preparing your car for the season every year. Call 312-321-3000 to obtain a copy of the most recent supplement. And of course, your owner's manual is a great source too.

If you plan on buying a new car, many residents advise waiting until after the cruel winter, which can put beyond normal wear and tear on even the best made vehicle. Many opt to never buy new, not while driving the streets of Chicago. If potholes and salt from the winter streets don't catch up to your car, a grocery cart or a carelessly opened car door at the Jewel parking lot surely will.

It's always a good idea to investigate the local automobile club that offers its members emergency road service. Ask your friends and co-workers for the organization they use or call AAA.

- **AAA Chicago Motor Club**, www.autoclubgroup.com, Chicago office: 312-372-1826

CONSUMER PROTECTION—RIP-OFF RECOURSE

Got a beef with a merchant or company? There are a number of agencies that monitor consumer related businesses and will take action when necessary. It goes without saying that the best defense against fraud and consumer victimization is to read the fine print, including all the terms and exclusions in whatever contract you sign; save all receipts and canceled checks; get the name of telephone sales and service people with whom you deal; and check a contractor's license number with the Department of Consumer Affairs for complaints. But at times, despite your best efforts, you still may fall victim to unfair practices. A dry cleaner returns your blue suit, but now it's purple and he shrugs. A shop refuses to provide a refund, as promised, on an expensive gift that didn't suit your mother. After $898 in repairs to your automobile's engine, the car now vibrates wildly, and the mechanic claims innocence. Negotiations, documents in hand, fail. You're angry, and embarrassed because you've been had. There *is* something you can do.

- **Better Business Bureau of Chicago and Northern Illinois**: 312-832-0500; takes complaints by consumers about area businesses.
- **Chicago Bar Association**, Consumer Law Program, 312-554-2000, www.chicagobar.org
- **City of Chicago, Department of Consumer Services**, 312-744-9400, TTY 312-744-9385, complaint hotline, 312-744-9400, www.cityofchicago.org/consumerservices/index/html
- **The Consumer Action Web Site**: www.pueblo.gsa.gov/crh/state the online handbook provides a listing of the government agencies dealing with consumer complaints.
- **Illinois Attorney General, Consumer Fraud Division**, 312-814-3580, www.ag.state.il.us; maintains a public inquiry unit that reviews and mediates consumer complaints.
- **Illinois Attorney General Consumer Protection Division**, 800-243-0618, TTY 877-844-5461; Chicago Office, 312-814-3000, TTY 312-814-3374; mediation services between a business and a consumer.
- **Illinois Department of Professional Regulation**, 312-814-4500, www.dpr.state.il.us, the place to go when your beef is with a professional licensed by the state of Illinois (architects, barbers, chiropractors, cosmetologists, dentists, nurses, security companies, veterinarians, etc).

- **State of Illinois/Department of Insurance**, 312-814-2427; is a state agency that investigates insurance complaints.
- **www.consumeraffairs.com**

For consumer protection information regarding utilities see **Consumer Protection—Utility Complaints** in the **Getting Settled** chapter. For landlord/tenant issues go to **Finding a Place to Live**.

LEGAL MEDIATION/REFERRAL PROGRAMS

LOW COST/FREE

- **AIDS Legal Council of Chicago**, 188 West Randolph Street, Suite 2400, Chicago, 312-427-8990
- **Chicago Kent College Of Law Legal Clinic**, 565 West Adams, Suite 600, 312-906-5050; employment, criminal, tax, and health law only.
- **Center for Conflict Resolution**, 200 North Michigan Avenue, 312-372-6420; mediation only.
- **Chicago Lawyers Committee for Civil Rights Under the Law**, 100 North LaSalle, Suite 600, 312-630-9744; class actions, civil rights, employment, housing and lending.
- **Chicago Legal Clinic**: 2938 East 91st Street (South), 773-731-1762; 1914 South Ashland (Pilsen), 312-226-2669; 118 North Central Street (Austin), 773-854-1610; 205 West Monroe, 312-726-2938
- **Chicago Volunteer Legal Services Foundation, Inc.**, 100 North LaSalle, Suite 900, 312-332-1624; all issues except criminal, civil rights, and environmental.
- **Community Economic Development Law Project**, 188 West Randolph, Suite 2103, 312-939-3638; contract, employment, tax, real estate, and environmental only.
- **DePaul Legal Law Clinic**, 25 East Jackson Blvd., Suite 950, 312-362-8294; only Family Law and domestic violence.
- **Evanston Community Defender Office**, 828 Davis Street, Evanston, 847-492-1410; criminal, juvenile, probate, and public aid only.
- **Lawyers for the Creative Arts**, 213 West Institute Place Suite 411, 312-944-2787; artists, art organizations, and entertainers only. **Lawyers Committee for Better Housing**, 220 South State Street, Suite 1700, 312-347-7600; eviction, sexual harassment/discrimination regarding housing, landlord retaliation only.
- **Legal Aid Bureau of Metropolitan Family Services**, 14 East Jackson 15th floor, 312-986-4200, TDD 312-986-4237; family law only.
- **Legal Assistance Foundation of Metropolitan Chicago**; all issues except class action, criminal, environmental, real estate, probate and tax. **General Intake Offices**: 111 West Jackson, 312-341-1070, TDD

312-431-1206; 828 Davis Street (Evanston), Suite 201, 847-475-3703, TDD 847-475-5580

- **Pro Bono Advocates**, 28 North Clark Street, Suite 630, 312-827-2420; orders of protection for domestic violence cases.

LEGAL ASSISTANCE FOR THE ELDERLY

- **City of Chicago, Department on Aging**, 312-744-4016; investigates elder abuse and nursing home problems.
- **Illinois Attorney General**, advocacy division/consumer protection, 217-782-1090, 800-243-0618, TTY 217-785-2771, www.ag.state.il.us (Chicago office: 312-814-3000, TTY 312-814-3374)
- **Illinois Department on Aging**, 800-252-8966 (senior help line), www.state.il.us/aging

SOCIAL SECURITY

If you are a US citizen, no doubt you already have a social security card, and can skip this section. But for those who are not, this might be new information. Non-citizens who are working or studying here need will a Social Security Number. This can be done through the mail by first calling 800-772-1213 for the necessary forms. Or go online to www.ssa.gov. You can also visit the nearest Social Security office, no appointment necessary.

Things to bring to the Social Security Office:
- A certified birth certificate (with its raised stamp, not a copy)
- A translation of your birth certificate if it was not originally printed in English.
- Two other pieces of identification, which can be a passport, driver's license, school or government ID, health insurance card, military records, or an insurance policy with your name on it.

A Social Security employee will complete the application, and you should receive a card with your number within several weeks. Non-citizens will need a birth certificate and/or a passport and a green card or student documentation. It will most likely take more than a month to receive a card.

If you already have a number but have lost your card, call the number above to apply for a new card.

SERVICES FOR THE DISABLED

The City of Chicago would like all its new residents, physically challenged or not, to experience the best Chicago has to offer. Below is a mix of services that you may want to investigate, sign up for, or just know about, in order to make your transition to Chicago easier.

- **Mayor's Office for People with Disabilities (MOPD)**, 312-744-6673, TTY 312-744-7833, is an excellent resource offering services and programs to Chicagoans with disabilities. MOPD provides case management services, employment services, skills training, information on how to find accessible housing, emergency home-delivered meals, and a host of other services for the disabled. They even have a pamphlet for business owners, which details the tax-incentives available for making facilities accessible to people with disabilities. For a complete list of services, call, or write them at City Hall, 121 North LaSalle Street, Room 1104, 60602.

- **Chicago Lighthouse**, 1850 West Roosevelt Road, 312-666-1331, TTY 312-666-8874, as well as the **Guild for the Blind**, 180 North Michigan Avenue #1700, 312-236-8569, provides employment and independent living services for the blind and visually impaired. Check the Yellow pages under "Disabled Persons" for more resources.

Free or low cost **legal services for the disabled** include:
- **Center for Disability & Elder Law**, 710 North Lake Shore Drive, 3rd floor, 312-908-4463, TTD 312-908-8705; all issues for disabled clients except criminal, domestic relations, environmental, immigration, and tax.
- **City of Chicago Mayor's Office for People With Disabilities**, 312-744-6673
- **Illinois Attorney General's Office**, 800-382-3000, www.ag.state.il.us
- **Equip for Equality, Inc.**, 20 North Michigan Avenue, Suite 300, 312-341-0022, 800-537-2632, TTY 800-610-2779, www.equipforequality.org; non-profit organization, operates the federally mandated Protection & Advocacy System for Illinois. Offers information on disability resources, services, rights, and advocacy.
- **Guardianship and Advocacy Commission**, 160 North LaSalle, 312-793-5900, TTY 866-333-3362

GETTING AROUND

- **CTA Customer Service**: many CTA 'L' stations are equipped with elevators. Call the RTA customer service center at 312-836-7000 for a list of handicap accessible train stations. Most buses are equipped to handle wheelchairs. For more information about special services, contact the CTA at 312-432-7025, TTY 888-282-8891.

COMMUNICATION

- **Illinois Telecommunications Access Corp.**, (**ITAC**), provides Illinois Relay Service, www.illinoisrelay711.com, and conducts a free TTY program (a teletypewriter allows those who cannot communicate through a conventional telephone the ability to do so with ease) for Illinois residents who are hard of hearing, deaf, or speech impaired. ITAC is governed by the Consumer Advisory Council and monitored by the Illinois Commerce Commission. Other agencies (see below) also provide free TTY equipment. In order to be eligible for a free TTY you must be an Illinois resident, your disability must be certified by a licensed audiologist, physician or speech pathologist, or by a certified DHS/ORS counselor. The last requirement: you must have working telephone service at the address you provide on your application. Request an application through the ITAC web site: www.itactty.org; or you may write to: ITAC, 3001 Montvale Drive, Suite D, Springfield, IL 62704. Or call 800-841-6167 (voice/TTY). To learn how to communicate with a person using TTY while you are using a conventional telephone, log on to www.illinois relay711.com.

- **Illinois Relay Center** enables hearing/speech-impaired TTY callers to call individuals or businesses who do not have TTY equipment. Service is 24/7. Calls are confidential and billed at regular phone rates. Call TTY: 800-526-0844 or voice: 800-526-0857.
- **TechConnect** is a state funded project whose mandate is to help the physically challenged obtain the proper devices (communication, daily living, etc.), and funding to pay for those devices. Contact them at 800-852-5110 (voice/TTY); 217-522-7985 voice; 217-522-9966 TTY, for more information. Or visit www.iltech.org.
- **Chicago Public Library** provides services for the hard of hearing and visually impaired. If you need a sign reader for a special event hosted by the library, please provide the library with 10 business-days' notice. Contact the CPL at 312-747-4252, TTY 312-747-4066. Headphones for special events, programs in the auditorium, or Video Theater are available by contacting the Library's Marketing Department at 312-747-4130 or the TTY Administrative Telephone service: 312-747-4066. A talking book center, computers with enlarged monitors, and power Braille catalogs are available on the 5th floor of the Harold Washington Library.
- **Chicago Hearing Society**, 2001 North Clybourn, teaches young children sign language, offers assistance in obtaining hearing aids, and assists in establishing a TTY in home: 773-248-9121 or 773-248-9174. For interpreter services contact the society at 773-248-9173.

ADDITIONAL RESOURCES

Following is a variety of resources, both governmental and non-profit, that may be of use to those with special needs. Their services include advocacy, referrals, training, assistance towards independent living, family resources, housing assistance and information. Those using TTY phones may receive operator and directory assistance by calling 800-855-1155. For a copy of the **US Government TTY Directory**, visit www.gsa.gov/frs, or write to: Federal Citizen Information Center, Department TTY, Pueblo, CO 81009, phone, 877-387-2001.

- **DuPage County Center for Independent Living**, 739 Roosevelt Road, Building 8, Suite 109, Glen Ellyn, 630-469-2300 (voice and TTY)
- **Family Resource Center on Disabilities**, 312-939-3513, TTY 312-939-3519, www.frcd.org
- **Federal Citizen Information Center**, 800-FED-INFO, TTY 800-326-2996, www.firstgov.gov; for questions about federal agencies, programs, benefits, or services. Staff will answer your question or get you to someone who can: 9 a.m. to 8 p.m., Monday-Friday. Recordings of frequently requested information available around the clock.
- **National Library Service for the Blind and Physically Handicapped**, 800-424-8567, www.lcweb.loc.gov/nls

GAY AND LESBIAN LIFE

Chicago is a good place to live if you're gay or lesbian. It's determinedly tolerant, from inclusive governmental policies, to friendly gay and/or lesbian neighborhood enclaves, to the annual gay pride celebration that takes place each June. In Cook County are anti-bias statutes that protect gays and lesbians from housing and workplace discrimination. Progressive suburb Oak Park was the first municipality in Illinois to offer domestic partner benefits to city employees (Chicago followed suit in 1996). Recently, Chicagoans elected the first openly gay Illinois State Representative. In June 2003, the Cook County Board agreed to establish a domestic partnership registry as a recordplace for gay and lesbian couples. While the registry does not provide any legal benefits to gay or lesbian couples, it does allow official recognition and validates same sex partnerships. Registration costs $30. For more information check with the Office of County Clerk at www.cookctyclerk.com or call 312-603-6566.

If you're looking for gay nightlife, the answer is easy. While it may not have the reputation of New York's Greenwich Village or San Francisco's Castro, Boystown in Wrigleyville/Lakeview is out and proud. The neighborhood, which is centered on Halsted Street between Belmont Avenue and Irving Park Road, is the backbone of gay Chicago. Also check Logan Square, west of Wrigleyville/Lakeview. But the boys don't have all the fun. Andersonville, just two miles to the north along Clark Street, is a preferred nesting ground for the city's lesbian community.

The weekly **Windy City Times**, 1115 West Belmont Avenue, 2D, 773-871-7610, www.windycitymediagroup.com, is an excellent resource for finding out what is happening in the gay, lesbian, bisexual, and transgender (GLBT) community; free and available at coffeehouses, bookstores, and music stores throughout Chicago. Also look for the **Pink Pages**, the GLBT version of the Yellow Pages, www.pinkpages-usa.com.

The **Gerber/Hart Library**, 1127 West Granville Avenue, phone 773-381-8030, is a private, community-supported library and archive, open to the public and devoted exclusively to gay and lesbian publications and concerns. It offers discussion groups, photography and archival displays, a visiting author series and "a free cup of coffee." Closed Mondays and Tuesdays. (See **Literary Life** in the **Cultural Life** chapter for more information.)

Join the hordes of Chicagoans—gay, straight, and everything in between—for the **Gay & Lesbian Pride Parade,** which takes place at the end of June. It starts at the corner of Halsted and Belmont. Everyone dresses: up, down, in drag, in leather, chests bared, in costume—and a great time is had by all. Check the *Windy City Times* for the exact day and times. Other resources geared toward gay life include:

- **Area hospitals and medical centers** in Chicago's gay and lesbian communities (Wrigleyville and Edgewater) include: NorthStar Medical Center, 2835 North Sheffield, 773-296-2400; Northwestern Memorial Physicians Group, 3245 North Halsted, 312-926-3627, www.nmpg. com; Brasch Medical Center, 3260 North Clark; Weiss Memorial Hospital, 4646 North Marine Drive, 773-878-8700; St. Joseph Hospital and Health Care Center, 2900 North Lake Shore Drive, 773-665-3000; Illinois Masonic Medical Center, 836 West Wellington Avenue, 773 975-1600; Thorek Hospital & Medical Center, 850 West Irving Park Road, 773-525-6780.
- **AWARE Talk Radio**, 312-541-8255, and **Windy City Radio** are programs geared towards the GLBT community. Aired on WCKG-FM, 105.9, Sundays from 10:30 p.m. to midnight. Visit www.windycityvoices.com, or www.awaretalkradio.org for more program information.
- **Fairy Gardeners' Guild**, 773-237-5981, www.fairygardeners.org; lesbigay gardening group, citywide and in the suburbs.
- **Gay and Lesbian Chamber of Commerce**, 773-303-0167
- **PinkAgenda.com**, clearinghouse of information for Chicago's GLBT community.
- **Windy City Gay Chorus/Unison: Windy City Lesbian & Gay Singers**, www.windycitysings.org, 773-404-9242

POLICE COMPLAINTS

If you feel you were abused or mistreated by a Chicago police officer, and you want justice, your first response should probably be to file a complaint with the city. Try the Mayor's office by dialing 311 or go online to www.cityofchicago.org. You can also call the Chicago Police Department directly at 312-746-6000 or the Police Superintendent's "hotline" at 312-939-5555, and there's the office of the Inspector General at 773-478-7799 established to "detect and prevent misconduct ... " Don't hold your breath, though. According to one report, few of the complaints and allegations of police misconduct filed with the city result in any disciplinary action.

Fortunately, you can seek redress in other ways. First of all, consider contacting the media (see **Broadcast and Print Media** in the **Getting Settled** chapter for a list); *The Chicago Reporter*, in particular has a long history of reporting on abuse by the Chicago Police Department. They can be found at 332 South Michigan Avenue, Suite 500, 312-427-4830, and on the web at www.chicagoreporter.com.

Other organizations to try:

- **American Civil Liberties Union**, www.aclu-il.org
- **Chicago Bar Association**, 312-554-2000, www.chicagobar.org
- **Cook County State's Attorney**, 312-341-2743 or 773-869-7200, www.statesattorney.org
- **State of Illinois, Attorney General**, 312-814-3000, www.ag.state.il.us
- **US Department of Justice**, 202-353-1555, www.usdoj.gov

Law school clinics might be interested to know about what happened to you. See the **Higher Education** chapter of this book for a list of institutions of higher learning.

If all else fails, and you have the stomach and the money, you can hire an attorney and seek justice the American way: file a lawsuit.

W HEN MOVING TO A NEW AREA, ONE OF THE MOST IMPORTANT tasks parents face is finding good childcare and/or schools for their children. The results of this search can be a deciding factor in, among other things, choosing a community in which to purchase a home. Key factors to consider when looking for a daycare center or school are affordability, convenience, safety, and, most importantly, the quality of care and instruction. *Please note: listing in this book is merely informational and is **not** an endorsement.*

CHILDCARE

First **daycare**. In Illinois, childcare centers are arranged in the following types:
- **Childcare Homes** are small facilities (in Illinois, eight or fewer children) which are run out of the house of the provider. The care here is more individualized and the setting more familiar than the larger centers, and the prices tend to be lower. Though some may advertise in neighborhood papers, many get their business through word of mouth; ask around your neighborhood or at work, or call your area childcare resource and referral agency. Childcare resource and referral agencies typically recruit potential day care home providers, and provide technical support and assistance to them (both in terms of start-up, and in maintaining a quality program).
- **Group Childcare Homes** are also run out of the house of the provider, but the number of children allowed is greater (up to twelve). These homes usually employ one or more assistants, along with the operator, to care for the children.
- **Childcare Centers** are what most people think of when they think "daycare." These are larger, more school-like facilities, which tend to be

around much longer, though the staff may change. Because of the number of employees and the higher overhead required to operate a separate building, the prices are higher than daycare homes. Frequently there are waiting lists to get in, especially for the infant and toddler age groups. Many centers have a capacity in the range of 50 children, although some are larger, with space for around 100 children, or, in a few instances, 200 children.

- **License Exempt Childcare** facilities are either too small (three children or fewer) to be regulated or are operated by non-profit organizations such as churches.
- **Non-Traditional Options,** such as religious institutions, neighborhood churches and synagogues, often provide good care at a reasonable price, and you do not necessarily have to be a member. Universities, too, may offer quality pre-school with fees on a sliding scale for the children of parents who are attending classes. Chicago Public Schools now offer some fee-based all day preschool programs in several neighborhood schools. Contact CPS for more information (see below under **Schools**). Parent Networks, which work like co-ops offer great options for those in need of part-time childcare. Or, along the same lines, trading childcare time with friends can be a great economical way to be a part-time caregiver while still working. Finally, of course, some parents use the informal option of care from relatives, most often a grandparent.

In Illinois, the state agency responsible for licensing and regulation of childcare centers and daycare family homes is the **Department of Children and Family Services** (**DCFS**), a state agency whose primary function is investigating possible child abuse, child abuse prevention through parenting classes, family counseling, foster care, and adoption services. The Department of Children and Family Services also publishes two useful pamphlets: "A Message to Parents of Children in Day Care Centers," and "Child Care Choices." Both outline DCFS regulations regarding child-staff ratio, group size, and caregiver qualifications, as well as checklists of quality factors to look for in childcare programs, and the phone number of the Child Abuse Hotline. The "Child Care Choices" pamphlet also provides a list of Child Care Resource and Referral Agencies statewide (see below), and information on subsidized day care: eligibility standards, application procedures, and availability. For more about services in your area call one of the **Greater Chicago Area DCFS Offices**: City of Chicago, 312-808-5060; Aurora, 630-844-8400; Aurora Region, 630-801-3400; Glen Ellyn, 630-790-6800; Joliet, 815-730-4000; Elgin, 847-888-7620, Round Lake Beach, 847-546-0772 and 847-249-7800; Woodstock, 815-338-1068; Tinley Park, 708-633-5300. Or call their daycare information hotline at 877-746-0829.

Child Care Resource and Referral Agencies offer a phone referral service to parents, usually for a small fee, where they can discuss their childcare needs with them and receive a list of facilities meeting their criteria, along with helpful information on choosing childcare. Some companies, particularly large employers, may have a contract with their local Child Care Resource and Referral Agency to provide referrals to employees in need of this service. **Childcare Resource and Referral Agencies** include:

- **YWCA of Metro Chicago** (DuPage and Kane counties), 630-790-8137
- **United Way of Will County**, 800-552-5526
- **Cook County, Day Care Action Council**, 773-769-8000

For parents who want a comprehensive list of childcare centers or daycare family homes in the greater Chicago area, they can be ordered by mail from the State of Illinois (Office of Policy, 406 East Monroe Street, Station 65-D, Springfield IL 62701, 217-524-1983). The cost for the childcare center list is $7, and $16 for the list of family daycare homes.

State Licensing Standards are as follows:

- **Staff/Child Ratios** for childcare centers: 4:1 (infants to 15 months); 5:1 (toddlers to 2 years); 8:1 (2 years); 10:1 (3-4 years); 20:1 (5 years and up).
- **Maximum Group Size** for childcare centers: 12 (infants to 15 months); 15 (toddlers to 2 years); 16 (2 years); 20 (3-4 years, 5 years and kindergarten); 30 (school-age).
- **Teacher Qualifications** for childcare centers: directors must be at least 21 years of age with two years of college including 18 semester hours of child development or equivalent experience and credentials.
- **Childcare workers (lead teachers)** must be at least 19 years of age with two years of college including six hours of child development or equivalent experience and credentials. **Teacher assistants** or **aides** must have a high school diploma or equivalent and work under the direct supervision of a teacher.
- **Training requirements**: beyond the above-mentioned qualifications, 15 hours of in-service training each year for each staff member is required. A staff member trained in first aid, CPR, and the Heimlich maneuver must be on the premises at all times.

ONLINE RESOURCES—DAYCARE

There are several helpful online agencies and organizations that can assist with the details of finding quality childcare, a good school, etc. in communities across the United States. **Care Guide**, www.careguide.com, offers assistance to those needing childcare or eldercare. This free service provides pertinent care-related news articles and advice. The **National Child Care**

Information Center's site, www.nccic.org, provides links to other child-care sites on the web. **Child Care Aware**, 800-424-2246, provides free referrals to childcare agencies in your community. The **National Parent Information Network**, sponsored by the ERIC Clearinghouse for Elementary and Early Childhood Education, offers information on parent-ing, child development, family life, and parent-education partnerships. Call them at 800-583-4135 or go to www.npin.org. And locally, the "**Chicago Area Town Profiles**" web site, www.northstarnet.org/regional/educonn, provides basic information, including name, address, phone number, ages, hours, and fees for child care centers and preschools across the region. The web site is maintained by **ParentLink Information Services**, which can be reached at 630-499-5810.

NANNIES

Hiring a nanny is probably the most expensive daycare option, with a monthly cost of $1,400 to $2,000+ for a full-time or live-in, but if the right person is found this can be a rewarding experience for everyone involved. A number of nanny agencies exist in the Chicago area (some of which also provide other domestic services such as eldercare and housekeeping). Likely services when using an agency include background checks on crimi-nal and driving records and credit information. Be sure the nanny agency you use is licensed and bonded. Also, there are several childcare consul-tants locally who can assist families with background checks, tax issues, and other matters related to employing a nanny. If you prefer to have private screenings done of prospective nannies, **Infotrack Information Services, Inc.**, 111 Deerlake Road, Deerfield, IL 60015, 847-808-9990, 800-275-5594, is a private investigative company that conducts back-ground investigations for pre-employment screening. They do a driving record, criminal record, and social security check for $75.

   Nanny services around Chicago include:

- **A+ Domestic**, 7703 West Belmont Avenue, Suite B, Elmwood Park IL 60707, 708-456-3143, www.apluschildcare.com
- **American Registry for Nurses & Sitters, Inc.**, 800-240-1820, www.american-registry.com
- **Better Homecare Service**, 630-650-1855
- **Childminders Inc.**, 4350 Oakton Street, Suite 204, Skokie, IL 60076, 847-673-8998, www.childmindersinc.com
- **Family Perfect Care, Inc.**, 773-545-5352
- **Gold Coast Domestic Employment Agency**, 3257 North Sheffield, Chicago IL 60657, 773-525-4273
- **Lakeview Domestic Agency, Inc.**, 3166 North Lincoln, Suite 214, Chicago, IL, 773-404-8452

- **Loretta's LTD**, 773-283-9927, 773-283-9933
- **Margaret's Employment Agency**, 708-403-8707 (childcare and elder care)
- **Midwest Nannies, LTD**, P.O. Box 103, St. Charles, IL 60174, 630-513-9034, www.midwestnanny.com
- **Nanny Sitters**, 200 West Higgins Road, Suite 233, Schaumburg, IL 60195, 847-885-1700, www.nannysittersinc.com
- **Nurture Network, Inc.**, 773-561-4610
- **Sandy's Nannies & More, Inc.**, 847-679-7766, www.sandysnannies.com
- **TeacherCare**, 847-240-2900, 630-545-CARE, 312-214-6411, www.teachercare.com
- **Teri A. Burgess, Childcare Specialist**, 319 Harding Avenue Libertyville, IL 60048, 847-918-8111
- **Traycee Nannies**, 448 Sheridan Road, Highwood, IL 60040, 847-432-6111, www.traycee.com
- **Village Nannies (Wilmette)**, 847-256-6162

The **Northside Parents Network**, 1218 West Addison, Chicago, IL 60613, 312-409-2233, www.northsideparents.org, offers a new "nanny-share" program. This program is predominantly for member families who have hired a nanny independently (not through an agency), for, perhaps three days a week, and will "share" the nanny with another family for the other two days. There are no fees involved.

Eisenberg Associates, 800-777-5765, www.eisenbergassociates.com, offers health insurance and other fringe benefits for nannies.

NANNY TAXES

For those hiring a nanny directly (not using a nanny agency) there are certain taxes that will need to be paid, specifically social security and Medicare, and possibly unemployment. For help with such issues check the Nanitax web site, www.4nannytaxes.com, 800-NANITAX, provider of household payroll and employment tax preparation services, or The Nanny Tax Company, 312-377-7770, www.nannytaxprep.com. Or check the IRS's household employer page, www.irs.gov/individuals/household, which discusses taxes for household employees (topic 756).

AU PAIRS

The US Information Agency oversees and approves the organizations that offer this service. Younger women (between 18 to 25) provide a year of in-home childcare and light housekeeping in exchange for airfare, room and board, and a small stipend ($110 to $120 per week). The program is certainly valuable for the cultural exchange that goes on between the host family and the (usually European) au pair. The downside is that the program only lasts one year and the au pairs don't have the life or work experience of a career nanny. Any of the following national agencies will connect you with a local coordinator who will match up your family with the right au pair.

- **Au Pair Homestay**, 800-479-0907
- **Au Pair in America**, 800-928-7247 www.aupairinamerica.com/
- **Au Pair International**, 800-654-2051
- **Au Pair USA**, 800-287-2477 www.interexchange.org
- **EF Au Pair**, 800-333-6056, www.efaupair.org

BABY-SITTING

References from co-workers/friends is usually the best way to go when looking for a competent and reliable baby-sitter. The average range for babysitters is $8 to $10/hour. Many park districts offer babysitting classes to children ages 12 and up, and may be a source of referrals. Other organizations that will assist with locating a baby-sitter are nanny services, and college job referral services, sometimes called the campus employment office. The **Parent and Child Education Society (PACES)**, headquartered at 1920 South Highland Avenue, Suite 300, in Lombard, IL 60148, 630-916-3190, www.pacesmoms.org, and with chapters across the Chicago area, includes babysitting co-ops among its programs and services. The Northside Parents Network (see above), 312-409-2233, also runs a babysitting co-op.

CHILD SAFETY

There are national, as well as local resources available for parents looking to make their child's new environment safer. The Board of Health, 312-747-9875, www.ci.chi.il.us/Health, provides safety pamphlets, especially with regard to lead paint in older homes. Local hospitals host emergency training classes (infant and child CPR). Local companies offering home safety inspections and products include **A & H Child Proofers** in Vernon Hills, IL, 847-680-1924, and **Safety Matters**, 478 Barberry Road, Highland Park, IL 60035, 800-972-3306, www.safetymatters.com. The local SAFE KIDS chapter, a national organization dedicated solely to preventing accidental injuries to children, is **SAFE KIDS Chicagoland**, 5841 South Maryland Avenue, Chicago, 773-702-0714, www.uchospitals. edu/community/safe-kids. The University of Chicago Children's Hospital is the coalition leader for the Chicago area. It teaches children and caregivers about bicycle helmets, child safety seats and seat belts, fire and burn prevention, and other ways to keep children safe from injury. A safety seat inspection site is at the University of Chicago's Children's Hospital 5839 South Maryland Avenue MC-1056, 773-702-7032. Or you can contact the Chicago Department of Public Health's Health Protection Division, 312-864-2016, which, for a small fee, provides infant and toddler seats and installation instruction to residents through its neighborhood health centers.

GENERAL RESOURCES

- **Child Care Connections** offers a 280-page spiral bound book with detailed listings of nearly 1,000 childcare centers and preschool programs in the greater Chicago area. Available for $24.95 from ParentLink Information Services, 1674 Cumberland, Aurora, IL 60504, 630-499-5810.
- The **Northside Parents Network**, 1218 West Addison, Chicago, IL 60613, 312-409-2233, www.northsideparents.org, is a group of around 650 parents that offers babysitting co-ops, playgroups, a new moms group, a "nanny-share" program (see above), and parenting advice. They put out a newsletter as well as an excellent information booklet that profiles local schools (both public and private).
- **Parent and Child Education Society (PACES)**, 1920 South Highland Avenue, Suite 300, Lombard, IL 60148, 630-916-3190, www.pacesmoms.org, has chapters throughout the Chicago area; offers a variety of programs, seminars, publications, and services such as babysitting co-ops. Memberships are available, though their meetings and many of their events and programs are available to the public.
- *Chicago Parent* magazine (and *Valley Kids*, its counterpart in the farwest suburbs along the Fox River); published monthly, the magazine contains articles on child- and family-related issues, a directory of events across the area, and special sections or separate publications (published annually at various times of the year) including *Chicago Baby, Going Places, Healthy Child, Healthy Woman, Camp Guide,* and *School Guide. Chicago Parent* is available free of charge at libraries, park districts, and some childcare centers, retail stores, and doctors' offices throughout the area. Subscriptions are also available, call 708-386-5555. *Chicago Parent* is online at www.chicagoparent.com.

SCHOOLS

There are approximately 2,000 public and private schools in the greater Chicago area. To check out the range of religious and secular private schools, you will need a guidebook or plenty of time to surf the web, but even enrolling your children in public school might warrant some scouting beyond your neighborhood school. The public school systems in the City of Chicago, and in a few suburban districts, offer a growing range of choices, with the proliferation of magnet programs and public charter schools.

SCHOOL RESOURCES

Before you begin your search, you might want to first collect as much print-ed information as possible. Begin with the following resources:

- **"School District Reports"** (school district information including cur-riculum and programs and test score data), and **"School's In—Chicago"** (a 160-page book with detailed listings of private and parochial schools in the greater Chicago area, price $16.55); both are available from ParentLink Information Services, 1674 Cumberland, Aurora, IL 60504, 630-499-5810.
- **Chicago High Schools**; a ranking of 235 public and private schools in Chicago and suburbs on 15 to 20 criteria, including class size, gradua-tion rate, average years of teacher experience, and test scores. Published by *Chicago Magazine*: call 312-222-8999 to order; the cost is $6.45.
- **A Guide to Chicago-area Independent Schools**: online guide, www.independentschools.net, containing descriptions of about 30 member schools, including application deadlines, and the availability or type of financial aid, transportation, summer school and before- and after-school programs. Their web site has a brief overview of member schools in a chart form. Each listing has a link to a page with a more detailed description, as well as links to school web sites and/or e-mail addresses when available.
- The **Northside Parents Network**, 1218 West Addison, Chicago IL 60613, 312-409-2233, www.northsideparents.org, puts out a newslet-ter as well as an annual "School Information Booklet" that profiles local schools (both public and private), and offers guidelines for choosing a school for your child. The cost is $5 for members and $15 for non-members.
- **School Match**, 800-992-5323, www.schoolmatch.com, offers a vari-ety of school information. The web site offers basic information includ-ing the name/address/phone of the school system, along with the grade range, enrollment, and number of full-time teachers and schools in a district at no charge. Prices for their school reports range from $10

to $97.50, according to the comprehensiveness of the report and whether it's ordered online or by phone or fax. Sample snapshots and school report cards are provided on the web site.

STATE OF ILLINOIS GUIDELINES AND FEES

Illinois schools are primarily funded through property and sales taxes. Reliance on local property taxes creates wide disparities in the amounts spent per pupil across the Chicago area. School districts that lack a substantial amount of commercial or industrial development, particularly in areas where property values are lower, can have high residential property tax rates, but still struggle to fund their schools adequately. Currently, many school districts are struggling financially. According to Illinois State Board of Education Chairman Ron Gidwitz, "Most of our districts are faced with staggering financial problems and we must provide greater state support or they will continue to run deficits and be forced to cut vital programs necessary to help students achieve state standards as required by federal law." (See the Illinois State Board of Education's web site for more, www.isbe.state.il.us.)

Some districts are having a hard time keeping up with the local growth and subsequent overcrowding. Districts across the region have cut programs and services (in areas often regarded as "peripheral," such as extracurricular activities, art, music, gifted education, etc.) in response to budgetary problems. In some cases, staffs have been reduced, resulting in larger class sizes.

Public schools in Illinois can, and do, charge an instructional fee (usually in the $50 to $100 range at the elementary school level, and somewhat higher for high schools). Extracurricular activities, particularly sports, often carry a "user fee," and high schools require the purchase of many of the textbooks (with a few exceptions the textbook loan program ends after 8th grade). Fees can be waived or reduced for families whose children qualify for the free or reduced rate lunch program (contact your local school district for specifics). Funding for special programs or equipment (field trips, computers, etc.) often comes through school-related organizations such as the Parent Teacher Association (PTA), and a district's Educational Foundation, both of which obtain money from dues, donations, and fundraising efforts.

All Illinois public schools use the Illinois School Achievement Test (ISAT) for grades K-8, and the Prairie State Assessment Exam (PSAE), which now includes the ACT, for grade 11. Students are assessed in the areas of reading, math, writing, science, and social studies. Student performance is grouped into four categories: Exceeds Standards, Meets Standards, Below Standards, and Academic Warning. The percentage of students in each category is included for individual schools, school districts, and for the entire state. Scores are recorded for all students in a school, as well as for subcategories such as race, ethnic background, limited English proficient, low-income, and students with disabilities. The "School Report Card" with the test scores and other school data, is available online at the Illinois State Board of Education's web site, www.isbe.state.il.us. All school districts that have a web site are required to post their district's information on their site (though this may take weeks or months beyond the state release of the scores in November). The school reports are also published as paper copies, available from school districts upon request (some districts charge a small fee to recover their printing costs).

For the City of Chicago Schools, check their web site, www.cps.k12.il.us, for test score data as well as other information about the Chicago Public Schools. You can also call their main number, 773-553-1000.

CHICAGO PUBLIC SCHOOLS

Chicago Public Schools have long suffered from a number of problems, including the poor physical condition of many schools, low educational achievement of students, as evidenced by poor test scores, and high dropout rates at the high school level. In the mid-1990s, Mayor Richard M. Daley, and then-school chief Paul Vallas took direct control of the schools, and addressed chronic financial problems, repaired the worst physical conditions, and implemented and revised a number of initiatives designed to increase student achievement. Though problems persist, some schools have made considerable progress at increasing student academic achievement, in spite of the larger social and economic factors such as poverty and crime that impact the schools.

One of Chicago Public School's initiatives to enhance its educational program (which is also, not coincidentally, an attempt to keep students in the system who would likely enroll in private schools or leave the area all together), is the magnet school program. About three-quarters of Chicago's high schools offer **magnet programs**, as do just over half of the elementary and middle schools. At the high school level, **Whitney Young Magnet High School**, 773-534-7500, provides a well-regarded six-year program offering gifted and talented students a chance to move through course material at their own pace. The new **Northside College Prep High School**, 773-534-3954, www.northsideprep.org, is a multi-million dollar facility that has attracted many applicants. Facilities include a swimming pool, outdoor stadium, science labs, computer labs, library, and art and music rooms. It's a college preparatory school and all core courses are offered at the honors and advanced placement level. The school offers a number of student services, including tutoring, health/wellness education, counseling, and service learning. Special Education services are available for students with diagnosed learning disabilities (LD), speech/language impairments (SPL), emotional/behavioral disorders (EBD), health impairments (OHI), and severe/profound cognitive delays (SPH). Northside College Prep has selective enrollment.

About 15 elementary schools are magnet schools, drawing pupils from throughout the City of Chicago. Elementary school magnet programs are arranged into "magnet clusters." Each magnet cluster consists of two to five neighborhood schools that together offer enhanced instruction in areas such as math/science, fine/performing arts, world language, and the International CPS Scholars and International Baccalaureate Middle School programs. Because these magnet programs are in place in neighborhood schools, children have a greater chance of taking advantage of these programs in schools close to where they live.

Magnet program information is available online at www.chicagomagnetprograms.org or by calling 773-553-2060 and requesting a copy of the "Options for Knowledge" booklet. A computerized lottery system of selection is used for all magnet programs/schools, except for Classical Schools (magnet schools designed to provide a challenging liberal arts course of instruction for students with high academic potential), 7th/8th grade programs for academically talented students, International Baccalaureate Programs, and regional gifted centers, which have specific academic criteria for entrance. Schools for 7th/8th grade academically talented students, International Baccalaureate Programs, and Regional Gifted Centers provide full transportation, all others provide only restricted transportation (for residents living from 1.5 to 6 miles from the school). No transportation is provided for high school students. Applications are not required for admission to Advanced Placement, Education to Careers, and/or Bilingual Education Programs.

Another program initiative by the Chicago Public Schools is "Small Schools," which is either a "school within a school" or a freestanding building of no more than 350 students (elementary level) or 500 students (high school level). The aim is to provide a more personal, theme-based educational program that will improve the attendance, behavior, and achievement levels (grades) of enrolled students, particularly at the high school level. The school system is also addressing poor reading skills in the primary grades with a system-wide intensive reading program, focusing primarily on grades K-3.

The Chicago Public School System instituted local school councils some years ago as a way to provide the community, parents, and school personnel input into governing the local schools. While many local school councils operate successfully, others suffer from lack of participation, and, in a few instances, financial mismanagement.

SCHOOL REGISTRATION

Public school enrollment/registration in Illinois is fairly simple, at least for neighborhood schools; policies vary for magnet school programs. You will need a proof of residency (such as a lease or closing papers on a house, and a recent utility bill in your name), and your child's birth certificate and immunization records. Medical and dental exams are required before entry into kindergarten, and again before high school. **Immunizations** (MMR, DPT, HIB, Hepatitis B, and now the chicken pox vaccine) are required prior to kindergarten entry, and a D/T booster before entering high school. Waivers to the requirement are possible for parents who object on religious grounds or whose child has a health condition putting him/her at risk from the immunization. To obtain a waiver, parents should check with the school district.

SUBURBAN SCHOOLS

Suburban schools, in general, have a better reputation for quality education than do the Chicago Public schools. Some districts, particularly in the southern Cook County region, are plagued by the same problems related to lower income levels that affect the city schools. Despite the day-to-day difficulties of funding, suburban schools in most areas offer consistent quality schooling.

SCHOOL CONTACTS

CHICAGO
- **City of Chicago**: Chicago School District 299, 125 South Clark Street, Chicago, IL 60603, 773-553-1000, www.cps.k12.il.us

SUBURBAN COOK COUNTY
- **Arlington Heights School District 25**, 1200 South Dunton Avenue, Arlington Heights, IL 60005, 847-758-4900, www.ahsd25.n-cook.k12.il.us
- **Arlington Township High School District 214**, 2121 South Goebbert Road, Arlington Heights, IL 60005, 847-718-7600, www.dist214.k12.il.us
- **Avoca School District 37**, 2921 Illinois Road, Wilmette, IL 60091, 847-251-3587, www.avoca.k12.il.us
- **Bannockburn School District 106**, 2165 Telegraph Road, Deerfield, IL 60015, 847-945-5900, www.bannockburnschool.org
- **Brookfield School District 95**, 3524 Maple Avenue, Brookfield, 708-485-0606, www.d95.w-cook.k12.il.us

- **Burbank School District 111** (elementary): 7600 South Central, 708-496-0500; high school: Reavis/District 220, 6034 West 77th Street, Burbank, 708-599-7200; www.burbank.k12.il.us
- **C.C. School District 59**, 2123 South Arlington Heights Road, Arlington Heights, IL 60005, 847-593-4300, www.elk-grove.k12.il.us
- **Community High School District 218**, 10701 South Kilpatrick Avenue, Oak Lawn, IL 60453, 708-424-2000, www.chsd218.org
- **Consolidated High School District 230**, 15100 South 94th Avenue, Orland Park, IL 60462, 708-745-5203, www.d230.org
- **Deerfield School District 109**, 517 Deerfield Road, 847-945-1844, www.dps109.org
- **Des Plaines C.C. School District 62**, 777 Algonquin Road, Des Plaines, IL 60016, 847-824-1136, www.d62.org
- **East Prairie School District 73**, 3907 West Dobson Street, Skokie, IL 60076, 847-673-1141, www.eps.n-cook.k12.il.us
- **Evanston C.C. School District 65**, 1500 McDaniel Avenue, Evanston, IL 60201, 847-859-8000, www.d65.k12.il.us
- **Evanston Township High School District 202**, 1600 Dodge Avenue, Evanston, IL 60201, 847-424-7000, www.eths.k12.il.us
- **Evergreen Park School District 124** (elementary), 708-423-0950; Evergreen Park Community High School District 231, 708-424-7400; www.d124.s-cook.k12.il.us
- **Flossmoor School District 161**, 41 East Elmwood Drive, Chicago Heights, IL 60411, 708-647-7000
- **Glencoe School District 35**, 620 Greenwood Avenue, Glencoe, IL 60022, 847-835-7800, www.glencoe.k12.il.us
- **Glenview C.C. School District 34**, 1401 Greenwood Road, Glenview, IL 60025, 847-835-7800, www.ncook.k12.il.us; also see Northbrook School District.
- **Golf School District 67**, 9401 Waukegan Road, Morton Grove, IL 60053, 847-966-8200, www.golf67.net
- **Highland Park District 113**: 847-926-9327, www.d113.lake.k12.il.us; **District 112**: 847-681-6700, www.nssd112.k12.il.us; Special Education: 847-831-5100
- **Homewood School District 153**, 18205 Aberdeen Street, Homewood, IL 60430, 708-799-5661, www.homewoodsd153.org
- **Homewood-Flossmoor High School District 233**, 999 Kedzie Avenue, Flossmoor, IL 60422, 708-799-3000, www.hfhs.s-cook.k12.il.us
- **Indian Prairie School District 204**, 780 Shoreline Drive, Aurora, 630-375-3000, www.ipsd.org
- **Kenilworth Elementary District 38 - Sears School**, 542 Abbotsford Road, Kenilworth, IL 60043, 847-256-5006, www.kenilworth.k12.il.us

- **La Grange Highlands School District 106**, 1750 Plainfield Road, La Grange, IL 60525, 708-246-3085, www.d106.k12.il.us
- **La Grange School District 102**, 333 North Park Road, La Grange Park, IL 60526, 708-482-2400, www.dist102.k12.il.us
- **LaGrange School District 105 (South)**, 1001 South Spring Avenue, La Grange, IL 60525, 708-482-2700, www.d105.w-cook.k12.il.us
- **Leyden High School District 212**, 3400 Rose Street, Franklin Park, IL 60131, 708-451-3000, www.leyden212.org
- **Lyons Township District 204**, 100 South Brainard Avenue, LaGrange, IL 60525, 708-579-6300, www.lths.net
- **Maine Township District 207**, 1131 South Dee Road, Park Ridge, IL 60068, 847-696-3600, www.maine207.k12.il.us
- **Morton Grove School District 70**, 6200 Lake Street, Morton Grove, IL 60053, 847-965-6200, wwwparkview70.net
- **New Trier High School District 203**, 7 Happ Road (Administration, grade 9), Northfield IL 60093; 385 Winnetka Avenue (grades 10-12), Winnetka, IL 60093, 847-446-7000 (both campuses), www.nths.newtrier.k12.il.us
- **Niles School District 71**, 6921 West Oakton Street, Niles, IL 60648, 847-966-9280
- **Niles Township School District 219**, 7700 Gross Point Road, Skokie, IL 60077, 847-626-3000, www.niles-hs.k12.il.us
- **North Palos School District 117**, 7825 West 103rd Street, Palos Hills, IL 60465, 708-598-5500, www.d117.s-cook.k12.il.us
- **Northbrook School District 27**, 1250 Sanders Road, Northbrook, IL 60060, 847-498-2610, www.northbrook27.k12.il.us
- **Northbrook School District 28**, 1475 Maple Avenue, Northbrook, IL 60062, 847-498-7900, www.district28.k12.il.us
- **Northbrook-Glenview School District 30**, 2374 Shermer Road, Northbrook, IL 60062, 847-498-4190, www.district30.k12.il.us
- **Northfield Township District 225**, 1835 Landwehr Road, Glenview, IL 60025, 847-998-6100, www.glenbrook.k12.il.us
- **Oak Forest, Arbor Park District 145**, 708-687-8040 (elementary), www.arbor.s-cook.k12.il.us; Bremen High School District 228, 708-389-1175, www.bhsd228.s-cook.k12.il.us, also check Tinley Park High School.
- **Oak Lawn Community High School District 229**, 9400 SW Hwy, Oak Lawn, IL 60453, 708-424-5200
- **Oak Lawn-Hometown District 123**, 4201 West 93rd Street, Oak Lawn, IL 60453, 708-423-0150, www.d123.s-cook.k12.il.us
- **Oak Park and River Forest School District 200**, 201 North Scoville Avenue, Oak Park, IL 60302, 708-383-0700, http://oprfhs.org

- **Oak Park Elementary School District 97**, 970 West Madison Street, Oak Park, IL 60302, 708-524-3000, www.op97.org
- **Orland Park School District 135**, 15100 South 94th Avenue, Orland Park, IL 60462, 708-349-5700, www.orland135.org
- **Palos Heights School District 128**, 12809 South McVicker, Palos Heights, IL 60463, 708-597-9040, www.d128.k12.il.us
- **Palos School District 118**, 8800 West 119th Street, Palos Park, IL 60464, 708-448-4800, www.palos118.org
- **Park Ridge-Niles School District 64**, 164 South Prospect Avenue, Park Ridge, IL 60068, 847-318-4300, www.d64.org
- **River Forest School District 90**, 7776 West Lake Street, River Forest, IL 60305, 708-771-8282, www.district90.org
- **Riverside-Brookfield Township High School District 208**, 160 Ridgewood Road, Riverside, IL 60546, 708-442-7500, www.rbhs.w-cook.k12.il.us
- **Rosemont School District 78**, 6101 Ruby Street Rosemont, IL 60018, 847-825-0144
- **Schaumburg School District 54**, 524 East Schaumburg Road, Schaumburg, IL 60194, 847-885-6700, www.sd54.k12.il.us
- **Skokie Fairview School District 72**, 7040 Laramie Avenue, Skokie, IL 60077, 847-929-1050, www.fairview.k12.il.us
- **Skokie School District 68**, 9440 Kenton Avenue, Skokie, IL 60076, 847-676-9000, www.sd68.k12.il.us
- **Skokie School District 69**, 5050 Madison Street, Skokie, IL 60077, 847-675-7666, www.skokie69.k12.il.us
- **Skokie School District 73-5**, 8000 East Prairie Road, Skokie, IL 60076, 847-673-1220, www.skokie735.k12.il.us
- **Sunset Ridge School District 29**, 525 Sunset Ridge Road, Northfield, IL 60093, 847-446-6383, www.sunset.k12.il.us
- **Tinley Park: C.C. School District 146** (elementary), 708-614-4500, www.ccsd146.k12.il.us; **Kirby School District 140** (elementary), 708-532-6462, www.ksd140.org; **Bremen High School District 228**, 708-389-1175, www.bhsd228.s-cook.k12.il.us (also see Oak Forest and Orland Park information).
- **Township High School District 211**, 1750 South Roselle Road, Palatine, IL 60067, 847-755-6600, www.d211.org
- **West Northfield School District 31**, 3131 Techny Road, Northbrook, IL 60062, 847-272-6880, www.dist31.k12.il.us
- **Wilmette School District 39**, 615 Locust Road, Wilmette, IL 60091, 847-256-2450, http://wilmette.newtrier.k12.il.us, www.nttc.org
- **Winnetka School District 36**, 1235 Oak Street, Winnetka, IL 60093, 847-446-9400, www.winnetka.k12.il.us

LAKE COUNTY

- **Deerfield School District 109**, 517 Deerfield Road, Deerfield, IL 60015, 847-945-1844, www.dps109.org
- **Highland Park Township High School District 113**, 1040 West Park Avenue, Highland Park, IL 60035, 847-432-6510, www.d113.lake.k12.il.us
- **North Shore School District 112**, 1936 Green Bay Road, Highland Park, IL 60035, 847-681-6700, www.nssd112.k12.il.us

DUPAGE COUNTY

- **Bolingbrook** (Will and DuPage counties), 815-886-2700 (administration), www.vvsd.org
- **Butler School District 53**, 2801 York Road, Oak Brook, IL 60523, 630-573-2887, www.sd53.k12.il.us
- **Community High School District 99**, 6301 Springside Avenue, Downers Grove, IL 60516, 630-795-7100, www.csd99.k12.il.us
- **Downers Grove School District 58** (elementary and middle school), 1860 63rd Street, 630-719-5800, www.dg58.dupage.k12.il.us; **Community High School District 99**, 6301 Springside Avenue, 630-795-7100, www.csd99.k12.il.us
- **Glen Ellyn Community School District 89**, 789 Sheehan Avenue, Glen Ellyn, 630-469-8900, www.ccsd89.org
- **Hinsdale School District 181**, 5905 South County Line Drive, Hinsdale, IL 60521, 630-887-1070, www.schooldistrict181.org
- **Hinsdale Township High School District 86**, 55th and Grant Street, Hinsdale, IL 60521, 630-325-2950, www.district86.k12.il.us
- **Indian Prairie School District 204**, 780 Shoreline Drive, Aurora, IL 60504, 630-375-3000, www.ipsd.org
- **Lisle C.U. School District 202**, 5211 Center Avenue, Lisle, IL 60532, 630-493-8000, www.lisle.dupage.k12.il.us
- **Lombard School District 44**, 150 West Madison Street, Lombard, IL 60148, 630-827-4400, www.district44.dupage.k12.il.us
- **Naperville C.U. School District 203**, 203 West Hillside, Naperville, IL 60540, 630-420-6300, www.ncusd203.org
- **Westmont C.U. District 201**, 200 North Linden Street, Westmont, IL 60559, 630-969-7741, www.westmont.dupage.k12.il.us
- **Wheaton/Warrenville Community School District 200**, 130 West Park Avenue, Wheaton, 630-682-2000, www.cusd200.org; **Community School District 89**, 789 Sheehan Avenue, Glen Ellyn, 630-469-8900, www.ccsd.89.org

KANE COUNTY

- **Aurora East Unit School District 131**, 417 5th Street, Aurora, IL 60506, 630-299-5550, www.d131.kane.k12.il.us

- **Aurora West Unit School District 129**, 80 South River Street, Aurora, IL 60506, 630-844-4400, www.sd129.org

SPECIAL EDUCATION

All public schools provide special education and related support services (speech, physical and occupational therapy, counseling) to children ages 3-21 who have special needs. The core of the special education system is the Individual Education Plan (IEP), which determines where the child will be placed (regular education classroom, special education class in the regular school, special school, etc.) and what services he or she will receive (for babies and toddlers, this is called the Individual Family Service Plan or IFSP). Parents can request testing of their child, or school personnel can recommend it and then proceed only with parental permission. Parents who disagree with the type of placement and/or level of services proposed can obtain private testing of their child (at the parents' expense), and have outside professionals (such as a therapist), accompany them to the IEP conference.

Virtually all school districts provide screenings of preschoolers for developmental delay, annually and/or by appointment. Many districts band together into special education co-ops to provide services to children with less common ("low-incidence") conditions such as autism, blindness, deafness, multiple handicaps, etc., for which a small district may have too few children to operate an entire classroom or employ full-time therapists independently. Participating districts in each co-op provide classroom space and other support for the special education students in their districts. Early intervention services for children birth to three years are now available through some of the special education co-ops and through some private therapy agencies, such as Easter Seals.

- **Aero Special Education Co-op**, 7600 South Mason Avenue, Burbank, IL, 708-496-3330
- **Cooperative Association for Special Education** (**CASE**), 1464 South Main Street, Lombard, IL, 630-932-5200; serves: DuPage County School Districts 15, 16, 41, 44, 87, 89, and 93 (Glen Ellyn, Glendale Heights, Lombard, Carol Stream).
- **DuPage West Cook Low Incidence Programs**, 1500 South Grace Street, Lombard, IL, 630-629-7272; serves: DuPage and Western Cook counties. Services for children with vision, hearing, and physical disabilities (SASED Highland Hills School program), testing for children birth to three.
- **Early Childhood Development Center**, 7431 Astor Avenue, Hanover Park, IL, 630-837-6445; serves: Hanover Township, Bartlett, Streamwood, Hanover Park. Assessment and outpatient services for children up through age 12.

- **East DuPage Special Education District (ESSED)**, 502 East Van Buren Street, Villa Park, IL, 630-279-4726 or 630-617-2647; serves school districts 4, 45, 88, and 205 (Addison, Villa Park, Elmhurst).
- **La Grange Area Department of Special Education (LADSE)**, 1301 West Cossitt Avenue, La Grange, IL, 708-354-5730; serves DuPage County School Districts 53, 61, 62, 86, 181 (Hinsdale, Oakbrook, Burr Ridge, Darien, Clarendon Hills); Western Cook County School Districts 94, 95, 96, 101, 102, 103, 105, 106, 107, 204, 208 (LaGrange, Riverside, North Riverside, Brookfield, Lyons).
- **Niles Township Department of Special Education (NTDSE)**, 8701 Menard Avenue, Morton Grove, IL, 847-965-9040; includes school district 68 and 69 in Skokie.
- **North DuPage Special Education Cooperative (NDSEC)**, 132 East Pine Street, Roselle, IL, 630-894-0490; serves school districts 2, 7, 10, 11, 12, 13, 100, 108 (Roselle, Itasca, Bensenville, Medinah, Wood Dale, Bloomingdale).
- **Northern Suburban Special Education District (NSSED)**, 760 Red Oak Lane, Highland Park, IL, 847-831-5100, www.nssed.k12.il.us; serves school districts 27, 28, 29, 30, 31, 34, 35, 36, 37, 38, 39, 65, 67, 106, 109, 112, 113, 203, 225 (Deerfield, Glenview, Glencoe, Highland Park, Kenilworth, Lake Forest, Lake Bluff, Northbrook, Northfield, Wilmette, Winnetka). Programs and services for children, birth to 21. Early childhood (birth to three) services provided in collaboration with Glenkirk (3504 Commercial Avenue in Northbrook, 847-272-5111).
- **Proviso Area for Exceptional Children (PAEC)**, 1000 Van Buren Street, Maywood, IL, 708-450-2100
- **School Association for Special Education in DuPage County (SASED)**, 6S331 Cornwall Road, Naperville, IL, 630-778-4500; serves School Districts 20, 25, 33, 34, 58, 60, 63, 66, 68, 69, 94, 99, 180, 201, 202 (Lisle, Westmont, West Chicago, Winfield, Downers Grove, Darien, Clarendon Hills).
- **Southwest Cook Cooperative**, 6020 151st Street, Oak Forest, IL, 708-687-0900
- **Special Education District of Lake County (SEDOL)**, 18160 Gages Lake Road, Gages Lake, IL, 60030, 847-548-8470, www.sedol.k12.il.us; 37 member school districts in Lake County.
- **Special Education District of McHenry County (SEDOM)**, 1200 Claussen Drive, Woodstock, IL, 815-338-3622, www.sedom.org; school districts: 3, 11, 12, 13, 15, 18, 26. 36. 46, 47, 50, 154, 155, 156, 157, 158, 165, 200 (Fox River Grove, Spring Grove, Richmond, Johnsburg, McHenry, Alden-Hebron, Cary, Harrison, Crystal Lake, Harvard, Marengo, Union, Huntley, Woodstock). Classes in districts in Cary, Crystal Lake, Huntley, Johnsburg, McHenry, Union, and Woodstock.

- **SPEED Coop (Special Education Joint Agreement #802)**, 1125 Division Street, Chicago Heights, IL, 708-481-6100, www.speedschldist802.com; programs for children and families from birth to 21. School districts: 144, 153, 161, 162, 163, 167, 168, 169, 170, 172, 194, 201U, 206, 207, 233 (South Suburbs including Markham, Homewood, Flossmoor, Park Forest, Glenwood, Sauk Village, Ford Heights, Chicago Heights, Park Ridge, Harvey, Steger, Crete, Olympia Fields, Hazel Crest, Matteson)

SPECIAL EDUCATION SCHOOLS

Special education schools serve children with a variety of special needs, including learning disabilities, hearing impairment, mental retardation, autism, and emotional/behavioral problems. In some instances, such as when a child is placed at the school as mandated by his or her Individual Education Plan (IEP) as the only program that can meet his/her needs, the referring district picks up the costs. Some **Special Education Schools** in the greater Chicago area:

- **Acacia Academy**, 6425 West Willow Springs Road, La Grange, IL 60525, 708-579-9040
- **Alexander Graham Bell Montessori**, 2020 East Camp McDonald Road, Mt. Prospect, IL 60056, 847-297-3206, www.aehi.org
- **The Bridge High School**, 2318 Wisconsin Avenue, Downers Grove, IL 60515, 630-964-1722
- **Cove School**, 350 Lee Road, Northbrook, IL 60062, 847-441-9300, 800-453-2683, http://homepage.interaccess.com/~cove
- **The Day School**, 800 West Buena Avenue, Chicago, IL 60613, 773-327-6000
- **Elim Christian School**, 13020 South Central Avenue, Palos Heights, IL 60463, 708-389-0555
- **Gateway to Learning School**, 4925 North Lincoln Avenue, Chicago, IL 60625, 773-784-3200
- **Krejci Academy**, 619 East Franklin Avenue, Naperville, IL 60540, 630-355-6870
- **Shore School**, 2525 Church Street, Evanston, IL 60201, 847-869-6610

PRIVATE AND PAROCHIAL SCHOOLS

Many parents, out of concern for the quality of the public schools, or other reasons, consider alternative schooling for their children. For them, there are several options, including parochial schools, Montessori and Waldorf schools, and college-prep programs.

CATHOLIC SCHOOLS

The Catholic school system is the largest non-public system in the Chicago area. The Archdiocese of Chicago has closed some schools, mostly on the south and west sides of Chicago, nonetheless Catholic schools remain a viable alternative to the public system for many parents. Average tuition at the grade school level is in the range of $2,500 for one child, while high school tuition and fees run around $3,500 to $4,000, on average. The Archdiocese of Chicago is currently looking into the financial feasibility of opening a new co-ed Catholic high school in the Southwest Cook County suburb of Orland Park. **Catholic School Directories** can be had from the **Office of Catholic Education, Archdiocese of Chicago**, 312-751-5200, http://schools.archdiocese-chgo.org (serves Catholic schools in the City of Chicago, and suburban Cook and Lake counties), and the **Archdiocese of Joliet School Directory**, 815-727-4674, www.diocese-ofjoliet.org/cso (serves the Catholic schools in DuPage, Will, and Kankakee counties).

Sampling of Catholic schools in Chicago:

- **Brother Rice High School**, 10001 South Pulaski Road, Chicago, IL 60642, 773-779-3410, www.brrice.chi.il.us
- **Cristo Rey Jesuit High School**, 1851 West Cermak Road, Chicago, IL 60608, 773-890-6800, www.cristorey.net
- **Maria High School**, 6727 South California Avenue, Chicago, IL 60629, 773-925-8686, www.mariahighschool.org
- **Marist High School**, 4200 West 115th Street, Chicago, IL 60655, 773-881-5300, www.marist.net
- **Mt**. **Carmel High School**, 6410 South Dante Avenue, Chicago, IL 60637, 773-324-1020, www.mchs.org
- **Sacred Heart Schools**, 6250 North Sheridan Road, Chicago, IL 60660, 630-839-1444, www.shschicago.org
- **St**. **Ignatius College Prep**, 1076 West Roosevelt Road, Chicago, IL 60608-1594, 312-421-5900, www.ignatiuschicago.com
- **St**. **Juliana School**, 7400 West Touhy Avenue, Chicago, IL 60631, 773-631-2256, www.stjuliana.org
- **St**. **Patrick High School**, 5900 West Belmont Avenue, Chicago, IL 60634, 773-282-8844, www.stpatrick.org
- **St**. **Rita of Cascia High School**, 7740 South Western Avenue, Chicago, IL 60620, 773-925-6600, http://stritahs.com

OTHER RELIGIOUS SCHOOLS

To find a private school in your area, check the Yellow Pages, under "Schools" for listings. For Jewish schools you might first contact the **Community Foundation for Jewish Education (CJFE) of Metropolitan Chicago**, 312-913-1818, www.cfje.org. Those interested in Lutheran schooling should go to www.valpo.edu/lutheran, www.lcms.org. There are several Islamic schools operating in the Chicago area, including the **Averroes Academy** in Northbrook, 847-272-3557, the **Islamic Foundation School** in Villa Park, 630-941-8800, www.islamicfoundation.org, and in Bridgeview, the **Universal School**, 708-599-4100, and **AQSA**, 708-598-2700.

PRIVATE SCHOOLS

Private schools in the Chicago area are mostly non-sectarian, and provide what most people think of as a good, "well-rounded" education. Some programs have a special emphasis on a particular area of the curriculum, such as foreign language or fine arts. The independent schools tend to be expensive, with tuition in some cases around $10,000 or more annually, especially at the high school level. Two such private programs include The Latin School of Chicago and Francis Parker School in Lincoln Park. **The Latin School of Chicago**, 59 West North Boulevard, Chicago, IL 60610, 312-573-4500, www.latin.pvt.k12.il.us, was founded in 1888, and serves grades K-12. The school emphasizes an interdisciplinary curriculum at all levels, and features foreign language instruction starting in junior kindergarten. The Upper School (high school) provides a college preparatory curriculum, and features an interdisciplinary humanities class for ninth-graders. Facilities at the Middle/Upper School include a middle school center, two gymnasiums, a performing arts center, and a 19,000 volume, online library complex. The Lower School features an early childhood learning center, gymnasium and play/performance space, a rooftop playground, and a library. **Francis Parker School**, 330 West Webster Avenue, Chicago, IL 60614, 773-549-0172, www.fwparker.org, was founded in 1901, and serves grades K-12 with a lower school for grades K-5, a middle school for grades 6-8, and a high school for grades 9-12. Located on 5.2 acres on the near North Side of Chicago, the school features three gymnasiums, a science center, a large auditorium, a conference center, an outdoor playground, an athletic field, and a new library. The school seeks diversity among its student body in terms of students' economic, cultural, and social backgrounds, and requires student involvement in social service activities. An after-school program

(Parker PM) is available for grades K-5. Those looking for a private fine arts school in Chicago should check out the **Chicago Academy for the Arts**, located at 1010 West Chicago Avenue, 312-421-0202.

Additional **private independent schools in greater Chicago** include:

- **Baker Demonstration School**, 2840 Sheridan Road, Evanston, IL 60201, 847-256-5150, ext. 2581, http://baker.nl.edu
- **The Catherine Cook School**, 226 West Schiller Street, Chicago, IL 60610, 312-266-3381
- **The Chicago City Day School**, 541 West Hawthorne Place, Chicago, IL 60657, 773-327-0900, http://independentschools.net/chicago/city-day
- **The Children's School**, 2010 Dewey Street, Evanston, IL 60201, 847-424-0748, www.thechildren.org
- **Hinsdale Junior Academy**, 631 East Hickory Street, Hinsdale, IL 60521, 630-323-9211
- **Joseph Academy**, 7530 North Natchez Avenue, Niles, IL 60714, 847-588-2090
- **Lake Forest Academy**, 1500 West Kennedy Road, Lake Forest, IL 60045, 847-234-3210, www.lfa.lfc.edu
- **Lake Forest Country Day School**, 145 South Green Bay Road, Lake Forest, IL 60045, 847-234-2350
- **Lake Shore Schools**, 6759 North Greenview, Chicago, IL 60626, 773-561-6707
- **Lycee Francais de Chicago**, 613 West Bittersweet Place, Chicago, IL 6013, 773-665-0013, www.edufrance.org/chicago
- **Morgan Park Academy**, 2153 West 111th Street, Chicago, IL 60643, 773-881-6700, http://independentschools.net/chicago/morgan-park
- **North Park Elementary School**, 2017 West Montrose, Chicago, IL 60618, 773-327-3144, www.npeschool.org
- **North Shore Country Day School**, 310 Green Bay Road, Winnetka, IL 60093, 847-446-0674, www.nscds.pvt.k12.il.us
- **Plato Academy**, 8101 West Golf Road, Niles, IL 60714, 847-470-8500
- **Roycemore School**, 640 Lincoln Street, Evanston, IL 60201, 847-866-6055, www.roycemoreschool.org
- **The Willows Academy**, 1012 Thacker Street, Des Plaines, IL 60016, 847-824-6900, http://willows.org

PRIVATE GIFTED SCHOOLS

- **Avery Coonley School**, 1400 Maple Avenue, Downers Grove, IL 60515, 630-969-0800

- **Quest Academy**, 500 North Benton Street, Palatine, IL 60067, 847-202-8035
- **Science & Arts Academy**, 1825 Miner Street, Des Plaines, IL 60016, 847-827-7880

MONTESSORI SCHOOLS

Montessori schools follow the hands-on educational philosophy of Maria Montessori, and use specified Montessori materials in their schools. Most Montessori schools in the United States are members of the American Montessori Society, www.amshq.org, and are accredited by, or affiliated with them. All teachers in accredited Montessori schools are Montessori trained and certified. For a complete list of Illinois schools, visit the **American Montessori Society's** web site at www.rpmschool.org, or check the Yellow Pages under "Schools" for listings.

WALDORF SCHOOLS

Waldorf schools are based on the educational philosophy and instructional methods of Rudolph Steiner, which emphasizes the importance of the arts in the curriculum. The web site of the Association of Waldorf Schools in America, www.awsna.org, goes into detail about the Waldorf philosophy and curriculum, and has links to other Waldorf-related web sites. Waldorf Schools in the greater Chicago area include **Chicago Waldorf School**, grades pre-K-12, 1300 West Loyola Avenue, Chicago, IL 60626, 773-465-2662, www.chicagowaldorf.org, **Great Oaks School**, 933B Chicago Avenue, Evanston, IL 60202, 847-864-9980, grades pre-K-8, and **Four Winds Waldorf School**, 30W160 Calumet Avenue, Warrensville, IL 60555, 630-836-9400, pre-K-8.

HOME SCHOOLING

Some parents prefer to educate their children at home. In Illinois, home schools are considered to be private schools, and the only state requirements are that children are taught, in English, the same broad subjects as are taught in the public school curriculum. Curriculum and other resources for home-schoolers are available online at web sites such as **Homeschool World**, www.home-school.com, which provides news articles, information, resources and notices of events related to home schooling. **Chicago area homeschooling organizations** include:

- **A.K. Nuni-Hudson, Interfaith Home Education**, 986 Grand Avenue, Aurora, IL 60506, lurningathome@aol.com

- **Cathy Wagner, Joliet Area Home School Fellowship**, 815-723-9315, carlw0851@aol.com
- **CHESS of Illinois**, 129 Webb Street Calumet City, IL 60409, 708-802-1996
- **Christian Home Educators Coalition (CHEC) of Illinois**, P.O. Box 47322, Chicago, IL 60647, 773-278-0673, www.chec.cc
- **Christian Home-Oriented Individualized Curriculum Experience (CHOICE)**, P.O. Box 425, Wheaton, IL 60189, 630-415-3609
- **Illinois Christian Home Educators**, P.O. Box 775, Harvard, IL 60033, 815-943-7882, www.iche.org
- **Islamic Homeschool Education Network**, 241 Meadowbrook Drive, Bolingbrook, IL 60440, mshgofil@aol.com
- **Jewish Homeschool Association of Greater Chicago**, 847-884-1480, bhp@bnoshenya.org, www.bnoshenya.org
- **Kane County Christian Home Schoolers**, P.O. Box 48, Sugar Grove, IL 60554, jjmew4@yahoo.com
- **Restore Our Catholic Kids (ROCK)**, 773 Pleasant Avenue, Glen Ellyn, IL 60137, 630-858 4877
- **Teaching Homes for Christ**, P.O. Box 113, West Chicago, IL 60186, info@teachinghomes.org, www.teachinghomes.org
- **Tri-County Christian Home Educators**, 40 West Timbercreek Drive, Yorkville, IL 60560, 888-470-4513, karlrpfizenmaierjr@prodigy.net
- www.homeschoolnewslink.com
- www.chicagokids.com/resources/homeschooling.cfm

This group is not Chicago-based, but may also be useful: **Muslim Home School Network & Resource (MHSNR)**, P.O. Box 803, Attleboro MA, 02703, www.muslimhomeschool.com.

WHEN SHOPPING IN CHICAGO, DON'T FORGET ABOUT THE recently renovated **State Street** shopping area (www.greater-statestreet.com). In the late 1990s, the city routed car traffic back down State Street—it had been a buses only route for years—hoping that more traffic to the area would naturally revitalize this once hopping shopping district. The city was right. With its turn of the century gas light lampposts and the grandeur of the original Marshall Field's and Carson Pirie Scott Department stores, it's once again a popular and pleasant shopping destination. For shopping of a headier nature, head a little north and toward the lake to **North Michigan Avenue**, the "Magnificent Mile." Up and down the avenue are dozens of boutiques, vertical malls, restaurants, and retails stores of every kind. The **Gold Coast**, west of Michigan Avenue, offers boutiques selling luxury goods and jewelry, beauty services, and designer clothing. But you don't have to head to the heart of the city for good shopping. Nearly every neighborhood and surrounding community has its own little retail area, and there are many fine shopping malls in the city and suburbs. Indulge yourself and explore them all.

Unless otherwise noted, all listings are in Chicago.

SHOPPING MALLS

CHICAGO

- **900 North Michigan Shops**, 312-915-3916, www.shop900.com
- **The Atrium**, 100 West Randolph Street, 312-346-0777, www.atriummallchicago.com
- **The Century**, 2828 North Clark Street, 773-929-8100
- **Chicago Place**, 700 North Michigan Avenue, 312-642-4811, www.chicago-place.com

- **Ford City**, 7601 South Cicero Avenue, 773-767-6400, www.shopford city.com
- **Harlem/Irving Plaza**, 4104 North Harlem, 708-453-7800, 773-625-3036, www.shopthehip.com
- **Harper Court**, 5211-25 South Harper Avenue, 773-363-8282, www.harpercourt.com
- **North Bridge**, 520 North Michigan, 312-327-2300, www.north bridgechicago.com
- **Piper's Alley Mall**, 210 West North Avenue, 312-337-0436
- **Water Tower Place**, 835 North Michigan Avenue, 312-440-3165, www.shopwatertower.com

SUBURBS

- **Chicago Ridge Mall**, 444 Chicago Ridge Mall Drive, Chicago Ridge, 708-422-0897, www.chicagoridgemall.com
- **Deer Park Town Center**, 20530 North Rand Road, Deer Park, 847-726-7755, www.deerparktowncenter.tv
- **Edens Plaza**, Lake Avenue & Skokie Boulevard, Wilmette
- **Evergreen Plaza**, 9500 South Western Avenue, Evergreen Park, 773-857-5760, www.evergreenplaza.com
- **Fox Valley Mall**, 195 Fox Valley Center, Aurora, 630-851-7200
- **Golf Mill Shopping Center**, 239 Golf Mill Center, Golf & Milwaukee roads, Niles, 847-699-1070, www.golfmill.com
- **Gurnee Mills Mall**, 6170 West Grand Avenue, Gurnee, 847-263-7500, www.millsmall.com
- **Hawthorn Center**, 122 Hawthorn Center, Vernon Hills, 847-362-6220, www.westfield.com/us/centres/illinois/hawthorn
- **Lincoln Mall**, Route 30/Lincoln Highway, Matteson, 708-747-5600, www.lincoln-mall.com
- **Northbrook Court**, 2171 Northbrook Court, Northbrook, 847-498-5144, www.northbrookcourt.com
- **Oak Brook Center**, 100 Oakbrook Center, Route 83 and Cermak Road, Oak Brook, 630-573-0700, www.oakbrookcenter.com
- **Old Orchard**, 34 Old Orchard Center, Skokie Boulevard & Old Orchard Road, Skokie, 847-673-6800, www.westfield.com/us/centres/illinois/oldorchard
- **Orland Square Mall**, 288 Orland Square Drive, Orland Park, 708-349-1646, www.shoporlandsquare.com
- **Plaza del Lago**, 1515 Sheridan Road, Wilmette, 847-256-4467, www.plazadelago.com
- **Randhurst Shopping Center**, 999 Elmhurst Road, Mt. Prospect, 708-259-0500, www.randhurstmall.com

- **River Oaks Center**, 96 River Oaks Center Drive, Calumet City, 708-868-5574, www.simon.com
- **Stratford Square**, 152 Stratford Square, Army Trail Road & Gary, Bloomingdale, 630-539-1000, www.stratfordmall.com
- **Woodfield Mall**, 5 Woodfield Shopping Center, Golf Road at Route 53, Schaumburg, 847-330-1537, www.shopwoodfield.com
- **Yorktown Shopping Center**, Butterfield Road & Highland Avenue, Lombard, 630-629-7330, www.yorktowncenter.com

OUTLET MALLS

Outlet shopping malls are not conveniently located to Chicago, but their discounts may make a trip worthwhile.
- **Lighthouse Place**, 601 Wabash Street, Michigan City, IN, 219-879-6506, www.premiumoutlets.com; if you are willing to travel out of your way (consider taking the Skyway, a bit scary if you are afraid of heights, but there will be no traffic), come spend the day at the Michigan City malls. Many find it to be worth the hour's drive from Chicago. Dozens and dozens of upscale outlets and trendy boutiques.
- **Original Outlet Mall**, 7700 120th Avenue, Kenosha, WI, 262-857-7961, www.originaloutletmall.com; located across the highway from Prime Outlets, this mall is a bit older than its competitor but it offers more stores within a mid-range price. Good source of electronics, children's clothing, and lingerie.
- **Prime Outlets at Huntley**, 11800 Factory Shops Blvd., Huntley, 847-669-9100, www.primeoutlets.com; Jeffersonian architecture, food court, playground and over 40 brand-name stores. Fifty miles west of Chicago along the Interstate 90 corridor.
- **Prime Outlets at Pleasant Prairie**, 11211 120th Avenue, Kenosha, WI, 262-857-2101, www.primeoutlets.com; offers 65 upscale name-brand stores, halfway between Chicago and Milwaukee.

DEPARTMENT STORES

- **Bloomingdale's**, 900 North Michigan Avenue, 312-440-4460, www.bloomingdales.com; home furnishings available at 600 North Wabash Avenue, 312-324-7500.
- **Carson Pirie Scott & Company**, www.carsons.com; offers everything from clothing and furniture to bridal wear to stamps and coins to jewelry. Carson's has stores throughout Chicago and the suburbs, including the flagship store at 1 South State Street, 312-641-7000, and a second city location at Gateway Shops, 120 South Riverside Plaza, 312-744-5380.

- **Lord & Taylor**, 835 North Michigan Avenue, 312-787-7400, www.mayco.com; also located at Woodfield, Old Orchard, Northbrook Court and other suburban malls.
- **Marshall Field's**, www.marshallfields.com; a Chicago institution that offers everything—from designer clothing to gourmet food and their famous chocolate mints, to home furnishings—topped with friendly service. During the Christmas season, visitors come from around the country to see the window displays at the beautifully renovated State Street store. Chicago locations include the flagship store in the Loop, 111 North State Street, 312-781-1000, and the Water Tower Place at 835 North Michigan Avenue, 312-335-7700. Many suburban locations which include: Lake Forest, 682 North Bank Lane, 847-735-2100, Oak Brook, 1 Oak Brook Center Mall, 630-684-2400, and Schaumburg, 1 Woodfield Mall, 847-706-6000.
- **Neiman-Marcus**, 737 North Michigan Avenue, 800-642-4480 or 312-642-5900, www.neimanmarcus.com; the opulent Texan retailer carries expensive non-necessities that many with cash and/or room on their credit cards find they absolutely must have. Nice restaurants and a good gourmet food department.
- **Nordstrom**, 55 East Grand Avenue, 312-464-1515 (as well as many suburban locations), www.nordstrom.com; employees at this upscale Seattle-based retailer have a reputation of being motivated and enthusiastic. Merchandise ranges from shoes and clothing for the entire family to jewelry and cosmetics. Perhaps most popular here are the women's shoe sales. Their online service is also top-notch.
- **Saks Fifth Avenue**, 700 North Michigan Avenue, 312-944-6500, www.saksfifthavenue.com
- **Sears**, www.sears.com; Sears stores are located in malls in the suburbs, or as stand-alone stores, including one at 2 North State Street, 312-373-6000. Check their web site for the closest store to your area.

DISCOUNT DEPARTMENT STORES

- **Filene's Basement**, www.filenesbasement.com, two locations: One North State Street, 312-553-1055, and 830 North Michigan Avenue, 312-482-8918.
- **K-Mart**, www.kmart.com: many of these stores have been liquidated, the remaining metro stores are located at 1360 North Ashland Avenue, 773-292-9400, and 3443 West Addison, 773-478-1334. In the suburbs, check 537 North Hicks Road, Palatine, 847-358-8181; 1155 Oakton Street, Des Plaines, 847-296-6136.

- **Marshalls**, www.marshallsonline.com, (two metro locations, many in the suburbs): 600 North Michigan Avenue, 312-280-7506, 1834 West Fullerton, 773-296-4494.
- **T.J. Max**, www.tjmaxx.com, (many in suburbs too): 11 North State Street, 312-553-0515; 1745 West Fullerton, 773-327-1124; 2840 North Broadway, 773-975-2347; 6456 West Irving Park Road, 773-725-9400.
- **Target**, www.target.com; an excellent choice for stylish but reasonably-priced lighting, smaller furniture, kitchen wares, clothing, simple electronics, and, of course, the irresistibly priced package of 200 rolls of toilet paper. Now if you can only figure out how to get it into the car. The Chicago stores are located at 2656 North Elston Avenue, 773-252-1994; 7100 South Cicero Avenue, 708-563-9050; and 2901 South Cicero Ave, Cicero, 708-863-6830. Suburban locations include: 2209 West Howard Street, Evanston, 847-733-1144; 6150 West Touhy, Niles, 847-588-2800; 2002 Golf Mill, Niles, 847-768-9217; 1700 East Rand Road, Arlington Heights, 847-222-0925. Others are located in Chicago Ridge, Chicago Heights, Park Ridge, Skokie, River Forest, and Lincolnwood.
- **Walmart**, www.walmart.com: many suburban locations including Niles, Bedford Park, Forest Park, Northlake, Villa Park.

SPECIALTY STORES

APPLIANCES, ELECTRONICS, CAMERAS

- **Best Buy**, www.bestbuy.com, has a large selection and good prices. Salespeople definitely won't pester you here, in fact, it may be hard to find them. The Chicago store is located at 1000 West North Avenue, 312-988-4067; suburban sites include Evanston, 2301 Howard Street, 847-570-0450, and Skokie, 5425 Touhy Avenue, 847-933-9170.
- **Central Camera**, 230 South Wabash Avenue, 312-427-5580
- **Circuit City**, 2500 North Elston, 773-772-0037
- **Hammacher Schlemmer & Co.**, www.hammacher.com, 445 North Michigan Avenue, 312-527-9100; offers an eclectic collection of things you never knew you didn't have.
- **Helix Camera & Video** has two locations: main store (the largest camera store in the United States), 310 South Racine Avenue, 312-421-6000; 2 Illinois Center, 312-565-5901.
- **Mid-State Camera Service** (for camera repair), 407 South Dearborn, #300, 312-939-2272
- **Tweeter Home Entertainment** has three Chicago-area locations: 900 North Michigan Avenue, 312-664-3100; the Century Shopping Center (level 4), 2828 North Clark Street, 773-525-7005; Edens Plaza in Wilmette, 847-251-1860.

- **Wolf Camera & Video**, www.wolfcamera.com; has locations throughout the Chicago metropolitan area and suburbs. In Chicago: The Atrium, 100 West Randolph Street #102, 312-269-9992; 750 North Rush Street, 312-943-5531; 1919 North Clybourn Avenue, 773-528-5585; 42 South Clark Street, 312-759-8030. The suburbs include: Evanston, 616 Davis Street, 847-328-0111; Oak Park, 135 North Oak Park Avenue, 708-848-2451; and Skokie, 7933 North Lincoln Avenue, 847-673-2530.

BEDS AND BEDDING

- **Arrelle Fine Linens & Down**, 445 North Wells Street, 312-321-3696, www.arrelle.com
- **Bed, Bath and Beyond**, www.bedbathandbeyond.com, has three locations: 530 North State Street, 312-755-9890; 1800 North Clybourn Avenue, 312-642-6596; 2838 North Broadway, 773-528-5055; also located in Naperville, Schaumburg, Orland Park, Downers Grove, Wilmette, Skokie, Deerfield, Kildeer.
- **Futonair**, 3154 North Clark Street, 773-281-0215
- **Jennifer Convertibles,** www.jenniferfurniture.com, has five locations: 180 North Wabash Avenue, 312-553-0260; 814 West North Avenue, 312-951-9377; 730 West Diversey Parkway, 773-281-9991; 2907 West Addison Street, 773-583-2171; 8101 South Cicero Avenue, 773-767-1605; and suburban locations such as Orland Park, Naperville, Evergreen Park, and Niles.
- **Linen 'n Things**, 3131 Clark Street, 773-388-5409, www.lnt.com; also in the suburbs including Schaumburg, Naperville, Gurnee, Joliet, Batavia, Crystal Lake, and Downers Grove.
- **Private Lives**, Chicago's largest selection of bed and bed linen, is at 56 East Oak Street, 312-337-5474, and 622 West Diversey Parkway, 773-525-6464

CARPETS AND RUGS

- **Caspian Oriental Rugs**, 700 North LaSalle Street, 312-664-7576
- **Home Carpet & Linoleum Center**, 3071 North Lincoln Avenue, 773-935-9314
- **Peerless Imported Rugs**, www.peerlessrugs.com, 3033 North Lincoln Avenue, 773-472-4848
- **Rexx Rug & Linoleum Co.**, www.rexxrug.com, 3312 North Lincoln Avenue, 773-281-8800; has a large discounted inventory of carpeting for immediate installation.

COMPUTER EQUIPMENT

The listings for computer sales and support go on and on. Check the Yellow Pages under "Computers."
- **C.D. Warehouse**, 315 Grand Avenue, 312-527-2700
- **Chicago Computer Supply**, www.chicagocomputersupply.com, 27 North Wacker Drive, 630-541-0004, or toll free 877-474-7774
- **Comp USA**, www.compusa.com, 101 East Chicago Avenue, 312-787-6776; 7011 Central Avenue, Skokie, 847-933-4700, and other suburban locations.
- **Hyde Park Computers, Inc.**, 133 Emerson, Evanston, 773-248-6200
- **Micro Center**, 2645 North Elston Avenue, 773-292-1700

FURNITURE/HOUSEHOLD GOODS

Chicago has stores to accommodate every taste and pocketbook.
- **Affordable Portables** located at 2608-10 North Clark Street, 773-935-6160, and Evanston, 924 Davis Street, 847-866-8124.
- **At Home Furniture**, www.nakedfurniturebydesign.com, 1330 South Milwaukee, Libertyville, 847-367-0009
- **Bloomingdale's**, 600 North Wabash Avenue, 312-324-7500; home furnishings, luggage, bridal registry.
- **The Container Store**, www.containerstore.com, 908 North Avenue, 312-654-8450, offers Chicagoans that most precious of urban commodities: more efficient (and stylish) use of scarce living space. Also in Northbrook, Schaumburg, and Oak Brook.
- **Crate & Barrel**, www.crateandbarrel.com; a notable company that offers contemporary furniture and household accessories. Crate & Barrel stores are located at 646 North Michigan Avenue, 312-787-5900; 850 West North Avenue, 312-573-9800; 3757 North Lincoln Avenue, 773-755-3900; 1515 Sheridan Road, Wilmette, 847-256-2726; 54 Oak Brook Center Mall, Oak Brook, 630-572-9199; and in Northbrook, Woodfield, Naperville, Vernon Hills, Michigan City, and Skokie. There's also an outlet store at 800 West North Avenue, 312-787-4775.
- **Ethan Allen Home Interiors**, www.ethanallen.com, 1700 North Halsted, 312-573-2500, and in the suburbs including Orland Park, Gurnee, Skokie, Arlington Heights, and Wheaton.
- **European Furniture**, 2145 West Grand Avenue, 312-243-1955
- **The Great Ace**, www.greatace.com, has furniture, bedding, and an excellent hardware department. Located at 2639 North Elston Avenue in Webster Place, a mall at the southwest corner of Webster and Clybourn avenues, 773-342-0300.

- **Hammacher Schlemmer**, 445 North Michigan Avenue, 312-527-9100, www.hammacher.com
- **Ikea**, www.ikea-usa.com, one location in the Chicagoland area, a gigantic store filled with stylish, well-made and affordable Finnish furniture and home items, at 1800 East McConnor Parkway, Schaumburg, 847-969-9700.
- **John M. Smyth Homemakers Furniture, Inc**. located in: Schaumburg, 1733 Woodfield Road (opposite Woodfield Shopping Center), 847-619-6800; Downers Grove, 1013 Butterfield Road, 630-852-6880; Orland Park, 66 Orland Square Drive, 708-349-5800; and Niles, Naperville, Joliet, and Sleepy Hollow.
- **Pier 1 Imports, Inc**., www.pierone.com, has many locations, including 1350 North Wells Street, 312-787-4320; 2112 North Clybourn Avenue, 773-871-6610; 651 West Diversey Parkway, 773-871-1558; and 2868 North Ashland Avenue, 773-975-1033, as well as many suburban locations.
- **Pottery Barn**, www.potterybarn.com, several metro and suburban locations: 734 North Michigan, 312-587-9602; 865 West North Avenue, 312-587-9837; 111 Old Orchard Road, Skokie, 847-673-8416; 21 Oak Brook Center, Oak Brook, 630-572-3307; 1850 Second Street, Highland Park, 847-681-9873; 20530 North Rand Road, Deer Park, 847-550-6763; also in Naperville and Geneva.
- **Scandinavian Designs**, 501 West North Avenue, 312-337-4200
- **Williams-Sonoma**, www.williams-sonoma.com, has several locations within Chicago and suburbs including 900 North Michigan Avenue, 312-587-8080; 113 Old Orchard Center, Skokie, 847-933-9803; 142 Oak Brook Center, Oak Brook, 630-571-2702; 2100 Northbrook Court, Northbrook, 847-291-3626; Woodfield Mall, Schaumburg, 847-619-0940; 121 Town Square, Wheaton, 630-665-7250; 9 West Jackson Avenue, Naperville, 630-369-4167; also in Lake Forest and Deer Park.

HARDWARE, PAINTS, AND WALLPAPER

Hardware stores can be found in every neighborhood. Chicago's biggest chains are ACE and True Value, in the suburbs you can also go to Home Depot and Menards.

- **ACE Hardware**: besides **The Great Ace**, listed above, here are a few locations with many more listed at www.acehardware.com: 4654 North Broadway, 773-334-7146; Ashland Paint & Hardware, 1013 North Ashland Avenue, 773-486-1271; Imperial ACE Hardware, 1208 West Grand Avenue, 312-421-0475; Lakeview ACE Hardware, 3921 North Sheridan Road, 773- 525-1700; Meyer's ACE Hardware, 315 East 35th Street, 312-225-5687; Stauber ACE Hardware, 3911 North Lincoln

Avenue, 773-281-1777; Streeterville ACE Hardware, 680 North Lake Shore Drive, 312-266-0900.

- **True Value Hardware (TVH)**, many more listed at www.truevalue.com: Clark-Devon Hardware, 6401 North Clark Street, 773-764-3575; Edward's TVH, 2804 North Halsted Street, 773-525-6104; Imperial TVH, 1208 West Grand, 312-421-0475; Klein TVH, 3737 North Southport Avenue, 773-525-2291; Lehman's TVH, 3473 North Broadway, 773-472-4435; Tenenbaum H.A. Hardware Company, 1138 West Belmont Avenue, 773-935-7374; N. Turek and Sons TVH, 333 South Halsted Street, 312-263-3560; Wahler Brothers TVH, 2551 North Halsted Street, 773-248-1349; Zweifel TVH, 345 West 25th Place, 312-842-1924.

- **Home Depot**, www.homedepot.com; is perfect for the do-it-yourself home repair handyman as well as the professional contractor. It has an extensive garden center for spring and fall landscaping. There are locations in Bedford Park, Niles, Chicago Ridge, Mt. Prospect and Evanston. In Chicago try: 1232 West North Avenue, 773-486-9200; 7200 South Cicero Avenue, 773-586-0032; 1500 North Dayton, 312-694-2400; 2570 North Elston Avenue, 773-289-4615; 2555 North Normandy, 773-745-9900; 2665 North Halsted, 773-472-7740; 1919 North Cicero, 773-622-8860.

- **Menards**, www.menards.com; "save big money" here: 4626 West Diversey, 773-685-8677; 2601 North Clybourn, 773-880-5954. Suburban locations include Hanover Park, Hillside, Mt. Prospect, Hoffman Estates, Morton Grove, Mundelein, Naperville, Palatine, Tinley Park, and Gurnee.

ONLINE SHOPPING SERVICES

Online shopping is the way to go if you don't like crowded malls or sitting in traffic. Three local web shopping sites:

- **Chicago Store Online**, www.chicagostore.com, 800-679-8810; this is the online version of the City of Chicago's retail shop. Here you will find city surplus and salvage memorabilia, as well as selected items from the museum shops around the city. Interested in buying a parking meter? Look no further! If your curiosity is piqued, you can visit the retail store at the Water Works Visitor Center, 163 East Pearson Street, 312-742-8811.

- **Greater North Michigan Avenue Association**, www.themagnificentmile.com; what better way to purchase gift certificates to the stores located within the Magnificent Mile without having to fight the crowds. Subscribe to their newsletter to keep current on special events happening in the area.

- **Urbanstyle Shopping Guide**, www.urbanstyle.com, will get you up to speed about where to buy what in a flash. Organized by neighborhoods, it will provide you with the retailers within your zip code.

SPORTING GOODS

- **Active Endeavors**, www.activeendeavors.com, 935 West Armitage Avenue, 773-281-8100; 55 East Grand Avenue, 312-822-0600; 1527 Chicago Avenue, Evanston, 847-869-7070
- **Ed Shirley Sports**, www.edshirley.com; sporting goods for fishermen: 3509 West 159th Street Markham, 708-331-5711; 5404 South LaGrange Road Countryside, 708-352-5712; 5802 West Dempster, Morton Grove, 847-966-5900; 1272 East Dundee Road Palatine, 847-705-8707; 691 North LaGrange Road Frankfort, 815-469-4060
- **REI**, www.rei.com, 8225 West Gold Road, Niles, 847-470-9090; 17W160 22nd Street, Oakbrook Terrace, 630-574-7700
- **Sportmart**, www.sportmart.com; 620 North LaSalle Street, 312-337-6151; 3134 North Clark Street, 773-871-8500; 6420 West Fullerton Avenue, 773-804-0044
- **Sports Authority**, www.thesportsauthority.com, 1801 West Fullerton, 773-935-7729, and in several suburban areas including Arlington Heights, Downers Grove, Gurnee Mills, Schaumburg, Northbrook, and Niles.
- **Vertel's Chicago Running Athletics and Fitness**, 2001 North Clybourn Avenue, 773-248-7400

THRIFT AND VINTAGE SHOPS

There are three kinds of second-hand stores: thrift stores, where the merchandise is plentiful, cheap but not necessarily trendy; vintage stores, where the clothes are more fashionable and more expensive; and antiques stores where the merchandise may be exquisite, with prices to match. You can find forgotten gems at thrift stores (the exciting challenge) but you may have to dig through a lot of sand along the way.

VINTAGE STORES

- **Disgraceland**, 3338 North Clark Street, 773-281-5875
- **Flashy Trash**, 3524 North Halsted Street, 773-327-6900
- **Hubba-Hubba**, 3309 North Clark Street, 773-477-1414
- **Strange Cargo**, 3448 North Clark Street, 773-327-8090
- **Wacky Cats**, 3012 North Lincoln Avenue, 773-929-6701

THRIFT STORES—CHICAGO

- **Brown Elephant Resale Shop** for the Howard Brown Memorial Clinic, 3651 North Halsted Street, 773-549-5943.
- **The Salvation Army** operates dozens of thrift shops in Chicago and suburbs. Check out 2258 North Clybourn Avenue, 773-477-1300; 2941 North Central, 773-283-1315 or 4315 North Broadway, 773-348-1401. For other locations look in the Yellow Pages under "Thrift Shops."
- **Unique Thrift**, 3748 North Eston, 773-279-0850; 4441 West Diversey, 773-227-2282; 4445 North Sheridan Road, 773-275-8623; as well as nine other locations.
- **Village Discount Outlet** has stores throughout Chicago including, 2032 North Milwaukee Avenue, 2855 North Halsted Street, 4898 North Clark Street, and 2043 West Roscoe Street. Same number for all stores: 708-388-4772.
- **White Elephant Shop** of Children's Memorial Hospital, 2380 North Lincoln Avenue, 773-883-6184

SUBURBAN THRIFTS

- **Bethesda Thrift Shop**, 26 Crystal Lake Plaza, Crystal Lake, 815-455-2325
- **Lafemmena**, 1022 North Boulevard, Oak Park, 708-386-8830
- **Lambs Farm Thrift Shop**, 14245 West Rockland Road, Libertyville, 847-327-9053
- **Little Mexico Thrift Shop**, 111 North Wolf Road, Wheeling, 847-419-8935
- **Simply Sensible Shoppe**, 17010 Oak Park Avenue, Tinley Park, 708-633-9180
- **Treasure Chest**, 105 South Genesee Street, Waukegan, 847-625-8460
- **Unique Thrift Shop**, 3316 Chicago Road, Chicago Heights, 708-756-1774
- **Upscale Resale of Libertyville**, 330 North Milwaukee Avenue, Libertyville, 847-918-9988

ANTIQUE STORES

There are plenty of opportunities to shop for antiques around Chicago, from auctions and galleries to antique warehouses. Be sure to call and inquire about store hours before dropping in; many shops keep odd hours and some serve by appointment only. Check the Yellow Pages under "Antiques" for listings.

AUCTION HOUSES

Auctions are a fun way to decorate your home. If you have an eye for design and know the market value, you can create a unique environment in your home by visiting auction houses. You will find announcements in the *Tribune* on Fridays and Sundays. Check the business section of the Sunday paper. Usually you will get a week's notice, but sometimes just a few days as some events are held mid-week. Try to get to the site before bidding starts so you can examine close up what will be on the block.

GARAGE SALES

As soon as the weather hints of warmer days, sale signs start popping out on lawns all over the suburbs, beckoning drivers to their yards. Garage sales are very popular in the Chicagoland area. There are a number of ways people advertise their wares. Some place an ad in the local community paper, but those who really want to draw a crowd will place an ad in the *Sun Times*, *Daily Herald* or *Chicago Tribune*. Most ads are placed on Wednesdays for Friday and Saturday sales, or Fridays, for Saturday and Sunday sales. Some don't advertise except for small hand-made signs posted at intersections near their home. Often neighbors join forces and coordinate their sales so that you can hit two or three sales without having to get back into your car and drive down the road. Garage sales are like golfers; they linger until it's too cold to be outdoors. You may find some sales as late as November, if the weather holds out.

Some communities get together each year, sometimes under the umbrella of a local church, and host an annual garage or rummage sale. You will see signs advertising the dates and times in front of the location.

DUMPSTER DIVING (ALLEY SHOPPING)

Many a funky Chicago apartment has been accented, or even primarily outfitted, with recycled material from alleys and dumpsters. Every neighborhood has a specific day for garbage pickup and the ideal time to go scrounging is the day or morning, before the blue Streets & Sanitation trucks cart it all away. The best times of the year to go hunting are the last weekends of April and September, when many leases expire and the alleys are piled high with whatever didn't make the cut. But the pickings are good at the end of any month. Another rewarding time to covet thy neighbor's trash is in springtime when people clean out their garages, basements, attics, etc. All in all, the alleys of Chicago offer the widest possible selection of used furniture, appliances, and household and decorative items at the lowest possible prices. Look out your back window for the one nearest you.

FOOD

GROCERY STORES

Chicago has corner grocers, vast supermarkets, specialty markets, farmers' markets, and everything in between. For big shopping trips many choose a neighborhood Dominick's, Jewel, or Cub Foods. These supply everything from meat and deli items to laundry soap and fresh produce. Check the Yellow Pages for one closest to you. If you're looking for that tough-to-find cheese or pasta, try Treasure Island. Another popular specialty store that is reasonably priced is Trader Joe's. Here you will find a wide assortment of exotic frozen vegetables, terrific frozen desserts, vegetarian specialties, and wine, all affordably priced. There is one store in Chicago on North Lincoln near Grace, and more in the suburbs. If you just need a few items, check your neighborhood grocers, many of which will offer a great variety of ethnic ingredients, depending on the neighborhood. If eating organic food is important to you, you'll find organic selections at most large grocers, and there are plenty of health food markets throughout the area including several Whole Foods, the formidable national chain. Bulk purchasing often appeals to those with large families; membership warehouses such as Costco or Sam's Club offer bulk foods and household items.

- **Costco** (membership fee), 2746 North Clybourn, Lincoln Park, 773-360-2054, www.costco.com; suburban locations include: Bedford Park, Oak Brook, Niles, and Glenview. Similar to Sam's Club; high quality meats, liquor department, prescription drugs, baked goods, and household items.
- **Cub Foods**, in Chicago at 2627 North Elston Avenue, 773-252-6400. Also in the suburbs. The least expensive of the three large supermarket chains and has a good produce section.
- **Dominick's**, www.dominicks.com; has many Chicago and suburban locations, including 3012 North Broadway, 773-549-6100; 3350 North Western Avenue, 773-929-8910; 5235 North Sheridan Road, 773-728-4300; and 6009 North Broadway, 773-769-2300. The larger stores have excellent bakeries.
- **Jewel**, www.jewelosco.com; has scores of stores in and around Chicago, including 1210 North Clark Street, 312-944-6950; 3033 South Halsted, 312-225-1010; 1240 West Harrison Street, 312-243-2370; 3531 North Broadway, 773-871-1054; 1341 North Paulina Street, 773-342-3410; 3630 North Southport Avenue, 773-281-1521; 438 West Madison, Oak Park, 708-383-7111. Most have decent bakeries, good deli departments, and fresh produce sections.

- **Sam's Club** (membership fee), suburban locations including 2450 Main Street in Evanston, 847-491-9000, and 101 Oakton, Des Plaines, 847-296-5050; online at: www.samsclub.com. Warehouse-like setting, offering everything from baked goods and high quality meats to televisions.
- **Trader Joe's**, 3745 North Lincoln Avenue, 773-248-4920, www.traderjoes.com; smallish, discount supermarket that offers healthy alternative eating. Organic foods, excellent variety of frozen vegetables and fish, small liquor department, interesting assortment of cheeses. Several suburban locations include: 17 West Rand Road, Arlington Heights, 847-506-0752; 1407 Waukegan Road, Glenview, 847-657-7821; 577 Waukegan Road, Northbrook, 847-498-9076; 735 West Main Street, Lake Zurich, 847-550-7827; 1942 West Fabyan Parkway, Batavia, 630-879-3234; also in Orland Park, Glen Ellyn, La Grange, Arlington Heights, Downers Grove and Naperville.
- **Treasure Island,** www.tifoods.com: 75 West Elm Street, 312-440-1144; 1635 North Wells Street, 312-642-1105; 680 North Lake Shore Drive, 312-664-0400; 3460 North Broadway, 773-327-3880; and 2121 North Clybourn Avenue, 773-880-8880. In Wilmette at 911 Ridge Road, 847-256-5033. Upscale supermarket offering ethnic produce, organic foods, a wide range of cheeses, and staples.
- **Whole Foods**, www.wholefoods.com; health and organic foods including fresh meat and fish, deli, and baked goods. The North Avenue location has an excellent cafe on the upper level, 1000 West North Avenue, 312-587-0648. Also at: 3300 North Ashland Avenue, 773-244-4200, 30 West Huron, 312-932-9600. In the suburbs: 760 Waukegan Road, Deerfield, 847-444-1900; 1640 Chicago Avenue, Evanston, 847-733-1600; 1331 North Rand Road, Palatine, 847-776-8080; 7245 Lake Street, River Forest, 708-366-1045; 151 Rice Lake Square, Wheaton, 630-588-1500; 201 West 63rd Street (between Route 83 and Clarendon Hills Road), Willowbrook, 630-655-5000.
- **Oberweis Dairy**, www.oberweisdairy.com; located in Aurora, Oberweis delivers premium dairy products, and select high quality meats, cheeses and specialty items, including ice cream. Milk is produced from small, locally owned farms. For more information call 888-645-5868. See the web site for one of their 26 store locations.

FARMERS' MARKETS

The City of Chicago sponsors 30 farmers' markets during the summer in various locations, including Daley Plaza in the Loop. Farmers come to sell their wares mid-May through November on Tuesday, Wednesday, Thursday, Saturday, and Sunday. For example, on Saturdays it's the Lincoln Park High School's parking lot (Armitage Avenue east of Halsted Street).

Further north on Tuesday mornings, head to Lincoln Square (just south of Lawrence Avenue on Lincoln Avenue). For a list of all the markets, locations, hours of operation and dates, visit the city's web site at www.ci.chi.il. us/SpecialEvents, or call 312-744-3315.

Many suburbs host farmers' markets as well. Evanston, Palatine, Park Ridge, Schaumburg, and Mt. Prospect are just a few in the northwest suburbs that hold them regularly. Check your local city hall for information about your area, or visit www.localharvest.org and search for locations nearest you.

ETHNIC DISTRICTS

With all the different kinds of people that immigrate to Chicago, you would be correct in expecting it to be a land of a thousand flavors. The restaurants and eateries here reflect both the taste of the new generation of Chicagoans as well as those that helped make Chicago what it is today. While you can find ethnic food in nearly every neighborhood, some are more solidly made up of one type of cuisine.

In general, on South Halsted, starting around the 200 South block, is Greek Town with its Mediterranean styled restaurants and back yard seating. The Taylor Street neighborhood offers mostly Italian and French bistro style cooking. River West offers cuisine with a Mediterranean touch and a few trendier restaurants as well. Lincoln Square holds on to its Middle European roots; come here for a solid selection of German/Austrian restaurants. The Lakeview East area is your first stop for authentic Thai cuisine. If the hearty dishes of Poland are more to your liking, look for the all-you-can-eat buffets in and around Logan Square—also here, and in Pilsen, are wonderful Mexican eateries. In Skokie, it's Middle-Eastern cuisine or kosher delis. Oak Park, Morton Grove, and Highland Park have good delis as well. Try Wrigleyville for Ethiopian and North African dining. Hyde Park is the place to go for southern cooking, whether it's Cajun style, Creole, or barbecue. Of course, Chinatown offers authentic Cantonese and Mandarin fare, but between Uptown and Rogers Park, and around Lakeview, you'll find other Asian delights, including a good selection of Vietnamese and Thai cuisine, and terrific noodle shops. To read reviews or to get acquainted with any particular area, refer to *Chicago Magazine* (either hard copy or online at www.chicagomagazine.com), or go to www.metromix.com for the latest on local eateries.

If you looking for a quintessentially Chicago meal it will probably be approved by the American High Cholesterol Society: ribs, steak or deep-dish pizza (unless it's vegetarian). Twin Anchors in Old Town or Ribs and Bibs in Hyde Park are good choices for ribs. Many go to Harry Carey or Gibson's for a nice steak dinner, and you (along with just about every tourist who visits Chicago) won't be disappointed with the pizzas at Pizzeria Uno.

If you are a college graduate and female, and enjoy tasting a variety of foods, you might consider joining the **American Association of University Women's Ethnic Dining Club**. They meet once a month, nine months of the year, each time at a different ethnic restaurant. They post their schedule online. For more information go to www.aauw-il.org.

And finally, what is a meal without dessert? Listed here are just a few of the scrumptious **ethnic bakeries** scattered throughout the city:

- **Artopolis**, 306 South Halsted, 312-559-9000, offers terrific Greek and French pastries.
- **Cafe Selmarie**, 4729 North Lincoln Avenue, 773-989-5595; located in the heart of Lincoln Square, this charming cafe serves light food as well as delicious French and German style desserts. Wedding cakes, too! Affordable and peaceful with nice art.
- **Marie Gold Bakery and Fast Food**, 5752 North California Avenue, 773-561-1978; Philippine food and bakery.
- **Middle East Bakery and Grocery**, 1512 West Foster Avenue, 773-561-2224; Andersonville has been traditionally known for Swedish pastries, but more recent immigrants have brought new traditions.
- **New Hong Kong Bakery**, 1050-52 West Argyle Street, 773-878-3226; Philippine and Chinese delights.
- **Panderia Ayutla Bakery**, 6963 North Clark Street, 773-764-9077; not much English spoken here, but if you can revive your rusty Spanish you will be rewarded.
- **Swedish Bakery**, 5348 North Clark Street, 773-561-8919; finely crafted European delectables, this bakery put Andersonville on the map. Everything here is mouthwatering.
- **Tahoora**, 2326 West Devon Avenue, 773-743-7272; Pakistani/Indian treats.
- **Vienna Pastry Shop**, 5411 West Addison Street, 773-685-4166; excellent German pastries.

O NE OF THE GREAT PLEASURES OF LIVING IN CHICAGO IS THE enormous number and variety of events and cultural offerings. Despite inclement weather, the drive, or the lack of parking, people come into the city in droves to experience the cultural riches the city has to offer. Unless otherwise noted, all listings are in Chicago.

So, where to start? Check with the following publications for listings of area events:

- **Chicago Magazine**, www.chicagomag.com; offers an extensive entertainment section in each monthly issue. You can also find museum exhibits, new restaurants, and art gallery openings. Occasionally it will review new clubs and new happenings in trendy neighborhoods as well.

- **Chicago Reader**, www.chireader.com; comes out every Thursday. You will find this free publication in bookstores, banks, movie theaters, coffee shops, etc. The *Reader* publishes a comprehensive guide to the upcoming events of the week. In the suburbs look for the *Reader's Guide to Arts and Entertainment*.

- **Metromix.com**, www.metromix.com; is an online entertainment guide from the Tribune Company. Check here for schedules of independent movies, club acts, plays, festivals, concerts, and even sports.

- Most of the traditional daily papers have a Friday/Weekend and an Arts Sunday section. Check the **Chicago Tribune**, **Chicago Sun Times**, and the **Daily Herald**.

- **New City**, www.newcity.com; is another weekly free alternative that publishes an entertainment guide.

- Your **neighborhood newspaper** is often a source of local happenings. These weeklies can be found in most chain drugstores, and convenience stores, alongside the traditional daily newspapers.

Entertainment hotlines are also popular for finding out more about area events:

- **Chicago Dance and Music Alliance Hotline**: 312-987-1123 or www.chicagoperformances.org
- **Concert Line**: 312-666-6667 for rock, country, blues
- **Hot Tix**: www.hottix.org for daily listings of shows offering discounted day-of-performance tickets. The Hot Tix offices are at 78 West Randolph, 163 East Pearson and 9501 North Skokie Blvd. in Skokie; and at Tower Records locations in suburbs.
- **Chicago Fine Arts Hotline**: 312-346-3278
- **Mayor's Office of Special Events Hotline**: 312-744-3370 or go to www.cityofchicago.org/specialevents.

TICKETS

Tickets for most events and performances may be purchased at the venue box offices or through **Ticketmaster** at 312-559-1212, 312-902-1500, 312-902-1400, online at www.ticketmaster.com, or at Ticketmaster outlets. It's always a good idea to get your tickets as far in advance as possible since many shows, concerts, exhibits, and events sell out. When calling have your credit card ready and be prepared to pay service fees. (See Hot Tix above for information about discounted day-of-performance tickets.)

MUSIC

PROFESSIONAL AND COMMUNITY SYMPHONIC, CHORAL, OPERA, CHAMBER

There may be more than one reason the French declared Chicago the "Paris of the Midwest"—the level of artistry here is extraordinary. Included in this section are professional groups as well as community ensembles. If you are a musician or singer, and are interested in performing, these groups are a good place to start your inquiries. Or check the Classical Studio web site, www.classicalstudio.com, which will lead you to community based musical events and groups interested in acquiring new musicians.

- **Artist Series at Wheaton College**; their calendar offerings can resemble a who's who in the classical music world. In the past, soprano Kathleen Battle and guitarist Christopher Parkening have been included on the roster. For tickets call, 630-752-5010.
- **Chamber Music Society of the North Shore**, www.cmsns.org; performances are held at Evanston's Pick-Staiger Concert Hall on Northwestern University's campus. Tickets or subscriptions can be purchased by calling 847-835-5084.

- **Chicago Chamber Musicians/Chicago String Ensemble**, www.chicagochambermusic.org; Sunday performances at the Pick-Staiger Concert Hall, Evanston; Monday performances take place at the DePaul University Concert Hall. You can order tickets online or by calling, 312-225-5226.

- **The Chicago Symphony Orchestra (CSO)**; highly acclaimed, when in town they perform at Orchestra Hall, 220 South Michigan Avenue, from September until June. For ticket sales information: 312-294-3040, www.cso.org.

- **College Church**; this Wheaton based non-denominational church features concerts on select Sundays, usually at 4 p.m. Offerings include organ recitals and piano trios—usually focused on sacred music. Check their web site for a calendar listing: www.college-church.org or call 630-668-0878.

- **Elgin Symphony Orchestra**, www.elginsymphony.org; nation's fastest growing orchestra with over 50 concerts annually in several locations. For tickets call the box office: 847-888-4000.

- **The Grant Park Symphony and Chorus** plays summer concerts at the Petrillo Band Shell in Grant Park (Jackson Boulevard between Lake Shore and Columbus drives). You can purchase a reserved seat or listen for free on several acres of grass (bring a blanket). Call 312-742-4736 or check www.grantparkmusicfestival.com, for more information.

- **Illinois Philharmonic Orchestra** is based in Park Forest, 708-481-7774, www.ipomusic.org; offers classical, pops, family and community concerts as well as educational programs.

- **Lakeshore Symphony of Chicago**, www.lsso.org, 312-409-5670; calling itself, "Chicago's Community Orchestra," this ensemble offers selections that are geared toward seniors and families, at very reasonable prices. Concerts are held at the Copernicus Center Gateway Theatre on Chicago's northwest side.

- **Network Chicago** is a terrific source of small, less expensive classical music programs. You will find a variety of musical genres along with classical performances listed here under "nc connections": www.networkchicago.com.

- **Performing Arts Chicago (PAC)**, 410 South Michigan Avenue, Suite 911, Chicago, 312-663-1628; this organization brings local, national, and international talent to Chicago in a variety of mediums—theater, music, performance. PAC members receive an array of benefits such as discounts on tickets, invitations to special events and more. You can buy tickets from their web site, www.pachicago.org.

- Small but entertaining musical groups are the **Chicago Chamber Orchestra**, 312-922-5570, and the **Chicago Sinfonietta**, www.chicagosinfonietta.org, 312-236-3681.

The city also sponsors separate blues, jazz, gospel, and Celtic festivals during the summer months, as well as free ballroom dances that are accompanied by a live band. Call the **Mayor's Office of Special Events Hotline** at 312-744-3370 for more information, or go to www.ci.chi.il.us/SpecialEvents.

CHORUSES

- **Chicago Master Singers**, www.chicagomastersingers.org; in Barrington, 847-604-1067; originally known as The New Oratorio Singers, this group presents concerts in northwest suburban Chicago communities.
- **Chicago Symphony Singers**, www.css.org; this choral group comprised of members of the Chicago Symphony Chorus, debuted in 2002. For tickets call 312-294-3000 or go online.
- **Downers Grove Choral Society**, 630-515-0030; full spectrum of major choral works, including contemporary masterpieces and commissioned premieres.
- **DuPage Chorale** is a community group with the College of DuPage, www.cod.edu. Major works are performed with the professional group, DuPage Chorale Orchestra and soloists. Tickets can be purchased online or by calling, 630-942-4000.
- **Elgin Chorale Union**, www.elginchoralunion.org; Fox Valley area's oldest performing arts group. For tickets call 847-622-0300.
- **Elmhurst Chorale Union** is a community chorus that performs twice a year in addition to occasional appearances with the Elmhurst Symphony Orchestra and special events. For more information visit www.elmhurst.edu/mus/ensembles/choralunion or call 630-617-3338 to purchase tickets.
- **Glen Ellyn-Wheaton Chorale**, www.ge-wtnchorale.org: not-for-profit, non-audition adult chorus. Call 630-415-3066.
- **Naperville Chorus and Chamber Singers**, www.napervillechorus.org; chamber singers provide musical entertainment for intimate settings: dinners, organizational events, and community events.
- **North Shore Choral Society**, www.northshorechoral.org; community chorus for over 60 years. Call 847-328-5158.
- **Northwest Choral Society**; located in Park Ridge, this community chorale of 50 generally performs three times a year. Visit their web site at www.nwchoralsociety.org. Call 847-577-7147 for information and 630-837-1666 for tickets.
- **Oak Park Concert Chorale**, www.oakparkconcertchorale.org; performs a variety of works a cappella and with accompaniment. Call 708-383-4742.
- **West Suburban Chorale Union**, www.choraleunion.ws/WSCU, in

Wheaton. Check their web site for schedule information and instructions on how to audition.

OPERA

The **Lyric Opera of Chicago** performs at the Civic Center for the Performing Arts (also known as the Civic Opera House), 20 North Wacker Drive in downtown Chicago. Their calendar generally runs from September through February. For information, call the box office at 312-332-2244 ext. 5600, or visit their web site at www.lyricopera.org.

DANCE—BALLET, JAZZ, MODERN

You won't find dance, be it ballet, tap, jazz, or classical, or modern, in just one concert hall. It's everywhere in Chicago; showcased in art galleries, museums, and outdoor festivals. Be sure to check your local community colleges, libraries, and theaters in addition to the listings here. For news about upcoming dance events, try the **Chicago Dance and Music Alliance Hotline**: 312-987-1123 or www.chicagoperformances.org or call 312-987-9296 to ask questions. You can also review *Chicago Magazine's* entertainment section, which has a special section for dance performances.

- **Athenaeum Theatre**, www.althenaeum.livedomain.com, 2936 North Southport, often hosts dance performances created by local choreographers. Tickets at Ticketmaster 312-902-1500. Box office information at 773-935-6860.
- **Ballet Chicago**, www.balletchicago.org, 312-251-8838; school with a studio company.
- **Gus Giordano Jazz Dance Chicago**, www.giordanojazzdance.com, 847-866-6779; founded in 1953, international touring company, professional dance school and active educational outreach program.
- **Hubbard Street Dance Chicago** is a home grown group that has achieved international recognition. The Hubbard Street often performs in town at such venues as the **Ford Center for the Performing Arts** and the **Cadillac Palace Theatre**. You can also visit the company's web site, www.hubbardstreetdance.com, or call their office at 312-850-9744 for more information.
- **Joffrey Ballet of Chicago**; often performs at the Auditorium, 50 East Congress Parkway, 312-902-1400. Call them at 312-739-0120 or check their web site, www.joffreyballet.org.
- **The Dance Center**, 1306 South Michigan Avenue, 312-344-8300; part of Columbia College, The Dance Center is home one of the city's leading promoters of contemporary dance. Check their web site for a schedule of events: www.dancecenter.org.

THEATER

Chicago is a city of drama and it loves actors. Experimental theater abounds, as well as community theater, and bigger productions that are working out the kinks before heading to Broadway. And don't forget the terrific ensemble theater here. Groups such as Steppenwolf work with core groups of actors, writers, directors, and invite guest performers for limited runs. The resulting work is often riveting, capturing nationwide attention. The variety and competition here means you can easily enjoy a solid performance without breaking the bank. Discounted fares and reduced rates are available with subscriptions or through the last minute Hot Tix route (see above). Check the local paper, the **Chicago Reader**, and **www.metromix.com** for reviews and ticket information.

PROFESSIONAL AND COMMUNITY THEATER

Provided here is a sampling of local production companies. Soon you will compile a list of favorites.

- **Arie Crown Theatre**, McCormick Center, 2301 South Lake Shore Drive, www.ariecrown.com, 312-791-6190
- **Bailiwick Repertory**, 1229 West Belmont, www.bailiwick.org, 773-883-1090
- **Briar Street Theatre**, 3133 North Halsted Street, www.foxtheatricals.com, 773-348-4000
- **Court Theatre**, 5535 South Ellis Avenue, www.courttheatre.org, 773-753-4472
- **Eclipse Theatre Company**, 2000 West Fulton, www.eclipsetheatre.com, 312-409-1687
- **Ford Center for the Performing Arts**, Oriental Theatre, 24 West Randolph Street, www.broadwayinchicago.com, 312-977-1700, for box office information.
- **Goodman Theatre**, 170 North Dearborn, www.goodman-theatre.org, 312-443-3800
- **Lookingglass Theatre Company**, world-renowned for their innovative performances, their new home is at the Water Tower Water Works. Theatre and Box Office: 821 North Michigan Avenue, 312-337-0665, www.lookingglasstheatre.org
- **North Shore Center for the Performing Arts**, 9501 Skokie Blvd., Skokie, www.northshorecenter.org, 847-673-6300
- **Royal George Theatre**, 1641 North Halsted, 312-988-9000

- **The Second City**, 1616 North Wells Street in the Old Town neighborhood, www.secondcity.com, 312-337-3992
- **Steppenwolf Theatre Company**, 1650 North Halsted Street, www.steppenwolf.org, 312-335-1650
- **The Theatre Building**, 1225 West Belmont Avenue, www.theatre-buildingchicago.org, 773-327-5252
- **Victory Gardens**, 2257-63 North Lincoln Avenue, www.victorygardens.org, 773-871-3000

For a comprehensive listing of theater in and around Chicago, go to **www.centerstage.net**, for profiles of theaters, scheduled performances and links to other performing art events.

FILM

Chicago has a few art houses that showcase independent and art films. The Sunday section of the *Sun Times* and the *Chicago Tribune* list the (mostly) mainstream films being shown at the multiplex theaters. Occasionally art films are reviewed in those newspapers, especially in the Friday Weekend sections. You can check the *Chicago Reader* and *New City* for film reviews and showings. In this book, check **A Chicago Year** for information regarding annual film festivals in Chicago. For commercial theaters, drive-ins, second-run cinema, and suburban locations visit www.centerstage.net.

ART FILM HOUSES

- **Century 12 & CineArts 6**, 1715 Maple Avenue, 847-492-0123
- **Chicago Filmmakers**, 5243 North Clark Street, www.chicagofilmmakers.org, 773-293-1447
- **Facets Multimedia**, 1517 West Fullerton Avenue, www.facets.org, 773-281-4114
- **Fine Arts Theatre**, 418 South Michigan Avenue, 312-939-3700
- **Gene Siskel Film Center** (located at the School of the Art Institute, www.artic.edu), 164 North State Street, www.artic.edu/webspaces/siskelfilmcenter, hotline: 312-846-2800, tickets: 312-846-2600
- **Lake**, 1022 Lake Street, Oak Park, 708-848-9088
- **Music Box Theatre**, 3733 North Southport, www.musicboxtheatre.com, 773-871-6604

COMEDY

Chicagoans love to laugh hard and long, so it comes as no surprise that comedians flock to Chicago and its environs. Here is just a sampling of area clubs. Call for times, cover charges, drink minimums and other up to the minute details:

- **All Jokes Aside**, 1000 South Wabash Street, 773-922-0577
- **Barrels of Laughs**, 10345 South Central Avenue, Oak Lawn, 708-499-2969; a little out of the way for downtowners, but this club attracts local and national talent to its stage.
- **Chase Café**, 7301 North Sheridan Road, 773-743-5650
- **Cherry Red**, 2833 North Sheffield, www.cherryredchicago.com, 773-477-3661
- **Comedy Comedy**, Wyndham Lisle Hotel, 3000 Warrenville Road, Lisle, www.comedycomedylive.com, 630-226-9700
- **ComedySportz Theatre**, 2851 North Halsted Street, www.comedysportzchicago.com, 773-549-8080
- **Cotton Club & All that Jazz**, 1710 South Michigan Avenue, 773-438-1104 or 312-341-9787
- **The Comedy Spot** under **Famous Freddies Roadhouse**, 1799 South Busse, Mount Prospect, www.thecomedy-spot.com, 847-652-7145
- **Gamekeepers**, 345 West Armitage Street, 773-549-0400
- **Hidden Lounge**, 651 West Washington, 312-627-0409
- **Hog Head McDunna's**, 1505 West Fullerton Street, 773-929-0944
- **Holiday Club**, 1470 North Milwaukee Avenue, www.swingersmecca.com, 773-486-0686
- **ImprovOlympic**, 3541 North Clark Street, www.improvolympic.com, 773-880-0199
- **Lincoln Restaurant**, 4008 North Lincoln Avenue, 773-248-1820
- **Lyons Den**, 1934 West Irving Park Road, www.lyonsdenlive.com, 773-871-3757
- **Phyllis' Musical Inn**, 1800 West Division, 773-486-9862
- **Red Pepper Masquerade**, 428 East 87th, 773-873-5700
- **Riddles**, 15750 South Harlem, Orland Park, www.riddlescomedyclub.com, 708-444-0234
- **Second City**, 1616 North Wells, www.secondcity.com, 312-337-3992 (call for suburban locations); is the legendary improvisational comedy theater where aspiring John Belushis and Bill Murrays perform nightly for locals and tourists alike.
- **Touch Of The Past**, 947 Mannheim Road, Bellwood, 708-493-9236
- **Zanies**, www.zanies.com,1548 North Wells, 312-337-4027; some consider this club the best in the city. Also at Pheasant Run Resort,

4051 East Main, Saint Charles, 630-513-1761; and 230 Hawthorn Village Commons, Vernon Hills, 847-549-6030.

- **Zella's**, 1983 North Clybourn, 773-549-2910

CONTEMPORARY MUSIC

Many newcomers are simply amazed at the music in Chicago. Enjoy...

CONCERT FACILITIES

Chicagoland plays host to concerts big and small. Most facilities offer tickets through TicketMaster and its outlets. Check the web sites listed below; most offer a diagram of the seating arrangements, which is a big help when ordering. Two questions you will want to ask are, is it partial view, and will you need binoculars? If you want more personal attention and have questions, call the venue directly.

- **AllState Arena** (a.k.a. Rosemont Horizon), 6929 North Manheim Road, Rosemont, www.allstatearena.com; more than 150 events are hosted at the arena each year. Tickets can be purchased through Ticketmaster: 312-559-1212, at the box office, or online. Parking fees range from $11 to $15 for cars. Limos and buses are extra.
- **Alpine Valley Music Center**, Highway D, East Troy, WI, 262-642-4400, www.alpinevalleymusic.com; purchase tickets at all Chicagoland Ticketmasters or order by phone: 312-559-1212. On the day of the event you may purchase tickets at the box office.
- **Arie Crown Theatre**, 2301 South Lake Shore Drive, Chicago, 312-791-6190, www.ariecrown.com; parking costs $20. The theater is wheelchair accessible. Tickets can be purchased through Ticketmaster or from the theater's web site.
- **Auditorium Theater**, 50 East Congress Parkway, Chicago, www.auditoriumtheatre.org; purchase tickets through Ticketmaster or in person at the box office.
- **Bradley Center**, 1001 North 4th Street, Milwaukee, WI, www.bradleycenter.com: events hotline: 414-227-0700, customer service: 414-227-0893. Tickets can be purchased through Ticketmaster or at the box office.
- **Verizon Wireless (Deer Creek) Music Center**, 12880 East 146 Street, Noblesville, IN, www.verizonwirelessmusiccenter.com, 317-776-3337; tickets available at all Tickemaster locations, online at www.cc.com, or at the Music Center box office. A parking fee of $2.75 is added to each ticket; $4 to each ticket for festival shows. The $10 lawn ticket available for selected events includes the parking fee.

- **Marcus Amphitheater**, 200 North Harbor Drive, Milwaukee, WI, 414-273-2600; enjoyable space with a view of Lake Michigan and the Milwaukee skyline. Tickets can be purchased at Ticketmaster or at the amphitheater box office in person. Visit www.summerfest.com, under "entertainment," for more information.
- **Ravinia**, Lake Cook and Green Bay roads, Highland Park, www.ravinia.org; tickets can be ordered by downloading a form and faxing it to 847-266-0641, or by phone after May 25th at 847-266-5100. The box office opens on May 24th and tickets may be purchased there as well. A $6 service fee is added to all faxed, phoned, and online orders.
- **Rosemont Theatre**, 5400 North River Road, Rosemont, 847-671-5100; with over 1,200 on-site parking spaces, this facility can pack 'em in. Large-scale productions include the Radio City Rockettes Christmas Spectacular. Tickets also available from Ticketmaster.
- **Soldier Field Concerts**, 425 East McFetridge Drive, Chicago; call the box office at 312-747-1285 or purchase tickets through Ticketmaster. You may not want to get seats on the south end as the stage is usually set up on the north end.
- **Tweeter Center** (a.k.a. New World Music Theatre), 19100 South Ridgeland Avenue, Tinley Park, www.tweetercenter.com, 708-614-1616; tickets can be purchased online at www.cc.com, through Ticketmaster or through the center's web site. Pavilion area is handicap accessible. VIP box or sky suites for private parties are available. No charge for parking.
- **UIC Pavilion**, 525 South Racine, Chicago, www.uic.edu; parking available across the street and in the parking structure next door. Ticket information at 312-413-5700.
- **United Center**, 1901 West Madison Street, www.united-center.com, 312-455-4500 for tickets. Parking ranges from $12 to $15 for cars; $20 for limos, buses, and RVs. Wheelchair accessible. Group and kid friendly.

NIGHT CLUBS

If you're a party animal, you'll be happy to know that many clubs stay open very late in Chicago, some as late as 4 a.m. You should consider how you will be getting home at that hour, before hitting the scene. While CTA buses and trains run around the clock, night owl service is less frequent, and some lines do not run at all. Consider calling the CTA for a late night bus or 'L' schedule if you know where you are heading on a particular night, or be prepared to hail a cab.

Take your pick for a night out from those listed here or be adventurous and find something new.

ROCK

- **Cubby Bear**, 1059 West Addison Street, www.cubbybear.com, 773-327-1642
- **Double Door**, 1572 North Milwaukee Avenue, www.doubledoor.com, 773-489-3160
- **Empty Bottle**, 1035 North Western Avenue, www.emptybottle.com, 773-276-3600
- **The Metro**, 3730 North Clark Street, www.metrochicago.com, 773-549-0203
- **Park West**, 322 West Armitage Avenue, www.parkwestchicago.com, 773-929-1322
- **Riviera**, 4746 North Racine, corner of Broadway and Lawrence Avenue, 773-275-6800

JAZZ

- **Andy's Jazz Club**, 11 East Hubbard Street, www.andysjazzclub.citysearch.com, 312-642-6805
- **The Backroom**, 1007 North Rush Street, 312-751-2433
- **Chicago Jazz Ensemble**, www.chijazz.com, 312-344-6245; in residence at Columbia College in downtown Chicago, but performances are held in Barrows Auditorium, Billy Graham Center, and at Wheaton College.
- **Green Dolphin Street**, 2200 North Ashland Avenue, www.jazzitup.com, 773-395-0066
- **The Green Mill**, 4802 North Broadway, 773-878-5552
- **Jazz Institute of Chicago**, www.jazzinstituteofchicago.org, 312-427-1676; has sponsored the Jazz Fair for over 20 years and has programmed the Chicago Jazz Festival from its inception. They commission new works, sponsor musician residencies and workshop, collect oral histories from the greats and almost greats. Members enjoy discounts at record stores, clubs, on music lessons, and free concerts. Their web site provides a calendar of events, and a full listing of membership benefits.
- **Jazz Showcase**, 59 West Grand Avenue, www.jazzshowcase.com, 312-670-2473

BLUES

You have come to the right part of the country if you like to hear live blues.

- **B.L.U.E.S.**, 2519 North Halsted, www.chicagobluesbar.com, 773-528-1012
- **Blue Chicago**, www.bluechicago.com, 536 North Clark Street, 312-661-0100, and 736 North Clark Street, 312-642-6261
- **The House of Blues**, 329 North Dearborn Street, www.hob.com, 312-923-2000

- **Buddy Guy's Legends**, 754 South Wabash Avenue, www.buddy guys.com, 312-427-0333
- **Kingston Mines**, 2548 North Halsted Street, www.kingston mines.com, 773-477-4646; traditional blues: two bands on two stages every night of the year.

FOLK/COUNTRY/COFFEEHOUSES

- **Abbey Pub and Restaurant**, 3420 West Grace Street, www.abbey pub.com, 773-478-4408
- **Old Town School of Folk Music**, 4544 North Lincoln Avenue, www.oldtownschool.org, 773-525-7793
- **Schubas Tavern**, 3159 North Southport Avenue, www.shubas.com, 773-525-2508
- **University of Chicago's annual Folk Festival** takes place in February. For three days and nights, folk musicians from all over the country come and perform in Ida Noyes Hall. Saturday and Sunday workshops open to the public. Call 773-702-7300 for more information.

LATE NIGHT CLUBS

If you like to party into the wee hours, you'll want to head to the River North section of town. The crowd here, for the most part, is a bit younger than in the Division Street area clubs. Many of the lounges, clubs, and trendy hangouts stay open until 4 a.m., some with late kitchens.

- **Baton Show Lounge**, 436 North Clark Street, 312-644-5269
- **Brehon Pub**, 731 North Wells Street, 312-642-1071
- **Buzz**, 308 West Erie Street, www.buzztheclub.com, 312-475-9800; a trendy spot for dancing and people watching.
- **Club 720**, 720 North Wells Street, www.club720.com, 312-397-0600; a club where Latin beats reign.
- **Excalibur**, 632 North Dearborn Street, www.excaliburchicago.com, 312-266-1944
- **Harry's Velvet Room**, 56 West Illinois Street, 312-527-5600
- **Le Bar**, 20 East Chestnut Street, www.sofitel-chicago.com, 312-324-4000; located in the Hotel Sofitel Chicago Water Tower, this club has a great view and a sophisticated crowd.
- **Minx Café & Lounge**, 111 West Hubbard Street, 312-828-9000; courts a young crowd. Kitchen leans towards Asian and Latin-influenced dishes.
- **Nacional 27**, 325 West Huron Street, 312-664-2727; salsa, merengue, and lambada are spoken here.
- **Redhead Piano Bar**, 16 West Ontario Street, www.redheadpiano bar.com, 312-640-1000

- **Spy Bar**, 646 North Franklin Street, 312-587-8779
- **Swank**, 710 North Wells Street, www.swankchicago.com, 312-274-9500; if you love leopard prints, you will feel right at home here. Good food and service.
- **Vision Nightclub**, 640 North Dearborn Street, www.visionnight club.com, 312-266-2114; strobe lights, VIP level, dance floor below, you know the place.
- **Voyeur**, 151 West Ohio Street, 312-832-1717
- **White Star Lounge**, 225 West Ontario, www.whitestarlounge.com, 312-274-9500; adjacent to the rather sophisticated and expensive restaurant, Magnum, this club is a good people watching spot.

REGGAE
- **Exedus Lounge**, 3477 North Clark Street, www.exeduslounge.com, 773-348-3998
- **The Wild Hare**, 3530 North Clark Street, www.wildharereggae.com, 773-327-4273

POP
- **Dragon Room**, 809 West Evergreen, 312-751-8700
- **Funky Buddha Lounge**, 728 West Grand Avenue, www.funkybud dha.com, 312-666-1695
- **Smart Bar**, 3730 North Clark, 773-549-4140
- **The Note**, 1565 North Milwaukee Avenue, www.thenotechicago.com, 773-489-0011

For more **club-hopping information**, visit www.chicagoscene.com.

MUSEUMS

Chicago has some of the finest museums in the country, and is on touring schedules for both national and international exhibitions.

ART

- **The Art Institute of Chicago**, Michigan Avenue at Adams Street, 312-575-8000, www.artic.edu; incredible masters' works on display, including Picasso, Renoir, Matisse, Van Gogh, as well as ancient works from classical Greece and Rome. Be advised: touring shows often sell out. Admission is free on Tuesdays. Admission on other days: $10/adults, $6/children/students/seniors, children age five and under free. Memberships available.

- **David and Alfred Smart Museum of Art**, University of Chicago, 5550 South Greenwood Avenue, 773-702-0200, www.smartmuseum.uchicago.edu
- **The Illinois Institute of Art Chicago**, the Apparel Center, 350 North Orleans Street, #16, 312-280-3500, www.artinstitute.edu; admission to the art gallery is free and open to the public.
- **Intuit, The Center for Intuitive and Outsider Art**, 756 North Milwaukee Avenue, www.outsider.art.org, 312-243-9088, free admission.
- **Mexican Fine Arts Center Museum**, 1852 West 19th Street, 312-738-1503, www.mfacmchicago.org; admission $7, free Wednesdays.
- **Museum of Contemporary Art**, 220 East Chicago, 312-280-2660, www.mcachicago.org; admission: $10/adults, $6/students/seniors/military, children 12 and under free. Also free on Tuesday evenings.
- **National Vietnam Veterans Art Museum**, 1801 South Indiana Avenue, www.nvvam.org, 312-326-0270; admission $5/general, $4/seniors/students.
- **Terra Museum of American Art**, 664 North Michigan Avenue, 312-664-3939, www.terramuseum.org; admission free, suggested donation of $5 per adult.
- **Chicago Artists' Coalition**, www.caconline.org, 312-670-2060; resource for community art events. Also exhibits and sells art work of over 140 members for artists, collectors or art enthusiasts.
- **Illinois Art Council**, www.state.il.us/agency/iac, 800-237-6994; publishes an annual art fair directory.

GALLERIES

In recent years, especially with the rejuvenation of the River North neighborhood, Chicago's art scene has blossomed. While it has a ways to go before it can rival New York City's SoHo, there is a level and quality of activity here that can't be ignored. Many galleries are located between Chicago and Grand streets, on the "Lake" Streets, i.e., Superior, Huron, and Erie. Generally, these galleries hold open evening hours on the first Thursday, or Friday of the month. During that time, you can often meet artists exhibiting their work and other art lovers as well. If you want to experience the art scene up close, attend the **free Saturday gallery tours** led by local art gallery owners in the River North neighborhood. Coordinated by The Chicago Art Dealers Association (CADA), gallery owners or directors and those interested in a tour, meet each Saturday at the Starbucks located at 750 North Franklin Street. There are four different tours that go from 10:30 a.m. to noon. No reservations are required.

A few **galleries in the River North area** are:

- **Alan Koppel Gallery**, 210 West Chicago Avenue, 312-640-0730
- **Aldo Castillo Gallery**, 233 West Huron Street, 312-337-2536
- **Ann Nathan Gallery**, 218 West Superior Street, 312-664-6622
- **Carl Hammer Gallery**, 740 North Wells Street, 312-266-8512
- **Catherine Edelman Gallery**, 300 West Superior Street, 312-266-2350
- **Douglas Dawson Gallery**, 222 West Huron Street, 312-751-1961
- **Geschiendle**, 300 West Superior Street, 312-654-0600
- **Gruen Galleries**, 226 West Superior Street, 312-337-6262
- **Habatat Galleries**, 222 West Superior Street, 312-440-0288
- **Melanee Cooper Gallery**, 740 North Franklin Street, 312-202-9305
- **Oskar Friedl Gallery**, 300 West Superior Street, 312-867-1930
- **Primitive Art Works**, 706 North Wells Street, 312-943-3770
- **Roy Boyd Gallery**, 739 North Wells Street, 312-642-1606
- **Schneider Gallery**, 230 West Superior Street, 312-988-4033 (photography)
- **Tigerman Himmel**, 212 West Chicago Avenue, 312-337-8300
- **Vale Craft Gallery**, 230 West Superior Street, 312-337-3525
- **Zg Gallery**, 300 West Superior, 312-654-9900
- **Zolla/Leiberman**, 325 West Huron Street, 312-944-1990

HISTORY MUSEUMS, CULTURAL CENTERS

- **Balzekas Museum of Lithuanian Culture**, 6500 South Pulaski Road, 773-582-6500; this museum includes exhibits on Lithuanian history and culture as well as the largest Lithuanian research center outside of Lithuania.
- **Cantigny**, Wheaton, 630-668-5161, www.rrmtf.org; the 500 acre former estate of Colonel Robert R. McCormick dedicated to golf and the history of the 1st Infantry Division from WWI to the present.
- **Charnley-Persky House Museum**, 1365 North Astor Street, 312-915-0105; this house was designed by Frank Lloyd Wright while he was employed by Louis Sullivan and is now owned by the Society of Architectural Historians. Limited tours available.
- **Chicago Cultural Center**, Randolph and Michigan Avenue, 312-744-6630; the nation's first free municipal cultural center. An architectural showplace that houses the city's official visitor center.
- **Chicago Historical Society**, Clark Street at North Avenue, 312-642-4600, www.chicagohistory.org; exhibitions, collections, and programs about Chicago, Illinois, and select areas of American history (such as the Lincoln era); admission $5/adults, $3/seniors/students, $1/children ages 6-12. Free on Mondays.

- **Cuneo Museum & Gardens**, Vernon Hills, 847-362-3042; Venetian style mansion is home to many art collections and is surrounded by 75 acres of lakes, fountains, formal gardens, antique classical statuary and conservatory housing exotic plants. Grounds admission $5/car; mansion tours: $10/adults, $9/seniors, $5/children. Closed Mondays.
- **DuSable Museum of African-American History**, 740 East 56th Place, 773-947-0600, www.dusablemuseum.org; admission is free on Sunday, otherwise: $3/adults, $2/seniors, $1/children 6 to 13, under six free.
- **Garfield Park Conservatory**, 300 North Central Park Avenue, 312-746-5100, www.garfield-conservatory.org; six multi-faceted greenhouses, two grand exhibition halls, hands-on, interactive children's garden and demonstration garden for learning about urban gardening.
- **Glessner House Museum**, 1800 South Prairie Avenue, 312-326-1480, www.glessnerhouse.org; the only surviving building by architect Henry Hobson Richardson and home to the Glessner family's outstanding collection of 19th and early 20th century furniture and decorative art objects. Wednesday is free. Thursday-Sunday admission is $9/adults, $8/students/seniors, $5/children (ages 5-12), tour sizes are limited and can include Clarke House and/or a walking tour for an additional cost.
- **Mitchell Museum of the American Indian**, Evanston, 2600 Central Park Avenue, 847-475-1030, www.mitchellmuseum.org; museum's collections range from the Paleo-Indian period through the present day. Permanent exhibitions depict the Native American cultures of the Woodlands, Plains, Southwest, Northwest, and Arctic. There are "touching tables" in each gallery as well as two thematic temporary exhibits; suggested admission donation of $5/adults, $2.50/students/seniors/children, $10/family maximum.
- **Museum of Contemporary Photography**, Columbia College, 600 South Michigan Avenue, 312-663-5554, www.mocp.org; over 6,000 photographs and related items since 1945 as well as rotating exhibits; admission is free.
- **Naper Settlement**, Naperville, 523 South Webster Street, 630-420-6010, www.napersettlement.org; a museum village where 19th century homes, shops, public buildings, children's activities and costumed interpreters tell the story of daily life in Naperville as it changed from a frontier outpost to a bustling turn-of-the-century community. Admission: $6.50/adults, $5.50/seniors, $4/youth (ages 4-17), $3 optional tour, discounts during the winter months.
- **Oriental Institute**, 1155 East 56th Street, 773-702-9514, www.oi.uchicago.edu; stunning collection of ancient artifacts from the cradle of civilization: Egyptian, Sumerian, Mesopotamian; admission is free, suggested donation of $5/adult and $2/children under 12.

- **Peace Museum**, 100 North Central Park Avenue, www.peacemuseum.org, 773-638-6450; more than 10,000 artifacts that explore the impact of war and peace and educational opportunities to enhance the development of peace making and conflict management skills.
- **Schingoethe Center for Native American Cultures**, Aurora University, Aurora, www.aurora.edu/museum, 630-844-5402, call for information about their annual Memorial Day weekend pow-wow.
- **Spertus Institute of Jewish Studies**, 618 South Michigan Avenue, 312-322-1747, www.spertus.edu; houses a collection of over 10,000 objects, artifacts, and works of art spanning 3,500 years of Jewish history including the nation's first permanent museum exhibition on the Holocaust. Admission: $5/general, $3/students, $10/family. Free on Friday.
- **Swedish American Museum**, 5211 North Clark Street in the Andersonville neighborhood, 773-728-8111, www.samac.org; this three-story museum includes a Children's Museum of Immigration and Swedish library, and is *the* place to celebrate Swedish holidays. Admission: $4/adults, $3/children/students/seniors. Free on the second Tuesday of each month.

SCIENCE

- **Adler Planetarium and Astronomy Museum**, 1300 South Lake Shore Drive, 312-922-STAR, www.adlerplanetarium.org; galleries, theaters and other exciting areas where you can learn about the stars. Admission package with one show is $13/adults, $12/seniors, $11/children (ages 4-17), discounts of $1 to $2 for residents. Mondays and Tuesdays are free in the fall.
- **Air Classics Museum**, Sugar Grove, 630-466-0888, www.airclassicmuseum.org; unique exhibits and educational programs for all ages chronicling the role of aviation; admission $5/adults, $4/seniors, $3/children six and over.
- **Cernan Earth & Science Center**, River Grove, 708-583-3100; located at Triton College this space-age facility has multi-functional 100-seat dome theatre and a Space Hall. Most shows $5/adults, $2.50/seniors, children 12 and under, laser light shows slightly higher.
- **The Field Museum**, 1400 South Lake Shore Drive, 800-FIELD-54, www.fieldmuseum.org; admission is $8, free Mondays and Tuesdays, September-February.
- **International Museum of Surgical Science**, 1524 North Lake Shore Drive, 312-642-6502, www.imss.org; housed in a landmark status mansion are artifacts which span over 4,000 years of important developments in surgery and medicine. Admission: $6/adults, $3/students, seniors. Free Tuesday with a suggested donation.

- **Jurica Nature Museum**, Lisle, 630-829-6546; small natural history museum located on the campus of Benedictine University, animal and bird specimens, African savanna diorama and educational programs. Limited afternoon hours.
- **Milano Model & Toy Museum**, Elmhurst, 630-279-4422, www.toys-n-cars.com; an eclectic collection of vintage models from kits, toys, and advertising artifacts.
- **Museum of Holography**, 1134 West Washington Boulevard, 312-226-1007, www.holographiccenter.com; 10,000 square feet of holograms representing significant historic, artistic and experimental advances in holography as well as lab facilities and a school. Admission: $4/adults, $3/children (ages 6 - 11).
- **Museum of Science and Industry**, 57th Street and Lake Shore Drive, 773-684-1414, www.msichicago.org; over 2,000 interactive units and 800 exhibits such as spacecraft, planes, trains, cars, a submarine, walk through model of a heart, baby-chick hatchery and an Omnimax theater. Admission: $9/adults, $7.50/seniors, $5/children (ages 5-11), discounts for residents. See web site for select free days.
- **Peggy Notebaert Nature Museum**, 2430 North Cannon Drive, 773-755-5100, www.naturemuseum.org; with wildflowers, trees, wildlife, and animal dress up for children, since the 1850s this venue has been helping urban dwellers connect with the natural world; parking available at the Lincoln Park Zoo. Admission: $7/adult, $5/seniors/students, $4/children (ages 3-12), $1 discount for residents. Thursdays free.
- **Scitech Hands On Museum**, Aurora, 630-859-3434, www.scitech.mus.il.us; teaming with activities that will really appeal to kids such as a virtual reality room and outdoor science park. Admission: $7/adults, $6/seniors/children (ages 3-17).
- **Shedd Aquarium**, 1200 South Lake Shore Drive, 312-939-2426, www.sheddaquarium.org; open since 1929 it is one of the oldest and still the largest public aquariums in the world. See sharks, turtles, beluga whales, a coral reef, a Napolean Wrausse ... in thousands of gallons of sea water. Admission: $21/adults, $15/seniors/children (ages 3-11).
- **Volo Auto Museum & Antique Mall**, Volo, IL, 815-385-3644, www.volocars.com; Hollywood star's, muscle and antique cars as well as an antique mall and auto sales showroom. Admission: $6.50/adults, $5/seniors, $3/children (ages 6-12).

LITERARY LIFE

Chicago has a strong literary bent—from highly acclaimed authors and poets who grew up in Chicago, (David Mamet, William Goldman, Michael

Crichton), to those who found their inspiration here (Carl Sandburg, Saul Bellow). From area universities, vast public and private libraries, and a solid selection of chain and independent booksellers, you will come to understand that this is a reading town. Every May/June, thousands of booklovers from across the Midwest attend the Printers Row Book Fair held outdoors on Dearborn (Congress to Park streets). For more information: www.chicagotribune.com/extras/printersrow.

GENERAL INTEREST BOOKSTORES

- **Afterwords**, 23 East Illinois Street, 312-464-1110; new and used titles.
- **Barbara's Bookstore**, 1350 North Wells, 312-642-5044; 233 South Wacker Drive, 312-466-0223; Navy Pier, 312-222-0890, 1100 Lake, Oak Park, 708-848-9140
- **Barnes & Noble** offers literary, reference, trade, and children's books, plus a wide selection of magazines and newspapers. Author readings and signings and other events are common. Some locations have in-store cafes and live music. Locations: Chicago, Skokie, Evanston, Orland Park, Oak Terrace, Deerfield, Downers Grove, Mount Prospect, Arlington Heights, Wheaton, Schaumburg, Naperville, and Vernon Hills. See the Yellow Pages or check www.barnesandnoble.com.
- **Borders Books & Music**, many locations throughout the region, offer a wide range of events from readings to book groups, all of which are free and open to the public. Many have cafes and live music on selected days and evenings. Check www.borders.com for a location near you.
- **Sandmeyers Bookstore**, 714 South Dearborn Street, 312-922-2104
- **Seminary Co-op**, 5757 South University Avenue, 773-752-4381
- **57th Street Books**, 1301 East 57th Street, 773-684-1300; at the Newberry Library, 312-255-3520; general interest and scholarly bookstores.
- **Tower Records**, several Chicago locations including: 2301 North Clark Street, 773-477-5994, 214 South Wabash Avenue, 312-663-2303; pop culture: music, sci-fi, some fiction.
- **Unabridged Books**, 3251 North Broadway Street, 773-883-9119
- **Waldenbooks**, national chain owned by Borders, typically located in shopping malls throughout the Chicagoland area. Good children's books section. Check in the Yellow Pages under "Bookstores" for a location near you.

SPECIAL INTEREST BOOKSTORES

For academic specialty books, head to any university campus bookstore. Other specialty bookstores include:

- **Beck's Book Store**, several locations, including: 4522 North Broadway, 773-784-7963; 6550 North Sheridan Road, 773-743-2281; 481 North Roosevelt Road, Glen Ellyn, 630-469-9080; college text books.
- **Chicago Architecture Foundation**, 224 South Michigan Avenue, #116, 312-922-3432, www.architecture.org
- **Rand McNally Map & Travel**, 2 locations: 444 North Michigan Avenue, 312-321-1751, and 150 South Wacker Drive, 312-332-2009
- **The Savvy Traveller**, 310 South Michigan Avenue, 312-913-9800, www.thesavvytraveller.com
- **Something Wicked Mystery Bookshop**, 816 Church Street, Evanston, 847-328-1300
- **Stern's Psychology Book Store**, 2004 West Roscoe Street, 773-883-5100
- **UIC Medical Bookstore**, 828 South Wolcott Avenue, # 1, 312-413-5550
- **Women and Children First**, 5223 North Clark Street (in Andersonville), 773-769-9299, www.womenandchildrenfirst.com; store specializing in books by women for women; also has a well-stocked children's section.

USED BOOKSTORES/SALES

- **Brandeis Used Book Sale**, Old Orchard Shopping Center, Skokie, www.brandeisusedbooks.org; make plans to do nothing on the second weekend of June, but attend this sale. Over 400,000 books and magazines are placed on sale in tents. If you have books to sell, call 847-724-9715 for information about pick-up service, and drop off sites.
- **Friends of West Chicago Public Library**, West Chicago, 630-231-1552, holds an annual fall book sale, as does the **Friends of Arlington Heights Memorial Library**, Arlington Heights, 847-392-0100, on a quarterly basis. Contact your local library for information regarding their book sales.
- **Powell's**, 2850 North Lincoln Avenue, 773-248-1444; 828 South Wabash, 312-341-0748; 1501 East 57th Street, 773-955-7780, www.powellschicago.com; specializes in second-hand, out-of-print and collector's editions.
- Each June the *Chicago Tribune* sponsors the **Printers Row Book Fair**. It's a well attended two days of literary programs on seven stages for children and adults. Close to 200 booksellers set up booths, offering rare, used, old, and new books. This free outdoor fair is held in the Printers Row neighborhood, on the blocks surrounding Dearborn and Polk streets. For more information call: 312-222-3986.

LIBRARIES

In addition to the specialty bookshops mentioned above, museum gift shops are excellent sources of books that are sometimes hard to find. If you need to do research, the libraries of the major universities in town are **DePaul**, 312-362-6020, the **University of Chicago**, 312-464-8650, **Northwestern**, 847-491-3741, and **Loyola**, 312-915-6520. Many universities extend library privileges to students registered in another university. Check the university library of your choice for its policy or if you are a matriculating student, check with university's library for policy information. If you are not a student, you may be able to use a university library, but not check out materials, or for a fee, you may be able to do both. Again, check with your local university library for details.

For public libraries, check the listings at the end of the **Neighborhood Profiles** for a branch library near you. Or visit one of these **regional branch libraries**:

- **Harold Washington Library Center**, 400 South State Street, www.chipublib.org, call 773-LIBRARY for hours. More than just a depository of books, in the ten floors that make up the Washington Library Center, there are classrooms, theaters, auditoriums, video theaters, meeting rooms, a language lab, books for the blind, computer connections, a restaurant, a winter garden and more. There are plenty of parking lots nearby, but public transportation is so convenient to this area that, unless you are coming from the suburbs, CTA is the way to go.
- **Des Plaines Library**, 1501 Ellinwood Avenue, Des Plaines, 847-827-5551, www.desplaines.lib.il.us; this new facility contains over 200,000 magazines, books, audio books, CDs, and periodicals. It offers bus tours to cultural events, seasonal reading clubs, children's programs, crafts and lectures. Conveniently located, steps away from the Metra train stop.
- **Arlington Heights Memorial Library**, 500 North Dunton, 847-392-0100, www.ahml.lib.il.us; one of the largest libraries in the state, this facility is a great community resource offering a variety of programs for children and adults. It is well-known for its excellent book sales.
- **Evanston Public Library**, 1703 Orrington, Evanston, 847-936-0300, www.evanston.lib.il.us

Listed here are private and public libraries in Chicago and surrounding suburbs. Please note that many of these institutions are *not* open to the public:
- **Art Institute of Chicago Library**, Michigan Avenue at Adams Street, 312-443-3666

- **Charles Deering McCormick Library of Special Collections**, 847-491-7658, www.library.northwestern.edu
- **Chicago Historical Society Library**, 1601 North Clark Street, 312-642-4600, www.chicagohs.org
- **Columbia College Library**, 624 South Michigan Avenue, 312-344-7900, www.lib.colum.edu
- **DePaul University Libraries**: Lincoln Park, 2350 North Kenmore Avenue, 773-325-7862; Loop Campus, 1 East Jackson Drive, 312-362-8433; Law Library, 25 East Jackson Drive, 312-362-8121, www.lib.depaul.edu
- **Dominican University/Rebecca Crow Library**, 7900 West Division Street, River Forest, 708-524-6875, http://domweb.dom.edu/library/crown
- **Evanston Public Library**, 1703 Orrington Avenue, Evanston, 847-866-0300, www.evanston.lib.il.us
- **Field Museum of Natural History**, 1400 South Lake Shore Drive, 312-922-9410, www.fieldmuseum.org
- **Garrett-Evangelical & Seabury Western Theological Seminary (United Library)**, 2121 Sheridan Road, 847-866-3900, www.unitedlibrary.org; for a comprehensive listing of theological library links, go to www.unitedlibrary.org/other_libraries.
- **Gerber/Hart Library**, 1127 West Granville Avenue, 773-381-8030, www.gerberhart.org; this unique library is a depository for the records of homosexuals, bisexuals, and transgendered individuals and the organizations which serve them. It is the largest library of its kind in the Midwest.
- **Government Publications and Maps**, 847-491-3130, www.library.northwestern.edu/govpub
- **Loyola University Library**, 6525 North Sheridan Road, 773-508-2631: Science Library: 773-508-8411; Humanities Library: 773-508-2654; Health Sciences Library: 708-216-9192; Law Library: 312-902-7205
- **National-Louis University**, library locations in: Evanston, 847-256-5150 ext. 2505; Wheeling, 847-465-0575 ext. 5503; Wheaton, 630-668-3838 ext. 4530; Elgin, 847-695-6070; Chicago, 312-621-9650 ext. 3376; www.nl.edu/ulibrary
- **Newberry Library**, 60 West Walton Street, 312-943-9090, www.newberry.org; a free, independent library with an emphasis on the humanities. It maintains a large, non-circulating collection of rare maps, manuscripts, and books. Anyone conducting research, over the age of 16, is welcome to become a reader. The Newberry holds many events for the public, including concerts and exhibitions.
- **Northern Suburban Library System**, North Suburban Library System, 200 West Dundee Road, Wheeling, 847-459-1300, www.nslsilus.org

- **Northwestern University Library**, 1970 Campus Drive, Evanston, 847-491-7658
- **Spertus Institute of Jewish Studies/Asher Library**, 618 South Michigan Avenue, 312-322-1749, www.spertus.edu/library
- **Suburban Library System**, www.sls.lib.il.us, provides a list of over 600 suburban libraries and phone numbers.
- **Transportation Library**, Evanston, 847-491-5273, www.library.north western.edu/transportation
- **University of Chicago/Regenstein Library**, 1100 East 57th Street, 773-702-4685, www.lib.uchicago.edu
- **University of Illinois-Chicago**, 801 South Morgan Street, 312-996-2726

MISCELLANEOUS

For those of you who can relate to the less than traditional ways to have a night out, may we suggest:

- **Beer School** at the Siebel Institute of Technology, 1777 North Clybourn Avenue, Suite 2F, 312-255-0705, www.siebelinstitute.com; forget the flavored martinis, you will soon discover that Chicago is a beer town. And now that it is both fashionable and legal to brew your own, consider taking a professional brewing class.
- **Nightmares Inc.**, Melrose Park, 708-344-2084, www.dream reapers.com; are you the kind of person whose favorite holiday is Halloween? You no longer have to wait until October to be scared out of your wits. This 14,000 square foot haunted house, rated the best in Illinois for three years running, is staffed by professional actors and is open several times throughout the year. They are also happy to oblige corporate groups and small parties. Visit their web site for more details.

CULTURE FOR KIDS

Living in Chicago gives you the opportunity to expose your child to a rich cultural life. From bookstore events to performing arts, the Chicago child is offered a wealth of exciting opportunities. Don't overlook your local public library and park district as a source for enriching programs for your children. For information about **Mayor Daley's Book Club** for students, go to http://mdbc.cps.k12.il.us/about.html.

MUSIC

- **Chicago Children's Choir**, 78 East Washington Avenue, 312-849-8300, ext. 321

- **Glen Ellyn Children's Chorus**, www.gechildrenschorus.org, 630-858-2471; this talented troupe has achieved international recognition, having performed in concert with the Chicago Symphony Orchestra, at the Ravinia Festival, and tours throughout the United States, Canada, New Zealand, Brazil, and Europe. Activities include pre-choral training for the youngest children, summer workshops, an annual festival workshop and more.
- **Elgin's Children's Chorus**, www.elgchch.org, over 200 children ages eight to sixteen perform three major concerts each year, in addition to performing with the Elgin Symphony Orchestra. For tickets call 847-622-0300. For information call 847-931-SING.
- **Metropolis Youth Symphony**, 847-577-5982 ext. 240; performs at Metropolis Performing Arts Center, 111 West Campbell Street, Arlington Heights, www.metroploisarts.com, 847-577-2121.

MUSEUMS

- **Bronzeville Children's Museum**, Evergreen Park, 708-636-9504, www.bronzevillechildrensmuseum.com; first and only African-American children's museum in the country houses interactive exhibits and programs for learning in the areas of the arts, humanities, and sciences. Admission $3/adults, $2/children.
- **Chicago Children's Museum**, 700 East Grand Avenue at Navy Pier, 312-527-1000, www.chichildrensmuseum.org; fifteen permanent exhibits and programming spaces provide innovative learning experiences for families in a large, inviting building. Admission: $7/general, $6/seniors, free Thursday evenings.
- **DuPage Children's Museum**, 301 North Washington Street, Naperville, 630-637-8000; admission fees: $6.75 (ages one to 59), $5.75 for those 60 and over. Plenty of hands-on stimulating exhibits combining science and fun. Visit their web site for calendar details: www.dupagechildrensmuseum.org.
- **Health World Children's Museum**, 1301 South Grove, Barrington, 847-842-9100, www.healthworldmuseum.org; offers a hands-on opportunity to learn more about the importance of a healthy lifestyle through programming, exhibits and discovery zones; admission $5, free for those under two.
- **Kohl's Children's Museum**, 165 South Green Bay Road, Wilmette, 847-512-1300, www.kohlchildrensmuseum.org; exhibits encourage the building of strong social skills by creating situations which require children to help each other and work as a team. Admission: $6/children and adults, $5/seniors, children under one are free.

- **Lake County Discovery Museum**, Lakewood Forest Preserve, Rte. 176 and Fairfield Road, Wauconda, 847-968-3400, www.lake countydiscoverymuseum.org; a life-sized mastodon statue guards the entrance to this collection of hands-on interactive exhibits which present the history of Lake County. Located on the Lakewood Forest Preserve. Admission: $5.50/adults, $2.50/children (ages 4-17). Discounts on Tuesdays and for seniors after 2 p.m.
- **Scitech Hands-On Museum**, see information above under science museums.

OUTDOOR

- The **Forest Preserve District of Cook County** operates six nature centers. Visitors can learn about native plants and animals from the professional naturalist on staff. Group visits must be scheduled in advance. Picnicking is permitted in designated areas. Visit the Forest Preserve District's web site at www.fpdcc.com or see **Greenspace and Beaches** for more information.

ZOOS

- **Lincoln Park Zoo**, 2001 North Clark Street, 312-742-2000, www.lpzoo.com; this small but wonderfully situated free zoo is a welcome respite to adults and families alike. Many animals at the Pritzker Children's Zoo may be touched under supervision.
- **Brookfield Zoo**, 8400 West 31 Street, Brookfield, 708-485-1434, www.brookfiledzoo.org; with 200 acres of animals, this is *the* zoo in the Chicago area.

THEATER

- **American Girl Theatre**, American Girl Place, 111 East Chicago Avenue, 877-AG-PLACE, www.americangirl.com
- **Emerald City Theatre**, 773-529-2690, www.emeraldcitytheatre.com; most performances at the **Apollo Theatre**.
- **Northbrook Musical Theatre for Young Audiences**, 3323 Walters Avenue, Northbrook, 847-291-2367, northbrooktheatre.org

OTHER

- **ESPN Zone**, 43 East Ohio Street, 312-644-3776; sporting entertainment complex

- **Donley's Wild West Town**, Rte. 20 and South Union Road, Union, 815-923-9000; recreated wild west town: train rides, pony rides, and shows.
- **Six Flags Great America**, I-94 at 132 Grand East Avenue, Gurnee, 847-249-1776, www.sixflags.com
- **Enchanted Castle Restaurant & Entertainment Center**, 1103 South Main Street, Lombard, 630-953-7860

WHETHER YOU ARE JUST GETTING STARTED ON YOUR COLLEGE degree, contemplating a second degree, or just interested in taking continuing education courses, the colleges and universities in and around Chicago offer a wide range of options. Whether it's a doctorate in medieval history or a weekend pottery class, you can find it here. In addition, concerts, plays, lecture series, and many other cultural opportunities await you at these institutions of higher learning.

The following list of larger and better-known institutions is far from comprehensive. Look in the Yellow Pages under "Schools—Universities and Colleges" for those in or close to your neighborhood.

CHICAGO

- **Barat College**, Lake Forest, 847-234-3000, www.barat.edu; now part of DePaul University, the Barat College campus offers many programs for the working professional, especially those interested in telecommunications, software engineering, and information systems.
- **City Colleges of Chicago**, 773-265-5343, www.ccc.edu; has seven campuses throughout the city. A variety of two-year associate degrees are offered.
- **Columbia College**, 312-663-1600, www.colum.edu; an art school which is highly regarded for its dance, film, writing, and photography programs.
- **DePaul University**, 312-362-8000, www.depaul.edu; Lincoln Park, Loop, and O'Hare Airport-area campuses. The largest Catholic university in the country, well known for its business and theater departments.
- **DeVry Institute of Technology**, 773-929-8500, www.devry.edu; Addison, Chicago, and Tinley Park campuses. Offers career-oriented programs such as business, information/computer technology, and engineering degrees.

- **Illinois Institute of Art**, 800-351-3450, www.ilic.artinstitutes.edu; Chicago and Schaumburg campuses.
- **Illinois Institute of Technology**, 312-567-3000, www.iit.edu; Chicago, Wheaton, and Summit campuses. Wide range of technology-based academic certificate and degree programs.
- **Loyola University**, 773-274-3000, www.luc.edu, is Chicago's other major Catholic university. Founded in 1870, it is located on the lake in East Rogers Park. If you live on the far North Side, this is a convenient place to take classes.
- **North Park University**, Chicago, 773-244-6200, www.northpark.edu; evangelical Christian university and seminary. Colleges include schools of nursing, business, education, and music.
- **Robert Morris College**, 800-225-1520, www.rmcil.edu; Chicago, DuPage County, Orland Park and Lake County campuses. Career designed programs and certificates.
- **Roosevelt University**, 847-619-8600, www.roosevelt.edu; Chicago Loop and Schaumburg campuses. Private, liberal arts college.
- **Saint Xavier University**, 773-298-3000, www.sxu.edu; Chicago, Orland Park and Tinley Park campuses. Offers undergraduate and graduate programs, including nursing and education.
- **School of the Art Institute of Chicago**, 312-899-5219, www.artic.edu; highly regarded art school. Though connected to the famous Art Institute Museum, the course offerings aren't limited to painting and sculpture. Performance art, video, and poetry are just some of the fine arts options.
- **The University of Chicago (UofC)**, 773-702-1234, www.uchicago.edu; the area's premiere institution of higher learning. Founded in 1890 by John D. Rockefeller and located in Hyde Park, seven miles south of the Loop, its stern, gothic campus is home to more Nobel Prize winners than any other educational institution in the world.
- **The University of Illinois at Chicago (UIC)**, 312-996-7000, www.uic.edu; just west of downtown, offers a variety of degree programs. It has a large, modern, and growing campus and is convenient to public transit and all major expressways.

NORTH AND NORTHWEST SUBURBS

- **College of Lake County**, 847-543-2000, www.clcillinois.edu; offers 40 career preparation programs in which students earn an associate degree or career certificates. Well known for its BA program for transfer students.
- **Finch University of Health Sciences/The Chicago Medical School**, North Chicago, 847-578-3000, www.finchcms.edu; four dif-

ferent schools/colleges for physicians, podiatric medicine, and health science areas.

- **Harper College**, Palatine, 847-925-6000, www.harpercollege.edu; community college with branch campus in Prospect Heights. Strong IT and career-oriented certificate programs and degrees.
- **ITT Technical Institute**, 847-375-8800, www.itt-tech.edu; Burr Ridge, Mount Prospect and Matteson campuses. Associate and bachelor degrees in such fields as IT, industrial design, electronics.
- **Kendall College**, Evanston, 847-448-2000, www.kendall.edu; offers career oriented programs: hospitality management, human services, business and technology, culinary school, criminal justice management and early childhood education.
- **Knowledge Systems Institute**, Skokie, 847-679-3135, www.ksi.edu; graduate school for computer information and sciences.
- **Lake Forest College**, Lake Forest, 847-234-3100, www.lfc.edu; private liberal arts college.
- **National-Lewis University**, 847-256-5150, www.nl.edu; Evanston and Wheeling campuses. Highly regarded education program.
- **Northwestern University**, 847-491-3741, www.northwestern.edu, is a well-regarded private university whose main campus is in leafy Evanston. The downtown Chicago campus is home to its law, medical, and dental schools.
- **Oakton Community College**, Des Plaines, 847-635-1600, www.oakton.edu; career programs resulting in an AAS or certificate, and BA oriented college transfer programs.
- **Shimer College**, Waukegan, 847-623-8400, www.shimer.edu; well-regarded, small liberal arts and science college.
- **Trinity International University**, Deerfield, 847-945-8800, www.tiu.edu; four year college with an emphasis on its divinity and law schools.
- **Westwood College of Technology**, www.westwood.edu; River Oaks, DuPage, O'Hare and Loop campuses. Computer-based technology and design programs, CAD, and engineering.

WEST SUBURBS

- **Aurora University**, Aurora and Lake Geneva campuses, 630-892-6431, www.aurora.edu; undergraduate, graduate, and doctoral programs.
- **Elmhurst College**, Elmhurst, 630-617-3500, www.elmhurst.edu; private, four year college affiliated with the United Church of Christ.
- **Northeastern Illinois University**, 815-753-1000, www.niu.edu; is primarily a commuter school located in DeKalb. Part of the state university system, nearly 25,000 students attend this affordable institution

best known for its teacher-training program.

- **Wheaton College**, Wheaton, 630-752-5000, www.wheaton.edu; well-regarded interdenominational Christian college. Strong music, theology, education, and psychology departments.

SOUTH/SOUTHWEST SUBURBS

- **Benedictine University**, Lisle, 630-829-6000, www.ben.edu; Catholic liberal arts college that prides itself on its campus diversity.
- **Concordia University**, River Forest, 708-771-8300, www.curf.edu; Lutheran liberal arts college.
- **Dominican University**, River Forest, 708-366-2490, www.dom.edu; Catholic liberal arts college and university. Student-faculty ratio of 13:1, with an average undergraduate class size of 15.
- **Fox College**, Oak Lawn, 866-636-7711, www.foxcollege.com; offers ten sixteen-month certificate programs in accounting and administration.
- **Midwestern University**, Downers Grove, 630-969-4400, www.midwestern.edu; university for osteopathic studies, pharmacology, and health sciences.
- **National University of Health Sciences**, Lombard, 630-629-2000, www.nuhs.edu; programs in alternative healing practices.
- **North Central College**, Naperville, 630-637-5100, www.noctrl.edu; independent college of liberal arts and sciences affiliated with the United Methodist Church, emphasizes academics, leadership, ethics and values.
- **Trinity Christian College**, Palos Heights, 800-748-0085, www.trnty.edu; four-year liberal arts college "in the Reformed tradition"; offers a variety of majors as well as professional programs.
- **University of Saint Francis**, Joliet, 800-735-7500, www.stfrancis.edu; sixty undergraduate programs including nursing and education. Ten graduate programs. Strong athletic division.

WHETHER YOU ARE A PARTICIPANT OR A FAN, CHICAGO IS a sports crazed town. There's even a sport that is popular nowhere else in the United States—or the world—and that's 16-inch softball, a game that requires only a bat and a 16-inch Clincher softball.

SPORTING RESOURCES

Chicagoans can get their minimum daily requirement of sports news from several places. The *Chicago Tribune, Chicago Sun-Times,* and the *Daily Southtown* devote lots of coverage to professional sports. Chicago City Newsstand, 4018 North Cicero, 773-545-7377 and at 860 Chicago Avenue/Main Street in Evanston, 847-425-8900, claims to have the biggest and best collection of sports publications in Chicago. Visit them directly, or check their virtual newsstand at www.citynewsstand.com. Your local community newspaper will be especially informative about high school sports. Dozens of high school teams are highlighted at www.hssp.cc/Illinois. For college teams, check www.collegesports.com, where each team has its own page, and you can have your sports news e-mailed to you via the web site's newsletter. If you are interested in a particular professional team, check their web site. Many teams have an e-mail newsletter service.

Most area colleges and universities with sports programs produce press releases and publications to keep the public aware of their activities. Here are a few:

- **University of Chicago,** Sports Information Office, 773-702-4638
- **Saint Xavier University,** Women's Basketball, Men's Basketball/ Cougars; sports Information, 773-298-3586
- **Loyola University,** Sports Information Office, 773-508-2575
- **University of Illinois,** Sports Information Office, 312-413-8199

- **DePaul University**, Sports Information Office, 773-325-7525
- **Northwestern University**, Department of Athletics, 847-491-3205

Finally, if you are interested in enrolling your youngster in a team sport, check with your local parks and recreation program. Youth and adult leagues are also popular throughout the area. Many leagues work in cooperation with the park districts; the districts will offer registration for team sports through their catalogues, while the leagues will provide the coaches, gear, and training.

PROFESSIONAL AND COLLEGE SPORTS

BASEBALL

Baseball season begins in early April and lasts until the first week in October, unless the Cubs or White Sox find themselves in post-season play. You'll find quickly that your place of residence aligns you as either a Cubs fan (North Side) or Sox fan (South Side). And you should know that the rivalry between the North Siders and the South Siders is sometimes taken to the extreme. So, don't be caught on the South Side cheering for the Cubbies!

- **Chicago Cubs** (National League) Wrigley Field, 1060 West Addison Street, 60613, 773-404-2827, www.cubs.com; will accommodate group outings of 50 persons or more. Call 773-404-CUBS for group sales information. You can purchase single game tickets at the Wrigley Field box office, at Tickets.com outlets (expect a service charge), or order by phone until two hours before game time using American Express, Discover, MasterCard or VISA. Call Tickets.com at 800-843-2827; out of state at 866-652-2827. Phone orders will be mailed or, if time does not permit mailing they will be held at the special "will call" window. Tickets.com also has kiosks located in Sears full-line and hardware stores throughout the Chicago area, Wisconsin, and northwest Indiana, at select Sports Authority retail stores, and at the Chicago Tribune Tower. Logon to the Cubs' web page and follow the link for Ticket.com for specific locations. The Cubs' Box Office, 773-404-CUBS, is open 8 a.m. to 6 p.m., Monday-Friday, and Saturday and Sunday 9 a.m. to 4 p.m. There are wheelchair seating areas in the Field Box behind home plate and in the rear section of the Terrace Reserved section. If you need this kind of seating, make arrangements by calling 773-404-4107. Senior citizen tickets are discounted for Wednesday afternoon games in the Terrace Reserve section. MasterCard, VISA, Discover, and American Express, and cash are accepted for ticket purchases at Wrigley Field.

- **Chicago White Sox** (American League) US Cellular Field (formerly Comiskey Park), 333 West 35th Street, 60616, 312-674-1000, TDD 312-451-5188, www.chisox.com; for season tickets, call 312-674-1000. Will accommodate group outings of 50 persons or more—call for details. All Monday night home contests are Family Night Half-Price games; Pepsi Tuesdays are also half-priced; and select Sundays are Willy Wonka days—tickets purchased at the field window that day are only $1 for kids. Other specials are listed on the web site. You can purchase White Sox tickets at the US Cellular Field box office, by phone: 866-SOX-GAME or 312-559-1212, until three hours before game time using American Express, Discover, MasterCard or VISA; at Ticketmaster outlets (locations include Carson Pirie Scott, Tower Records, Hot Tix, select Coconuts and Record Town locations); and online at the White Sox web site. The post-game fireworks schedule is posted on the web site. Wheelchair seating is available on each level; all levels accessible by elevators behind home plate. Wheelchair guests may make prior seating arrangements by calling 312-674-1000 ext. 5225, TDD 312-674-5235. For assistance during the game, or for the use of head-sets, contact the guest relations booth.

BASKETBALL

The professional basketball season begins in October, when baseball ends, and continues through April, with the NBA playoffs extending well into June.
- **Chicago Bulls** (NBA) United Center, 1901 West Madison Street, 60612, www.bulls.com, 312-455-4000; with their precipitous and long-lasting fall from glory, tickets are now available, even last-minute from scalpers, for those who wish to sit in the house that Michael built. For individual games, tickets go on sale the last weekend of September at the United Center box office; online at www.bulls.com; or through Ticketmaster outlets or at Ticketmaster.com; or call 800-4NBA-TIX. Group tickets (25 or more) go on sale through the Bulls front office in August. Call 312-445-4000 and ask for group sales. Purchase tickets by phone, until three hours before game time with a credit card by calling Ticketmaster at 800-462-2849. Phone orders will be held at the "will call" window. There is a service charge added to the price of each ticket ordered by phone.

Chicago also has several **Division I men's college basketball** teams, including the DePaul Blue Demons, who play at the Rosemont Horizon; the Loyola Ramblers, who play at Loyola University; and the Northwestern Wildcats, who play at McGaw Hall. **Women's college basketball** teams include the Chicago Blaze, who play at DePaul's Athletic Center and the Flames, who play at the UIC Pavilion.

FOOTBALL

The Bears' popularity is evidenced by the approximately 60,000 die-hard Bears fans who, despite the team's less than stellar record, brave Chicago's notorious winter, a.k.a. "Bear weather," to attend home games at Soldier Field. Pre-season games start in August; the regular season ends in mid-December. The Bears began playing in their newly renovated stadium in 2003. Despite an overall consensus that the new stadium does not do justice to the classic lines of the original, which opened in 1924, the grounds surrounding Soldier Field offer 19 pleasant acres of green space and includes an outdoor museum, a terraced garden, sledding hill, and a winter garden.

- **Chicago Bears** (NFL) Ticket Office is at 1000 Football Drive, Lake Forest, 60045, 847-615-2327, www.chicagobears.com. Bears tickets are tough to come by because season ticket holders hold most seats. If you want to get on the waiting list, go online to www.chicago bears.com and download a wait list form. It will cost you a $100 non-refundable deposit and there are only about 9,000 people ahead of you. You can purchase Bears single game tickets by mail every year by sending a self-addressed stamped envelope to the Bears ticket information office in early May. You will receive an order form, which you fill out and send back with a check on or after June 1. Any remaining tickets from the mail-order sale—and there aren't many—go to Ticketmaster for sale in July. You can (try to) purchase Bears tickets through Ticketmaster outlets or by phone with American Express, Discover, MasterCard or VISA cards by calling 312-559-1212. There is a service charge added to the price of each ticket.

HOCKEY

Although not as high profile as the Bears, Cubs, and White Sox, the Chicago Blackhawks have a definite following. Like basketball, the regular NHL season runs from October until April with the Stanley Cup playoffs extending through the spring. Also in Chicago are the International Hockey League's Chicago Wolves and the US Hockey League's Chicago Steel.

- **Chicago Blackhawks** (NHL) United Center, 1901 West Madison Street, 60612, 312-455-7000, www.chicagoblackhawks.com; you can purchase Blackhawks tickets at the Stadium box office, at Ticketmaster outlets or Ticketmaster phone service, 312-559-1212. With its loyal fan base of season ticket holders, tickets are difficult to come by, but not impossible. Call 312-943-7000. You can also download an order form from their web site. Groups of 15 or more will get you some benefits. If you are interested in getting regular news about the Blackhawks, sign up for an e-mail newsletter at their web site.

- **Chicago Wolves** (IHL), home games are played at the Allstate Arena, Rosemont Horizon, 10550 Lunt Avenue, Rosemont, 60018, 847-724-4625 or 800-THE-WOLVES, www.chicagowolves.com. Tickets are not as expensive as those for the Blackhawks games. Expect families and groups of Boy Scouts here. Ticket sales of 15 or more receive group benefits. For individual tickets, call Ticketmaster at 312-559-1212 or stop by the Allstate Arena's box office at 6920 North Mannheim Road, 847-635-6601, 11 a.m. to 7 p.m., Monday-Friday, Saturday, noon to 5, and Sundays three hours before game time. Go to their web site for a ticket order form and then mail it to Chicago Wolves, 2301 Ravine Way, Glenview, IL 60025, or fax it to 847-724-1652.

- **Chicago Steel** (USHL), 735 East Jefferson Street, Bensenville, 60106, www.chicagosteelhockey.com; home games are played at the Edge Arena in Bensenville. Members of this 21 year-old and younger team are recruited by college hockey teams. The tickets for these games are the least expensive of the three teams. To buy tickets by phone, call 630-594-1111. You can also order tickets through the team's web site.

SOCCER

Although the 1994 World Cup brought international fans to town for much of the summer, temporarily increasing the sport's visibility, professional soccer in Chicago has remained an acquired taste. First there was the outdoor Sting, then the indoor Power, now the city again has the outdoor Major League expansion team, the Chicago Fire. Soccer season runs from early April through late September, with twenty home games.

- **Chicago Fire** (MLS) www.chicago-fire.com; home games are played in Cardinal Stadium at North Central College in Naperville. For ticket information call the Fire's general information number at 312-705-7200. Single tickets for home games go on sale in late March. To order by phone, call 312-559-1212. You can download a single ticket order form via the web site and fax your order to 312-705-7393 (orders must be received 48 hours before game). You can mail your order to the Chicago Fire, 980 North Michigan Avenue, Suite 1998, Chicago, 60611. Or contact Ticketmaster. There is a discount for ticket sales of 15 or more, plus priority seating with advance purchase. To purchase group sales by phone, call 888-MLS-FIRE. Or download the group ticket order form and fax it or mail it (see above). Season ticket passes can be purchased via e-mail: firetickets@mlsnet.com, a fax order, or snail mail. There are many incentive plans so contact the ticket sales department for more information at 312-705-7200.

- The **Chicago Cobras** are the **W-League** team, the semi-professional women's soccer team in the area. They have training teams for young girls and teenagers. Home games are played in a number of stadiums including Mooseheart Memorial Stadium, in Mooseheart, IL. If you want to learn more about this organization, visit www.eclipseselect.org or call 847-680-9762. You may also try the league's office at 630-377-9292 and the W-1 League's web site, www.USLsoccer.com.

There are a number of strong **college soccer** teams in the area as well:
- **Augustana College**—men's and women's soccer, both NAIA, Division 1: women's link: www.augie.edu/athletics/soccer; men's link: www.augustana.edu/sports/msoccer
- **Benedictine University**—men's and women's soccer, both NAIA, Division 1: www.ben.edu/Athletics
- **College of St. Francis**—men's soccer, NAIA, Division 1, www.stfranciscollege.edu/sports/soccer
- **DePaul University**—men's and women's soccer, both NCAA, Division1: www.depaulbluedemons.com
- **Loyola University**—men's and women's soccer, both NCAA, Division 1: www.loyolaramblers.com
- **Northern Illinois University**—men's and women's soccer, both NCAA, Division 1: www3.niu.edu/athletics
- **Northwestern University**—men's and women's soccer, both NCAA, Division 1: www.nsudemons.com/soccer

DRAG RACING

- **www.trackchaser.com** lists tracks, of all kinds, across Illinois and the country.
- **Raceway Track**: 130th and Ashland; racing season runs April through October.
- **Route 66 Raceway**, www.route66raceway.com; Chicago Speedway, 500 Speedway Boulevard, Joliet. Races usually take place during summer weekends. For tickets by phone: 815-727-RACE, by fax: 815-727-7895; also available at the box office or online through Ticketmaster.com.

HORSE RACING

Prefer to play the ponies rather than ride them? There are five racetracks in the Chicago area:
- **Balmoral Park Racetrack**, Rte. 394 and Calumet Expressway, Crete, 708-672-7544; harness racing year-round.

- **Hawthorne Race Course**, 3501 South Laramie Avenue, Cicero, 708-780-3700; thoroughbred racing starts in October and runs through December. Harness racing is held in January.
- **Maywood Park Race Track**, 8600 West North Avenue, Maywood, 708-343-4800; harness racing February through May.
- **Sportsman's Park**, 3301 South Laramie Avenue, Cicero, 773-242-1121; thoroughbred racing starts in February and runs into May. Harness racing runs from May until October.
- **Arlington Park Racetrack**, 2200 West Euclid, Arlington Heights, 847-255-4300, www.arlingtonpark.com, is a beautiful, family-friendly park. Many event days throughout the season, with petting zoos, face painting for kids. Season runs May to September. Handicap accessible, general parking is free.

If you can't make it to the tracks, there are two **off-track betting parlors** in the Loop at 177 North State Street, 312-419-8787, and 233 West Jackson Boulevard, 312-427-2300.

More information on Illinois racetracks and racing schedules can be found at the **Illinois Racing Board**, 100 West Randolph Street, 312-814-2600.

PARTICIPANT SPORTS AND ACTIVITIES

PARKS AND RECREATION DEPARTMENTS

If you are looking for a neighborhood park that might offer something special—tennis courts, baseball diamonds, a kiddie pool—start with the Chicago Park District, www.chicagoparkdistrict.com, 312-742-PLAY. If they don't know the details of your neighborhood park, they will be able to direct you to someone who can help. For a complete list of greater Chicago area parks and recreation departments, see the **Greenspace and Beaches** chapter.

REGIONAL OFFICES
- For West Side parks contact: **Central Region, Garfield Park**, 100 North Central Park Avenue, 312-746-5092.
- For information on lakefront parks, beaches, harbors, trails, Museum Campus, and more, contact the **Lakefront Region, South Shore Cultural Center**, 7059 South Shore Drive, 312-747-2474.
- For information on 146 playgrounds and parks from Edison Park to Near North, and from Rogers to Portage Park, contact: **North Region, Warren Park**, 6601 North Western Avenue, 312-742-7888.
- From Chinatown to Lake Calumet, from the lakefront west to Englewood, to the southern limits of the city, Chicago offers 102 parks,

13 swimming pools, a recording studio, an ice rink, theater, and more. Contact **Southeast Region, Kennicott Park**, 4434 South Lake Park Avenue, 312-747-7138.

- From Bridgeport to Beverly, from Chatham to Clearing, Chicago offers golf courses, swimming pools, playlots, lagoons, boxing centers and batting cages. Contact: **Southwest Region, Tarkington Park**, 3344 West 71st Street, 312-747-6727.

BICYCLING

A few years ago, *Bicycling Magazine* named Chicago the best big city in the US for cycling. Mayor Daley, a bicycling enthusiast himself, promotes the bike to work movement, and has even assembled what his office calls Bike Ambassadors, to spread the good news about the bipedal. Since 1991, Chicago has established more than 100 miles of bike-ways and spent millions on bike-related improvements, including more than 8,000 bike racks across the city, with more in the works.

But having said all that, the biking experience in Chicago is decidedly urban for most Chicagoans. With the exception of the spectacular lakeshore path, the rest of the city's designated bike routes are on city streets. If you plan on doing much biking, you should be prepared for inconsiderate—or, even worse, oblivious—motorists. Still, there are some good reasons why people choose to get around by bike. Speed for one. During rush hour, you'll often get home faster on a bike than you will in a car. Whizzing by a quarter-mile long line of cars can be quite exhilarating. And you can forget about parking issues. You've got a guaranteed spot right outside your place of employment and it doesn't cost a dime. Last but not least, it's good for you. If you need to go farther than your legs can take you, remember bikes are allowed on the CTA trains during weekday rush hours, and at any time on the weekends.

Get a good bike lock and use it. Bikes get stolen in Chicago all the time, and the thieves are talented and committed. Buy a U-lock and make sure you lock your bike to a fixed object (if you can't find a bike rack, parking meters work well). Look out for "dummy poles" which are regular street sign poles where the bolts holding the base to the pole have been removed; the thief merely lifts up the pole and your bike is gone. More importantly, make sure you lock your frame and both wheel rims (if your wheels are of the quick-release variety) to the rack. Anything that isn't secure is fair game. Finally, buy a good bike helmet—and use it! While there is no current city or state law requiring cyclists to wear a bike helmet, your local township may have one, especially for residents under 14. Check with your local city hall for details.

As for specific routes, the lakefront path is almost 20 miles long and runs from the northern tip of Lincoln Park to south of Hyde Park. Bicycle rentals are available in stores and at various locations along the path. Take care, the paths can get very congested on summer afternoons and weekends with foot, in-line skate, and skateboard traffic. Inland from the lake, ride on the smaller north-south and east-west streets which run parallel to the busy main drags. Avoid the heavy traffic on Ashland Avenue, Western Avenue, Addison Street, Irving Park Road, and Sheridan Road north of Hollywood.

The **Chicagoland Bicycle Federation**, www.biketraffic.org, 312-427-3325, publishes a seven-county map of government-designated off-road bicycle trails in the Chicago metropolitan area as well as bicyclist-recommended roads for cycling through the Chicago area. The map is available in most bike shops and at the Rand McNally Map & Travel stores. For weekend riding, check out the seven bike trails in various **Cook County Forest Preserves**. Call 800-870-3666 for free maps and brochures, or visit their web site for downloadable maps, www.fpdcc.com. You can also visit the City of Chicago's bike page at www.cityof chicago.org/trans/BikeInfo for downloadable maps, and other bike-related information.

Remember that on a bicycle you are subject to the same rules of the road as motor vehicles: you are expected to ride with traffic, not against it; signal your turns, do not weave in and out of traffic, and do not run red lights. In addition, it's an especially good idea to wear a helmet and bright reflective clothing when riding at night.

BILLIARDS AND POOL

Just as Chicago has more bars and taverns per capita than any city in the United States, the ratio surely must extend to pool tables. Many pool halls are recent additions to the cityscape, but most bars in town will have a table or two in back. Here's a short list of places that are more billiards than booze:

- **Breaktime Bar and Billiards**, 3635 North Halsted Street, 773-281-0095
- **The Corner Pocket** (nine tables), 2610 North Halsted Street, 773-281-0050
- **Stix** (21 tables), 3416 North Sheffield Avenue, 773-404-7849
- **Shark City Billiards and Sports Bar** (23 tables), 2240 Bloomingdale Road, Glendale Heights, 847-51-SHARK
- **Southport Lanes and Billiard** (six tables), 3325 North Southport Avenue, 773-472-6600

BOATING

Lake Michigan is arguably Chicago's greatest asset. During the summer, the Chicago Park District and several lakefront yacht clubs offer sailing lessons and rentals. Call 312-742-8520, for more information. (Classes fill by spring.)

For private lessons try the **Chicago Sailing Club**, 773-871-7245, www.chicagosailingclub.com, at Belmont Harbor. Gillson Park hosts the **Chicago Corinthian Yacht Club** at 601 West Montrose Drive. Contact their information hotline at 773-395-5306 or visit www.corinthian.org. The **Chicago Yacht Club**, www.chicagoyachtclub.org, offers boating lessons; two locations: 400 East Monroe Street, 312-861-7777, and 300 West Belmont Avenue, 773-477-7575. The Evanston Township High School Sailing Club, www.missa.net/evanston/, meets every Sunday afternoon from June through September. **Gillson Sailing Beach**, at Lake Avenue/Lake Michigan in Wilmette, offers private and group sailing lessons. Call Wilmette Park District at 847-256-6100 for information. You can also rent kayaks, hobbies, and sunfish through the Wilmette Park District at Gillson Beach.

If you already know a thing or two about sailing, and wish to brush up on your skills, or even find a crew assignment, contact the **Chicago Women's Sailing Network** for more information, www.torresen.com/cwsn.

The members of the **Lincoln Park Boat Club** paddle, scull and row. Visit their web site at www.lpbc.net.

If you own a boat and want to dock it in any of Chicago's 5,200 boat slips, you must lease a space through the **Chicago Park District's Marine Department**, 312-742-8520. For a mooring permit, visit www.westrec.com for an application and information about fees. There is a long waiting list for docking space, and some Chicagoans opt for an alternative—the northern suburbs or an Indiana harbor. Check with the park district offices of the lakefront suburb in which you are interested.

BOWLING

If you placed Chicago's bowling alleys end to end, they would circle the globe. Actually, this may not be true, but it sure seems like it. There are bowling alleys in nearly every neighborhood and many that sponsor leagues. Here are just a few recommendations:

- **Diversey/River Bowl** (36 lanes), 2211 West Diversey Avenue, 773-227-5800; features a Saturday night Rock-n-Bowl. Open 24 hours on weekends.
- **Marigold Bowling Alley** (32 lanes), 828 West Grace Street, 773-935-8183; has a junior bowling program for ages 8 to 18.
- **North Center Bowl & Billiards** (12 lanes), 4017 North Lincoln Avenue, 773-549-2360; the entrance of North Center is tough to find. Look for the door under the Old Style sign and go up the stairs.
- **Southport Lanes & Billiards** (four lanes), 3325 North Southport Avenue, 773-472-6600; if you see a pair of legs standing where you've just hurled your bowling ball, you may not be drunk. Southport Lanes, a 75-year old institution, is the last bowling alley in Chicago to use human pin setters.

- **Spencer's Marina City Bowl** (38 lanes), 300 North State Street, 312-527-0747; if you're looking for a place to unwind after work, Marina City Bowl is perfect, conveniently located in the Marina City complex.
- **Waveland Bowl** (40 lanes), 3700 North Western Avenue, 773-472-5900; for those who need to kegel at 3 a.m. in the middle of the week, Waveland Bowl is the place for you. Open 24/7, 365 days.

In the **northwest suburbs,** look for:
- **Skokie Lanes**, 8146 Floral Avenue, Skokie, 847-673-2425
- **Fair Lanes**, 4833 Oakton, Skokie, 847-676-1700
- **Brunswick Deerbrook Lanes**, 10 South Waukegan Road, Deerfield, 847-498-3575
- **AMF Bowling Center**, 3245 Kirchoff Road, Rolling Meadows, 847-259-4400
- **Bowling Beyond Arlington Heights**, 3435 North Kennicott Avenue, Arlington Heights, 847-255-6373
- **Beverly Lanes**, 8 Beverly Lane, Arlington Heights, 847-253-5238; not modern or showy, but pleasant staff, and kid friendly.
- **Brunswick Zone of Palatine**, 519 South Consumers, Palatine, 847-392-8290; recently remodeled, many adult leagues play here. Children's area.
- **Brunswick Niles Bowl**, 7333 North Milwaukee Avenue, Niles, 847-647-9433
- **River Rand Bowl** (21 lanes), 191 North River Road, Des Plaines, 847-299-1001
- **Sy's Lane** (24 lanes), 6670 North Lincoln Avenue, Lincolnwood, 847-675-1050; has a cocktail lounge.

In the **south suburbs**:
- **Country Lanes Bowling Center**, 1009 West Laraway Road, New Lenox, 815-485-3916
- **Crete Bowling Lanes**, 1338 Main Street, Crete, 708-672-6262
- **Eagles Bowling Lanes**, 2427 Grove Street, Blue Island, 708-388-9739
- **Oak Forest Bowl**, 15240 Cicero Avenue, Oak Forest, 708-687-2000
- **Tinley Park Bowling Lanes**, 7601 183rd Street, Tinley Park, 708-532-2955

CHESS

Whether you are eight or 80, you will find a chess club to suit your needs here.
- **Chicago Industrial Chess League**, www.cicl.org, organizes team chess matches between downtown and suburban commercial, govern-

ment and educational organizations. The league has 21 six-member teams within its four divisions. Chess match season runs from August through April, with special festivities held in May and June.

- **Chess in Chicago**, www.chessinchicago.org, is a scholastic focused group whose web site serves as a portal for chess activities around the Chicagoland area. You can learn about upcoming tournaments, local clubs, and sign up for their e-mail newsletter.
- **Illinois Chess Association (ICA)**, www.illinoischess.org, is an excellent portal for chess information beyond Chicago. Provides chess club information for suburbs and neighboring states, high school teams and tournament information, as well as links to other chess sites. Membership forms must be sent via snail mail to: ICA Membership, 7042 North Greenview Avenue, 1-S, Chicago, IL 60626.
- **Pick-up Games**: where do you go when you are suddenly struck with the urge to play chess and don't have a partner? Try:
  - Java Oasis, 2240 South Michigan Avenue
  - Oak Street/North Avenue Beach Chess Pavilion.
  - Hyde Park: 52nd and Harper Avenue has concrete chess tables. In the summer, it's said chess is played here around the clock.
  - Borders Bookstore, Crystal Lake, Tuesdays, 7 p.m. to 10:30 p.m.

DANCE

If you are interested in inexpensive dance lessons, for either yourself or your children, check with your local park district. They often have good basic dance programs for young children, and even a few hip-hop classes as well. You may also find ballroom or Latin dance classes for adults at these facilities. If you are looking for something more demanding, you might explore **Chicago Dance**, 3660 West Irving Park Road, Chicago, 773-267-3411, www.chicagodance.com. The owners, Gregory Day and Tommye Giacchino, are one time US and World Dance champions. Latin, ballroom, and swing lessons are offered. If you are looking for salsa lessons, visit www.chicagodancenews.com, for links to a variety of Latin dance programs. In some instances you can find lessons provided free of charge in area dance clubs/bars (see **Cultural Life**). **Windy City Jitterbug Club** in Franklin Park (dance hotline: 708-456-6000), offers lessons in West Coast swing, shag, bop and of course, the jitterbug. For lesson information call 630-231-7644. **Chicago Rebels Swing Dance Club** offers West Coast swing dancing lessons, as well as hustle and motion study. They are located at 6137 North Northwest Highway, and 5919 North Knox Street, Chicago, 773-736-8109. You can find a link to their organization through www.chicagodance.com.

If you are interested in dancing to live swing music, try the Coffee Bar at the University of Chicago, 773-702-6238. In Naperville, try Frankie's Blue Room, 16 West Chicago Avenue, 630-416-4898.

FISHING

Fishing is popular in Chicago and you'll find plenty of places to do it. There are roughly 100 lakes and ponds, 10 significant rivers, and six dams in the six-county area that allow fishing, and that is in addition to the lakes and streams you will find in the forest preserves and state parks. Online, go to the **Chicago Area Paddling and Fishing Guide**, http://pages.ripco.net/~jwn, which will provide you with links to these fishing areas as well as information about water depth, the kind of fish you are most likely to find in a particular body of water, boating restrictions, and information about fishing licenses. It is the best! If you would like to compare notes with other sites, the **Illinois Department of Natural Resources** has a web site with a fishing link; visit: www.dnr.state.il.us. You can also call their hotline: 800-ASK-FISH.

For **chartered fishing** try:

- **Waukegan Charterboat Association**, 847-BIG-FISH; excellent salmon and trout fishing, April through September, on Lake Michigan.
- **Northpoint Charterboat Association**, Winthrop Harbor, 800-247-6727; operates out of Northpoint Marina in Winthrop Harbor. Fish Illinois and Wisconsin waters. Charters available May through October.
- **Free Spirit Charters**, 5219 North Virginia Street, 773-616-7799, offers salmon and trout fishing, mornings or afternoons.
- **Chicago Sportfishing Association**, www.great-lakes.org/il/fish-chicago/, is a charter boat captain's organization operating out of three downtown harbors, April through October.

And now, if you don't know already, you should know about **smelt fishing**. Every spring millions of these finger-sized delectables head towards the lakeshore to spawn. It doesn't take much skill to fish for smelt—just a dipping net. The trick is you have to do it at about 3 a.m., so bring a lantern and some warm clothes. You will find many Chicagoans lined up along the shore, chatting and laughing as they dip their nets. Many people like the area south of Navy Pier for smelting but you are almost guaranteed to get lucky standing anywhere along the shore—there are that many! If you find yourself shoulder to shoulder with an experienced smelter, ask him for his favorite smelt recipe. The most common way to cook smelt is to deep-fry them whole. Add a sprinkle of salt, mmmmmm.

FRISBEE

Another hybrid sport, Frisbee golf, or some call it, disc golf, this is actually a sport, not just a backyard game. There are bona fide courses in which to play—30 in Illinois alone—some are 18 hole courses, others nine. There are even state championships. Rules are similar to golf, but most most places do not charge, and you don't have to make reservations. Go to the **Professional Disc Golf Association** web site, http://pdga.com, for more information. Area **disc golf courses** include:

- **West Park**, Bellevue and Wheeler avenues, Joliet, 815-741-7275
- **Koch Knolls Park**, Naperville; disc course with picnic tables and restrooms.
- **Madison Meadow**, East Wilson/South Fairfield Avenue, Lombard, 630-627-1281
- **Centennial Park**, 3100 Trailway Drive, Highland Park, 847-831-3810; bring bug repellent!
- **Larry Fink Memorial Park**, 701 Deercreek Park, Highland Park, 847-831-3810; nine holes, beautiful setting.
- **Willow Stream Park**, Farmington Drive South, off old Checker Road, Buffalo Grove
- **Lippold Park**, IL-176/IL-14, Crystal Lake, 815-459-0680

CASINO GAMBLING

While not a sport, casino gambling is certainly a serious form of recreation for many. If playing the lottery isn't enough for you, you don't have to go far. Riverboat gambling is immediately available on the scenic Des Plaines river 15 miles south of Chicago in Joliet, or head just over the state line to Indiana for "lake boat gambling" on Lake Michigan. In Joliet, try: the **Empress Casino**, 888-436-7737, **Harrah's**, 800-427-7247. Other Illinois establishments include: **Argosy's Alton Belle Casino** in Alton, 800-336-7568, **Casino Queen** in, East St. Louis, 800-777-0777, **Grand Victoria Riverboat** in Elgin, 847-888-1000, **Hollywood Casino** in Aurora, 800-888-7777, and further west, **Par-a-Dice Hotel/Casino** in Peoria, 800-727-2342, and **Jumer's Casino** in Rock Island, 800-477-7747. In Indiana it's the **Trump Casino**, 888-218-7867 in Buffington Harbor.

GOLF

Surprising to many, the Chicago metropolitan area has miles and miles of fairways for your golfing pleasure. The Chicago Park District runs six public courses: **Robert A. Black** (9 holes), 2045 West Pratt Avenue; **Columbus**

Park (9 holes), 5200 West Jackson Boulevard; **Jackson Park** (18 holes), 63rd and Stony Island; **Sydney A. Marovitz** née Waveland (9 holes), 3600 North Lakefront (at Lake Shore Drive); **Marquette Park** (9 holes), Marquette Road and Kedzie Avenue; and **South Shore Country Club** (9 holes), 71st Street and South Shore Drive. To make reservations or for more information call the Park District at 312-245-0909. In addition to golf courses, the Chicago Park District has driving ranges in Lincoln Park at Diversey and at its Jackson Park and Robert A. Black courses.

The Cook County Forest Preserve also runs a number of golf courses. They include: **Billy Caldwell** (9 holes), 6200 North Caldwell Avenue, Chicago, 773-792-1930; **"Chick" Evans** (18 holes), 6145 Golf Road, Morton Grove, 847-965-5353; **Edgebrook** (18 holes), 5900 North Central Avenue, Chicago, 773-763-8320; and **Indian Boundary** (18 holes), 8600 West Forest Preserve Drive, Chicago, 773-625-9630.

Dozens of public golf courses dot the suburbs. For a comprehensive list of Chicagoland area public courses, visit www.centerstage.net, and look for the golf link. Some of the more popular public courses include:

NORTH
- **Bonnie Brook Golf Course** (18 holes), 2800 North Lewis Avenue, Waukegan, 847-360-4732
- **Glenview Park** (18 holes), 800 Shermer Road, Glenview, 847-724-0250
- **Midlane Country Club** (27 holes), 4555 West Yorkhouse Road, Wadsworth, 847-623-4653
- **Pine Meadow** (18 holes), One Pine Meadow Lane, Mundelein, 847-566-4653
- **Sportsman Country Club** (18 holes), 3535 Dundee Road, Northbrook, 847-291-2351

NORTHWEST
- **Arlington Lakes** (18 holes), 1211 South New Wilke Road, Arlington Heights, 847-577-3030
- **Chevy Chase** (18 holes), 1000 North Milwaukee Avenue, Wheeling, 847-537-0082
- **Golf Club of Illinois** (18 holes), 1575 Edgewood Road, Algonquin, 847-658-4400
- **Kemper Lakes**, Old McHenry Road, Hawthorn Woods, 847-320-3450
- **Old Orchard Country Club** (18 holes), 700 West Rand Road, Mt. Prospect, 847-255-2025
- **Villa Olivia Country Club** (18 holes), US Highway 20 and Naperville Road, Bartlett, 630-289-1000
- **Wilmette** (18 holes), Lake Ave/Harms Road, Wilmette, 847-256-6100

WEST
- **Cantigny Golf** (27 holes), 27 West 270 Mack Road, Wheaton, 630-668-3323
- **Indian Lakes Resort** (18 holes), 250 West Schick Road, Bloomingdale, 630-529-6466

SOUTH AND SOUTHWEST
- **Carriage Greens** (18 holes), 8700 Carriage Greens Drive, Darien, 630-985-3730
- **Cog Hill** (4 to 18 holes), including the infamous Dubsdread, 12294 Archer Avenue, Lemont, 630-257-5872
- **Evergreen Golf Club**, (18 holes), 9140 South Western Avenue, Evergreen Park, 773-238-6680
- **Gleneagles Country Club** (36 holes), 13070 McCarthy Road, Lemont, 630-257-5466
- **Hickory Hills Country Club** (1 to 18; 1 to 9 holes), 8201 West 95th Street, Hickory Hills, 708-598-6460
- **Silver Lakes** (45 holes), 147th Street and 82nd Avenue, Orland Park, 708-349-6940

HORSEBACK RIDING

Believe it or not, there is a place in Chicago where you can not only ride a horse, but you can board one and take riding lessons as well. The **Noble Horse Equestrian Center**, 1410 North Orleans Street, 312-266-7878, is the last riding center in the City of Chicago. It has an indoor riding arena and space to board more than 60 horses. Riding lessons, dressage, jumping and hunt seat lessons also are available. Group lessons begin at $24 per hour; private lessons start at $25 per half-hour.

In addition to the Noble Center, there are many stables in the northwest and southwest suburbs, which offer everything from equestrian- to trail-riding for riders of all ages and skill levels. Check the Yellow Pages under "Stables." Or visit the **Midwest Horse Stables Directory** at www.centaur.org. By providing your area code or zip code, you can access dozens of stables in your area. This portal also categorizes stables according to the type of riding lessons they provide, whether there is rental space available, and if they breed horses as well.

IN-LINE AND ICE SKATING

During the summer, in-line skaters abound on the lakefront, so many in fact that it can be hazardous for pedestrians. If you want to participate but don't have the gear, there are rental shacks dotting the lakefront and Lincoln Park, or try **Londo Mondo**, 1100 North Dearborn Street, 312-751-2794.

If ice is your element, Chicago has outdoor skating rinks in many parks throughout the city. Downtown, try **Skate on State** and the **Daley Bicentennial Plaza** at the north end of Grant Park. Navy Pier, 600 East Grand Avenue, has an outdoor ice skate rink at the **Skyline Stage**, open December to April. Call 312-595-5189. Another outdoor city rink is **Millennium Park**, 55 North Michigan Avenue, 312-742-PLAY. **Chicagoblader.com/events** is a good source of information about in-line and outdoor skating events, competitions, maps and links to other skate web sites. You can also subscribe to their newsletter.

Head to the suburbs for **indoor ice rinks**:

- **Addison Ice**, 475 South Grace Street, Addison, 630-543-9200
- **All Season Ice Rinks**, 31 West 330 North Aurora Road, Naperville, 630-851-0680
- **Barrington Ice Arena**, 28206 West Commercial Drive, Lake Barrington, 847-381-4777
- **Carol Stream Ice Rink**, 540 East Gunderson Drive, Carol Stream, 630-682-4480
- **Centennial Ice Rink**, 3100 Trailway, Highland Park, 847-432-4790
- **Center Ice of DuPage**, 1N450 Highland Avenue, Glen Ellyn, 630-790-9696
- **Darien Sportsplex**, 451 Plainfield Road, Darien, 630-789-6666
- **Downers Grove Ice Arena**, 5501 Walnut Avenue, Downers Grove, 630-971-3780
- **Fox Valley Ice Arena**, 1996 South Kirk Road, Geneva, 630-262-0690
- **Glenview Indoor Ice Center**, 1851 Landwehr Road, Glenview, 847-724-2800
- **Rocket Ice Arena**, 180 South Canterbury Lane, Bolingbrook, 630-679-1700
- **Rolling Meadows Ice Rink**, 3900 Owl Drive, Rolling Meadows, 847-818-3210
- **Seven Bridges Ice Arena**, 6690 Route 53, Woodbridge, 630-271-4423
- **Skatium Indoor Ice Arena**, 9300 Weber Park Place, Skokie, 847-674-1500
- **Sports Center Ice Rink**, 1730 Pfingsten Road, Northbrook, 847-291-2993
- **Twin Rinks Ice Pavilion**, 1500 Abbott Court, Buffalo Grove, 847-821-7465

INDOOR SUBURBAN ROLLER SKATING

- **Orbit Skate Center**, 615 Consumers Avenue, off the Northwest Highway in Palatine, 847-394-9199; indoor rink that rents in-line skates, as well as the old-fashioned roller skate kind.
- **Aurora Skate Center**, 34W113 Montgomery Road, Aurora, 630-898-5830
- **Lombard Roller Rink**, 201 West 22nd Street, Lombard, 630-953-2400
- **Mt. Prospect Park District-CCC Indoor Inline Skating Rink**, 1000 West Central Road, Mt. Prospect, 847-255-5380
- **Triple R Skate Park**, 1025 Campus Drive, Mundelein, 847-549-9950

HOCKEY

Chicago Freeze (North American Hockey League/Western Division, www.chicagofreeze.com); this league helps transition young players from midget and high school teams to college and major junior hockey teams. The players are male athletes under 20 years of age, and games are generally played on weekends to avoid school conflicts. Games are played at the Fox Valley Ice Arena, 1996 South Kirk Road, Geneva, IL 60134, 630-262-0690. Ticket prices are very reasonable. You can order tickets by phone with a VISA or MasterCard by calling the box office at 630-262-0690. You can also use the Ticketmaster web site or call Ticketmaster at 312-559-1212. Seating discounts are given to groups of 20 or more.

If you are interested in your youngster getting involved in hockey, contact your local park district.

RUGBY

Chicago has rugby clubs for both men and women. The season runs from late March until late May and then again in the autumn from Labor Day into November. If having your brains beaten out on the field and then drinking your brains out with your erstwhile opponents sounds like your kind of fun, call:

- **Chicago Condors Rugby Club**; practices are Tuesday and Thursday evenings at Columbus Park. Visit www.condorsrugby.com for more information.
- **Chicago Lions Rugby Club**; home games are played either at Revere Park or Schiller Woods. Clubhouse is located at 1801 West School Street, 773-404-1441. Visit www.chicagolions.com for more information.

- **Chicago Women's Rugby Football Club**; practices are held Mondays and Thursdays at Austin-Foster Park. Visit their web site for more information: www.cwrfc.com. Hotline: 312-409-5297

RUNNING

Chicago's lakefront provides an ideal place for running all year round, although you should be prepared for the blasting winds off the lake in the winter. In the summer you would do best to run in the morning, otherwise you'll be competing with bikers, roller bladers, and slow pedestrians. There are competitive races throughout the year, and some parks hold weekly events. Check the *Sun-Times* or the *Tribune* for schedules. It goes without saying that you should avoid running after dark in areas where there are few people.

If you're really serious about running, check out the **Chicago Area Runners Association** (**CARA**), 203 North Wabash Avenue, 312-666-9836, www.cararuns.org, the largest association of runners in the Midwest. It organizes races and training runs and actively works for runners' rights. The group successfully lobbied a lakefront alderman to keep the Lincoln Park running paths plowed through the winter. To keep up with runners' news in the region, visit Chicago Athlete at www.chicagoaa.com. They also feature a magazine, *Chicago Athlete* that you can subscribe to online.

The Chicago Marathon is held every year on the last Sunday in October (see **A Chicago Year**). It's a world-class event where you'll find the best runners in the world as well as 10,000 others participating.

SOFTBALL

There are hundreds of softball players—16-inch, 12-inch fast and 12-inch slow-pitch—in leagues across the Chicago area. Call the Chicago Park District at 312-747-2200, or your local park district for information on the league nearest you. The **Chicago Metropolitan Sports Association** is the largest non-profit gay and lesbian sports organization in the Midwest. Contact them at 312-409-7932, or visit their web site at www.chicagomsa.com, for more about their softball leagues and other sports they organize. Area employers, bars, and restaurants sponsor most softball teams.

SOCCER

If your youngsters want to play soccer and you live in the suburbs, contact the **Northern Illinois Soccer League**, 545 Consumers Avenue, Palatine, 847-398-4545, for information about outdoor and indoor leagues. Or visit their web site at www.northernillinoissoccerleague.com. The outdoor season starts in April and runs through September; indoor leagues run from autumn to spring. In Chicago, check with your local park district office. Most park districts offer some soccer instruction.

Other area **soccer clubs and associations** include:

- **American Youth Soccer Organization**: 800-USA-AYSO, www.soccer.org
- **Chicago Area Soccer League**, 708-802-CASL, www.casl.org (southwest suburbs, youth)
- **Chicago Celtic Soccer Club**, www.chicagocelticsoccerclub.com
- **Chicago Latin American Soccer League**, www.clasa.org (metro, adults and youth)
- **Hispanic Youth teams**: visit **Illinois Youth Soccer's** link at www.iysa.org/web/soccerstart
- **Illinois Soccer Association**, 773-283-2800 (metro, adults)
- **Illinois Women's Soccer League**, 847-985-4975, www.iwsl.com (metro, girls, and youth)
- **Illinois Youth Soccer Association**, 847-290-1577, www.iysa.org (youth to age 19)

SWIMMING

Despite its easy access, **Lake Michigan** might not be the place you want to go to swim—for many it's just too darn cold! For those hardy souls who prefer the lake to pool laps, many swim parallel to the shoreline from Ohio Street to the Oak Street curve and from Oak Street Beach to North Avenue Pier. Check www.chicagoparkdistrict.com under "swim report" for a list of Chicago beaches and conditions. Also see **Greenspace and Beaches**.

The Chicago Park District has **outdoor pools** throughout the city, but these are usually filled with screaming kids enjoying summer vacation. It's a good idea to check to see if the pools have reserved lap times. The district's **indoor pools** are one of Chicago's best-kept secrets. They are free, well maintained, and there are more than 30 scattered throughout the city. They lack the luxury and amenities of health clubs and private pools, but they'll get you in shape just as quickly. Call 312-747-2200 or check www.chicago parkdistrict.com for the pool nearest you, or look in the White Pages under "Chicago Park District." Hours, frequency, and duration of lap swims vary from facility to facility. Here are a few you might want to investigate:

- **Austin Town Hall Park,** 5610 West Lake Street, 312-746-5006; call for open swim times.
- **Blackhawk Park**, 2318 North Lavergne Avenue, 312-746-5014; extensive swim times, categorized by age. Special senior swim hours on Saturday mornings and Wednesday afternoons.

- **Gill Park**, 825 West Sheridan Road, 312-742-7802, in Wrigleyville, is the place for serious swimmers. Lap swimming is available three times a day and the pace can be blistering; if you're a novice, you'll want to stay in the slow lane.
- **Portage Park**, 4100 North Long Avenue, 312-742-7634; with its Olympic size pool, this facility hosted the 1972 Olympic Swim trials in which Mark Spitz set new world records. Pool was rennovated in 1998.
- **Shabbona Park**, 6935 West Addison Street, 312-742-7608
- **Welles Park**, 2333 West Sunnyside Avenue, 312-742-7515, in the Lincoln Square neighborhood, is a full-sized pool in a beautiful building with many windows and lots of natural light.

Health clubs and YMCAs throughout the city also have pools for the serious swimmer, and many high-rise apartment buildings have their own pools, but these are more for quick dips while sunning on a nearby chaise lounge than a serious workout. **Private swimming pool clubs** include:

- **Lakeshore Athletic Club—Streeterville**, 333 East Ontario Street, 312-944-4546
- **South Plymouth Court Swimming Pool**, 1151 South Plymouth Court, 312-427-4950

If you are looking for a little competition, visit www.chicagomasters.com. **Chicago Masters** team members practice in the University of Illinois' Olympic-size pool in the Physical Education Building located at 901 West Roosevelt Road.

If you live in the suburbs, check with your local parks program. In the suburbs you can expect an admission fee, and many park districts support summer camps, which generally have use of the pools in the afternoons. Some allocate 15 minutes each hour to adult swims after 3 p.m. Most suburban park districts offer residents a discounted season pass if it is purchased pre-season.

TENNIS

The Chicago Park District has nearly 700 tennis courts in parks throughout the city, but be warned: the good ones are packed and the bad ones look like the surface of the moon. The most popular public tennis courts are in Lincoln Park, between Addison Street and Irving Park Road, and at the south end of Grant Park, east of Columbus Drive.

There are also courts at some private health clubs, including the **Lakeshore Athletic Club**, 1320 West Fullerton Avenue, 773-477-9888, and the **Mid-Town Tennis Club**, 2020 West Fullerton Avenue, 773-235-

2300, www.midtowntennisclub.com. Many suburban park districts feature tennis courts. Check with your parks program for more information.

WHIRLYBALL

Not exactly basketball, not quite lacrosse but it's fast-paced fun played in electric bumper cars! You can only play whirlyball in two locations in the Chicago area, and you must make a reservation weeks in advance, but it is worth it: call WhirlyBall, 1880 West Fullerton, 773-486-7777, in Chicago or in Lombard, 800 East Roosevelt Road, 630-932-4800. For more information about "the world's only totally mechanized team sport" you can go online to www.whirlyball.com.

HEALTH CLUBS

If you're used to working out at a health club or if you want to start doing it, you're in luck: Chicago has an abundance of workout centers ranging from little more than weight and machine rooms to gigantic and luxurious mega-clubs that offer the latest fitness class, tennis courts, basketball courts, swimming pools, saunas, indoor jogging tracks, juice bars ... even climbing walls.

Get a tour, and if possible a free pass or two, before signing on the dotted line—you may decide that the reality of exercising to skull-pounding "music" is not so healthful after all. When you're told that this week the club you're visiting is having a "sale," take it with several grains of salt; with few fixed prices, words like "special," and "discount" are next to meaningless in the fitness business. The person on the treadmill next to you may have paid double or half what you paid. Ask at your place of work if they offer an employer-sponsored program. Finally, don't let yourself be pressured into signing up for a long-term commitment—unless you're *really* sure you want that multi-year membership!

- **Bally's Chicago Total Fitness Centers** are located throughout Chicago and the suburbs—check the White Pages for the one closest to you. The pulsating TV commercials notwithstanding, quality of service and equipment at Bally's varies considerably. Tour/try the place before splurging. For general information visit www.ballyfitness.com.
- **Chicago Athletic Association (CAA)**, 12 South Michigan Avenue, 312-236-7500; the address says it all, and the dress code too (no jeans). As much social club as health club, the CAA has been around for over a century.
- **Chicago Fitness Center**, 3131 North Lincoln Avenue, 773-549-8181, www.chicagofitnesscenter.com

- **Chicago Sweat Shop**, 3215 North Broadway, 773-871-2789, www.chicagosweatshop.com
- **East Bank Club**, 500 North Kingsbury Street, 312-527-5800, www.eastbankclub.com; three blocks long, this monument to fitness claims to be the largest health club in the United States.
- **Lakeshore Athletic Club** has four locations: 441 North Wabash, 333 East Ontario Street, 1329 West Fullerton, 211 North Stetson Avenue; 312-477-9888; go to http://lsac.com for more information.
- **Lehmann Sports Club**, 2700 North Lehmann Court, 773-871-8300, www.lehmannsportsclub.com
- **Lincoln Park Athletic Club**, 1019 West Diversey Avenue, 773-529-2022, www.lpaconline.com
- **Metropolitan Fitness Club**, 200 West Monroe Street, 312-444-1040, www.metfitclub.com
- **Webster Fitness Club**, 957 West Webster Avenue, 773-248-2006

Chicago YMCAs are a good place if you're looking for a no-frills health club. Many Ys have all the amenities of the popular health clubs at a fraction of the cost, and some of the suburban locations are very plush. Call the **YMCA of Metropolitan Chicago**, 312-932-1200, for the Y nearest you. Two of the more popular Ys are the **New City YMCA**, 1515 North Halsted Street, 312-440-7272, and the **Lakeview YMCA**, 3333 North Marshfield Avenue, 773-248-3333. In the suburbs try **Latoff YMCA**, 300 East Northwest Highway, Des Plaines, 847-296-3376.

Finally, you might want to call your local hospital and see if they have a fitness center. An increasing number of hospitals operate non-profit fitness centers both as preventive/rehabilitative medicine and as a marketing tool. These hospital gyms can be mellower and more affordable than the commercial gyms. In the northwest suburbs, contact **Northwest Community Healthcare-Wellness Center**, 900 Central Road, Arlington Heights, 847-618-3500.

CHICAGO PARKS

IN A CITY AS URBAN AND INDUSTRIALIZED AS CHICAGO, IT IS TRULY remarkable that it has been able to sustain its ambitious efforts to balance nature and man-made facilities in the same space. The number of parks, nature centers, forest preserves, and pockets of greenery that exist are amazing. From rooftop gardens above city hall, to seating along the Chicago River, to baskets of blooming greenery on lampposts all over the city, Chicago is a green city and becoming more so all the time.

The Chicago Park District is responsible for over 550 parks—and that doesn't include sports fields, diamonds, field houses, county preserves, lagoons, and golf courses.

Bikers, in-line skaters, walkers, and runners head to the lakeshore trails for exercise. For those who like team sports, there are sports leagues and teams scattered throughout the parks. Like volleyball? Head out to North Avenue Beach. Baseball your game? Then it's the diamonds across from Waveland Avenue. Sold on soccer? Try out the fields north of Montrose Avenue. Rowers can test their might in the lagoon near Lincoln Park Zoo, while sailors head to Burnham Harbor. Golfers can tee up at the 18-hole course at Jackson Park (among others—see **Sports and Recreation** for a list of public golf courses). Whatever your outdoor needs, you can probably find a place to do it in Chicago. Call the Park District, 312-742-7529, or visit their web site at www.chicagoparkdistrict.com for more information.

SOME FAVORITE PARKS

- **Columbus Park**, 500 South Central Avenue, 312-746-5046; now restored, is considered to be Jens Jensen's masterpiece. This park pulled together many of the ideas he had been developing through other projects in Chicago. Located downtown near the Congress Expressway, it features a wildflower prairie, with stepping stone paths, a meandering river, waterfalls, and an outdoor theater. Though it lost some acreage to the Eisenhower Expressway, it is still a popular and beautiful place.

- **Douglas Park** (3000W/2100S), 1401 South Sacramento Avenue, 312-747-7670; what was once a swamp was transformed into a lagoon surrounded by lawns and trees, thanks to William LeBaron Jenney and later to Jens Jensen, who added the Flower Hall and Gardens. Their work here is identified as the Prairie-style of landscape architecture.
- **Garfield Park**, 100-300 North Central Park Avenue, 312-746-5092; this park was originally one of three large parks that were designed with inter-linking boulevards in 1869 by William LeBaron Jenney, the father of the skyscraper. When it became apparent that the plans were too ambitious to be realized at once, it was decided that Garfield Park would be developed in stages, beginning with its east lagoon. For a number of reasons the three parks were neglected for years until Jens Jensen was named Chief Landscape Architect of the parks in 1905. Experimenting with his Prairie-style landscaping designs, he created the Garfield Park Conservatory, which opened in 1908. Today the Conservatory is still one of the jewels in the park district system; its programs and events continuously draw visitors to the Garfield Park neighborhood. Garfield Park also features the Garfield Park Formal Gardens, designed by the highly respected landscape designer, Chris Woods of the Chanticleer Gardens in Philadelphia.
- **Grant Park**, 331 East Randolph Street, 312-742-7648; is perhaps the best known of all Chicago's parks. It owes its existence to the foresighted citizens who fought against development projects for the space along the shore. In 1927, the Buckingham Fountain was added. Today the park is part of the Museum Campus Project and plans are underway to add more gardens, sculptures and performance spaces, without obstructing its breathtaking views of Lake Michigan and beyond.
- **Hamilton Park**, 513 West 72nd Street, 312-747-6174; part of a 10-park project designed to provide some recreation for those living in South Side tenements, Hamilton Park was the first. Designed by Daniel Burnham in 1904, it included a new type of building—the field house, which included classrooms, a cafeteria, public bathing area, meeting rooms, an indoor gym, locker room, and one of the city's earliest library branches. In 1916, Chicago artist John Warner Norton painted a series of murals in the field house's lobby, depicting scenes from American political history.
- **Jackson Park**, 6401 South Stony Island Avenue, 312-747-6187; after Frederick Law Olmsted and Daniel Burnham transformed this area into the "White City" for the 1893 World's Fair, Olmsted returned the site to parkland. While his original plans were never fully realized, the results

were still impressive. The city added 10 acres of landfill to create the 63rd Street Beach. The beach's Classical-style bathing pavilion was recently restored. Beyond the beach, the park contains a golf course, and the Japanese-styled Osaka Gardens, hidden behind the Museum of Science and Industry. Its Wooded Isle attracts many migratory birds.

- **Lincoln Park**, 2045 North Lincoln Park West, 312-742-7726; what began as a lakeside cemetery for cholera and smallpox victims was transformed into a 1,200-acre park/zoo/conservatory/garden and more. Throughout the park's history, renowned artists have contributed to its development. The roster includes: sculptor Augustus-Saint Gaudens, landscape designers Ossian Cole Simonds and Alfred Caldwell, and architects Dwight Perkins and Joseph Lyman Silsbee. The park offers many programs for adults and children, camps and cultural events.
- **Olive Park** is a small park just north of Navy Pier. As it juts out onto Lake Michigan it is not accessible by car, making it an especially quiet and restful area. Don't be surprised to find a few tired bicyclists napping on the grass.
- **Washington Park**, 5531 South King Drive, (just off 55th Place); once again, Daniel Burnham was called upon to work his magic in Chicago. He designed the refectory that is now used for meetings, special community events, and locker rooms. The 1910 administrative building he designed was converted into the DuSable Museum (see **Cultural Life**). This park has an outdoor swimming pool, winding paths, the beautifully sculpted Fountain of Time, and a lovely grove of trees.

DOG FRIENDLY PARKS

Most parks do not allow dogs to roam without a leash, some don't allow dogs at all. But in the parks below they are welcome. Check with your local park district (see listing below) to find out your community's rules about pets and parks. In off-leash areas, for the protection of fellow pooches, only allow your dog off-leash if it is a well socialized animal.

If you would like your dog to get an opportunity to strut his or her stuff, check into the Anti-Cruelty Society's annual "Bark in the Park" walkathon. Usually held in the spring, this 5K walk includes free doggie snacks, parades, demonstrations and educational tips. Visit www.barkinthepark.org to learn more. For a comprehensive list of dog friendly areas beyond Chicago, visit www.chicagolandtails.com.

- **Coliseum Park**, 14th Place and Wabash Avenue, 312-747-7640 (South Lakeshore Drive/West 15th Street); nestled among the Amtrak and Illinois Central Railroads, this park has one playground, a small recreation area, and a dog-friendly space. Off-leash area.

- **Grant Park**, Congress/Columbus Drive, 312-742-7648 (downtown Chicago); dogs are allowed but only on leashes. The Lakefront Trail Park is close by.
- **Hamlin Park**, 3035 North Hoyne Street, 312-742-7785 (Hamlin Park neighborhood, Belmont/Lincoln); dogs can roam free inside the fenced in area at Hoyne and Wellington.
- **Lakefront Trail Park**, Lake Shore Drive, 312-742-7529; 18 miles of paved walkway accommodates cyclists, strollers and leashed dogs. You can start your dog run at any number of points—Lake Shore Drive/Wacker is a common one. While you may be tempted to let your dog romp on the beach, resist. Except for Doggie Beach (see below), dogs are not allowed on any Chicago beaches. (That said, many still come to the beaches with pooches in tow on early summer mornings or late evenings.)
- **Margate Park/Puptown**, 4921 North Marine Drive, 312-742-7522; is just south of Lincoln Park, off West Castlewood Drive. Off-leash area.
- **Walsh Park**, 1722 North Ashland Avenue, 773-384-0393 (West Town neighborhood); is a two-acre park built in memory of fireman John P. Walsh Jr., who gave his life fighting a fire in 1970.
- **Wicker Park**, 1425 North Damen, 312-742-7553 (Wicker Park neighborhood); in the southeast corner of the park, lies a fenced in area where dogs can wander off-leash.
- **Wiggly Field Dog Park**, 2645 North Sheffield Avenue, 773-348-2832; is a park with a sense of humor! This dog-friendly area is within Grace Noethling Park in the Lincoln Park neighborhood and offers dog-sized drinking fountains, and fake mailboxes for marking territory.

Chicago even has a beach set aside for canines:
- **Doggie Beach**, Lakeshore/Recreation drives, north end of Belmont Harbor, 312-742-DOGS; open daily during the season, sunrise-sunset. Small sandy beach for pets to romp. No facilities, and dog owners must clean up after their pets; owners must provide their own cleanup tools.

CHICAGOLAND PARK DISTRICTS

- **Arlington Heights**, 847-577-3000, www.ahpd.org
- **Barrington**, 847-381-0687, www.ci.barrington.il.us
- **Buffalo Grove**, 847-850-2100, www.bgparkdistrict.org
- **Chicago,** 312-742-PLAY, www.chicagoparkdistrict.org
- **Deerfield**, 847-945-0650, www.deerfieldparkdistrict.org
- **Des Plaines**, 847-391-5700, www.desplaines.org
- **Downers Grove**, 630-963-1304, www.dgparks.org
- **Elk Grove Village**, 847-437-9494, www.parks.elkgrove.org

- **Evanston**, 847-866-2900, www.cityofevanston.org
- **Glen Ellyn**, 630-858-2462, www.gepark.org
- **Glencoe**, 847-835-3030, www.glencoeparkdistrict.com
- **Highland Park**, 847-831-3810, www.pdhp.org
- **Hinsdale**, 630-789-7090, www.villageofhinsdale.org
- **LaGrange**, 708-352-1762, www.pdlg.org
- **Lisle**, 630-964-3410, www.lisleparkdistrict.org
- **Morton Grove**, 847-965-1200, www.mortongroveparks.com
- **Mt. Prospect**, 847-255-5380, www.mppd.org
- **Naperville**, 630-848-5000, www.napervilleparks.org
- **Northbrook**, 847-291-2960, www.nbparks.org
- **Oak Lawn**, 708-857-2222, www.olparks.com
- **Oak Park**, 708-383-0002, www.oakparkparks.com
- **Palatine**, 847-991-0333, www.palatineparkdistrict.com
- **Prospect Heights**, 847-394-2848, www.phparkdist.org
- **Rosemont**, 847-823-6685
- **Skokie**, 847-674-1500, www.skokieparkdistrict.org
- **Westmont**, 630-969-8080, www.wpd4fun.org
- **Wheaton**, 630-665-4710, www.wheatonparkdistrict.com
- **Wilmette**, 847-256-6100, www.wilmettepark.org
- **Winnetka**, 847-501-2040, www.villageofwinnetka.org
- **Woodridge**, 630-964-2100, www.woodridgeparks.org

FOUNTAINS

On a hot summer day, few things are more refreshing than to sit within view of a cool fountain.

- **Centennial Fountain**, 300 North McClurg Court, 312-751-6633, TDD 312-744-2947; from Memorial Day to Labor Day, seven days a week, this fountain is in action. Every 15 minutes after the hour it shoots a powerful spray of water. There are plenty of benches and seating around Cityfront Plaza to witness the display; you'll find many office workers, lunch in hand, vying for a spot too. While the fountain might be considered a kind of centerpiece, it's actually only part of a winding paved river walkway that extends around the southern edge of the Streeterville neighborhood and the Chicago River. Wheelchair accessible.
- **Buckingham Fountain**; designed in 1927 and set in a Beaux-arts styled garden in Grant Park, this bronze sculpture was declared a Chicago landmark in 2000. Its design is based on the Latona Basin in the gardens of Versailles. Its four sea horses represent the four states that touch Lake Michigan. What sets this fountain apart is its innovative use of technology to create a light and water display that has become synonymous with summer in Chicago. The colored light shows are dis-

played hourly from 8 p.m. to 11 p.m. during the summer months. Buckingham Fountain is one of the world's largest fountains, and is one of the state's leading attractions.

NATURE CENTERS AND SANCTUARIES

In addition to the hundreds of parks in Chicago, there are also 49 nature areas. These specially designed landscapes are all unique, some feature lagoons, others focus on recreating prairie-scapes. Here are a few:

- **Burnham Prairie Path**, 47th Street/Lake Shore Drive; part of Burnham Park, near the lakefront, these winding paths lead the walker through a butterfly garden, prairie path, and a woodland area, all planted with species native to the area.
- **Columbus Woodland and Lagoon**, Central Avenue and Adams Street; one of the many fine examples of Jen Jensen's Prairie-style realized here in the woodland setting. All footpaths lead to the lagoon, which was inspired by natural prairie rivers. There are also three manmade limestone waterfalls. By planting the woodland with local varieties of plants and flowers, the woodland has become home to many native birds.
- **Gompers Park Wetland Recreation**, a former oxbow in the North Branch of the Chicago River at Foster Avenue and Pulaksi Road; fed by Gompers Park Lagoon and a stretch of the North Branch of the Chicago River, the Gompers Park Wetland is now important to area flood control. Heron, butterflies, muskrat, frogs, and fish have been observed here. Nearby lies the one-acre **Gompers Park Lagoon**, a treasured fishing spot for many locals.
- **Hurley Park Savanna**, 1901 West 100th Street, in the Beverly neighborhood; is one of the state's few remaining oak savannas, and the only one within the Cook County Park District's network. In 1996 a joint effort between the Park District and the Morton Arboretum restored the Savanna's understory, recreating the natural grasses, brushes and plants that naturally occur in such an environ.
- **Jackson Park Bobolink Meadow**; located south of the Museum of Science and Industry, Jackson Park was host to the 1893 World's Fair. Once used as a Nike missile base, then neglected and nearly abandoned, this meadow is slowly being rehabilitated to encourage the return of the Bobolink, an Illinois songbird that enjoys open grasslands. Six acres have been restored and are a haven for birds and butterflies. A two-acre woodland section is still under restoration. The Park's East Lagoon has attracted turtles, muskrats, beavers, and dragonflies.
- **Lincoln Park Addison Migratory Bird Sanctuary**, 3600 North Addison; is the fenced area behind the totem pole. This is the only bird sanctuary in Chicago that denies public access. This is because many

birds roost in this six-acre sanctuary several months a year, and the sanctuary has become home to a variety of animals, including an occasional fox and coyote. However, newly expanded pool areas, along with extended viewing platforms will at least give the public a better view to the inside.

- **Lincoln Park Alfred Caldwell Lily Pool**; located directly north of the Lincoln Park Zoo, on Fullerton, this extensively rehabilitated landscape was reopened to the public in 2002. The Lily Pool is becoming a coveted spot for bird watchers.

- **Lincoln Park North Pond**, behind Peggy Notebaert Museum; is proof that you can make a silk purse out of a sow's ear. Through the efforts of the Park District and park volunteers, this pond, once a dumping ground, has become an important flyaway area for over 160 species of migrating birds. It was at this pond that Mayor Daley and the US Fish and Wildlife Service signed an Urban Conservation Treaty for Migratory Birds. In addition to the pond, there are 10 wooded acres that serve as home to a variety of animals and beneficial insects.

- **Marquette Park Ashburn Prairie** on the southwest side, is the city's largest prairie, encompassing over 300 acres. The park's field house is located at 6734 South Kedzie, and the prairie, which has an unusual history, is just east of Kedzie. While some of the other prairies in Chicago needed restoration, and heavy weeding, none of them were transplanted, as was the case with Ashburn. This prairie originally blossomed in a two-acre area near Evergreen Cemetery. But encroaching development threatened its existence. In 1993, the Park District dug up several large plugs of prairie—each were at least five feet across—and brought them to the Marquette Park's lagoon where the composition of the soil was similar to the prairie's original site. The prairie's continuing success is largely a measure of the volunteers who monitor, weed, and seed it.

- **Montrose Point Bird Sanctuary**, 4400 North Montrose/Lake Michigan; in Lincoln Park, this bird sanctuary attracts over 300 species of migratory birds each year. East of the bathhouse is a 150-yard stretch of hedge nicknamed "The Magic Hedge" for its ability to attract an especially large number of migratory birds. This hedge is recognized internationally as a birding area.

- **Nichol's Park Wildflower Garden**, 1300 East 55th Street in Hyde Park; a small blue/yellow sign signals entrance to the garden with its many native, prairie and woodland plantings. Nichol's Park Meadowlarks, a Hyde Park gardening group, contribute their energies to the maintenance of this garden.

- **Paul Douglas Nature Sanctuary in Jackson Park**; Jackson Park Lagoon is located at 6401 South Stony Island Avenue. The park contains an area called Wooded Isle, which can be reached over a bridge that is within walking distance from the parking lot off of Hayes Drive. If you take the bridge on the north side of the lagoon, you will find the Osaka Japanese Gardens. The Douglas Nature Sanctuary is a favorite with birders as the area attracts as many as 250 species of birds.

- **South Shore Cultural Center Nature Sanctuary**; located on Lake Michigan, at the peninsula of the South Shore Cultural Center. The field house is located at 7059 South Shore Drive. To reach the sanctuary, you must walk south along the beach. Construction of this sanctuary began in 2001. It includes a trail that takes hikers through a sand dune, over a wetland and into the three-acre prairie. The sanctuary has proven to be an important stopover for migrating birds.

If you are interested in keeping up with the various programs, activities, and efforts to rehabilitate the Chicagoland area's green spaces, subscribe to *Chicago Wilderness* magazine or visit their web site at www.chicagowildernessmag.org.

NATURE AND WILDLIFE GARDENS

In Chicago are a series of six gardens planted with native species, which are tagged for easy identification. These nature and wildlife gardens demonstrate the abundant beauty of midwestern flora and fauna. The plantings were selected according to an established criteria: providing food and shelter for wildlife, beneficial insects, and birds; native plant species that require little care after initial watering; plants that thrive in either sunny locations, wetlands, or wooded areas. Take note of the kinds of plants and the designs of these gardens; they can be easily adapted for backyard use.

- **Bessemer Park**, 8930 South Muskegon Avenue, 312-747-6023
- **Horner Park**, 2741 West Montrose Avenue, 312-742-7572
- **Ogden Park**, 6500 South Racine Avenue, 312-747-6572
- **Portage Park**, 4100 North Long Avenue, 312-742-7634
- **Prospect Gardens Park**, 10940-11000 South Prospect Avenue, 312-747-6163
- **Rutherford Sayre Park**, 6871 West Belden Avenue, 312-746-5368

OTHER CHICAGO–AREA GARDENS

- **Chicago Botanic Garden**, 1000 Lake Cook Road, Glencoe; perhaps the most famous of all Chicago gardens, the grounds are comprised of 385 acres of beautiful and unique cultivated gardens with over two million plants. Included are 81 acres of waterways, 100 acres of wooded land, nine islands, six miles of shoreline, and 15 acres of prairie. Owned by the Forest Preserve of Cook County but operated by the Chicago

Horticultural Society, the gardens feature over 20 different types of gardens, from English walled gardens to Japanese-styled gardens. The center offers a variety of programs, many hosted by internationally known experts, plant sales, horticultural classes, children's programs, an e-mail newsletter, and much more. Birders take note: over 250 species of birds have been sighted here. Admission is free with paid parking. Memberships are available. Visit www.chicagobotanic.org for more information or call 847-835-5440. Wheelchair accessible.

- **Garfield Park Conservatory**, 300 North Central Park Avenue, 312-746-5100; nation's largest public garden under glass. Visit www.garfield-conservatory.org.
- **Morton Arboretum**, 4100 Route 53, Lisle, 630-968-0074; this 1,700-acre outdoor museum delights its visitors with 3,300 different kinds of plants, trees, and shrubs in woodland, prairie, wetland, and garden settings. Open daily from 7 a.m. to 7 p.m. Admission: $7 per car, $3 per car on Wednesdays. The Arboretum offers many programs and events, publishes several booklets, calendars and handbooks. Visit their web site at www.mortonarb.org.
- **South Shore Cultural Center Gardens**, 7059 South Shore Drive, 312-747-2536; formal gardens set in a 65-acre park against the restored 1905 Cultural Center. Grounds include the South Shore Beach.

If you are interested in learning more about Illinois wildlife, including the efforts being made to preserve and protect it, contact the **Illinois Audubon Society** at 217-446-5085 or visit www.illinoisaudubon.org. If you would like some information on where to look for certain species of birds, try the **Chicago Audubon Society**, 847-299-3505. For those in the northwest suburbs, local chapters are **Prairie Woods Audubon Society** in Arlington Heights, 847-622-5321; **DuPage Audubon Society** in Winfield, 847-299-7882; and **Lake Cook Audubon Society** in Highland Park, 847-433-0083.

CEMETERIES

Peaceful walks can be experienced at Chicago's cemeteries. Generations ago, people often picnicked on cemetery grounds, and today cemeteries are still fascinating places to explore. Here you may find the tombs and headstones of some of Chicago's famous and infamous. Don't be surprised to discover the names of local streets on the tombstones; it is one way the city has honored the men and women that made Chicago what it is today. For a complete list of area cemeteries, visit www.graveyards.com or buy the book *Graveyards of Chicago* by Matt Hucke and Ursula Bielski.

- **Beth-El/Ridgelawn Cemeteries**, 5736 North Pulaski Road, 847-673-1584; small Jewish cemeteries, burials dating back to 1895.

- **Bohemian National Cemetery**, 5255 North Pulaski, 773-539-8442; holds what is considered by some as the finest funerary art in the city.
- **Calvary Catholic Cemetery**, 301 Chicago Avenue, 847-864-3050, on the lakefront behind Sheridan Road, Evanston; is the oldest cemetery in the Chicago Archdiocese.
- **Forest Home**, 863 South Des Plaines Avenue, Forest Park, 708-366-1900; originally the burial grounds of the Potawatomis Indians. Of particular interest is the Druid Monument erected in 1888, and the Haymarket Monument; many anarchists, socialists and labor party movement members are buried near this monument, including Emma Goldman.
- **Graceland Cemetery**, 4001 North Clark Street, 773-525-1105; is one of Chicago's best-known and most historic places of rest. The bodies exhumed from the lakefront cemetery were moved here in order to establish Lincoln Park. Among the buried here are Mies van der Rohe, Louis Henri Sullivan, Marshall Field, and Daniel Hudson Burnham.
- **Graveyards of Barrington**, Evergreen Cemetery is located at Dundee/Monument avenues, and White Cemetery on Cuba Road. Evergreen has burials dating back to the Civil War era, and White Cemetery is said to be haunted!
- **Jewish Graceland**, 3919 North Clark Street; collective name of four cemeteries adjacent to one another, but without borders. The Hebrew Benevolent Society, after which one of the four is named, was established in 1851, making it one of the oldest cemeteries in Chicago. These four cemeteries are poorly maintained and many stones are damaged beyond repair.
- **Montrose Cemetery and Crematorium**, 5400 North Pulaski, 773-478-5400; several sections devoted to specific ethnic groups, such as Japanese and Serbian.
- **Mount Carmel**, Harrison/Hillside Avenue, Hillside, 630-449-8300; a final resting-place for many Italian immigrants in Chicago. Cardinal Bernadin and Al Capone are both buried here.
- **Oak Ridge/Glen Oak Cemeteries**, 4301 West Roosevelt, Hillside; has several special sections: Showmen, members of the Salvation Army, Masons. Oak Ridge has a Jewish section. Blues fans will remember, Howlin' Wolf, a.k.a. Chester Burnett, who is buried here.
- **Rosehill Cemetery and Mausoleum**, 5800 North Ravenswood, 773-561-5940; the largest cemetery in the city. Opened in 1859, it is also one of the oldest. A number of Chicago mayors, Civil War generals and soldiers are buried here.
- **St. Boniface Cemetery**, 4901 North Clark Street, 773-561-2790; was dedicated in the 1860's to serve the German Catholic community.

- **St**. **Henry Cemetery**, Ridge Avenue/Devon, 847-864-3050; this small cemetery has a grave that is purported to be that of the boy on the Cracker Jack box.
- **Waldheim Jewish Cemeteries**, 1400 South Des Plaines, Forest Park, 708-366-4541; over 300 cemeteries are a part of this burial ground.

COOK COUNTY FOREST PRESERVES

Cook County is responsible for over 68,000 acres of land. Within the forest preserves, you will find picnic groves, horseback riding and hiking trails, ponds, swimming pools, model airplane flying fields, nature centers, golf courses, dog training areas, rivers, streams, and toboggan slides. The Forest Preserve's web site is chock-full of information about its facilities, license information, trail maps, as well as useful information for gardeners and naturalists. The Cook County Forest Preserve is always looking for volunteers. If you are interested, contact them at 800-870-3666. For more information about events and activities call the recreation department at 708-771-1550 or visit www.fpdcc.com.

COOK COUNTY NATURE CENTERS/FOREST PRESERVES

These six nature centers are free to the public and open year round (except Camp Sagawau).

- **Crabtree Nature Center**, 3 Stover Road, Barrington; has over 1,000 acres and is the newest of the county's nature centers. Since its purchase by the Cook County Forest Preserve in the mid-1960s, this glacier-formed landscape is slowly being returned to its natural state. Over 263 species of birds have been identified here, with at least 89 species breeding within its boundaries. There is an exhibit building and several miles of self-guided educational trails through the center. Groups are encouraged to make a reservation by calling, 847-381-6592. No bicycling, horseback riding, or cross-country skiing allowed. Picnicking is permitted only at designated areas: Deer Grove Forest Preserve, Shoe Factory Road Woods, and Barrington Road Pond. For more information, contact the Conservation Department at 800-870-3666.
- **North Park Village Nature Center**, 5801 North Pulaski Road, 312-744-5472, www.cityofchicago.org/environment; is a 46-acre preserve with woodlands, prairie, pond and savannas. Offers family and adult educational programs, bird walks, owl prowls.
- **River Trails Nature Center**, 3120 Milwaukee Avenue, Northbrook; walk through sugar maple woods on self-guided educational trails. There is an exhibit building, and naturalists are available to answer

questions. Groups are encouraged but reservations are recommended. Call 847-824-8360. For more general information, contact the Conservation Department at 800-870-3666.

- **Sand Ridge Nature Center**, 15891 Paxton Avenue, South Holland; this 235-acre preserve is located near Wampum Lake Woods. It has four easy, well-marked hiking trails, none longer than two miles. Each trail leads through a different habitat: an oak savanna, marsh, ancient sand dune, and a pond. The area is especially admired for its April/May spring blossoms, summer prairie flowers, and early autumn colors. Several events are celebrated at the center throughout the year, including Earth Day, Migratory Bird Day, and Settler's Day. Free nature programs are held in the exhibit building. Guided walks are available. Contact 708-868-0606 for reservations and more information.

- **Camp Sagawau**, 12545 West 111th Street, Lemont; containing the only rock canyon in Cook County, the preserve is home to over 100 migratory birds. Opened only for scheduled programs, though over 80 family programs and hikes are presented. For more information about programs, college credit courses, and workshops, call 630-257-2045.

- **The Little Red Schoolhouse Nature Center**, 9800 Willow Springs Road, Willow Springs; built in 1866 to replace a one-room log cabin school, this building was in use as a school until 1948. Today's hikers can still traverse trails used by former students. Fruit orchards planted in 1906 still bear fruit. Groups of 15 or more must make a reservation by calling 708-839-6897.

- **Harold Tyrell Trailside Museum**, 738 Thatcher Avenue, River Forest; the museum building, built in 1874, is located in a savanna prairie, and is used as a rehabilitation center for injured wildlife. Once the animals are well enough to live on their own they are released into the wild. Groups are welcome. November through February, reservations needed. Call 708-366-6530.

- **Wampum Lake Woods**; situated between the townships of Thornton and Lansing, this 375-acre wood is home to a variety of plants not normally found in the area. Its sandy soil fosters wildflowers, trees, and shrubs. This area is considered one of the best working archaeological sites in the Chicago area (off-limits to the public). Cross-country skiing, ice fishing, and hiking are popular here. Boating and swimming are prohibited. Dogs on leashes are welcome. Pick up a map at the Nature Center. For more information call 800-870-3666.

FOREST PRESERVES BEYOND COOK COUNTY

Neighboring counties also have extensive forest preserves.

DUPAGE COUNTY FOREST PRESERVE

The DuPage County Forest Preserve covers more than 23,000 acres with 60 mile of rivers and streams, 80 mile of trails, and over 600 acres of lakes. Each year, over one million visitors come to the forest preserves of DuPage County to hike, ski, bird watch, or ride horses. You can call 630-933-7200 or visit the web site www.dupageforest.com, for more information, but here are some areas you may wish to explore:

- **Egermann Woods Forest Preserve**, DuPage County Forest Preserve, Lisle; mowed turf trails follow paths originally set by Native Americans and European settlers more than 200 years ago. A great horned owl has been sighted along the Hobson Road trails. Hikers, joggers, and cross-country skiers are welcome.
- **Willowbrook Wildlife Center**, Glen Ellyn, Du Page County
- **Winfield Mounds** in DuPage County is the site of prehistoric mounds and earthworks.

WILL COUNTY FOREST PRESERVE

The Will County Forest Preserve, 815-727-8700, covers approximately 15,000 acres. At the preserve are nature programs for school groups, special events for the public, and a woodland and open grassland rehabilitation program. Go to the web site where you can download maps, learn about new programs, and register for a newsletter: www.fpdwc.org.

Other Will County sites of interest are:

- **Briscoe Mounds**, site of prehistoric mounds and earthworks.
- **Higginbotham Woods**, Joliet; full of mysterious and prehistoric mounds and formations.
- **Lake Renwick Heron Rookery Nature Preserve**, 23144 West Renwick Road, Plainfield; call 815-727-8700, or visit the county web site, www.fpdwc.org, for more information.
- **Monee Reservoir**, 27341 Ridgeland Avenue, Monee, 708-534-8499; is a 46-acre lake for fishing and boating. Boat rentals available April-October. Shoreline fishing, free. Ice-skating and cross-country skiing in the winter months. Visit www.fpdwc.org/monee for more information.
- **Oakwood Fischer** is the site of prehistoric mounds and earthworks.
- **Plum Creek Nature Center**, 27064 South Dutton Road, Beecher, 708-946-2216; includes family programs, night hikes, campfire programs.

LAKE COUNTY FOREST PRESERVE

A late bloomer, Lake County had no land set aside for forest preserves as recently as 1957. Thanks to Ethel Untermyer and a 1958 county referendum, today there are more than 23,000 acres of forest preserve lands in Lake County, with a 475-acre area named Ethel's Woods set aside in her honor. The Lake County Forest Preserve has been recognized as one of the nation's outstanding systems of parks, recreation and conservation facilities. It was awarded a Gold Medal from the National Association of Parks Association. Go to www.lcfpd.org for more information.

Some of the facilities within the Lake County Forest Preserve include:

- **Lake County Discovery Museum**, 272777 Forest Preserve Drive, Wauconda, 847-968-3400; admission: adults: $5.50, children, $2.50. Discounts on Tuesdays. Free parking. Be sure to visit the Curt Teich Postcard Archives, while you are there. It's the largest public collection of post cards and related material in the world. Visit, www.lakecountydiscoverymuseum.org, for more information.
- **McDonald Woods Forest Preserve**, Lake County; is comprised of 304 acres of woodland in the northern portion of Lake County. There are three ponds, and trails for walking and cross-country skiing.
- **Ryerson Woods Visitor Center**; housed in a Greek-Revival Style mansion, this building is listed on the National Register of Historic Places. Today it serves as the preserve's library and meeting space; the facility can be rented for special events. The visitor center is situated within the 552-acre Ryerson Conservation Area, at 21950 North Riverwoods Road, Deerfield. Call 847-968-3321 for information about programs or visit www.lcfpd.org.

BEACHES

Since 1909, the City of Chicago has operated public beaches along its shores. Initially many beaches along the lakeshore were privately-owned—some as late as the 1930s. The city's struggle to take over all the lakeshore beaches within city limits was advanced by the illicit activities that often took place on private beaches.

Beach season officially begins in Chicago on Memorial Day and ends on Labor Day. Most beaches open at 9 a.m. and close at 9:30 p.m. Chicago operates 33 beaches, all free to the public. One group, mostly in Rogers Park, includes 18 **street-end beaches**. These beaches are small tracts at the end of residential streets, used mostly by nearby residents. While they all have lifeguards on duty during the season, they do not have changing facilities or restrooms. Call 312-742-7857 or visit www.chicagoparkdistrict.com for more information. Here are a few street-end beaches:

- **Hartigan Beach**, 1031 West Albion Avenue
- **Jarvis Beach and Park**, 1208 West Jarvis Avenue
- **Juneway Terrace Beach and Park**, 7751 North Eastlake Terrace
- **Lane Beach and Park**, 5915 North Sheridan Road
- **Leone Park and Beach**, 1222 West Touhy Avenue
- **North Shore Beach Park**, 1040 West North Shore Avenue
- **Pratt Boulevard Beach and Park**, 1050 West Pratt Boulevard
- **Rogers Avenue Beach and Park**, 7800 North Rogers Avenue

The following beaches are **Chicago's most poplular beaches**. Facilities vary, and there is lots of foot traffic.
- **57th Street Beach**, 5700 South Lake Shore Drive, 312-742-7529; used by university staff, students, and locals alike. The nearby Promontory Point serves as a vast back yard for family picnics, biking, and dog walking. Look out for flying Frisbees and up for kites.
- **Calumet Park**, 9801 South Avenue G, 312-747-6039; this 198-acre park sits on Chicago's South Shore, where Illinois meets Indiana on Lake Michigan. A lakeside bicycle trail runs right along the beach. In addition to sun bathing and swimming, there are 16 tennis courts, two volleyball courts, and football, baseball, and soccer fields. In the field house you can play basketball, work in the woodshop or work out in the gym. In the basement of the field house, a model of Chicago's East Side, circa 1940, accompanied by a model train chugging along.
- **Foster Beach**, Lakeshore/Foster Avenue, 312-742-7507; open 9 a.m. to 9:30 p.m. This small but generally teen-free beach is a nice alternative to the need-to-be-seen action at some of the other downtown beaches. Beach house offers food stands, handicap accessible rest rooms, and outdoor showers. There is a large free parking lot just south of the beach.
- **Kathy Osterman Beach**, formerly Hollywood Beach, 5800 North Lake Shore Drive, 312-742-7529; a noisy, crowded beach, Osterman Beach attracts families on its north end where the water is a bit shallower, while the southern part has become a meeting place for men. You can bike over on the path that hugs the shoreline or take a bus.
- **Montrose Beach**; stretching from Montrose to Wilson avenues along Lake Shore Drive, Montrose Beach offers beach volleyball, baseball diamonds, soccer fields, horseback riding trails, along with a clean beach. There is a playlot for young children and a six-lane boat-launch. Rest rooms are closer to Wilson Avenue. Fishing is possible from the pier. Open 6 a.m. to 11 p.m. daily during the summer. Admission to the beach is free and street parking is available.
- **North Avenue Beach House**, 1603 North Lakeshore Drive, 312-242-7857; this beach is one of the most popular in the city. Its new beach

house resembles an ocean liner and features restrooms, outdoor showers, concession stands, eating areas, chess pavilion, rental offices. Some
say the beach house offers one of the best views in Chicago.

- **Oak Street Beach**, 1000 North Avenue, 312-742-5121; is the most
  famous of all the local beaches. It is wide, long, clean, and a favorite
  with locals and tourists. You can ride a bike on the path, (rentals are on-
  site), swim, sunbathe, skate, and jog right in the shadows of the
  Hancock building. You will have to walk up towards the North Avenue
  beach for a restroom. This beach is free to the public. There is some
  street parking, and lot parking too (try looking around the Palmolive
  Building, the Hancock Building or the Drake Hotel). The beach is
  wheelchair accessible.
- **Rainbow Beach Park**, 3111 East 77th Street, 312-745-1479; also
  offers tennis, baseball facilities and a gym.
- **South Shore Cultural Center Beach**, 7059 South Shore Drive,
  312-747-2536; facilities in this 65-acre park include tennis courts and
  a golf course.

BEACHES BEYOND CHICAGO

Many of the suburbs north of Chicago have outstanding beaches. Clean,
long sweeps of silky sand that are as beautiful as the mansions built along
them. North Shore beaches are not free; there is an admission and sometimes a parking fee as well. Fees change periodically, so check with the park
district for the latest information. The money goes to maintain the beaches,
which can be quite costly, especially in years when algae bloom or bacteria
threatens the quality of the water. Season passes are available or you can pay
per visit. In most communities, both residents and non-residents must pay.

- **Centennial Beach**, 500 West Jackson Avenue, Naperville, 630-848-
  5090; built from a limestone quarry, Centennial Beach has been a family destination for Naperville-area residents since 1931. Centennial has a
  large sandy beach and a playground facility. Floating rafts are in the
  middle of the quarry for rest. Supervised bathhouse with showers and
  coin operated lockers. Free off-street parking. Season passes available.
  Open June-July, 11 a.m. to 8 p.m., August 11 a.m. to dusk. Admission:
  $10 non-residents, $5 for residents with county ID; $3 after 6 p.m.
- **Centennial Park-Dog Beach**, Elder/Sheridan roads, Winnetka; dog
  friendly beach, but requires membership. No swimming allowed. Off-
  street parking. Check with the park district office for more information,
  847-501-2040.
- **Elder Lane Beach**, Elder/Sheridan roads, Winnetka; beach house with
  restrooms, off-street parking, and playground. Parking fee, $5/day, plus

admission fee. Season pass can be purchased, which includes parking. For more information, call the park district at 847-501-2040.

- **Forest Park Beach**, Lake Road, Lake Forest; this 29-acre park is open year-round. You can fish off the pier, grill in sheltered areas, or walk along the woodland paths. It is also equipped with a boat launch. Handicap accessible. Contact the park district for information regarding parking and admission fees: 847-234-6700.

- **Glencoe Beach**, Hazel/Park avenues, Glencoe; call for information about fees and parking, 847-835-1185.

- **Gillson Beach**, Wilmette, 847-256-9656; one of the biggest Lake Michigan beaches (60 acres) in the North Shore area, and the one with the most parking. Facilities include a snack bar, dunes, main beach, and sailboat rental. Open 9 a.m. to 8 p.m. during the season. Admission is $6.50 non-residents; after 6 p.m. admission is $3 for non-residents. Season passes are available for purchase at the Park District Administrative Offices, 847-256-6100, or through the Gillson Beach House.

- **Lloyd Place Beach**, Winnetka; launching ramp for boats.

- **Maple Beach**, Maple/Sheridan roads, Winnetka; beach house with restrooms and off-street parking.

- **Northwestern University Beach** (also known as **Evanston North Beach**); twelve miles north of Chicago, the rocky shoreline of this beach sets it apart from the rest. Since it is owned by the university, use of the beach is restricted to NU affiliates.

- **Riveria Beach**, Wrigley Drive, Lake Geneva, 262-248-3673; open May 1 to Labor Day, 9:30 a.m. to 6 p.m. Admission: $5 adults, $2 children 7-12. Metered parking available. A beach literally in the middle of town is an oddity to be sure but it's also quite handy. The beach has a bathhouse with showers. Fine shopping and dining nearby.

- **Tower Beach**, Winnetka; twenty miles north of Chicago, this beach is small and a bit out of the way, so it is easy to miss from the road. It offers the most facilities of all Winnetka beaches. The parking area sits on a bluff, and you walk down toward the shore. The beach house is equipped with restrooms, showers, concession stands and vending machines. There is a playground and two sand volleyball courts. Handicap accessible.

STATE PARKS

For more about Illinois State Parks, contact the **Department of Natural Resources** (**DNR**), www.dnr.state.il.us, 847-608-3100. The DNR is a good source of information about outdoor activities, state museums, campsites, and parks. Their free magazine, *Illinois State Parks*, includes information about park activities, camping facilities, lodges, beaches, and recreation areas. You can request a copy online, by e-mail: clearing@dnrmail.state.il.us, by fax 212-782-9552, or call 217-782-7498.

- **Illinois Beach State Park**, at the lakefront, Zion, 847-662-4828; situated on Lake Michigan, this beach has over six miles of quiet sandy beaches. The park, approximately 90 minutes north of the city, includes the beach plus over 4,100 acres of dunes, woodlands, and marshes. Fishing is allowed from the beach or Sand Pond. Depending on the season, you can bike, hike, and cross-country ski here. There are 240 campsites on the south end of the park, all equipped with electricity. Make reservations several months in advance. For boaters, North Point Marina is five miles north of the park with over 1,500 slips.

- **Starved Rock State Park**, Utica, 815-667-4726; ninety-two miles southwest of Chicago, Starved Rock State Park offers striking scenery that includes 18 canyons formed by melting glacier waters and stream erosion. Enjoy horseback riding, camping, fishing, and boating in lush vegetation that is full of wildlife. Visitor center is open daily; check for annual events schedule. Guided tours are available on weekends. Stone and log lodge offers luxury hotel rooms and comfortable cabins. Indoor swimming pools, sauna, and children's pool. Restaurant on premises. For lodge reservations, call 800-868-7625.

- **Chain O' Lakes**, 8916 Wilmot Road, Spring Grove, 847-587-5512; an hour and a half northwest of Chicago, this state park is bordered by the Fox River and three lakes. Hike some of its 15 plus miles of trails and you are likely to come across deer, pheasant, and a variety of waterfowl. There are also five miles of bike trails, grasslands, meadows, and woodlands. Fishing and camping are allowed but permits and reservations are necessary. On the northern end of the trail system is a two-mile section called Nature's Way, a self-guided interpretative trail. Along the way, you can see one of the few remaining American lotus beds. The park is open May-October, 6 a.m. to 9 p.m., and from 8 a.m. to sunset in the winter. Maps are available in the park office.

- **Jubilee College State Park**, 13921 West Route 150, Brimfield, 309-446-3758; this 3,200-acre park is a mountain biker's delight with over 40 miles of open dirt and grass trails. One hundred sixty species of birds, including wild turkeys, mink, fox, and other wildlife live in this park. Picnicking is available in sheltered areas equipped with electricity, water hydrants, and toilets. There are ten miles of hiking, cross-country skiing trails; fishing is allowed in Jubilee Creek and in the two ponds in the park, but swimming is not allowed. Camp facilities are open April-November. Download an application from DNR web site.

- **Moraine Hill State Park**, 914 South River road, 815-385-1624, McHenry, IL; nestled in the northeast corner of the state, a little more than an hour northwest of Chicago, this park offers three easy walking trails, each set in its own landscape: hickory/oak forest, bogs and marshes, or thick vegetation. Glacier Lake Defiance is the park's center-piece. Fishing is possible at the William Stratton Dam—kids fish free, adults for $5. There is a nature center that offers weekend programs. Park hours: dawn to dusk.

- **Rock Island Trail**, 311 East Williams Street, Wyoming, IL, 309-695-2228; offers twenty-six miles of hiking/walking trails from Alta (Peoria County) to Toulon (Stark County). These trails are easy traversing thanks to the former rail beds that once ran alongside it. You will see remnants of the railroad as you walk through this tree-canopied corridor. As the rail line was abandoned, the landscape reverted to its native prairie grasses. Water, parking, and pit toilets are located at access areas. The old Chicago Burlington/Quincy Depot serves as a visitor center and railroad museum. No motorized vehicles or horses allowed on the trails. Call first if you'd like to visit, as the Depot is open only as available staff permits. For more information call the Department of Natural Resources' Office of Public Services, 217-782-7454 or 800-720-0298.

NATIONAL LAKESHORE

- **Indiana Dunes National Lakeshore**, 1100 North Mineral Springs Road, Porter, Indiana, 219-926-7561; fifty miles southeast of Chicago, the dunes are an easy day trip to the beach. Twenty-five miles of beach on the southern shore of Lake Michigan, the park offers 45 miles of hiking and riding trails, an 18th-century French-Canadian farm house, and fishing along the lakeshore or from the Little Calumet River. West Beach is a favorite spot with its beachhouse showers, concession stands, and picnic areas. It also is one of the few beaches that has a lifeguard on duty. It can be a bit crowded so if you need some space, try the un-guarded Kemil, Porter, Central Avenue, or Mt. Baldy beaches (dogs are allowed at Mt. Baldy until October). The entire park is open 8 a.m. to 4:30 p.m.; West Beach Bathhouse is open from 9 a.m. to 9 p.m. There is a user fee for West Beach: $6 per carload, $1 for walk-ins. Wheelchair accessible. Entrance to the dunes is free. If you prefer not to drive, the Chicago South Shore and South Bend railroads make numerous stops through the lakeshore area. For more information visit the National Park System web site at www.nps.gov/indu.

ADDITIONAL RESOURCES–LAKES AND RIVERS

For more information about the dozens and dozens of lakes and rivers in the eight-county area, visit the **Chicago Area Paddling and Fishing Pages** at http://pages.ripco.net/~jwn. Here you will find information not only about the neighboring lakes and their location, but you will learn what kind of fishing you can expect in each lake, maps, links to areas with white-water rafting, sailing, canoeing, and more. Michigan's **Harbor Country** is very popular with Chicagoans. From New Buffalo to Warren Dunes State Park, it's all gorgeous. Visit their web site at www.harbor country.org/beaches. The **Great Lakes Information Network** is a great resource for outdoor recreation ideas, historical sights, shipwrecks, lake tours and a lot more: www.great-lakes.net.

For more information about Chicago parks and green space, check the **Sports and Recreation** chapter of this book and/or the pertinent **Neighborhood Profile**.

BEING IN THE MIDWEST, CHICAGO ENJOYS FOUR DISTINCT SEAsons, and though the city has a reputation for harsh winters, they are nothing like the winters in snowy Buffalo or semi-arctic Minneapolis-St. Paul. Some argue that the sweltering summers in Chicago can be much more unpleasant, not to mention dangerous, with high temperatures and humid conditions. While winter weather is often the product of cold Canadian air masses, Chicago summer weather is usually brought here courtesy of south and southwest winds—and therefore not tempered by the infamous "lake effect." When a summer lake effect breeze does come to the rescue, neighborhoods near the lake can be cooler than their suburban neighbors by as much as 10 degrees.

The story about how Chicago became known as the "windy city" has nothing to do with the weather. Legend has it that a New York editor came up with the nickname when he was describing Chicago politicians. While hot air and politicians go hand in hand, particularly in Chicago, you won't find many Chicagoans who will deny the might of Chicago's winds. Their effect on local temperatures is significant, whether cooling lake effect winds in the summer or those chilling arctic blasts from the Canadian plains.

FALL/WINTER

Fall can be a great time of year for outdoor activities in Chicago. Lovely autumn colors are a pleasurable sight in this tree-filled city. Some autumns are dry and sunny; in other years it can be cold and rainy. If you have out of town friends who want to come for a visit, fall is the perfect time. The weather is generally good, and the summer crowds are gone, making for easier shopping and site seeing.

Dickens might have been thinking of Chicago winters when he wrote, "it was the best of times, it was the worst of times." If you aren't afraid of weather, you will enjoy the Chicago winters, or at least be indifferent to them. If you are not a cold-weather lover, watch out! It can get cold here. Temperatures in the teens and even below zero are not uncommon, and the wind chill will make that seem even colder. The winter season typically lasts from late November to late March. Winter snowstorms usually take place in January and February, but long time residents will tell you that spring snowstorms are not out of the question either. The party line on winter dress for downtown commuters is "heavy and waterproof." If you are moving to Chicago from a warmer part of the country you will want to buy a good coat (lined, windproof, and on the longish side), boots, gloves, and a good hat.

If you have never driven in icy conditions, it can take some getting used to. To speed up your learning curve, visit www.icepack.org, a coalition of agencies in the Illinois and Indiana area whose main purpose is to prepare motorists for hazardous winter driving. For tips on winterizing your car, see **Automobiles** in the **Helpful Services** chapter.

SPRING

Springs vary in Chicago—some come in with balmy spring rains and sunny days, others are slow to come and are cold, rainy, and even snowy. Generally though, from March to May, it's wet and temperatures hover in the mid-60s. If it is early spring and a Chinook wind has just swept down from Canada, you can experience a balmy day with dramatic downpours—an inch of rain within a few hours is not uncommon. But on average, Chicago gets nine inches of rain each spring, accompanied by thunderstorms and lightning. Snow isn't unheard of either. Though the bulk of Chicago snowfalls occur in January and February, the only two months that snow hasn't been recorded are July and August! So, don't be surprised when a few sunny, warm days in mid or even late March turn fickle, bringing below-average temperatures and even a few white flakes. Typically there won't be anymore frosts after the end of April, but if you plan to set out young plants in your garden, most local nurseries will suggest you wait until May 10th, just to be on the safe side.

One consolation for Chicago's blustery spring weather is the return of green to the city. The parks and even the traffic islands in Chicago are wonderfully landscaped. The sight of flowering shrubs and trees, and colorful spring tulips and daffodils are a welcome and soothing treat after a long winter.

Weather that produces tornadoes, particularly in the spring, does happen here, though tornadoes seldom touch Chicago. However, watch it in the south suburbs, which are five times more likely to be hit by a tornado than the city.

SUMMER

Micro-climates in Chicago are not significant, except the term "cooler at the lake" is true—in summer, temperatures in the northwest and southwest suburbs can vary by as much as ten degrees from the temperature downtown. Chicago summers typically offer a good couple of weeks of above 90 degree temperatures: about 15 days in the northwest suburbs; 24 in the south suburbs; and only 11 at the lakefront. July and August are when Chicagoans really pay attention to the heat index. Death from summer heat and humidity is a leading weather-related killer. According to the Center for Disease Control, each year more people die from heat than from lightning strikes, hurricanes, flooding, and tornadoes combined! Over a two-week period in July 1997, Chicago temperatures ranged from 93 degrees to 104 degrees, and the heat index peaked at the city's record high of 119 degrees. In those two weeks 465 people died from heat related causes. In order to prevent such a tragedy from happening again, Mayor Daley has established emergency cooling centers around the city for dangerous heat index days, which are a particular concern for the elderly and disabled, many of whom live without air-conditioning. The concept of the heat index was created by the National Weather Service to give people a more accurate indication of how high temperatures actually feel when high humidity is factored into the equation. Keep in mind that the heat index was developed for shady, light winded areas. Exposure to sunlight can increase the heat index value by 15 degrees.

In the summer, most urban areas are key targets for **ozone alert** days. Ozone, a powerful lung irritant, is caused when the sun cooks air-carbon-based chemicals emitted by vehicle and industry exhaust, and other pollutants. While ozone alerts are not as frequent here as in other US metropolitan areas, they can still be a problem, particularly for those with lung sensitivities. Chicago's offshore breezes help to clear out the heavy air, and several of the mayor's clean air initiatives—promoting the planting of roof-top gardens, encouraging bicycling as an alternate means of transportation, tree-planting, installation of light-colored roofs, cleaning up industrial parks, and working closely with industry to facilitate the elimination of air pollutants—are pluses. The hottest, most humid months, August especially, are most challenging. According to the Environmental Protection Agency, Chicago has been successful in meeting EPA guidelines for ozone (smog) free days. According to data found in the 2001 Annual Air Quality Report, www.epa.state.il.us/air, the outdoor air quality of Illinois was in the "moderate to good" range, most of the time (89%), particularly for ozone levels, but Cook County struggled to maintain the EPA's "safe" levels for airborne carcinogens. The American Lung Association's State of the Air Report, http://lungaction.org/reports, was not as optimistic about Chicagoland's overall air quality, particularly for high risk groups—those with asthma and other lung conditions—and in 2003 gave Cook County a failing grade for its number of high-ozone days.

To check **current smog conditions**, go online to the MidWest Hazecam, www.mwhazecam.net, which provides near real-time air quality data, current air pollution levels, and information to determine whether natural or man-made pollutants are causing the present levels of visibility impairments. Daily air quality reports are available on the web at the EPA's AirNow site, www.epa.gov, and through the National Weather Service, www.crh.noaa.gov/lot.

If you are an **allergy sufferer**, brace yourself: in Chicago allergy season starts in the spring with the flowering of oak, elm, maple, and pine trees, followed by the summer bloom of ragweed and cottonwoods. If you live in an outlying area, agriculture-related pollen counts may also be an allergen factor. For a daily pollen and mold count in your area, check the American Academy of Allergy, Asthma & Immunology's pollen and mold report at www.aaaailorg.

CHICAGO AREA WEATHER STATISTICS

Below is a chart noting average daily temperatures for each month, but don't let these numbers fool you—as mentioned above, summertime temperatures can soar to the upper 90s, while winter temperatures often drop below ten degrees. The wind chill of course, dips the winter weather into the single digits on a regular basis. Weather averages according to the US National Climatic Data Center, www.ncdc.noaa.gov are:

TEMPERATURES
- **January** 13 degrees Fahrenheit
- **February** 18 degrees Fahrenheit
- **March** 28 degrees Fahrenheit
- **April** 39 degrees Fahrenheit
- **May** 48 degrees Fahrenheit
- **June** 57 degrees Fahrenheit
- **July** 63 degrees Fahrenheit
- **August** 62 degrees Fahrenheit
- **September** 64 degrees Fahrenheit
- **October** 42 degrees Fahrenheit
- **November** 31 degrees Fahrenheit
- **December** 20 degrees Fahrenheit

- **Annual average rainfall**: 35.2 inches
- **Annual average snowfall**: 38.2 inches
- **Annual average wind speed**: 10.4 mph

If you'd like more information on current Chicago weather conditions, visit the **National Weather Service** web site, www.crh.noaa.gov/lot.

I
F YOU CAME FROM A SMALL TOWN, YOU MAY HAVE GONE TO *THE*
Methodist church, *the* Catholic Church, or *the* synagogue. But here in
Chicago, there are more than 2,800,000 Roman and Orthodox
Catholics, 1,350,000 Protestants, 310,000 Muslims, 260,000 Jews, and
100,000 Buddhists. If you add Hindus, well, you get the idea—there are a
lot of places of worship in Chicago. You'll find some of them listed by
denomination in the Yellow Pages. The **National Council of Churches**,
212-870-2227, www.ncccusa.org, publishes the *Yearbook of American &
Canadian Churches,* a directory listings of thousands of Christian churches.
Order one for $35 at 888-870-3325 or browse the directory links at
www.electronicchurch.org. Other online directories of churches—generally limited to Christian denominations—include http://netministries.org,
http://churches.net, and www.forministry.com. Synagogues serving all
branches of Judaism are listed at www.jewish.com. If you are interested in
becoming involved in interfaith projects, you can visit the Illinois
Conference of Churches at www.ilconfchurches.org, or the Office of
Ecumenical and Interreligious Affairs that operates within the Catholic
Archdiocese of Chicago, 312-751-5325, www.archchicago.org.

Below we list a variety of religious institutions that are particularly
noteworthy—maybe because of their historical significance, their physical
beauty, or their spirit of community. Churches, synagogues, and temples
that have been given landmark status are noted, as well as some of those
known for their musicality.

BAHÁ'Í

- **Bahá'í House of Worship**, 100 Linden Avenue, Wilmette, 847-853-
  2300; only one of seven temples of its kind in the world. Construction
  on the nine-sided bell shaped temple began in 1920, but it took until

1953 for this now historic temple to be completed. The Bahá'í House of Worship is open to all. See www.us.bahai.org for more information.

BUDDHIST

The Buddhist Temple of Chicago's web site, www.budtempchi.org, offers links to other temples in the Chicago area.

- **Buddhist Temple of Chicago** (**BTC**), 1151 West Leland Avenue, 773-334-4661, is a non-sectarian temple. Established on Chicago's south side in 1944, it was moved to its current location in 1956. Services in English and Japanese are held separately. The temple offers its community a range of services, including religious teaching, martial arts instruction, and more. Go to www.budtempchi.org for more information.

- **Midwest Buddhist Temple**, 435 West Menomonee Street, 312-943-7801, is affiliated with the Buddhist Churches of America, which is headquartered in San Francisco. In the third week of August, the temple celebrates a Ginza holiday by bringing artisans from the Waza area of Japan to demonstrate their crafts.

CHRISTIAN

Some of the **oldest churches** in Chicago are:
- **Old St. Patrick Catholic Church**, 700 West Adams, 312-648-1021 (1856)
- **Episcopalian Cathedral of St. James**, 65 East Huron, 312-787-7360 (1857)
- **Holy Family Catholic Church**, 1080 West Roosevelt, 312-432-0986 (1860)
- **St. Michael Catholic Church**, 455 West Eugene, 312-642-2498 (1869)
- **Trinity Episcopal Church**, 125 East 26th Street, 312-842-7545 (1874)
- **Holy Name Cathedral**, 735 North State, 312-787-8040 (1875)

BAPTIST

- **First Baptist Congregational Church**, 60 North Ashland Avenue, 312-243-8047; this church, located near the Union Park Lagoon on Chicago's west side, is often featured in historical pictures of Chicago. Today it is sometimes referred to as the Union Park Congregational Church. What is especially noteworthy about this building is its interior:

a theater-like auditorium whose seating curves around the pulpit. This innovative design was very influential in church architecture. In 1869, the adjacent Carpenter's Chapel was built for the Chicago Theological Seminary. Founded in 1851 by abolitionists, it maintains its strong roots in community activism. Today this African-American church is home to a number of choirs, and hosts several community programs and schools. It achieved landmark status in 1982.

- **First Church of Deliverance**, 4315 South Wabash, 773-373-7700; designed by Walter T. Bailey, Chicago's first African-American architect in the Moderne style, this church was founded by Reverend Clarence Cobbs. Reverend Cobbs was influential in gospel music and was a key figure in Christian radio broadcasting. Another architect added the twin towers on in 1946. The church received landmark status in 1994.

- **Metropolitan Missionary Baptist Church**, 2151 West Washington Boulevard, 312-738-0053; this church is unique in that its design was a deliberate break with the then current church architecture. Originally designed as the Third Church of Christ, Scientist, by architect Hugh M.G. Garden, he combined elements of Classical and Modern influences to create a unique style—which is today sometimes referred to as "Gardenesque." The church was sold to the Metropolitan Missionary Baptist congregation in 1947.

- **Pilgrim Baptist Church**, 3301 South Indiana Avenue, 312-326-9828; this dramatic looking church is the result of the collaboration of one of the premier architects of the time, Louis H. Sullivan, and the engineering skills of Dankmar Adler. It is made with masonry and terra cotta panels, both inside and out. Originally built as a synagogue in 1890, it has been the home of the Pilgrim Baptist Church since 1922. The church has been a leader in developing gospel music; Mahalia Jackson and the Edwin Hawkin Singers are among some of its celebrated guest artists. The church received landmark status in 1981.

CHRISTIAN SCIENTIST

- **Eighth Church of Christ, Scientist**, 112 East 44th Street, 773-373-4126; designed by architect Leon Stanhope in 1910, and accorded landmark status in 1993, the Eighth Church of Christ is one of the country's oldest African-American Christian Scientist congregations. Built in the Classical-revival style, it features a beautiful broad dome that was made popular by the 1893 World's Columbian Exposition. The church is still active, offering children Sunday school services as well as regularly scheduled service for adults.

ECUMENICAL

- **Rockefeller Memorial Chapel**, 5850 South Woodlawn Avenue, 773-702-2100 (in Hyde Park); at the request of its benefactor, John D. Rockefeller, this 1928 chapel was designed to be the central, unifying element on the University of Chicago campus. Today, the chapel hosts study groups, performances of religious music, lectures, travel/study seminars, and community service. Religious services are held each Sunday during the academic year. In 1932, Rockefeller donated the Laura Spelman Rockefeller Carillon, the second largest such instrument in the world. The Carillon is played on Fridays and Sundays during the academic year, and during special events, especially during the summer months, when carillonneurs from the world over come to play the bells. A tour of the bell tower can be arranged by calling 773-702-2100. The chapel is a very popular wedding site. For wedding ceremony information call the chapel coordinator at 773-702-9202.

EPISCOPAL

- **All Saints' Episcopal Church**, 4550 North Hermitage Avenue, 773-561-0111, www.allsaintschicago.org; located in the Ravenswood neighborhood, All Saints' is the oldest wood frame church in the city. It was designed by John Cochrane, in what became known as the Stick Style; Cochrane is best known for designing the state Capitol in Springfield. The church was built in 1884 and is considered one of the best examples of this type of architecture. All Saints' attracts worshippers from all over the city; it's a youngish congregation with a liberal bent. The church dedicates one-third of its budget to outreach programs. It feeds over 130 people every Tuesday night, hosts community dinners each month, sponsors events that encourage teens to participate in fundraisers, and hosts Sunday school for small children. All Saints' is active in many social service programs throughout the area, and has many opportunities for volunteers. The church was declared a Chicago landmark in 1990.
- **Church of the Epiphany**, 201 South Ashland Avenue, 312-243-4242; built in 1885 in the Romanesque style, this church and a few row houses and town houses on the 1500 blocks of West Adams and West Jackson are all that is left of the once fashionable Near West Side. The rough-cut stone and rounded arches are typical of a style that has its roots in Spanish and French traditions. The church and the surrounding blocks were designated as landmarks in 1976.

EVANGELICAL

- **Wheaton Evangelical Free Church**, 520 East Roosevelt Road, Wheaton, 630-668-6490, www.wefc.org; has an extensive outreach program for adults and children. Includes Sunday school for children and teens, bible studies for adults, youth programs, and sports activities. Sermons archived on tape and online. Sunday services are broadcast live on Wheaton College Radio.

INDEPENDENT/INTERDENOMINATIONAL/CHRISTIAN

- **Moody Church**, 1630 North Clark Street, 312-943-0466, www.moodychurch.org, is an evangelical non-denominational church. Facilities include a 4,000-seat auditorium that is used for the Moody Bible Institute's Founder's Week conferences, services, and multi-evening crusades. Well-known for their inspiring, upbeat services, the church brings its influence to the community through live Sunday radio broadcasts, a television network, store, and magazine. It sponsors monthly Loop luncheons, and programs directed towards women's issues.
- **Park Community Church**, 108 West Germania Place (intersection of Clark and North Avenue), 312-280-8828, www.parkcommunity church.org; three services on Sunday. Offers an adult education program, a running club, a twenty-something group, and weekly prayer meetings.
- **Willow Creek Community Church**, 67 East Algonquin Road, South Barrington, 847-765-5000, www.willowcreek.org; offers over 100 ministries, Sunday morning breakfasts after services, a food pantry, premarital budget workshops, and bible classes for both adults and children. Church facilities feature a bookstore, café, and meeting rooms where classes are held and services geared for smaller children are conducted. Services are interdenominational and designed using multi-media, contemporary music, guest speakers and singers, mimes, full orchestras, wide screen projections and more.

LUTHERAN

- **Irving Park Lutheran Church**, 3938 West Belle Plaine Avenue, 773-267-1666; offers adult religious education, music lessons, youth groups including scouts, basketball, and children's choir.
- **Ebenezer Lutheran Church**, 1650 West Foster Avenue, 773-561-8496; this church began as a Lutheran Synod in 1892, founded by Swedish immigrants. At the height of Swedish migration the congregation numbered 2,000. But as Andersonville's ethnic mix began to

change, so did the church. In 1988 it became a member of the Evangelical Lutheran Church in America and made changes in its mission in order to serve the changing community. The church welcomes gay and lesbian members and will even bless these unions. Swedish traditions are a focus of December services; St. Lucia Day is observed on December 13th, and Christmas morning service is celebrated in the Swedish language. The chapel in which services are held was built in 1908.

- **Light of Christ Lutheran Church**, 7045 North Western Avenue, 773-262-7070; offers adult bible study, several groups dedicated to various ages of children and young adults, and occasional evening outdoor worship in the summer months.

METHODIST

FIRST UNITED METHODIST CHURCH
- **Chicago Temple**, 77 West Washington Street, 312-236-4548, www.chicagotemple.org; this First United Methodist Church of Chicago is the oldest congregation in Chicago, dating to 1831, before the city's incorporation. Their original meeting house was a log cabin, a far cry from their current structure, which was built in the 1920s. Located in the Loop, the Chicago Temple is easily recognizable in Chicago's night sky by its massive lighted spire.

AFRICAN METHODIST EPISCOPAL (A.M.E.)
In 1787, a disagreement between Richard Allen and the congregation of St. George's Methodist Church of Philadelphia (the first Methodist Church in the United States), forced Richard Allen and other black Christians in this community to form their own organization. What was first called the Free African Society would grow into the first black church in America, and the first major religious movement among African-Americans in this country. Richard Allen would go on to become the first bishop of the African Methodist Episcopal Church.

- **Greater Institutional A.M.E. Church**, 7800 South Indiana Avenue, 773-873-0880; has been located at its present site since 1956. What sets the Greater Institutional A.M.E. Church apart from other congregations is that it was organized as both a settlement house and a house of worship. In its early years, the church received financial support from such figures as Robert T. Lincoln, son of Abraham Lincoln, and Mrs. George Pullman, widow of the president of the Pullman Company. Offers congregation a credit union, Head Start program, Boy Scout Troop, a scholarship fund, Bible study, and a nursery. It was the first church in Chicago to offer a Head Start Program. In continuing its mission as a settlement house, the A.M.E. offers a variety of ministries to the community, along with support to many groups such as disaster victims, missionaries, and women's shelters.

- **Quinn Chapel**, 2401 South Wabash Avenue, 312-791-1846; built in 1892, Quinn Chapel received landmark status in 1979, and is the oldest African-American congregation in Chicago. It traces its roots back to 1844 when several black Americans gathered to form a prayer circle. In 1847, it organized as an A.M.E. church, and then played an important role in the Underground Railroad. Though the original church was destroyed in the Great Chicago Fire of 1871, the congregation purchased its current site in 1890. Today the congregation continues to be active politically and socially, as well as culturally—hosting recent performances by Wynton Marsalis and Patti LaBelle.

PRESBYTERIAN (USA)

- **Lincoln Park Presbyterian Church**, 600 West Fullerton Parkway, 773-248-8288; a popular church, it has a choir, and offers Lenten suppers, religious studies for children and adults, and retreats. Beautiful historic organ on site.
- **Second Presbyterian Church**, 1936 South Michigan Avenue, 312-225-4951; when it was first constructed in 1874, this city, state, and national landmark featured stained glass windows by Louis Comfort Tiffany. A fire in 1900 destroyed much of the original church, but it was reconstructed under Howard Van Doren Shaw. It received Chicago landmark status in 1977. Today, the church is very active in the South Loop community; it offers its gym facilities to a nearby charter school, feeds the poor, conducts Sunday school, and participates in several community organizations.

ROMAN CATHOLIC

Most Catholics attend mass near their home, but there are a few churches, which, for one reason or another, attract worshipers from beyond the parish confines. One of the following may suit you or call the Office of the Archdiocese of Chicago for assistance with choosing a church, 773-752-2632.

- **Holy Family Catholic Church**, 1019 May Street, 312-492-8442; Holy Family is known citywide for its extraordinary acoustics and numerous musical events.
- **St. Michael's Church**, 1633 North Cleveland, 312-642-2498, www.st-mikes.org; declared a city landmark in 1977, the original church was built on land donated by Michael Diversey, and was designed by August Waldbaum in the Romanesque style. During the Great Fire of 1871, the Church was destroyed. It was rebuilt by October 1872, and by 1886 five

tower bells and the 290-foot bell tower steeple were finished (restored in 1998). (There is a neighborhood saying that if you can hear the bells of St. Michael's, you know you are in Old Town.) Inside are hand-carved communion rails, seven altars, German stained glass windows, hand-carved stations of the cross, and commissioned frescoes. A special altar was constructed to house an icon of Our Mother of Perpetual Help, which somehow survived the fire and retains special significance to the parish. The church conducts several outreach programs, adult education classes, student groups, choirs, councils, a food panty, home visits, and offers many opportunities for volunteering. Sunday services are held in English or Spanish, some with a choir in attendance. Sunday evenings offer a less traditional mass. The Old Town Art Fair and St. Michael's Fest are celebrated each year on the church grounds.

- **St. Peter's in the Loop**, 110 West Madison Street, 312-372-5111; St. Peter's Catholic Church has been serving the downtown area for over 150 years; one million people pass through the doors each year. The Franciscan Friars built the present-day church in 1953. Programs include a broad range of services to the business and residential community: twelve step programs, counseling for the divorced, extended hours of weekday mass and penance, lecture series, in addition to services for the poor and homeless. Services are accompanied by a range of musical ensembles including the organ.

RUSSIAN ORTHODOX

- **Holy Trinity Orthodox Cathedral and Rectory**, 1121 North Leavitt Street, 773-486-6064; built in 1903 and designed by Louis H. Sullivan, Holy Trinity resembles a Russian provincial church. This elegant structure, built in a working class neighborhood, was partially funded by Csar Nicholas II. It is considered one of Sullivan's best smaller works. Holy Trinity holds a vintage 1909 Louis Van Dinter & Sons organ. The Church was declared a landmark in 1979.

UNITARIAN UNIVERSALIST

- **Lake Shore Unitarian Society**, 620 Lincoln Avenue, Winnetka, 847-441-6336, has made partnerships with over a half dozen Chicagoland area social agencies on behalf of its congregation. These include Evanston YMCA Shelter, and the Christopher House. Since the year 2000, it has been a sponsor of the North Shore/Skokie CROP Walk, an interfaith fundraiser to address hunger and homelessness. The Church hosts a wide variety of clubs including a movie club, book club, investment club and social groups for men and women.

- **Unitarian Unity Temple**, 875 Lake Street, Oak Park, 708-848-6225, www.unitytemple.org; one of Frank Lloyd Wright's personal favorites, he was commissioned to build this church for the Unitarian Universalist Congregation in 1906. It contains many cubist elements and the poured concrete frame was considered very unorthodox for its time. While the church is active in assisting in the preservation of this building as a work of art, it is also an active member of the community. As a religious force, it hosts a concert series, does fundraising, offers assistance to the gay and lesbian community, oversees a children's religious education program, and more.

ETHICAL SOCIETIES

Not a conventional religious organization, ethical societies offer a meeting place and fellowship to members and visitors. Their focus is on the "core ethical values that people have in common." Acknowledging that humans are both individualistic and social in nature, ethical societies explore what it means to understand the inner workings of self and how to relate to each other in a respectful/ethical/moralistic way. For more information go to www. ethicalsociety.org or contact the local **Ethical Humanist Society of Greater Chicago**, 7574 North Lincoln Avenue, Skokie, 847-677-3334, www.ethicalhuman.org.

HINDU

- **Hindu Temple of Greater Chicago**, 10915 Lemont Road, Lemont, 630-972-0300, www.ramatemple.org; the temple complex offers two buildings, the Rama Temple and the smaller, Ganesha-Shiva-Gurga Temple. The Rama Temple is built in the Chola Dynasty style, a 10th century style associated with Indian Kings, with an 80-foot tower. The Ganesha Temple is built in the tradition of the Kalinga Dynasty, known during the 1st century, BC. The temple offers daily worship, grand festivals, youth activities, children's programs, and fundraising events.

ISLAM

For a listing of mosques in Illinois, go to www.imbn.com/masajid.
- **Mosque Maryam**, 7351 South Stony Island Avenue, 773-324-6000; is the national center and headquarters for the Nation of Islam. Originally built as a Greek Orthodox Church, the building was purchased in 1972 by Elijah Muhammed and the Nation of Islam. In 1988, it was repurchased and rededicated by Louis Farrakhan. The National Center, located next to the mosque serves as a school for children ages preschool through the 12th grade. More information on the web at www.noi.org.

JEWISH

See Virtual Jewish Chicago, www.vjc.org and/or the *Chicago Jewish News*, www.chicagojewishnews.com, for more information about Jewish congregations, events, and activities.

- **Chicago Sinai Congregation**, 15 West Delaware Place, 312-867-7000, www.chicagosinai.org, is one of the oldest Reform Congregations in the United States. Its first service was held in 1861 in what is now the financial district of the city, and then for 45 years the temple was located in the Hyde Park neighborhood. In 1997 a new structure in a more central part of the city was constructed. The new building has the distinction of being the first Reform Temple built on the Near North Side since the Civil War. The temple offers a community nursery school, religious education, classes, a library, outreach programs for interfaith couples, and meeting rooms.
- **Congregation B'nai Shalom**, 701 Apatasic Road, Buffalo Grove, 847-541-1460, www.bnaishalom.org; B'nai Shalom was conceived in the late 1970s by a small group of Jewish families determined to find a permanent site for their new and growing congregation. Until 1981, services were held in makeshift facilities: park district buildings, community centers, etc. Their temple now has a community center and school, as well as a gorgeous antique European ark that had been custom made for the Albany Park Hebrew Congregation (now disbanded). The ark was refurbished, gold leafed, and reassembled in 1984.
- **K.A.M. Isaiah Israel**, 1100 East Hyde Park Boulevard, Hyde Park, 773-924-1234, www.kamii.org; this impressive Byzantine-styled temple was founded in 1847. K.A.M. is the oldest Jewish congregation in the Midwest. It serves the Reformed Jewish community through youth groups, services for families with small children, concerts. Designated a Chicago landmark in 1996.
- **Northbrook Congregation Ezra Habonim**, 2095 Landwehr Road, Northbrook, 847-480-1690; a traditional congregation offering Shabbat, Torah studies, Hebrew school, Sunday morning breakfasts, and other weekly events. Call about playing mah jong.
- **Temple Sholom**, 3480 North Lake Shore Drive, 773-525-4707, www.sholomchicago.org; founded in 1867, this Reform Temple is one of Chicago's oldest synagogues, and is well known throughout the Chicago Jewish community. Owns the Westlawn Cemetery and Mausoleum. Equipped with a 1930 Wurlizter organ.

OTHERS SITES OF INTEREST

MASONS

- **Scottish Rite Cathedral**, 929 North Dearborn, is situated in the Washington Square District, itself a landmark. Here you will find the Newberry Library and historic row houses, along with the park. Built in the 1870s, the cathedral has a remarkable E. & G.G. Hook & Hastings organ. Scottish Rite is not a religious sect, but a fraternal organization inviting men of different faiths and backgrounds to join in philanthropic pursuits. They are more commonly known as Masons.

SHRINES

- **Our Lady of the Snows**, 442 South DeMazenod Drive, Belleville, 618-397-6700, www.snows.org; operated by the Missionary Oblates of Mary Immaculate, it is one of the largest outdoor shrines in North America. Nearly one million people visit the more than 200-acre grounds each year, which include nine devotional areas for all faiths and denominations, as well as a restaurant, gift shop, and hotel. More than 50 shrine events are held, each year, in addition to masses and community programs. About 300 miles south of Chicago.
- **National Shrine of Mary Immaculate, Queen of Universe**, St. Pius X Church, 1025 East Madison Street, Lombard, 630-627-4526
- **Shrine of St. Maximilian Kolbe, Marytown**, 1600 West Park Avenue, Libertyville, 847-367-7800, www.marytown.com; offers full and half-day guided pilgrimages of the historic complex. The chapels are decorated with marble columns, stained glass, religious relics, and mosaics. Weekend retreats available.

ORGAN MUSIC

Some places of worship draw us to them through their music. Chicago has an abundance of houses of worship that possess vintage organs. The following religious houses all own antique or vintage organs and some have outstanding choirs as well.

- **Basilica of our Lady of Sorrows**, 3121 West Jackson Boulevard, 773-638-5800; this church is equipped with a 1902 Lyon & Healy organ.
- **Disciples Divinity House**, 1156 East 57th Street, University of Chicago, 773-643-4411, this church owns a 1930 Aeolian organ.
- **Epworth United Methodist Church**, 5253 North Kenmore Street, 773-561-6422; equipped with a 1930 M.P. Moller organ.

- **First Baptist Congregational Church**, 60 North Ashland Avenue, 312-243-8047; has a 1927 Kimball organ.
- **First Congregational Church of Evanston**, 1417 Hinman Avenue, Evanston, 847-864-8332, has a 1927 Skinner organ.
- **Good Shepherd Lutheran Church**, 4200 West 62nd Street, 773-581-0096; owns an 1891 Lancashire Marshall organ.
- **Holy Family Catholic Church**, 1019 May Street, 312-492-8442, Chicago's second oldest church, has an 1879 Steinmeyer.
- **Holy Trinity Russian Orthodox Church**, 1121 North Leavitt Street, 773-486-6064; this historic church has a 1909 Louis Van Dinter & Sons organ.
- **Lake View Presbyterian Church**, 716 West Addison Street, 773-281-2655; owns an 1888 Johnson & Sons organ, used with a variety of the church's choirs, and in performances.
- **Lincoln Park Presbyterian Church**, 600 West Fullerton Parkway, 773-248-8288; this church has a beautiful 1888 Johnson & Sons Tracker organ.
- **Pullman United Methodist Church**, 11211 South Saint Lawrence Avenue, 773-785-1492; has an 1882 Steere & Turner organ.
- **Scottish Rite Cathedral**, 929 North Dearborn, has an 1882 E & G.G. Hook & Hastings organ.
- **St. Andrews Episcopal Church**, 48 North Hoyne Street, 312-226-7205; has a 1905 Lyon & Healy organ.
- **St. James Catholic Church**, 2942 South Wabash, 312-842-1919; owns an 1891 Roosevelt organ.
- **St. John Evangelical Lutheran Church**, 305 Circle Avenue, Forest Park, 708-366-3226; this church owns a 1954 Aeolian organ.
- **St. Joseph Catholic Church**, 1107 North Orleans Street, 312-787-7174; owns an 1891 Hutchings organ, the only restored Hutchings in Chicago.
- **St. Luke's Episcopal Church**, 939 Hinman Avenue, Evanston, 847-475-3630, owns a 1922 Skinner organ.
- **St. Mary of Perpetual Help Catholic Church**, 1039 West 32nd Street, 773-927-6646; owns a 1928 Austin organ.
- **St. Paul Lutheran Church**, 5201 Galitz Street, Skokie, 847-673-5030; owns a 1974 Phelps organ.
- **Temple Sholom**, 3480 North Lake Shore Drive, 773-525-4707, www.sholomchicago.org; equipped with a 1930 Wurlizter.
- **University Church**, 5655 South University Avenue, Hyde Park, 773-363-8142; owns a 1928 Skinner organ.

VOLUNTEERING IN A NEW CITY IS AN EXCELLENT WAY TO MEET people who share similar interests. Whether you are skilled at building houses, caring for the elderly, tutoring underprivileged children, or canvassing neighborhoods, you can find a volunteer project that suits your interests. Chicago-area nonprofits are always in need of volunteers willing to give their time and energy. Your place of employment may even offer a corporate volunteering program; contact your human resources representative.

VOLUNTEER PLACEMENT SERVICES

The following organizations coordinate many volunteer activities in the Chicagoland area. Call them and they will help you find a place in need of your special talents:

- If you are a student at the **University of Chicago**, contact the student-run UCSC (University of Chicago Service Center), at 773-753-GIVE, or stop by their office located in the parking structure office suites. Visit their web site for a list of the organizations they assist: http://communityservice.uchicago.edu.

- **Chicago North Shore Section** is a branch of the National Council of Jewish Women. Several volunteer groups assist in a number of ways, from offering a teen dating violence awareness program to running a resale shop. Visit their web site for a list of their efforts: www.ncjwchicagonorthshore.org/volunteer, or call 847-853-8889.

- **Community Resource Network—Chicago Volunteer**, www.chicagovolunteer.net, 312-906-2425, is a volunteer referral service. When you visit their web site, you will be asked to provide your volunteer criteria (your area of interest and level of commitment), and they will provide you with a list of area opportunities, which cover both the city and suburbs (Outside of metropolitan Chicago, go to www.pointsoflight.org/centers.)

- **Chicago Wilderness**, 312-580-2137, www.chicagowilderness.org; being a "wilderness" volunteer in Chicago is not as unbelievable as it sounds, and is a great way to share your outdoor expertise. There are many organizations, from zoos to gardens to parks that appreciate the work of volunteers. Consider serving as a guide, caring for trees, working a community garden, or organizing cleanup days. There are several affiliated groups; we have listed a few here, which you may contact through Chicago Wilderness directly:
  - **Lincoln Park Zoo**, 312-742-2124, www.lpzoo.com
  - **Chicago Botanic Garden**, 847-935-8281, www.chicago-botanic.org
  - **The Morton Arboretum**, 630- 968-0074, www.mortonarb.org
  - **Volunteer Stewardship Network**, 312-346-8166, http://nature.org/wherewework/northamerica/states/illinois
  - **Open Lands Project**, 312-427-4256, www.openlands.org
  - **Forest Preserve District of Cook County**, 708-771-1574, www.fpdcc.com
  - **Chicago Park District**, 312-742-7529, www.chicagopark district.com
- If you live in the north or northwest suburbs and would like to donate your time in your area, contact **The Volunteer Center of Northwest Suburban Chicago**, 2121 South Goebbert Road, Arlington Heights, 847-228-1320.
- The national online database, **www.volunteermatch.org**, allows you to access thousands of non-profit organizations. Provide your zip code, and the site will list what is available in your area, matching your interests and schedule with their database.

AREA CAUSES

If you were involved in a volunteer effort before you moved, or if you already know the specific cause that sparks your interest, you can call the following organizations and inquire about donating your time.

AIDS

- **Better Existence with HIV (BEHIV)**, 847-475-2115, www.behiv.org; serves the North Shore communities, including Evanston.
- **Bonaventure House, Inc.**, 773-327-9921, www.bonaventurehouse.org
- **Chicago House and Social Service Agency**, 773-248-5200, www.chicagohouse.org
- **The Children's Place**, 773-826-1230, www.childrens-place.org
- **Research Alliance: Chicago**, 773-244-5800

ALCOHOL AND DRUG DEPENDENCY

- **Alcoholics Anonymous**, 312-346-1475, www.chicagoaa.org
- **Alliance Against Intoxicated Motorists (AAIM)**, 847-697-2246
- **Mothers Against Drunk Driving (MADD)**, 312-782-6266, www. madd.org

ANIMALS

- **Anti-Cruelty Society**, 312-644-8338, www.anticruelty.org
- **Lake Shore Animal Shelter**, 312-409-1162, www.lakeshoreanimal shelter.org
- **Lincoln Park Zoo**, 312-742-2124, www.lpzoo.com

CHILDREN

Also see **Health and Hospitals** below.
- **Big Brothers/Big Sisters of Metropolitan Chicago**, 312-427-0637; North Side Regional Office, 773-271-8196, www.bbbschgo.org
- **Boy Scouts of America, Chicago Area Council**, 312-421-8800, www.chicagobsa.org
- **Boys & Girls Clubs of Chicago**, 312-627-2700, www.bgcc.org
- **Girl Scouts of Chicago**, 312-416-2500, www.girlscouts-chicago.org
- **Shriner's Hospital**, 2211 North Oak Park Avenue, 773-622-5453; visit their web site for a downloadable volunteer form: www.shriner-shq.org/shc.chicago
- **YWCA of Metropolitan Chicago**, 312-372-6600, www.ywcachica go.org/volopp

COMMUNITY SERVICES

- **Ada S. McKinley Community Services**, 312-554-0600, www.adasm ckinley.org
- **Jane Addams Hull House Association**, 312-906-8600, www.hull house.org

CRIME PREVENTION

- **Chicago Crime Commission**, 312-372-0101, www.chicagocrimecom-mission.org
- **CAPS (Chicago's Alternative Policing Strategy)**, 312-746-6000, www.cityofchicago.org/police

- **Illinois Council Against Handgun Violence**, 312-341-0939, www.ichv.org

DISABLED ASSISTANCE

- **Access Living of Metropolitan Chicago**, 312-226-5900; TDD 312-226-1687
- **America's Disabled Inc.**, 773-685-7111, www.americasdisabled.com
- **Association for Retarded Citizens of Illinois**, 708-206-1930
- **Blind Service Association Inc.**, 312-236-0808
- **Chicago Association for Retarded Citizens**, 312-346-6230, www.chgoarc.org
- **Chicago Lighthouse for the Blind**, 312-666-1331, www.the chicagolighthouse.org
- **Contact Chicago**, 773-728-0780
- **A Gift from the Heart Foundation**, 773-777-2306
- **Guild for the Blind**, 312-236-8569, www.guildfortheblind.org
- **Illinois Society for the Prevention of Blindness**, 312-922-8710
- **Illinois Special Olympics**, 312-595-9138, www.ilso.org
- **Lester and Rosalie Anixter Center**, 773-273-1000, www.anixter.org

EDUCATION

For a list of local tutoring and mentoring programs go to the Tutor Mentor Connection, www.metrist.ovm/tutor, or contact one of the following:
- **Cabrini-Green Tutoring Program**, 312-397-9119, www.cabrini greentutoring.org
- **Midtown Educational Foundation**, 312-738-8300, www.mid town-metro.org
- **Tuesday's Child** (parent training program), 773-248-6394

ENVIRONMENT

- **Center for Neighborhood Technology (CNT)**, 773-278-4800, ext 127, www.cnt.org
- **Friends of the Park**, 312-922-3307, www.fotp.org
- **Greenpeace USA, Inc.**, 312-563-6060, www.greenpeace.org
- **Lake Michigan Federation**, 312-939-0838, www.lakemichigan.org
- **Nature Conservancy**, 312-346-8166, www.tnc.org
- **North Branch Prairie Restoration Project**, 312-409-5831, www.northbranchrestoration.org
- **Open Lands Project**, 312-427-4256, www.openlands.org
- **Sierra Club**, 312-251-1680, www.sierraclub.org

FOSTER CARE

- **Jewish Children's Bureau of Chicago**, 312-444-2090, www.jcb chicago.org
- **Lawrence Hall Youth Services**, 773-728-2807, www.lawrencehall.org
- **Volunteers of America**—Illinois, 312-707-8707, www.voamass.org

GAY AND LESBIAN

- **Gay & Lesbian Anti-Violence Project**, 773-871-2273
- **Horizons Community Services**, 773-472-6469, www.horizonson line.org
- **Howard Brown Health Center**, 773-871-5777, www.howard brown.org
- **Parents and Friends of Lesbians and Gays (PFLAG)**, 773-472-3079

HEALTH AND HOSPITALS

- **American Cancer Society**, 800-227-2345, www.cancer.org
- **American Diabetes Association**, 312-346-1805, www.diabetes.org
- **American Heart Association Greater Midwest**, 312-346-4675, www.americanheart.org
- **American Lung Association**, 312-243-2000, www.lungchicago.org
- **American Red Cross of Chicago**, 312-729-6128, e-mail: volun teer@chicagoredcross.org
- **Children's Memorial Hospital**, 800-KIDS-DOC, www.children smemorial.org/friends
- **Epilepsy Foundation of Greater Chicago**, 312-939-8622, www.efa.org
- **Juvenile Diabetes Foundation**, 312-670-0313, www.jdf.org
- **Les Turner ALS Foundation** (Lou Gehrig's disease), 847-679-3311, www.lesturnerals.org
- **Leukemia Research Foundation**, 847-808-1845, www.joeysan gels.org
- **Leukemia Society of America**, 312-726-0003, www.leukemia-lym phoma.org
- **Make a Wish Foundation of Northern Illinois**, 312-943-8956, www.wishes.org
- **National Kidney Foundation of Illinois**, 312-663-3103, www. nkfi.org

- **Northwestern Memorial Hospital**, 312-926-2070, www.nmh. org/jobs
- **United Cerebral Palsy of Greater Chicago**, 312-368-0380
- **University of Chicago Children's Hospital**, 773-702-0407, www.ucch.org/childlife

HISTORIC PRESERVATION

- **Chicago Historical Society**, 312-642-4600, www.chicagohs.org
- **Chicago Landmarks**, www.ci.chi.il.us/landmarks
- **Rogers Park/West Ridge Historical Society**, 773-764-4078, www. members.aol.com/rphistory
- **Skokie Historical Society**, 847-673-1888

HOMELESS

- **Chicago Coalition for the Homeless**, 312-435-4548, www.chicago homeless.org
- **Greater Chicago Food Depository**, 773-247-3663
- **Heartland Alliance**, 773-728-5960
- **Inspiration Cafe**, 773-878-0981
- **Lakeview Pantry**, 773-525-1777
- **Opening Doors Project**, 800-215-6379, www.homelessed.net/help
- **Pacific Garden Mission**, 312-922-1462, www.pgm.org
- **Voice of the People Uptown, Inc. (VOP)**, 773-769-2442
- **Windy City Habitat for Humanity Midwest**, 800-643-7845, www.windycityhabitat.org

Note: many religious organizations participate in PADS programs (Public Action to Deliver Shelter). These programs offer overnight shelter to the homeless and those in at-risk situations. Check with your local church or temple.

LEGAL

- **American Civil Liberties Union**, 312-201-9740, www.aclu-il.org
- **Chicago Lawyers Committee for Civil Rights Under Law**, 312-630-9744, www.crccrul.org
- **Lawyers for the Creative Arts**, 312-944-2787, www.law-arts.org
- **Legal Assistance Foundation of Chicago**, 312-949-5390, www. lafchicago.org

LITERACY

- **Literacy Volunteers of Chicago**, 312-236-0341, www.literacy chicago.org
- **Reading Is Fundamental**, e-mail: centralteam@rif.org

POLITICS—ELECTORAL

- **US Hispanic Leadership Institute**, 312-427-6220, www.ushli.com
- **Democratic Party of Cook County**, 312-263-0575, www. ildems.org.
- **Illinois Green Party** (HQ in Urbana, IL), www.ilgreenparty.org
- **League of Women Voters**, 312-939-5935, www.lwv.org
- **Libertarian Party**, 847-459-9246, www.il.lp.org
- **Reform Party**, 312-266-7431, www.reformpartyillinois.com
- **Republican Party of Cook County**, 312-977-1467, www.ilgop.org

POLITICS—SOCIAL

- **Amnesty International**, 312-427-2060, www.amnesty.org
- **Better Government Association**, 312-427-8330, www.bettergov.org

SENIOR SERVICES

- **Chicago Cares**, 312-780-0800, www.chicagocares.org, offers 100 different monthly programs for volunteer opportunities, including working with the elderly.
- **Home-Housing Opportunities & Maintenance for the Elderly**, 773-252-3200
- **Lincoln Park Senior Center**, 312-943-6776
- **Little Brothers Friends of the Elderly**, 312-455-1000, www.little brothers.org/chicago
- **Senior Centers of Metropolitan Chicago Affiliate of Hull House Assoc.**, 773-525-3480

WOMEN'S SERVICES

BATTERED WOMEN'S GROUPS, SHELTERS, COUNSELING
- **Chicago Abused Women Coalition**, 773-278-4110, www.cawc.org
- **Chicago Foundation for Women**, 312-266-1176, www.cfw.org
- **Chicago Metro Battered Women's Network**, 312-360-1924
- **Deborah's Place**, 773-722-5080, www.deborahsplace.org

- **A Friend's Place**, 773-274-5232
- **Sarah's Circle**, 773-728-1991, www.chicagovolunteer.net
- **Wing's**, 847-963-8910, www.wingsprogram.com
- **YWCA of Metropolitan Chicago**, 312-372-6600, www.ywcachica go.org

YOUTH SERVICES

- **Alternatives, Inc.**, a multi-service youth agency, 312-663-3574, http://chicagoareaproject.org
- **Big Brother/Big Sister**, 312-427-0637, www.bbsa.org
- **Chicago Youth Centers**, 312-795-3500, www.chicagoyouthcenters.org
- **Jobs for Youth/Chicago**, 312-782-2086, www.jfychicago.org
- **National Runaway Switchboard**, 773-880-9860, www.nrscrisis line.org
- **Omni Youth Center**, 847-353-1712, www.omniyouth.org
- **Youth Outreach Services**, 773-777-7112

GETTING AROUND BY CAR

CHICAGO HAS FOUR MAJOR EXPRESSWAYS THAT EXTEND FROM the heart of the city like outstretched arms to the suburbs and beyond. During rush hour, you want to be anywhere but these thoroughfares. But of course, that may not be possible. So here are a few tips to help you survive area traffic tangles.

- The **Kennedy Expressway** (Interstate 90) runs northwest to O'Hare International Airport and is reputed to be the busiest stretch of concrete in the country. Beyond O'Hare, I-90 (in Illinois called the Northwest Tollway) will take you to Rockford and on up to Madison, Wisconsin. For those who want a fast trip to the northern suburbs, take the **Edens Expressway** (North I-94), which splits from the Kennedy just north of the Irving Park Road ramps.

- The **Eisenhower Expressway** (Interstate 290) is your gateway to the western suburbs and the East-West toll road. As you leave the Loop on the Eisenhower, you will drive right through the US Post Office, (sounds scary, but don't panic, it's a tunnel). In Hillside, I-290 connects with **I-88**, which heads west to Aurora; I-290 then heads directly north to Palatine.

- The **Stevenson Expressway** (Interstate 55) is the least crowded of Chicago's interstates, although you'd never know it during rush hours. It's the route to Midway Airport, the western and southwestern suburbs, Joliet, and Springfield.

- The **Dan Ryan Expressway** (Interstate 94) extends straight south and then splits at 95th Street traveling either east to Indiana or south-south-west as **I-57** toward Kankakee, Champaign-Urbana, and ultimately, Memphis, Tennessee. The Tri-state Tollway **I-294** is an offshoot of I-94, running north/south from the north suburb of Northbrook all the way south to Harvey.

A map is a good idea. Rand McNally makes a great laminated folded map called, "Chicago & Vicinity." Look in bookstores and gas stations for one. If city street information is more pertinent to you than suburb layouts, get the Rand McNally "Chicago Easy Finder." For serious Chicagoland traveling, get their spiral bound "Chicago & Vicinity 6-County Street Finder." It's not as portable as the two other two but it is worth having for weekend trips. In Chicago, **The Savvy Traveller** on South Michigan Avenue across from the Art Institute, and the **Rand McNally Map & Travel Store** will have the maps (see **Literary Life** in the **Cultural Life** chapter), or go to First Books, www.firstbooks.com to place an order.

TRAFFIC

Traffic congestion in Chicago is bad and getting worse. The traditional suburb-to-Chicago commute is still the granddaddy of all traffic jams, but the growing number of city-dwellers who work in the suburbs, and the even larger number of suburbanites who work in other suburbs, are changing traffic patterns. These days congestion on roads that link suburb-to-suburb is competing for top billing on the list of most congested roadways. Many of the older throughways were not built to handle such heavy traffic. Before heading out in the morning or after work, you might want to check on road conditions. Call 800-452-IDOT for a prerecorded message from the Department of Transportation. The Mayor also has a traffic web site, www.cityofchicago.org/transportation. News radio stations will also give you frequent updates: try 780/WBBM AM or 720/WGN AM, or call radio station US99 at 312-222-9456 for a report. Another option, go to www.gcmtravel.com, which provides real-time traffic updates for the Gary, Chicago, Milwaukee corridor. (Made available to the public through IDOT, INDOT, WisDOT, in cooperation with UIC-EECS AI Laboratory.)

Chicago proper certainly is not without its own traffic headaches. Due to the gentrification of much of the North Side, the resultant increase in households with two or more cars, and the blossoming of strip malls and mega-stores, heavy traffic and the lack of parking are big problems. And it's just as bad on weekends. When possible, taking the CTA train or bus really is the way to go. Better yet, walk or take a bike.

If you plan to do a lot of highway driving, you might want to consider buying an **I-Pass**—it allows you to drive (slowly) through a tollway instead of having to stop, roll down your window and hand over the toll fee. You can open an I-Pass account with a credit card or check. There is a $40 minimum to start your account. Tolls are automatically deducted from your account, and if you sign up for automatic replenishment, your account is credited for an additional $40 once the account falls below $10. Contact the **Illinois State Tollway Authority** at 800-824-7277 for more information.

For a pleasant kind of driving excitement check out the justifiably famous view from Lake Shore Drive (during non-rush hour). The sight of the downtown at night or shimmering in the light of dusk, can raise goose bumps on the arms of even the most jaded Chicagoans.

CAR RENTALS

Chicago has car rental agencies throughout the city and suburbs. Call the following phone numbers for information, reservations, and the nearest location (Many more agencies are listed in the Yellow Pages under "Automobile Rental.")

- **AVIS**, 800-331-1212; O'Hare, 773-694-5600, www.avis.com
- **Budget**, 800-763-2999, www.budget.com
- **Enterprise**, in town, 800-736-8222; out of town, 800-325-8007, www.enterprise.com
- **Hertz**, 800-654-3131; O'Hare, 773-686-7272, www.hertz.com
- **Rent-a-Wreck**, north and downtown, 773-281-4242, www.rent-a-wreck.com

If you are considering renting a car and need to pick it up from a suburban location, you can try **Ace Rent a Car**: Libertyville, 847-362-6740; Schaumburg, 847-882-6424; Lombard, 630-889-1606, O'Hare, 847-297-3350; out-of-state, 800-323-3221. For a quick rate quote go to www.acerentacar.com.

I-GO

Called the "smarter way to drive" by its promoters, I-GO offers Chicago residents the convenience of easy access to a car, without the hassle of owning a car, such as cost of insurance, maintenance and upkeep, or storage. Pay a one-time membership fee and you can reserve a slot of time (minimum one hour) and then pay only for the hours and miles used. It is recommended for those who need a car only occasionally. Currently available in Edgewater, Wicker Park, Andersonville, Hyde Park (two locations), and Logan Square. Call 773-278-4800 ext. 227 or go to www.i-go-cars.org for details.

TAXIS

Taxis can be found at most hotels, transportation hubs such as Union Station and O'Hare International Airport, most Metra express station stops, and cruising the city's main thoroughfares. When hiring a cab, make sure it displays the driver's photo ID and the vehicle license. There should also be information about the rates, usually posted on one of the windows. If you have any complaints or feel you have been overcharged, you can contact the Department of Consumer Services at 312-744-9400, and file a complaint. You must provide the cab number to file a complaint, and the date, time, and location of the incident. All city-licensed cabs have a silver medallion on the hood. Here are a few of the cab companies in the Chicagoland area. For a complete list go to www.thecityofchicago.org/taxi/ or check the Yellow Pages.

- **5 Star Taxi Association, Inc.**, 773-774-7200
- **ABO Taxicab Association**, 773-873-9140
- **American United Cab Association**, 773-327-6161
- **Blue Ribbon Association, Inc.**, 773-508-0800
- **Checker Taxi**, 312-243-2537
- **Wolley Cab**, 877-888-8294, lost and found, 312-225-5411
- **Yellow Cab**, 312-829-4222, lost and found, 312-225-7456

If you are at the airport, check the kiosk at the taxi stand for a "share-a-ride" deal. Up to four passengers can share a cab from O'Hare or Midway airports to any downtown location (between 22nd Street and Fullerton Avenue, Lake Michigan and Ashland Avenue) Rates at last check for cab sharing were:

- O'Hare to downtown: $19/person
- Midway to downtown: $16/person
- Midway to O'Hare: $25/person

LIMOUSINES

Chicago has scores of limousine companies, many providing 24-hour service. While the Yellow Pages lists them all—check under "Limousines"—here are a few:

- **Crown Cars And Limousines**, 2726 South River Road, 773-286-2277
- **Five Star Limousine Service Inc.**, 5311 South Nagle, 773-586-8000
- **O'Hare Midway Limousine Service**, 1419 Lake Cook Road, Deerfield, 312-558-1111, 800-468-0211

CARPOOLING

Carpooling is a good thing. While, given job schedules and after work errands, it's not a good fit for everyone, it should be seriously considered for those who can make it work. Not only does it create less wear and tear on your car, it saves money and is better for the environment. If you'd like to know more, contact **Ride Share** at 800-920-RIDE, and they will assist you with a carpool match anywhere in the six-county Chicagoland area. It's free. To fill out their carpooling request form online, go to www.sharethe drive.org. If you don't think the savings from carpooling add up to much, you can figure out how much you are spending driving to work alone through Ride Share's cost calculator. Go to www.sharethedrive.org and do the math—the cost may surprise you. Also check with your human resources department at work. Many corporations have carpooling programs, and some offer incentives to those willing to forgo the solo drive to work.

PARK & RIDE

Park & Ride stations are CTA's 15 daily parking lots that make your daily commute on public transportation a little more convenient. Lots are situated right next to 'L' stations, and range in size from 38 spaces to over 1,600. Parking prices run from $1/24 hours to $10.75/24 hours, depending on the station. Check with the RTA for more information at 312-836-7000 or visit www.rtachicago.com.

BY BIKE

Mayor Daley has made great attempts to not only promote the benefits of riding your bike to work, but has also implemented plans to make biking in Chicago safer. The results of the city's efforts have been so well received that in 2001 Chicago was named the Best Big Cycling city in the United States by *Bicycling Magazine*. Every spring there are events to promote bicycling around the city, such as Bike the Drive, and Bike to Work. There is a large section on the city's web site devoted to bicycling—go to www.cityofchicago.org/Transportation/Bikes/bicycle. The state of Illinois has joined in as well. Check the Illinois Department of Transportation's web site for its special section on bicycling: http://dot.state.il.us. At this site you can purchase any of nine maps detailing regional bicycling trails. Another biking resource in Chicago is the Chicagoland Bicycle Federation; check them out at www.biketraffic.org, or call them, 312-427-3325. For more specifics on biking in the city, see **Sports and Recreation**.

BY PUBLIC TRANSPORTATION

The **Regional Transportation Authority** (**RTA**) is the coordinator for all methods of public transportation in and around Chicago—from CTA buses and 'L' lines to suburban PACE buses and Metra trains. Call them with questions about fares, schedules, transfer options, etc.: 836-7000, TTY 836-4949—using any Chicagoland area code. Or visit www.rtachicago.com for more details.

The **Chicago Transit Authority** (**CTA**) is an independent state-sponsored agency that governs all public transportation within the city limits, except Metra. Their general information number is 888-YOUR-CTA.

A Chicago Transit Authority map is an invaluable weapon in the battle against commuter confusion. You can get one at the Regional Transportation Authority Travel Information Center, 175 West Jackson Blvd.; at the CTA Main Offices, Merchandise Mart, 350 North Wells (phone number, 312-664-7200); or at the Visitor Information Booths at the Chicago Cultural Center, Chicago Waterworks, or inside Sears at Madison/State. If you want information about schedules, maps, fares, or information for special needs travelers, dial 888-968-7282 or go to www.transitchicago.com.

The CTA offers Transit Cards, which can be purchased from the automatic card machines at any CTA rail station, at neighborhood currency exchanges, or at select Jewel, Dominick's, and Cub Foods. Transit Cards automatically keep track of how much fare credit you have and are good on CTA and PACE lines. Each time you go through one of the automatic turnstiles (or fare card machines on the bus) the fare is deducted from your total and the card returned to you. An adult fare single trip costs $1.50 and a transfer (to another subway line or bus route within two hours of your original trip) will set you back 30 cents. A second transfer (within the two-hour time limit) is free. Transit Cards can be recharged with cash (machines accept change and $1, $2, $5, $10, and $20 bills) at any CTA station. There is also a bonus if you purchase enough fare credit—for every $10 you buy, you receive an additional $1 of fare credit. Children under seven ride free. Seniors and youths are half price, including transfers, and during the school year, students ride at a reduced rate. The CTA also sells monthly passes, an unlimited monthly adult pass is $75, and the Chicago Card™. The Chicago Card™ works like a Transit Card, but if it is lost or stolen it will be replaced by CTA and it can be shared by up to seven individuals. (To use, place it against the electronic pad; it is not swiped through the automatic turnstile.) Purchase online at www.transitchicago.com or at any CTA sales office. Go online or call 888-968-7282 for more information.

CTA rail stations are no longer staffed with cashiers, however, CTA Customer Assistants are available at all CTA rail stations to offer travel information and assistance.

THE 'L'

The 'L' is the quickest way to get around town, if it's going your way—and it very often is. Five main lines intersect in the Loop and extend to all corners of the city. They include the **Red Line** (north/south), **Green Line** (west/south), **Blue Line** (west/northwest), **Brown Line** (north/northwest) and **Orange Line** (southwest side and Midway Airport). (If you're trying to get to either airport during rush hour, the Blue or Orange lines will be your fastest bet.)

The CTA has several rider initiatives in place in order to make using the system more economically attractive to residents. Logon to www.transitchicago.com for more information about discounts for full-time students, seniors, new area residents, and those commuting by Metra train that require a connecting bus or train ride.

In addition to these city-bound lines, there also are two north suburban rapid-transit lines, the **Purple Line** and the **Yellow Line**. Both trains run from the Howard station at the north end of the Red Line. The Yellow Line runs directly west from the Howard station to the 4800 block, then continues north to just about Dempster (8800 North). The Purple Line runs north, making seven stops in Evanston and ending at Linden Avenue in Wilmette. During rush hours: 5:20 a.m. to 9:25 a.m. (southbound beginning at Linden); 3:40 p.m. to 7:10 p.m. (northbound from Clark/Lake), the Purple Line Express makes local Evanston stops and then runs express to and from the Loop—skipping stops between Howard Street and Belmont Avenue, and making all stops south of Belmont.

CTA BUSES

The CTA has bus routes running along most of Chicago's main arteries but not all lines have 24-hour service. (Lines with nighttime service are called "owl service"—look for the owl on the bus stop sign.) Exact fare of $1.50 or a transit card is required on buses. Drivers will not give out change. Of the 143 CTA bus routes, 126 of them are handicap accessible, and bus drivers are trained to assist with special needs passengers. Information on which bus routes are equipped with handicap seating and stair lifts is available at www.transitchicago.com, or call 836-7000, using any local area code.

PACE SUBURBAN BUS SERVICE

PACE is the suburban bus service and provides bus transportation throughout Chicago's suburbs. The types of service are: regular bus routes between suburban communities on a fixed route; local bus routes within a community; feeder bus routes providing morning and evening rush-hour service between residential areas and commuter train stations; and express routes providing direct service between suburbs and the Loop and between different suburbs. Exact fare is $1.50, and PACE transit cards are available. Bus schedules are posted in village halls, libraries, or you can get one from your bus driver, or the PACE office, 550 West Algonquin Road, Arlington Heights. They are also posted in most Metra train station waiting areas. To receive schedules by mail, call PACE at 847-364-7223, or the RTA Travel Information Center, 836-7000, using any Chicagoland area code. Or visit their web site at www.pacebus.com.

TRAINS

METRA COMMUTER RAILROAD SERVICE

Metra (Metropolitan Rail) is the commuter railroad service that runs from the Loop to 225 suburban stations near and far. Service generally operates all day, including holidays; frequency varies by as much as three hours during non-rush hour times. Trains do not run all night. Metra's fare system is separate from the CTA, and is based on distance traveled. The following Metra lines leave from these stations:

- Union Pacific, Ogilvie Transportaion Center (formerly North Western Station), 500 West Madison Street, 312-496-4777
- Milwaukee District, Union Station, 210 South Canal Street, 312-322-4269
- Burlington Northern, Union Station, 210 South Canal Street, 312-322-4269
- Norfolk Southern, Union Station, 210 South Canal Street, 312-322-4269
- Heritage Corridor, Union Station, 210 South Canal Street, 312-322-4269
- Rock Island, LaSalle Street Station, 414 South LaSalle Street, 312-322-8957
- Metra Electric, Randolph Street Station, 151 East Randolph Street, 312-322-7819
- South Shore Line, Randolph Street Station, 151 East Randolph Street, 312-782-0676

For information regarding Metra schedules, routes and fares, call 312-322-6777. For South Shore information, call 800-356-2079. Printed schedules are available at all Metra stations or you can request one to be sent in the mail by calling 312-322-6777. Visit their web site for detailed station information and PACE connections: www.metrarail.com.

AMTRAK

Amtrak, 800-USA-RAIL, www.amtrak.com, provides inter-city rail service. Trains leave Union Station, 210 South Canal Street; there are stops at the Glenview, LaGrange, and Naperville Metra stations. For affordable and efficient service to such nearby cities as Detroit, Indianapolis, Milwaukee, or St. Louis, Amtrak can't be beat. Go to their web site to sign up for e-mail promotions. Buy online and you can save up to 60% on long-distance coach train tickets. Late fall and early spring are good times to look for deals on Amtrak.

NATIONAL/REGIONAL BUS SERVICE

- **Greyhound Bus**, Chicago stations: 630 West Harrison, 312-408-5800; 14 West 95th Street, 312-408-5999; CTA Transit Building, 5800 Cumberland Avenue, 773-693-2474, www.greyhound.com

There are a number of **regional bus lines** (all go to and from the airports):
- **Bluebird Charter Coach Airport Services**, www.bluebirdcharter.com, call 800-400-5500 for schedule information to and from Champaign, Savoy, Bradley, or Rantoul, Illinois. From O'Hare: terminals 1, 2, 3; from Midway Airport: exit 3LL at the arrival area.
- **Coach USA/United Limo**, 800-833-5555, www.busville.com, service to and from O'Hare and Midway airports to Harvey, Matteson, and Crestwood in Illinois, and in Indiana to: Gary, Highland, Merrillville, Michigan City, Mishawaka, Portage, and South Bend (Notre Dame).
- **Coach USA/Wisconsin Coach Lines**, 877-324-7767, service to and from Gurnee, IL, and the Wisconsin cities of: Kenosha, Racine, Mitchell Airport, Marquette University, and Waukesha.
- **Coach USA/Van Galder**, 800-747-0994, www.vangalderbus.com, service to and from O'Hare Airport and Midway Airport to Rockford, Illinois, or Janesville and Madison, Wisconsin. Bus pickup from downtown Chicago is at the Amtrak Station at Jackson/Canal.
- **Peoria Charter**, 800-448-0572, www.peoriacharter.com; service to and from O'Hare and Midway airports to: Joliet, Schaumburg, Pontiac, Peoria, Morton, Oakbrook, River Road (CTA station), and Normal, Illinois.

AIRPORTS AND AIRLINES

O'HARE INTERNATIONAL AIRPORT

O'Hare International Airport (800-832-6352, www.ohare.com); with over 70 million passengers going through O'Hare each year, it has the dubious honor of being one of the busiest airports in the world. As you might expect, it can be crowded and confusing at times. O'Hare is the headquarters for United Airlines (the sparkling Terminal 1), and more than 50 other airlines have gates at one or more of O'Hare's five huge terminals. The airport is easy to get to via the 'L' or by car on the Kennedy (I-90)—if you're driving, watch it during rush hour! You can easily miss a flight by underestimating travel time to O'Hare. If you're coming from downtown by public transportation, the 'L' Blue Line is the fastest route—approximately 45 minutes. For drivers, there's plenty of short and long-term parking. Call Airport Transit Service (ATS), 773-686-3177 (main parking garage

773-686-7530) for parking information. Those taking a taxi from downtown should expect to pay $40 to $45—there are no flat rate runs to the airport—all cab rides are metered. (You can you share a cab from downtown but you will have to negotiate a shared fare with the other passenger at a flat rate. If you are at the airport and need to go downtown, flat rate/cab shares are available. See above under **Taxis**.)

But of course, there are more ways to get to the airport than by car or the 'L.' Suburban shuttles, trains, and buses also may be options. From 6 a.m. to 11:30 p.m., **Continental Airport Express** offers shuttle van transportation from downtown Chicago and the northern suburbs to the airport. From downtown to O'Hare, the fare is about $17, and departures are scheduled every five to ten minutes. There are discounts for even small groups. Call 800-Z-THE-VAN for more information or visit their web site at www.airportexpress.com. If you would like to board a Continental Express van from the airport, go to the baggage claim level of terminals 1, 2, and 3, or outside US Customs at Terminal 5. **Omega Airport Shuttle** offers service to and from O'Hare and Midway, and between Hyde Park and O'Hare Airport. Pick-up from the O'Hare Airport is at the Bus/Shuttle Center, door number four. One way fare between airports costs $17. Call 773-483-6634 or go to www.omegashuttle.com for more information. Regional bus lines (see above), including Owl Airport Service, 800-621-4153 (serves Lake Geneva, Lake Zurich, McHenry, Richmond, and Volo), and PACE, 847-364-7223, also offers service to and from O'Hare. The **Bus/Shuttle Center** is located on the ground level of O'Hare's elevated parking garage. From terminals 1, 2, 3, use the pedestrian tunnels; from Terminal 5, take the "people mover" to Terminal 3, then follow the signs.

LOST AND FOUND

If you lose something at the airport—as opposed to losing a piece of luggage in flight—you can contact O'Hare, but you should be aware that there is no central lost and found at the airport. If you think you left an item at a security checkpoint, try the Transportation Security Administration at 773-894-8760. Keep in mind they eventually turn lost items over to the police. For the parking lots, call 773-686-3177. If you left your belongings on an airplane or at the gate or ticket counter, you will need to contact that carrier. Here are a few lost and found phone numbers for three of the busier carriers at O'Hare: American: 773-686-4234, United: 773-601-3295/3290, and Northwest: 773-686-5550.

MAJOR AIRLINES SERVING O'HARE

- **Air Alaska**, 800-252-7522, www.alaska-air.com
- **Airtrain**, 800-247-8726, www.airtran.com
- **Aloha Air**, 800-367-5250, www.alohaairlines.com

- **American Airlines**, 800-433-7300, www.americanair.com
- **American Eagle**, 800-433-7300, www.americanair.com
- **American West**, 800-327-7810, www.americawest.com
- **Cathay Pacific USA**, 800-233-2742, www.cathay-usa.com
- **Colgan Air**, 800-428-4322, www.colganair.com
- **Continental**, 800-523-3273, www.continental.com
- **Delta**, 800-221-1212, www.delta.com
- **Island Air**, 800-225-6732, www.ambergriscaye.com/islandair
- **Jet Express**, 888-806-8833, www.jetexpress.com
- **Northwest Airlines**, 800-225-2525, www.nwa.com
- **United Airlines**, 800-864-8331, www.ual.com

MIDWAY AIRPORT

Midway Airport (773-838-0600, www.ohare.com/midway); one square mile on Chicago's southwest side—bounded by 55th and 63rd streets on the north and south, and Cicero and Central avenues on the east and west—is Midway Airport. Get there by car on the Stevenson Expressway (I-55) or by using CTA's Orange Line—the train ride from downtown is roughly 30 minutes. CTA's 55th Street/Garfield bus also ambles its way to and from Midway. Once easily overshadowed by O'Hare, the growth of discount airlines such as Southwest and AirTran, who use Midway, has turned this older airport into a bustling commuter hub. Get there early if you need to park in the long-term lot (a shuttle bus will bring you to the terminal). Park in the garage for $23/day or in the economy lots for $10/day. (For more parking information, call 773-838-0756.) For travel between Midway Airport and Chicago check the shuttles mentioned in the O'Hare section for transportation options. Regional bus service to and from Midway is also similar to that of O'Hare (see **Regional Bus Lines** above).

LOST AND FOUND

If you left something at one of the security checkpoints, you will need to contact the Transportation Security Administration's Lost and Found department at 773-948-6370. If your belongings were lost in the parking lot, contact Standard Parking at 773-838-0756. If you left your item at a ticket counter, on a plane or at a gate, you must contact the airline directly. Two airlines that service Midway and have lost and found phone numbers are Airtran, 773-948-6488, and Frontier Airlines, 773-948-6414. Southwest Airlines recommends calling their baggage service, 773-884-3039.

MAJOR AIRLINES SERVING MIDWAY AIRPORT

- **Airtran**, 800-825-8538, www.airtran.com
- **ATA**, 800-435-9282, www.ata.com

- **ComAir,** 800-221-1212, www.comair.com
- **Delta,** 800-221-1212, www.delta.com
- **Indigo Airlines,** 773-585-5155, www.flyindigo.com
- **Frontier Airlines,** 800-432-1359, www.frontierairlines.com
- **Mesa Airlines,** (known as US Airways Express in the Midwest), 800-637-2247, www.mesa-air.com
- **Mesaba** (a Northwest Airlines partner), 800-225-2525, www.nwa.com
- **Southwest Airlines,** 800-435-9792, www.iflyswa.com

MEIGS FIELD

This single runway on landfill extending south from Shedd Aquarium that was created for Chicago's 1933 Century of Progress Exposition is no longer. Much to the shock of many, particularly area business owners and executives, the field was destroyed on March 31, 2003, at Mayor Daley's direction. It was generally used by private planes, and government officials, most notably, the President of the United States, and business people who wanted to get in and out of the Loop quickly.

Plans are to erect a new lakefront park. Go to www.openlands.org for more information.

ONLINE AIR TRAVEL RESOURCES

There are a number of travel related web sites all touting great deals, including **Travelocity.com, Expedia.com, Lowestfare.com, Cheaptickets.com, Priceline.com, Qixo.com,** and **Sidestep.com**; take your pick. Also, many airlines post last minute seats at a reduced rate, usually online. In fact, booking online directly with the airline of your choice may be less expensive than what many of the so-called discount travel sites offer.

To **register a complaint against an airline**, the Department of Transportation is the place to call or write: 202-366-2220, Aviation Consumer Protection Division, C-75 Room 4107, 400 7th Street SW, Washington, DC 20590.

Information about **flight delays** can be checked online on your airline's web site, or at www.fly.faa.gov. Similarly, the site www.flightarrivals.com offers real-time arrival, departure, and delay details for commercial flights.

THERE ARE HUNDREDS OF HOTELS AND MOTELS IN CHICAGO, ranging from the bare bones room-with-a-bed motel to luxurious hotel suites with breathtaking views of Lake Michigan and the Chicago skyline. When making a reservation, always remember to ask about discounts or weekend packages, as many lodgings have daily, unadvertised specials. Also keep in mind that room rates vary by the season (off-season begins January 1 and ends March 31) and by the convention (no discounts during large events like the National Restaurant Convention which occurs each spring).

The following list of hotels and motels is by no means complete. With an eye to your pocketbook, we have shied away from most of the expensive hotels in favor of more reasonably priced accommodations in good locations. For a complete listing, check the Yellow Pages under "Hotels and Motels." Also check the **Chicago Convention and Tourism Bureau's** site, www.chicago.il.org/hotels (phone 877-244-2246), or the **Illinois Hotel & Lodging Association**, www.stayillinois.com. AAA travel guides (free to members) are another good source for hotel and motel recommendations. If you need a room in a hurry, call the Chicago-based **Hot Rooms**, 773-468-7666, www.hotrooms.com, a hotel-reservation service that offers special discounted rates. **Quikbook** is a national discount room reservation service that costs nothing to join. It offers reduced room rates for many hotels. For a list of cities and hotels and information about them, visit www.quikbook.com or call 800-789-9887. Other national reservation companies include: **Hotels.com**, 800-964-6835, www.hotels.com, and **Central Reservation Services**, 800-548-3311, www.reservation-services.com.

Online travel agents, which offer room reservation services, airline tickets, and sometimes car rentals, include:

- **BizTravel**, www.biztravel.com
- **Expedia**, www.expedia.com

- **Cheap Tickets**, www.cheaptickets.com
- **Click-It Weekends**, www.travelweb.com
- **LowestFare.com**, www.lowestfare.com
- **Tom Parsons' Best Fares**, www.bestfares.com
- **Travelocity**, www.travelocity.com
- **Travelhero.com**, www.travelhero.com

A word of advice: when making reservations through any discount site it is always wise to ask about the cancellation policy and if the rate quoted includes the **hotel tax**, which in Chicago is 14.9% per day. Also, some services require a full payment at the time of the reservation.

LUXURY LODGINGS

Hotels listed in this section charge $200 to $300 a night, unless otherwise noted. Rates vary greatly based on season and availability.

- **Four Seasons Hotel**, 120 East Delaware Place, 312-280-8800, 800-332-3442; room prices range from $390 to $3,500 for a presidential suite. Ask about the weekend package, which start at $305 a night.
- **Omni Ambassador East**, 1301 North State Parkway, 312-787-3700, www.omnihotels.com
- **The Drake**, 140 East Walton Street, 312-787-2200
- **Hotel Burnham**, One West Washington, 312-782-1111, toll-free, 877-294-9712; only 122 rooms.
- **Whitehall Hotel**, 105 East Delaware Place, 312-944-6300; Gold Coast location.
- **The Ritz-Carlton Chicago**, 160 East Pearson Street, 312-266-1000; this luxury property is set atop Water Tower Place, above North Michigan Avenue. It features fine furnishings and one of Chicago's best French restaurants, The Dining Room. Rooms always above $300.
- **Sofitel**, 20 East Chestnut Street, 312-324-4000; designed by renowned French architect Jean-Paul Viguier, this "Sofitel Water Tower" as it is named, offers 415 rooms (21 of them accessible for special needs) of European luxury at the corner of Chestnut and Wabash
- **Park Hyatt Chicago**, 800 North Michigan Avenue, 312-335-1234, 800-233-1234, www.parkhyattchicago.hyatt.com; elegant 202-room tower hotel, with an art gallery.
- **The Peninsula Chicago**, 108 East Superior Street, 312-337-2888; over 300 rooms.
- **The Westin/Michigan Avenue**, 909 North Michigan, 312-943-7200 or 800-228-3000; large hotel (over 700 rooms), recently renovated, lots of amenities (rates as low as $99 depending on availability).

MIDDLE RANGE LODGINGS

Following is a list of national hotel chains and local hotels with nightly fees ranging from about $90 to $250; suites cost more. Room rates vary by availability and type.

- **Belden-Stratford Apartments**, 2300 North Lincoln Park West, 773-281-2900; apartments and hotel styled rooms. Helpful staff, safe, secure, and clean. Near Lincoln Park.
- **Best Western**, 800-528-1234, www.bestwestern.com; 1100 South Michigan Avenue, 312-922-2900; **Best Western Inn Chicago**, 162 East Ohio Street, 312-787-3100; a moderately priced hotel one-half block east of North Michigan Avenue; **Best Western River North Hotel**, 125 West Ohio Street, 312-467-0800; spacious and airy rooms, free parking, and indoor pool.
- **Claridge Hotel**, 1244 North Dearborn Parkway, 312-787-4980; 164 rooms, recently renovated.
- **Comfort Inns & Suites Downtown**, 15 East Ohio Street, 312-494-1515, 888-775-4111
- **Days Inn Lincoln Park North**, 644 West Diversey Avenue, 773-525-7010, www.lpndaysinn.com; **Days Inn Gold Coast**, 1816 North Clark, 312-664-3040
- **Doubletree Hotels & Guest Suites**, 800-222-8733, www.doubletreehotels.com
- **The Drake Hotel**, 140 East Walton Street, 312-787-2200; this landmark hotel is in the heart of the Gold Coast, overlooking Lake Michigan.
- **Embassy Suites**, 800-362-2779, www.embassysuites.com; locations in downtown, Lombard, Deerfield, Rosemont, and Schaumburg.
- **Hampton Inn Chicago River-North**, 33 West Illinois Street, 312-832-0330, 800-426-7866; locations in the northwest and southwest suburbs.
- **Hilton Hotels**, 800-445-8667, www.hilton.com: **Palmer House Hilton**, 17 East Monroe Street, 312-726-7500; this downtown hotel is a Chicago landmark, known for its German food and festivities. Very convenient to downtown shopping, museums, and public transportation. **Hilton Chicago & Towers**, 720 South Michigan Avenue, 312-922-4400; suburban locations: Northbrook, Hoffman Estates, Evanston, Oak Brook Terrace, Lisle, Oak Lawn.
- **Holiday Inn**, 800-465-4329, www.ichotelsgroup.com
- **Hyatt Hotels & Resorts**, 800-233-1234, www.hyatt.com; four downtown locations and in the suburbs: Woodfield, Deerfield, Oak Brook, Lisle
- **Marriott Hotels**, 800-228-9290, www.marriott.com; **Marriott O'Hare**, 8101 West Higgins Road, 773-867-0000; other hotel locations in Schaumburg, Lombard, Elmhurst, Hoffman Estates, and Itasca.

- **Quality Inn & Suites**, 800-228-5151, www.qualityinn.com
- **Radisson**, 800-333-3333, www.radisson.com, 160 East Huron Street
- **The Talbot Hotel**, 20 East Delaware Place, 800-621-8506; European-styled hotel, recently renovated.
- **The Tremont Hotel**, 100 East Chestnut Street, 312-751-1900, 800-621-8133; small upscale hotel.
- **W Chicago Lakeshore Hotel**, 644 North Lake Shore Drive, 312-943-9200, www.whotels.com; located downtown on Lake Michigan.
- **Wyndham Hotels**, 800-WYNDHAM or www.wyndham.com, downtown 633 North St. Clair Street; suburbs: Oak Brook, Lisle, Buffalo Grove, Naperville, Itasca, two in Schaumburg.

INEXPENSIVE LODGINGS

Listings here include rooms with rates below $100 (also check the chains listed in the **Middle Range Lodgings** above, some suburban locations will have rooms for under $100):

- **Days Inn**, 800-329-7466, www.daysinn.com, suburban locations: Melrose Park, Niles, Schiller Park
- **LaQuinta Inns**, 800-221-4731; in the Chicago area this hotel chain is in the northwest and southwest suburbs. Call for locations.
- **Red Roof Inns**, 162 East Ontario, 312-787-3580; call 877-222-7663 for locations in the north and northwest suburbs.
- **Roadway Inn Downtown**, One South Halsted, 312-829-5000
- **Sleep Inn**, 1831 West Diehl Road, Naperville, 800-695-8284

EXTENDED STAY HOTELS

At Home Inn Chicago is a reservation service that will locate furnished apartments in downtown Chicago for extended stays: 312-640-1050, www.athomeinnchicago.com.

Extended stay hotels in Chicagoland include:

- **AAA Deluxe Weekly Penthouse Condos**, 1412 West Diversey Parkway, 312-226-5361; can be rented daily, weekly or monthly. Condos sleep eight to twelve: 3,000-sq. feet, three to four bedrooms.
- **Doral Michigan Avenue**, 151 North Michigan Avenue, 312-616-6005; offers furnished apartments for a minimum 30-day stay. The lease includes cable television, kitchen amenities, health-club memberships, linens, and weekly maid service. Furnished "corporate suites" start at $1,700 per month for a studio, $2,000 for a one-bedroom, $2,700 for a two-bedroom. Discounts are available for stays of three months or more. Unfurnished apartments can also be had for significantly lower rates, although a one-year lease is required.

- **Equity Corporate Housing**, 1434 Brook Drive, Downers Grove, 800-575-4050, www.equitycorporatehousing.com
- **Extended Stay America**, 800-398-7829, www.extendedstay.com, has locations in several suburbs including Rolling Meadows, Gurnee, Downers Grove, and Waukegan. A room with a queen-sized bed, kitchenette, utensils, and weekly maid service ranges from $200 to $400 a week (seven nights).
- **Flemish House of Chicago**, 68 East Cedar Street, 312-664-9981, www.chicagobandb.com; seven suites with kitchenettes; near Michigan Avenue/Oak Street Beach neighborhood. Facilities can be set up as corporate apartments for extended use.
- **Homewood Suites**, www.homewood-suites.com, 800-CALL-HOME; discounts may be available for stays of five nights or more: in downtown and Schaumburg.
- **Oakwood Corporate Housing**, 800-888-0808, www.oakwood.com; provides corporate housing and temporary lodgings: downtown and Lincoln Park location, also in Schaumburg, Arlington Heights, Naperville.
- **Residence Inn by Marriott**: located in southwest suburbs: Lombard: 2001 South Highland Avenue, 630-629-7800; Schaumburg: 1610 McConnor Parkway, 847-517-9200.

BED & BREAKFASTS

For nationwide listings, including the Chicago area, go to www.bbonline.com or www.bedandbreakfasts.com. Or call one of the following:

- **Gold Coast Guest House Bed and Breakfast**, 113 West Elm Street, Chicago, 312-337-0361, www.bbchicago.com; Victorian row house, rated AAA three Diamond. Five minute walk to Michigan Avenue. McCormick Place shuttles nearby. Ask about their furnished corporate studio apartments, available monthly. Recommended by *Travel & Leisure* magazine.
- **Inn on Early**, 1241 West Early Avenue, 773-334-4666; near Lake Michigan. All rooms equipped with phone and answering machine, air conditioning, and TV/VCR; daily continental breakfast.
- **Old Town Chicago Bed and Breakfast Inn**, 1442 North North Park Avenue, 312-440-9268, www.oldtownchicago.com; art deco styled city house; four non-smoking suites, large common areas. In downtown Chicago.
- **Under the Gingko Tree Bed and Breakfast**, 300 North Kenilworth Avenue, Oak Park, 708-524-2327; Queen Ann Victorian inn, 20 minutes from downtown Chicago.
- **The Wheeler Mansion**, 2020 South Calumet Avenue, 312-945-2020, www.wheelermansion.com; luxury boutique hotel. Eleven rooms/suites, each with spa bath. Decorated with 19th century

antiques. Lots of amenities including full gourmet breakfast, down pillows, comforters, cable TV, laundry/dry cleaning, on-site bike rental, twice daily chambermaid service, full concierge services.

- **Windy City Urban Inn**, 607 West Deming Place, 773-248-7091, www.windycityinn.com; five rooms, three suites; all non-smoking. Former mansion; located in Lincoln Park.
- **Wooded Isle Suites**, 5750 South Stony Island Avenue, 773-288-5578, 800-290-6844; 13 suites, non-smoking, full kitchens. Located between the Museum of Science and Industry and the University of Chicago.

HOSTELS/CLUBS/YMCAS

- **McGraw YMCA**, 1000 Grove Street, Evanston, 847-475-7400; this men-only residence offers temporary and long term housing. Call for rates and availability.
- **The Three Arts Club**, 1300 North Dearborn Parkway, 312-944-6250, www.threearts.org, is a non-profit women-only residence. Nightly rates are $45 (double) $50 (single); weekly $225. Breakfast and dinners provided.

For nationwide listing of hostels, including Chicago, go to **www.hostels. com**. Chicago **area hostels** include:

- **Arlington International House**, 616 West Arlington Place, 773-929-5380
- **Chicago International Hostel**, 6318 North Winthrop Avenue, (near Loyola University), 773-262-1011; four to eight beds per room with showers, with a full kitchen.
- **Hostelling International**, 24 East Congress Parkway, 312-360-0300, 500 bunk facility, no curfew, membership not required, 24-hour access and security, stays of longer than 30 days qualify for semi-private accommodations. Most rooms have private baths and showers, there is access to laundry and kitchen facilities, and the hostel has two in-house restaurants. The rate is $22 per day for long-term stays (30+ days), less than 30 days is $30 per day plus tax.

SUMMER ONLY

- **Illinois Institute of Technology**, 3241 South Wabash, 312-567-5075; three miles directly south of downtown, IIT offers its dorm rooms to travelers of all ages during summer. Private or rooms to share are available. Community bathrooms are located on each floor. Laundry and cafeteria on-site. One-time linen set-up included. Reservations accepted one week in advance with credit card guarantee.

- **Columbia College Chicago**, 731 South Plymouth Court, 312-344-6801, located in downtown Chicago in the South Loop area. From the second week of June through the last week of August, Columbia offers apartment style housing with private bedrooms, a bathroom, living room, dining area, and a kitchen. There is a laundry facility, workout room, and meeting room/TV lounge on site as well. For individual and group stays of less than a week there is a one time linen set offered (includes a sheet set, bath towel and face towel, but not pillows). If you need accommodations for more than a week you will need to provide your own linens. Reservations are accepted a month in advance, and the balance of your charge must be paid at least two weeks in advance of your arrival to guarantee your reservation.

ACCESSIBLE ACCOMMODATIONS

The following national chains own hotels in Chicago and have reputations for offering many services to the disabled: **Hilton Hotels**, 800-445-8667, TTY 800-368-1133, www.hilton.com; **Hyatt Hotels**, 800-532-1496, TTY 800-228-9548, www.hyatt.com; **ITT Sheraton**, 800-325-3535, TTY 800-325-1717, www.starwood.com/sheraton; **Marriott Hotels**, 800-228-9290, TTY 800-228-7014, www.marriott.com. However, accommodations may not be consistent from place to place, so be sure to call and talk over your specific needs in advance. Be aware that federal law requires that if a hotel guarantees reservations for its regular rooms, it must also guarantee reservations for handicapped-accessible rooms.

You may have the best luck finding fully accessible accommodations in the extended stay facilities located outside of Chicago proper. The following hotels all claim accessibility:

- **Best Western Inn Chicago**, 162 East Ohio Street, 312-787-3100; a moderately priced hotel one-half block east of North Michigan Avenue.
- **Days Inn Lincoln Park North**, 644 West Diversey Parkway, 773-525-7010
- **Doubletree Suites**, 198 East Delaware Place, 312-664-1100
- **The Drake Hotel**, 140 East Walton Place, 312-787-2200
- **Extended Stay America**, 800-398-7829; special rooms feature grab bars in the bathroom, fire alarms with lights, and Braille elevators.
- **Homestead Studio Suites Hotel**, 51 East State Parkway, Schaumburg, 847-882-6900, www.homesteadhotels.com
- **The Ritz-Carlton Chicago**, 160 East Pearson Street, 312-266-1000
- **Sofitel**, 20 East Chestnut Street, 312-324-4000; 21 rooms available for special needs
- **W Chicago Lakeshore Hotel**, 644 North Lake Shore Drive, 312-943-9200, www.whotels.com; located downtown.

FYI, the **Society for Accessible Travel & Hospitality**, 212-447-7284, www.sath.org, offers advice and publishes a magazine for disabled travelers called *Open World*.

For more information on services for the disabled, look in the **Helpful Services** chapter of this book.

C ONTRARY TO WHAT A NEW ARRIVAL MAY BELIEVE, NOT ALL OF Illinois is flat or filled with cornfields; to the west lie rolling hills and the beautiful Mississippi River Valley; to the north, wooded lake lands and, to the south, historical Indian lands and state parks.

A car makes getting to any of the following places a breeze, and Amtrak is an option to places like Springfield or Milwaukee, and even some of the state beaches in Indiana. Most of the following suggestions are perfect for a long day trip, although bed and breakfasts abound for those who choose to spend the night.

For those interested, legalized gambling has sprung up on riverboat casinos along the Ohio and Mississippi rivers as well as parts of Lake Michigan (see **Sports and Recreation**).

ILLINOIS

Call the **Illinois Department of Tourism** at 800-226-6632, for more information about area tourism, or visit their web site at www.enjoyillinois.com. Also check the **Greenspace and Beaches** chapter for additional details about area state and national parks.

GALENA

Galena is a lovely, pre-civil war town, with 85% of its buildings on the National Historic Register. It is located on the Mississippi River three hours west of Chicago, and is surprisingly hilly. Galena is the hometown of Ulysses S. Grant, whose house, presented to him by the community upon his triumphant return from the Civil War, is only one of the charms of this beautiful town. In the warmer weather, you can take a walking tour through Victorian homes, explore antiques shops, brush up on your tennis or golf game, or just sit in an outdoor café and watch the world go by at a slower pace. In the winter months, Chicagoans can be found in these parts snowmobiling and cross-country skiing. Stop into a jazz club after dinner or one of the resorts for some evening entertainment. The nearby Eagle Ridge resort, set in the hills, is a golfer's paradise. Contact the Galena Tourism Information Center, 800-747-9377, www.galena.com, for more information.

SPRINGFIELD

Home of Abraham Lincoln, as well as dozens of historical buildings, the state capital also hosts the Illinois State Fair every August. It's a long drive (about 4.5 hours)—best as a weekend trip. Call the Springfield Convention and Tourism Bureau, 800-545-7300, or visit www.visit-springfieldillinois.com.

STATE AND NATIONAL PARKS

Illinois is full of state and national parks, perfect for a one- or two-day nature excursion. Perhaps the closest park area to Chicago is the **Illinois and Michigan Canal Heritage Corridor**. Headquartered in Lockport, southwest of Chicago, the corridor is a network of parks, state trails, nature centers, and historical museums that mark the 97-mile canal that links the Chicago River to the Illinois River at Peru, Illinois. You can tour some of the parks by horseback, snowmobile or on foot. Contact the Heritage Center at 815-727-2323, or go to www.nps.gov/ilmi for more details on particular parks and other venues in the network.

The **Shawnee National Forest**, located in Harrisburg, is a pristine nature site with over 200 acres available for horseback riding. The park contains areas that are privately owned as well as government owned. It operates on a "leave no trace" guideline, and motorized vehicles are prohibited from traveling off-road. There are extensive hiking and backpacking trails. Climbing here is recommended for experienced climbers only. You must obtain a license before you fish or hunt. Horses can be rented from nearby vendors. For more information, check with the Harrisburg Chamber of Commerce at 618-252-4192; Shawnee National Forest Headquarters can be reached at 800-699-6637, www.fs.fed.us/r9/shawnee.

Two hours west of Chicago is **Starved Rock State Park**. The 18 canyons that make up this park include natural attractions such as waterfalls, 600 types of wildflowers, and incredible views. The area is known for its unusual rock formations, mostly St. Peter sandstone, laid down in a huge inland sea more than 425 million years ago. Starved Rock State Park hosts a number of events throughout the year, and guided hikes are available on most weekends. A good spot for camping, fishing or boating, the park is also worth a visit in the winter months for viewing frozen waterfalls, ice skating, or cross-country skiing. For more information, call 815-667-4906, or the Starved Rock Lodge and Conference Center, 800-868-7625, www.starvedrocklodge.com.

Illinois State Park boasts coveted beaches, including six miles of beach along the Lake Michigan shoreline in Zion, Illinois. You can camp, swim, hike, picnic, fish, and boat in the park. Reservations are advisable, even on non-holiday weekends. Call the Illinois Department of Natural Resources (DNR) for more information: 217-782-6752. You can also download a reservation form from the web site at www.dnr.state.il.us. If you prefer a more civilized end to your day, you can stay at the 96-room Illinois Resort and Conference Center in Lake Zion. Call 847-625-7300 for reservations.

An alternative to a state park is a road trip through the **National Historic Byway Road** of Illinois. The National Roads were in a sense, America's first highways. In 1806, Congress authorized the construction of the first federally supported roads, in an effort to link the eastern states with what was then the western frontier. Construction started in Cumberland, Maryland and was to end at the Ohio River. But the road resulted in an impetus of its own; bringing settlers, traders and new business to Illinois. As activity on the road increased, demand for its extension increased as well. Road construction proceeded across Ohio and through Vandalia, Illinois. But by 1840, the increasing interest in railroads stopped further development of the National Road, although it was not destined for obscurity. The invention of the automobile brought renewed interest in the road, and in the 1920s, it was renamed Route 40. It remained a major east-west roadway until the 1960s when construction of Interstate 70 replaced it. Today these old trails meander through a half a dozen states, passing by state parks, nature preserves, lakes, historic cemeteries, prehistoric archaeological sites, and districts, golf courses, quaint towns, and even a riverboat casino—the Casino Queen docked in East St. Louis. In Illinois, the Historic Road begins south of Springfield, at the Wabash River, and ends at the Mississippi. Contact the National Road Association of Illinois for maps and more information: 217-849-3188 or online at www.nationalroad.org. Or take a virtual tour at www.byways.org.

BICYCLE TRIPS

It's hard not to look at Illinois and think "bike trip!" The endless plains seem to have been made with a cyclist in mind. There are several terrific areas around Chicagoland to take a spin. Here are some favorites:

- **The Great Western Trail**: 18 miles of wetlands and prairie between St. Charles and Sycamore, taking you through DeKalb and Kane counties.

- **The Illinois Prairie Path**: a 40-mile trail through the southern suburbs, stretching from Elmhurst to Wheaton, where it splits four-ways as it heads towards the Fox River. This trail welcomes horseback riders and hikers.
- If you enjoy buffalo and bird watching, you can combine both pleasures at the **Fermilab National Accelerator Laboratory**. Fermilab is located in Batavia, about 45 miles west of Chicago. While its business is high energy physics research, its 6,800 acres of wetlands, forests, and fields offer one of the finest bird-watching areas around. You can take your bike and navigate the grounds any day of the week. For information, contact their Public Affairs Office at 630-840-3351 or online at www.fnal.gov.

INDIANA

INDIANA DUNES NATIONAL LAKESHORE AND STATE PARK

Forty-five minutes south of Chicago on the Indiana shore of Lake Michigan (near the City of Porter) is a little bit of heaven. Indiana Dunes is a popular spot for sun worshippers. With over 2,000 acres, the park boasts plenty of picnic spots, campgrounds, (reservations must be made about six months in advance for Memorial and Labor Day weekends), and of course, sand dunes, gorgeous soft and silky sand dunes. For park information: contact the National Lakeshore, www.nps.gov/indu, 219-926-7651 ext. 225, or the State Park, www.in.gov/dnr, 219-926-1952. Contact the Indiana Department of Tourism, 800-289-6646 or visit www.in.gov/enjoyindiana for even more ideas.

WISCONSIN

LAKE GENEVA

Less than two hours north, just across the Illinois/Wisconsin border, lovely Lake Geneva calls. It's been a favorite getaway for Chicagoans for generations. Stroll around part of the lake to admire the huge mansions built by wealthy vacationers in years past, listen to a concert, water-ski, take in an art fair, fish, or hunt for antiques—just a few of the ways you can spend your time. For more information, call the Wisconsin Department of Tourism, 800-432-8747, or visit their web site at www.travelwisconsin.com.

MADISON

If you continue past O'Hare on I-90, in two and a half hours you'll reach Madison, Wisconsin's vibrant capital city. With hills and lakes galore and home to the huge University of Wisconsin, Madison is an attractive place to visit, and with its first class schools and low crime rate it's a great place to raise kids. Madison is an hour south of the **Wisconsin Dells**, also along I-90, which appears to offer the largest collection of waterslides and "themed" entertainment this side of Gatlinburg. If you're car-less or just don't want to drive, an easy and affordable way to get to Madison is to hop on a Coach USA/Van Galder bus at O'Hare or at the Amtrak station downtown at Jackson/Canal (see **Transportation** for more information).

MILWAUKEE

Just two hours north of Chicago, past Gurnee, Milwaukee has been called a smaller version of Chicago. Its Central European heritage means there's plenty of taverns, restaurants, interesting neighborhoods, tempting cheeses, and of course, breweries. The Wisconsin State Fair is held in Milwaukee every summer and it is worth the trip just to see the racing piglets! For more information, contact the Milwaukee Visitor Information Center, 800-554-1448, or visit www.milwaukee.org.

KOHLER VILLAGE

Fifty-five miles north of Milwaukee, lies Kohler, Wisconsin. More than 75 years ago, Walter Kohler began creating what was to become one of the first planned cities in America. He drew his ideas from the garden cities of Europe and worked closely with the Olmsted Brothers, designers of New York City's Central Park. Today, Kohler Village still exists as a carefully planned community and home to the Kohler factory for kitchen and bathroom fixtures. Kohler Waters Spa is a first rate spa located at the American Club Hotel, in Kohler Village. It is the Midwest's only AAA Five Diamond rated resort. There are several museums around the resort, award winning golf courses, such as Blackwolf Run, and guided tours of the historic American Club Hotel, the Kohler Design Center, and the Kohler Factory. The American Club resort is listed in the National Register of Historic Places. Of course, there are the usual outdoor activities—fishing, canoeing, birding, dog sledding, cross country skiing, hiking, and much more. For more information contact Kohler Village by calling 800-344-2838 ext. 700, and visit their web site at www.destinationkohler.com.

SOUTHWEST MICHIGAN

A generation ago, the area was still full of family farms and sleepy towns, evoking little interest from Chicagoans. Today, Chicagoans have woken up to the beauty of southern Michigan, and it's a coveted summer weekend destination. Wealthy Chicagoans have bought large weekend homes in southwest Michigan, especially in the towns along the lakefront. But it's definitely a welcome respite for people of all income levels. If you are traveling without children, you might want to investigate the bed & breakfast inns, gourmet dining, and shopping outlets in New Buffalo, Union Pier, and Benton Harbor. Head further north, with children in tow, for the lovely beach towns of Saugatuck and Grand Haven. Holland offers a glimpse of the early Dutch settlers—tulips in the spring, and lots of wind mills. If you like wine tours, then Paw Paw and Traverse City (five to six hours north) are possibilities too. If this is a family trip, be sure to investigate the Sleeping Bear Dunes, St. Joseph, Mackinaw Island, Warren Dunes, and South Haven. Visit www.michigan.org for more information, or contact the Southwest Michigan Tourist Council: 269-925-6301, www.swmichigan.org.

C HICAGOANS LOVE TO CELEBRATE. SO WHETHER YOU LIVE IN THE heart of town or in the suburbs, you will find many, many reasons and ways to make merry in and around Chicago. Join in as much as you can; it's a great way to acclimate yourself to your new surroundings. To start you on the right foot, we have put together the following incomplete list of feasts, fairs, and festivals, check the newspaper for more. Also, if it's a Chicago-based event, check the city link at www.cityofchicago.org or contact the **Mayor's Office of Special Events** at 312-744-3315.

JANUARY

- **Chicago Boat, Sports & RV Show**, McCormick Place
- **Chicago Cubs Convention**
- **Chicago Winter Delights**, for details and schedule of events, visit www.cityofchicago.org.
- **Ice Sculpture Festival and Ice Carving Competition**, Downers Grove, 630-434-5921
- **Monthly Skywatch Program**, Cernan Earth & Space Center, River Grove, 708-583-3100

FEBRUARY

- **African-American History Month**, Chicago Cultural Center, DuSable Museum
- **Around the Coyote Short Film & Video Festival**, 773-342-6777, www.aroundthecoyote.org
- **Chicago Winter Delights**, for details and schedule of events, visit www.cityofchicago.org.

- **Chinese New Year Festival**, Chinatown (Cermak Road and Wentworth Avenue)
- **Festival of Cinema for the Deaf**, 847-332-2464, www.cinema forthedeaf.org
- **Irish Film Festival**, 773-445-3838
- **University of Chicago Folk Festival**, Hyde Park (see **Cultural Life** for more information).
- **Winter Break Festival, Chicago Cultural Center**, 312-744-6630
- **Winter Delights Speed Skating Classic**, McFetridge Sports Center, 312-744-3315

MARCH

- **Bangladesh Parade**, Devon Avenue, 773-616-1797
- **Big Ten Conference**, www.bigten.org
- **Chicago Flower and Garden Show**, Navy Pier
- **Chicago International Documentary Film Festival**, 773-486-9612
- **Chicago Winter Delights**, for details and schedule of events, visit www.cityofchicago.org.
- **Hellenic Heritage Greek Parade**, Halsted, Randolph to Van Buren, 773-994-2222
- **Hong Kong Film Festival**, 312-846-2600
- **LaSalle Bank Shamrock Shuffle**, 8K, Grant Park, www.shamrock shuffle.com
- **Maple Syrup Harvest**, Highland Park, 847-433-6901
- **Spring Dog Show**, McCormick Place
- **St. Patrick's Day Parade**, Columbus Drive, Balbo to Monroe streets, 312-942-9188; South Side parade: Western Avenue, 103 to 113th streets, 773-239-5934
- **Touch of Green**, Daley Civic Center
- **Tunes of Glory**, Columbus Drive, Balbo to Monroe streets, www.pipefest.com
- **Winnetka Antiques Show**, Winnetka Community House

APRIL

- **Asian-American Showcase**, 312-846-2600
- **Assyrian New Year Parade**, Western Avenue, 773-743-4027, www.aanf.org
- **Cheney Mansion Antique Show**, Oak Park
- **Chicago Latino Film Festival**, 312-431-1330, www.latinocultural center.org

- **Chicago Palestine Film Festival**, www.palestinefilmfest.com
- **Hop Around the Clock**, Kids Triathlon, www.caprievents.com
- **March of Dimes Walk**, www.walkamerica.org
- **MS Walk**, www.nationalmssociety.org

MAY

- **Annual Chicago Blues Fest**, Grant Park, 312-744-3315
- **Annual Mid-South Blues Fest**, Mandrake Park, 773-924-1330
- **Asian-American Festival**, Daley Plaza
- **Belmont-Sheffield Music Festival** on Sheffield Avenue, between Belmont/Barry avenues, 773-868-3010
- **Chicago International Art Exposition**, lakefront
- **Chicago Memorial Day Parade**, State Street, Randolph to Van Buren
- **Cinco De Mayo**, Douglas Park, 773-868-3010, www.chicagoevents.com; for parade information call 773-843-9738.
- **Great Chicago Places and Spaces**, Archicenter Plaza, 224 South Michigan Avenue, 312-744-3315
- **International Theater Festival**, (various locations)
- **Lakeview Mayfest**, 3100 North Ashland Avenue, 773-665-4682
- **Mayor Daley Annual Kids and Kites Festival**, Lincoln Park
- **Polish Constitution Day Parade**, Columbus Drive, Balbo to Monroe streets, 773-282-6700
- **St. Jude Police League March**, Michigan Ave, Chicago River to Oak Street, 312-745-5900
- **Unity Carnival**, Chicago Avenue/Armour streets, www.holyinnocents chicago.org, 312-666-3675
- **Walk & Roll Chicago**, Grant Park, 312-372-0471

JUNE

- **Andersonville MidSommarfest**, 500 North Clark Street, 773-665-4682
- **Annual Arts Experience**, Plaza of the Americas, 312-751-2500
- **Annual Country Music Festival**, Grant Park, 312-744-3315
- **Back Yard Bash**, 5100 West Belmont Street, 773-665-4682
- **Bike the Drive**, Lake Shore Drive, 312-744-3315; an annual one-day event, usually held on Father's Day.
- **Bike to Work**, Daley Plaza, 312-744-3315; part of a week of events dedicated to encouraging people to bike to work/school
- **Calumet/Giles/Prairie Historical Festival**, 3100 South Calumet Avenue, 312-225-2257
- **Chicago Blues Festival**, Grant Park

- **Chicago Quarter Marathon**, Midway Plaisance, 312-347-0233
- **Gay & Lesbian Pride Parade**, Wrigleyville/Lakeview, 773-348-8243, www.chicagopridecalendar.org
- **Gospel Festival**, Grant Park, 312-744-3315
- **Heart of Italy Food & Wine Festival**, 2400 South Oakely Avenue, 773-625-0506
- **Hyde Park Art Fair**, Hyde Park
- **"I Hear Music in the Air" Outdoor Concert**, 5100 West Quincy Avenue, 312-458-9372
- **Jammin' at the Zoo**, Lincoln Park, 312-742-2283, www.lp.zoo.org
- **Jefferson Park Community Festival**, 4850-4900 West Higgins Avenue, 773-868-3010
- **Lincoln Park Festival**, Lincoln Park West between Clark/Dickens streets, 312-868-3010
- **North Center Community Festival**, Lincoln Avenue, Irving Park Road-Warner Street, 773-868-3010
- **Old Town Art Fair**, 1763 North Park Avenue, 312-337-1938, www.oldtowntriangle.com
- **Park West Antiques Fair**, 600 West Fullerton, 773-935-3751
- **Pridefest**, Halsted, Grace/Waveland streets, 773-868-3010
- **Printers Row Book Fair**, Printers Row, 312-222-3986
- **Puerto Rican Day Parade**, 773-292-1414
- **Rainbow Beach Gospel Fest**, 3111 East 77th Street, 312-458-9109
- **Run for the Zoo**, Lincoln Park Zoo, 312-742-2283
- **Shades of Riverview 8**, Lane Tech Parking Lot, 773-935-9351
- **Southport Neighbors' Children's Festival**, 1420 West Grace, 312-458-0762
- **St. Frances De Sales Carnival**, 10210 Avenue J, 773-734-1383
- **St. Josaphat Summer Fest**, 2311 North Southport Street, 773-327-8955
- **St. Matthias Family Festival**, 4910 North Claremont, 773-784-0999
- **St. Michael's Celebration**, Old Town, 312-642-2498
- **St. Pascal Festival**, St. Pascal Church, 6143 West Irving Park Road, 773-725-7641
- **St. Priscilla Summer Fun Carnival**, 6969 West Addison Street, 773-545-6157
- **Taking it to the Streets**, Marquette Park, 773-434-4626, www.imancentral.org, bi-annual event
- **Taste of Chicago**, Grant Park
- **Weed Street Summer Festival**, Weed Street from Kingsbury/Sheffield/Fremont, 773-868-3010
- **Wells Street Art Festival**, Wells Street, North/Division streets, 773-868-3010

- **WVON's Juneteenth Festival**, Mandrake Park, 773-247-6200
- **YMCA Summer Kick-Off** Festival, North and Clybourn, 773-868-3010

JULY

- **African/Caribbean International Festival for Life**, 55th Street and South Cottage Grove, 312-427-0266
- **All American 8K**, Lincoln Park, 773-404-2372
- **An Arts Adventure**, Superior Street, State to Wabash streets, 312-751-2500
- **Annual Arts & Crafts Expressions**, Canal Street, Madison/Jackson streets, 312-751-2500
- **Annual Mayor's Cup Youth Soccerfest**, Montrose/Lake Shore Drive, 312-744-3315
- **Annual Race to Taste**, 5K Run, 2 mile Walk, Columbus Drive/Balbo, 312-744-3315
- **BenFest**, Irving Park Road/Leavitt Street, 773-665-4682
- **Broken Arrow High Noon Ride**, Washington Park, 773-469-3837
- **Chicago Folk & Roots Festival**, Wells Park, 773-728-6000
- **Chicago Park District Air and Water Show**, Grant Park
- **Children's Penny Cinema Theater**, 773-947-0600
- **Civil War Weekend**, Glenview, 847-299-6096
- **DuPage County Fair**, Wheaton, 630-668-6636, www.dupagecountyfair.org
- **Fiesta del Sol**, Pilsen, 312-666-2663
- **Fourth of July Celebration**, Grant Park
- **Ghana Fest**, Washington Park
- **Health Fair**, 7400 South Michigan Avenue, 773-487-4673
- **"I Have a Vision"** Community Gospel Fest, 6700 South Dorchester Avenue, 312-861-8990
- **Illinois State Fair Preview**, Daley Plaza, 312-744-3315
- **Independence Eve Fireworks**, Grant Park
- **Jam in the Park**, 312-749-8992
- **Jammin' at the Zoo**, Lincoln Park, 312-742-2283, www.lp.zoo.org
- **K.I.D.S. Zone Festival**, 6700 Halsted Street, 773-874-4901
- **Lifeway Bastille Day**, 5K Run/walk & Block Party, Aberdeen and Jackson streets, 773-868-3010
- **NBGC Family Festival**, Irving Park Road/Rockwell Avenue, 773-463-4161
- **Newberry Library Bughouse Square Debates**, Newberry Library, 312-255-3510
- **NWC Art Fair**, Naper Settlement, Naperville, 630-420-9680

- **Outdoor Film Festival**, Grant Park (Butler Field), 312-744-3315
- **Reeling: Chicago Lesbian & Gay International Film Festival**, 773-293-1447
- **Rock around the Block**, 3200 North Lincoln Avenue, 773-665-4682
- **Run for the Kids**, Arvey Field
- **Silent Film Festival**, 773-777-9438
- **Sizzlin' Craft Faire**, Naperville, 630-355-1708
- **Tall Ships**, Navy Pier, 312-744-3315
- **Taste of Chicago** (continued), Grant Park

AUGUST

- **47th Street Mexican Independence Parade**, 773-759-1200
- **African Festival of the Arts**, Washington Park, 773-955-ARTS
- **Air and Water Show**, lakefront at Grant Park
- **Annual Arts Experience**, Plaza of Americas, 312-751-2500
- **Annual Port Clinton Art Fair**, Highland Park, 847-444-9600
- **Annual Septemberfest**, Schaumburg, 847-923-3636
- **Annual Viva Chicago Latin Music Festival**, Grant Park, 312-744-3315
- **Argyle Street Fair**, 773-769-3776
- **Augustfest**, 2651 South Central Park Avenue, 773-522-0142
- **Belize Day in the Park**, Washington Park, 773-881-0412
- **Black Harvest International Film & Video Festival**, 312-846-2600
- **Bucktown Arts Fest**, Bucktown
- **Bud Billiken Parade**, King Drive, 312-225-2400
- **Chicago Underground Film Festival**, www.cuff.org
- **Come As You Are Music Festival**, 1923 West 51st Street, 773-476-0847
- **Croatian Fest**, 2823 South Princeton Avenue, 312-842-1871
- **Englewood Back to School Day Parade**, 773-881-8363 or 773-298-8619
- **Festival De Colores**, Western Boulevard/43rd Street, 773-259-1200
- **Fiesta Boricua**, Division Street, Western Avenue/Mozart Street, 773-276-4269
- **Fiesta del Sol**, Pilsen, 312-666-2663
- **Foster Park Community Celebration**, Foster Park, 773-238-6600
- **Ginza Holiday**, Midwest Buddhist Temple, 312-943-7801
- **Gold Coast Art Fair**, 847-444-9600
- **Gran Kermes De San Roman**, 2659 West 23rd Street, 773-247-6645
- **"It's Harvest Time"** Outdoor Crusade, 6900 South Green Street, 773-602-1677

- **Jammin' at the Zoo**, Lincoln Park, 312-742-2283
- **Jazzfest, South Shore Cultural Center**, 71st Street and South Shore Drive
- **Korean Street Festival**, 3200 West Bryn Mawr, 773-583-1700
- **Lakeshore Arts Festival**, Evanston, 847-491-0266
- **Michigan Avenue Arts & Crafts Experience**, Michigan Avenue, Randolph-Monroe streets, 312-751-2500
- **North Halsted Market Days**, Halsted, Belmont/Addison, 773-868-3010
- **Retro on Roscoe**, Roscoe and Damen streets, 773-665-4682
- **Southport Art Festival**, Southport, Waveland/Grace, 773-868-3010
- **St. Procopius Kermes**, 1641 South Allport Street, 312-226-7887
- **Summer Fest West**, Garfield Park
- **Summer on Southport Festival**, 3159 North Southport Street, 773-525-2508
- **Tall Ships** (continues), Navy Pier
- **Taste of Greece**, 100 South Halsted
- **Taste of Polonia**, 5216 West Lawrence Street, 773-777-8898
- **Venetian Night**, Lakefront at Grant Park, 312-744-3315
- **Wicker Park Festival**, Damen Street, Honore/Paulina streets, 773-868-3010

SEPTEMBER

- **26th Street Mexican Independence Day Parade**, 773-521-5387
- **57th Street Children's Book Fair**, 773-324-6926
- **Annual Celtic Fest Chicago**, Grant Park, 312-744-3315
- **Around the Coyote**, Short Film & Video, 773-342-6777, www.around thecoyote.org; a film/poetry/art/dance festival
- **Chicago's Half Marathon & Kids Fest**, Museum of Science & Industry, 312-347-0233
- **Chinatown Autumn Moon Festival**, 312-326-5320
- **German-American Fest**, Lincoln Square
- **Guinness Oyster Festival**, 1515 North Halsted Street, 773-868-3010
- **Harvest Festival, Belmont/Wolcott Street**, 773-665-4682
- **Ice Cream Social & Craft Fair**, Galena, 815-492-2238
- **Jazz Festival**, Grant Park
- **Kids and Kites Festival**, Museum of Science and Industry
- **Labor Day Parade**, Dearborn and Wacker Drive
- **Mexican Independence Day Parade**, Dearborn and Wacker Drive, 312-654-5314
- **Nichiren Temple Food Fest**, Nichiren Buddhist Temple, 773-493-9872

- **Old Fashion Holiday Craft Fair**, Glenview, 847-299-6096
- **Onion City Experimental Film & Video Festival**, 773-293-1447 (each fall, month varies)
- **Park Forest Art Fair**, 708-748-3377
- **Riverwalk Art Fair**, Naperville, 630-355-2530
- **Taste of Romania**, St. Alphonsus Church
- **The Berghoff Ocktoberfest**, Adams/Dearborn streets, 312-427-3170
- **Viva! Chicago Latin Music Festival**, Grant Park
- **Von Steuben Day Parade**, 630-653-3018

OCTOBER

- **Annual Halloween Pumpkin Plaza**, Daley Plaza
- **Apple Festival-Long Grove**, Mount Prospect, 847-634-0888
- **Chicago International Children's Film Festival**, 773-281-9075, www.cicff.org
- **Chicago International Film Festival**, 312-425-9400
- **Chicago Marathon**, 312-904-9800, 888-243-3344, www.chicago marathon.com
- **Chicagoween**, 312-744-3315
- **Columbus Day Parade**, Dearborn and Wacker Drive, 708-450-9050
- **Festival of Films from Iran**, 312-846-2600
- **Honey & Harvest Festival**, Northbrook, 847-824-8360
- **Old Town Haunted House**, 226 West Schiller Street
- **St. Charles Scarecrow Festival**, 800-777-4373
- **Village Scarecrow Festival**, Barrington

NOVEMBER

- **Harvest of the Hands Art & Crafts Fair**, Naperville, 630-355-1483
- **Brach's Holiday Parade**, Michigan Avenue
- **Candlelight Christmas**, Plainfield, 815-436-5510
- **Daley Plaza Santa House**, Daley Plaza, 312-744-3315
- **Field's Jingle Elf Parade**, 312-781-5678
- **Gingerbread Fantasy Factory**, Chicago Children's Museum, 312-527-1000 (November-December)
- **Holiday Celebrations** (through December), Botanic Garden, Glencoe, 847-835-5440
- **Magnificent Mile Lights Festival**, Michigan Avenue, 312-642-3570
- **Nouveau Wine Festival**, Galena, 815-777-3330
- **Polish Film Festival in America**, 773-486-9612
- **Tree Lighting Ceremony**, Daley Plaza, 312-744-3315

- **Veteran's Day Parade**, Dearborn Street and Wacker Drive
- **Wheeling Festival of Lights**, Wheeling, 847-459-2600

DECEMBER

- **63rd Street Holiday Parade**, 773-436-1000
- **Annual Holiday Celebration in Many Lands**, Aurora
- **Annual Winter Wonderland Light Show**, Cuneo Museum, Vernon Hills, 847-367-3700
- **Buckingham Fountain Fireworks**, Columbus Drive/Congress Parkway, 312-744-3315
- **Christmas Around the World Holiday of Lights**, Museum of Science and Industry, 773-684-1414
- **Christmas Tours of Frank Lloyd Wright Home and Studio**, Oak Park
- **Dreidelmania**: **A Family Hanukkah Party**, Buffalo Grove, 847-392-7411
- **Highland Park String Concert**, Highland Park, 847-831-3810
- **Holiday Science Workshops**, Sci-Tech Museum, Aurora, 630-859-3434
- **Julmark nad** (**Christmasfest**), Swedish American Museum Center
- **Kiddie New Year**, Shedd Aquarium
- **Lamb's Farm Holiday Arts & Crafts Show**, Rosemont
- **Long Grove Countryside Christmas**, Long Grove, 847-634-0888
- **Mayor Daley's Annual Holiday Sports Festival**, 312-744-3315
- **New French Cinema Film Festival**, 773-281-9075
- **New Year's Eve at the Pier**, Navy Pier, 312-595-7437
- **Peaceable Kingdom**, Field Museum, 312-665-7400
- **Star of Wonder Sky Show**, Adler Planetarium, 312-922-STAR
- **Toys for Tots Motorcycle Parade**, 773-866-8697

OOKSTORES AND LIBRARIES THROUGHOUT CHICAGO OFFER
hundreds of titles about the Windy City. Here are just a few that may
be of interest.

ARCHITECTURE

- ***Chicago Architecture and Design***, George A. Larson and Jay Pridmore (Harry N. Abrams)
- ***Chicago Bungalow***, Dominic A. Pacyga and Charles Shanabruch, co-editors (Arcadia)
- ***Chicago**: A Guide to Recent Architecture*, Susanna Sirefman (Konemann)
- ***The Sky's the Limit**: A Century of Chicago's Skyscrapers*, Pauline Saliga (Rizzoli)
- ***Unexpected Chicago***, Camilo Jose Vergara (New Press)
- ***A View from the River**: Chicago Architecture Foundation's River Cruise*, text by Jay Pridmore (Pomegranate Communications)

FICTION

- ***A Long Way From Chicago**: A Novel in Stories*, Richard Peck (Puffin Books)
- ***Devil in the White City**: Murder, Magic and Madness at the Fair that Changed America*, Erik Larson (Crown Publishers)
- ***House on Mango Street***, Sandra Cisneros (Vintage Contemporaries)
- ***Hunter and the Hunted**: The Ed & Am Hunter Novels*, Frederic Brown (Stewart Masters Publishing)
- ***Indemnity Only***, Sara Paretsky (Dell Books)
- ***The House of Seven Mable***, Jill Churchill (Avon Books)
- ***The Law Review***, S. Scott Gaille (Creative Art Books)

GETAWAYS

- *52 Adventures in Chicago*, Lynn Gordon (Chronicle Books)
- *Chicago Bicycle Guidebook Great Bicycle Riding Through Chicago's Lakefront Neighborhoods*, Michael Palucki (Pastime Publications)
- *Country Walks Near Chicago*, Alan Hall Fisher (Rambler Books)
- *Kids Explore Chicago: The Very Best Kids' Activities within an Easy Drive of Chicago*, Susan Moffat (Adams Media Corp.)
- *Kids in the Loop: Chicago Adventures for Kids and their Grownups*, Ann Basye (Independent Publishers Group)
- *Off the Beaten Path Chicago*, Cliff Terry (Globe Pequot)
- *Quick Escapes Chicago*, Bonnie Miller Rubin (Globe Pequot)
- *Somewhere Over the Dan Ryan: Day and Weekend Outings for Chicago-area Families*, Joanne Y. Cleaver (Chicago Review Press)
- *Visiting the Midwest's Historic Preservation Sites*, Majorie Grannis (Jameson Books)
- *Weekend Getaway Guide:160 Trips to take Within 200 Miles of Chicago*, Mike Michaelson (Rand McNally)

HISTORICAL

- *Chicago: Then & Now*, Elizabeth McNulty (Thunder Bay Press)
- *How Clout and Community Built Dearborn Park*, Lois Wille (Southern Illinois University Press)
- *Chicago Death Trap: The Iroquois Theatre Fire of 1903*, Nat Brandt (Southern Illinois University Press)
- *Jewish Chicago: A Pictorial History*, Irving Cutler (Arcadia)
- *Lost Chicago*, David Garrad Lowe (Watson-Guptill Publications)
- *Nature's Metropolis: Chicago and the Great West*, William Cronon (W.W. Norton & Co.)
- *Prairie Passage: The Illinois & Michigan Canal Corridor*, Edward Ranney (University of Illinois Press)
- *The Great Fire*, Jim Murphy (Scholastic, Inc.)
- *To Sleep with the Angels: The Story of a Fire*, David Cowan (Ivan R. Dee, Inc.)

REGIONAL NONFICTION

- *Chicago Home Book*, (Ashley Group)
- *Chicago Tribune Sunday Crossword Puzzles*, Wayne Robert Williams (Random House)

- **Eight Men Out: The Black Sox and the 1919 World Series**, Eliot Asino and Stephen J. Gould (Henry Holt)
- **Father Mac: The Life & Times of Father Ignatius D. McDermott, Co-founder of Chicago's Famed Haymarket Center**, Thomas Roeser (The McDermott Foundation)
- **Great Chicago Stories**, Tom Maday and Sam Landers (Twopress Publishing Co.)
- **Our Chicago: Life & Death on the South Side of Chicago**, Lealan Jones, Lloyd Newman, David Isay (Washington Square Press)
- **Return to the Scene of the Crime: A Guide to Infamous Places in Chicago**, Richard Lindberg (Cumberland House)
- **The Complete Chicago Cubs: The Total Encyclopedia of the Team**, Derek Gentile (Black Dog & Leventhal)
- **The Franklin Report: Chicago, An Insider's Guide to Home Services**, Elizabeth Franklin (Allgood Press)
- **The Gangs of Chicago: An Informal History of the Chicago Underworld**, Herbert Asbury (Thunder's Mouth Press)
- **True Stories from Chicago's Jewish History**, Walter Roth (Academy Chicago Publishers)
- **White Sox Encyclopedia**, Richard Lindberg, Mark Fletcher (Temple University Press)
- **Wrigley Field: A Celebration of the Friendly Confines**, Mark Jacob (McGraw Hill)
- **Zagat Chicago Restaurants** (Zagat Survey)

WALKING TOURS

- **Chicago In and Around the Loop, Walking Tours of Architecture and History**, Gerard R. Wolfe (McGraw-Hill Professional)
- **Chicago Street Guide to the Supernatural**, Richard T. Crowe (Carolanda Press)
- **A Guide to Chicago's Murals**, Mary Lackritz Gray (University of Chicago Press)
- **A Guide to Oak Park's Frank Lloyd Wright and Prairie School Historic District**, Molly Wickes (University of Chicago Press)
- **A Walk Through Graceland Cemetery**, Barbara Lanctot (Chicago Architecture Foundation)

ANIMALS

Area shelters, humane societies, and emergency animal clinics:
- **Abbott Animal Hospital**, 6721 West Archer Avenue, 773-788-9000
- **Anti-Cruelty Society**, 510 North LaSalle, 312-644-8338, www.anti-cruelty.org
- **Chicago Exotics Animal Hospital** (all animals), 3735 West Dempster, Skokie, 847-329-8709, www.exoticpetvet.com
- **City Animal Control**, 312-747-1406, www.ci.chi.il.us/AnimalCareControl
- **Cook County Department of Animal Control**, 708-974-6140, www.co.cook.il.us
- **Dead Animal Removal**, dial 311
- **Dog License** (City Clerk), 312-745-1100, www.chicityclerk.com
- **Dupage County Animal Control**, www.co.dupage.il.us, 630-682-7197
- **Hyde Park Vet House Calls**, 9333 South Escanaba Avenue, 773-538-4880
- **Lake Shore Animal Shelter**, 312-409-1162, www.lakeshoreanimalshelter.org
- **South Suburban Humane Society**, 1103 West End Avenue, Chicago Heights, 708-755-7387, www.sshpets.org
- **West Suburban Humane Society**, 1901 West Ogden Avenue, Downers Grove, 630-960-9600, www.wshs-dg.org

AUTOMOBILES

- **Abandoned vehicle removal**, dial 311
- **Automotive Repair Bureau**, Department of Consumer Services, 312-744-4006

- **American Automobile Association (AAA)**, 800-AAA-HELP, www. aaa.com
- **State Department of Motor Vehicles**, Licenses and Registration, www.sos.state.il.us
- **Tow lots**: first call 311 to find out where your car was towed. City tow lots: 400 East Wacker Drive; O'Hare Airport/Remote Lot E; 103rd Street and Doty Avenue; 701 North Sacramento Avenue.
- **Traffic Court**, Daley Center, Parking Ticket Inquiries, 312-744-PARK (7275), www.cookcountyclerkofcourt.org

CHAMBERS OF COMMERCE

- **Chicago Southland Chamber of Commerce**, 708-957-6950, www. chicagosouthland.com
- **Chicagoland Chamber of Commerce**, 312- 494-6700, www. chicagolandchamber.org
- **Cosmopolitan Chamber of Commerce**, 312-786-0212, www. cchamber.org
- **East Side Chamber of Commerce**, 773-721-7948
- **Edgebrook-Sauganash Chamber of Commerce**, 773-775-0378
- **Edison Park Chamber of Commerce**, 773-631-0063, www.edison park.com
- **Hyde Park Chamber of Commerce**, 773-288-0124, www.hpcham-ber.com
- **Illinois State Chamber of Commerce**, 312-983-7100, www.ilcham-ber.org
- **Jefferson Park Chamber of Commerce**, 773-736-6697, www.jef-fersonpark.net
- **Lake View East Chamber of Commerce**, 773-348-8608, www.lake-vieweast.com
- **Lincoln Park Chamber of Commerce**, 773-880-5200, www.lincoln parkchamber.com
- **Portage Park Chamber of Commerce**, 773-777-2020
- **Uptown Chamber of Commerce**, 773-878-1184, www.uptown chamber.com
- **West Chicago Chamber of Commerce & Industry**, 630-231-3003, www.wegochamber.org

CONSUMER COMPLAINTS AND SERVICES

- **Attorney General Consumer Fraud Division**, 800-386-5438 (Illinois only), 312-603-8700, www.ag.state.il.us

- **Better Business Bureau**, 312-832-0500, www.chicago.bbb.org
- **Chicago Bar Association**, 312-554-2000, www.chicagobar.org
- **City Ethics Board**, 312-744-9660
- **Consumer Affairs Department**, Chicago, 312-744-9400, TTY 312-744-9385
- **Consumer Protection Division** (Attorney Generals' Office), 800-386-5438, www.ag.state.il.us
- **Consumer Product Safety Commission**, 800-638-2772
- **County Ethics Board**, 312-603-4304
- **Department of Consumer Services**, Chicago, 312-744-4006, complaint hotline 312-744-9400, TTY 312-744-9385, www.ci.chi.il.us/ConsumerServices
- **Federal Trade Commission**, 877- 382-4357
- **Insurance Commissioner**, 312-814-2427
- **Office of Consumer Health Insurance**, 877-527-9431
- **US Consumer Product Safety Commission**, 800-638-2772, www.cpsc.gov

CRISIS HOTLINES

ALCOHOL & DRUG DEPENDENCY
- **Adolescent Addiction Programs**, 800-522-3784, 800-373-1700 (Illinois only)
- **Alcohol and Drug Hotline**, 800-ALCOHOL
- **Alcoholics Anonymous**, 312-346-1475
- **Narcotics Anonymous**, 708-848-4884, www.chicago.na.org
- **Substance Abuse Hotline**, 800-821-4357
- **Substance Abuse Services**, Chicago/Central Intake/Westside: 800-962-1126; Central Intake/Northside: 773-878-9999

CHILD ABUSE & FAMILY VIOLENCE
- **Abducted, Abused, and Exploited Children**, 800-248-8020
- **Boys Town National Hotline**, 800-448-3000
- **Child Abuse Hotline**, 800-422-4453, 800-252-2873
- **Childhelp USA**, 800-422-4453
- **Child Social Service Agency/Protective Services Hotline**, 800-232-3798 (Illinois only)
- **National Domestic Violence Hotline**, 800-799-7233
- **Rape Crisis Hotline**, 888-293-2080
- **Suicide Prevention Hotline**, 312-647-4357 (elderly), 800-SUICIDE
- **Youth Crisis Hotline**, 800-232-3798 (Illinois only)

CRIME
- **Chicago Alternative Policing Strategy (CAPS)**; local anti-crime/ neighborhood watch program. There are over 279 police beats participating in CAPS in Chicago. To find CAPS information about your area, visit the CAPS web site at www.ci.chi.il.us/CommunityPolicing
- **Crime in progress**, 911
- **Fraud reporting line**, 800-386-5438 (Illinois only)

DISCRIMINATION
- **City/County Human Rights/Human Relations Offices**, Chicago, 312-744-4111 or 312-814-6200, TTY 312-744-1088
- **Cook County Department of Human Rights**, 312-603-1100, www.co.cook.il.us
- **Discrimination in Housing**, 800-662-3942
- **Fair Employment and Housing Department**, 312-814-6200, www.state.il.us/dhr
- **State Commission on Human Rights**, 312-814-6269, www.state. il.us/ihrc
- **US Department of Fair Housing & Discrimination hotline**, 800-424-8590
- **Women's Commission**, 312-814-2121

ELECTED OFFICIALS/GOVERNMENT

CITY OF CHICAGO
- **City Council**, 312-744-0403
- **City Hall: Office of the Mayor**, 312-744-3300
- **City Ward Information**. available at www.chicityclerk.com

COOK COUNTY
- **Cook County home page**: www.co.cook.il.us
- **Cook County Board of Commissioners**, 312-603-6398
- **Cook County Clerk**, 312-603-5656, or 847-818-2850 (northwest suburbs)
- **Clerk of the Circuit Court**; contact the Circuit Court regarding the following: child support/protection, domestic relations, traffic, probate, juvenile justice, criminal, civil, county division issues: www.cookcounty clerkofcourt.org or 312-603-5030.
- **Cook County Recorder of Deeds**, 312-603-5050, www.co.cook.il.us

DUPAGE COUNTY
- **DuPage County Board**, 630-682-7282, www.co.dupage.il.us; many services can be found through the web site, including the following:

County Clerk, Coroner, Sheriff, County State Attorney, Auditor and Clerk of the Circuit Court.
- **County Clerk**, www.co.dupage.il.us/countyclerk, 630-682-7035

LAKE COUNTY
- **Lake County Home Page**, www.co.lake.il.us; provides links to many government services.

MCHENRY COUNTY
- **County Home Page**, www.co.mchenry.il.us, provides links to many county departments
- **Circuit Clerk**, 815-334-4310
- **County Clerk**, 815-334-4242
- **County Recorder**, 815-334-4110
- **Health Department**, 815-334-4510
- **State's Attorney**, 815-334-4159
- **Mental Health**, 815-455-2828
- **Sheriff**, 815-338-2144

STATE OF ILLINOIS
- **Governor's Office**, 217-782-0244, TTY 888-261-3336, www.state.il.us/gov
- **Illinois State Board of Elections**, www.elections.state.il.us
- **Secretary of State**, 800-252-8980, www.sos.state.il.us
- **State Senate**: Senate President Emil Jones, 217-782-2728; Frank Watson, Senate Minority Leader, 217-782-5755. To view a state senator's links, records and contact information, go to www.legis.state.il.us/senate
- **State Assembly**, Speaker of the House: Michael Madigan, 217-782-5350; Minority Leader, Tom Cross, 217- 782-1331. Visit General Assembly web site at www.legis.state.il.us for information on these assemblymen or any others representing Illinois.
- **State of Illinois web site**: www.illinois.gov
- **US House of Representatives**; Illinois has 19 Congressman in the House of Representatives. Some from the Chicagoland area include: Henry Hyde, Bobby Rush, Luis Gutierrez, and Jesse Jackson, Jr. The main number for the House of Representatives is 202-224-3121, or go to www.house.gov.
- **US Senate**: US Senator Richard Durbin, 202-224-2152, www.durbin.senate.gov; US Senator Peter Fitzgerald, 202-224-2854 or 312-886-3506, www.fitzgerald.senate.gov
- **www.finditillinois.org**, provides links to state government, public libraries, public safety, natural resources.
- **www.statelocalgov.net**, provides links to state government, including all state departments.

EMERGENCY

- **Fire, Police, Medical**, 911
- **FEMA Disaster Assistance Information**, 800-621-FEMA (3362), www.fema.gov

ENTERTAINMENT

Also see **Cultural Life**.

- **City Cultural Affairs Department**, visitor information, 312-744-2400, www.cityofchicago.org/CulturalAffairs
- **Chicago Dance and Music Alliance Hotline**, 312-987-1123, www.chicagoperformances.org
- **Chicago Fine Arts Hotline**, 312-346-3278
- **Concert Line**, 312-666-6667, for rock, country, blues
- **Lincoln Park Hotline**, 312-742-2283
- **Music & Theatre Hotline**, www.metromix.com, or www.ctcts.com
- **Hot Tix** (discount day-of-the-show tickets), www.hottix.org
- **Ticketmaster**, 312-559-1212, 312-902-1500, 312-902-1400, www.ticketmaster.com
- **Mayor's Office of Special Events Hotline**, 312-744-3370, 312-744-3315 or visit www.ci.chi.il.us/SpecialEvents
- **Newspaper entertainment listings**: www.chicagotribune.com, www.dailyherald.com, www.dailysouthtown.com, www.chicago reporter.com

FEDERAL OFFICES/CENTERS

- **Federal Citizen Information Center**, 800-FED-INFO, www.pueblo.gsa.gov, or www.info.gov
- **SSA**, 800-772-1213, TTY 800-325-0778 (both 7 a.m. to 7 p.m., Monday-Friday), www.ssa.gov

HEALTH AND MEDICAL CARE

- **AIDS/STD/TB Hotline**, 800-458-5231
- **Chicago Department of Public Health**, 312-747-9884; care van, 312-746-6122
- **Doctor referral lines**; pediatric doctors: www.childrensmemorial.org/findadoc; adults: www.chicagodrs.com. Or call your area hospital and ask for a referral for a specific specialty.

- **DuPage County Health Department**, 630-682-7400
- **HIV Testing**, 312-747-0184
- **Illinois Department of Public Health**, 217-782-4977, www.idph. state.il.us
- **Illinois Poison Control Center**, 800-222-1222, www.mchc.org/ipc
- **Kane County Health Department**, 630-208-3801
- **Lake County Board of Health**, 847-377-8000
- **National Health Information Center**, US Department of Health and Human Services, 800-336-4797, www.os.dhhs.gov
- **Nursing Home Information and Referral**, 800-252-8966 (Illinois only)
- **Office of Consumer Health Insurance**, 877-527-9431
- **Public Health Center**, 312-747-0184
- **Smokers Help-lines**: Illinois, 800-784-8937, National, 877-44U-QUIT, www.smokefree.gov

HOUSING

- **Chicago's Heat Hotline**, 312-744-5000
- **Chicago Department of Housing**, 312-747-9000, www.cityof chicago.org/housing
- **Chicago Rents Rights Hotline**, 312-742-RENT
- **Chicago Urban League**, 4510 South Michigan Avenue, 773-285-5800
- **Fair Housing and Equal Opportunity**, Chicago, 312-747-9000
- **Fair Housing Information Clearinghouse**, 800-343-3442, www.hud.gov/progdesc/fhip.cfm
- **Illinois Tenants Union**, 4616 North Drake Avenue, 773-478-1133, www.tenant.org
- **Landlord and Tenant Fact Sheet from the Office of the Attorney General**, www.ag.state.il.us
- **Lawyers' Committee for Better Housing** (Edgewater and Rogers Park), 312-347-7600
- **Legal Assistance Foundation of Chicago**, 312-341-1070, www. lafchicago.org
- **Metropolitan Tenants Organization**, 773-292-4988, www.tenants-right.org
- **Rogers Park Community Action Network (RPCAN)**, 1545 West Morse, 773-973-7888
- **US Department of Fair Housing and Discrimination**, 800-477-5977, www.fairhousing.com

LEGAL REFERRAL

- **American Civil Liberties Union**, 312-201-9740, www.aclu-il.org
- **Legal Assistance Foundation of Chicago**, 312-341-1070, www.lafchicago.org
- **Public Defender Information Line**, 312-603-0600

LIBRARIES

For the local branch of your public library, check your community's resources, which follow each **Neighborhood Profile**. Also see **Literary Life** in the **Cultural Life** chapter.
- **Arlington Heights Memorial Library**, 500 North Dunton Avenue, 847-392-0100, www.ahml.info
- **Des Plaines Library**, 1501 Ellinwood Street, 847-827-5551, www.dppl.org
- **Harold Washington Center**, 400 South State Street, 312-747-4396, www.chipublib.org
- **Naperville Library**, 200 West Jefferson Street, 630-961-4100, www.naperville-lib.org
- **Suburban Library System**, www.sls.lib.il.us, provides a list of over 600 suburban libraries and phone numbers.

PARKING

- **Booted vehicles**, dial 311
- **City Clerk's Permit Sales Unit for residential parking permits**, 312-744-6774, www.chicityclerk.com
- **City Clerks' Offices** (city stickers), 312-744-6861, TTY 312-744-2939
- **Parking and Compliance Violation Center**, 312-744-PARK (7275)
- **Pay your ticket online**, www.cityofchicago.org
- **Ticket Inquiries**, 312-744-7275
- **Traffic Court**, 312-603-2000

PARKS AND RECREATION DEPARTMENTS

Refer to listings in the **Neighborhood Profiles, Sports and Recreation**, or **Greenspace and Beaches** chapters.

POLICE

Check the **Neighborhood Profiles** for branch stations.
- **Police Emergencies**, dial 911
- **Cook County Sheriff Department**, 708-865-4700
- **Illinois State Police**, Des Plaines, 847-294-4400, www.isp.state.il.us
- **Non-emergency Chicago City Police Department**, dial 311

POST OFFICE

Refer to the **Neighborhood Profiles** for post offices in your area.
- **US Postal Service**, 800-275-8777, www.usps.com

SANITATION AND GARBAGE

- **Blue Bag Recycling**, www.cityofchicago.org/Environment, 312-744-1614
- **Chicago Department of Streets and Sanitation**, www.cityof chicago.org/StreetsAndSan/Sanitation/WardOffices
- **Department of Environment**, 312-744-7606
- **Recycling hotlines and general information**, 312-744-1614
- **Resource Center**, 773-821-1351
- **Uptown Recycling**, 773-769-5579

SCHOOLS

Check the community resources listings following the **Neighborhood Profiles** chapter for your local school office or check the **Childcare and Education** chapter.
- **Chicago Public Schools Superintendent**, 312-814-2220
- **Chicago Board of Education**, 773-553-1000
- **General information** web site for Chicago Public Schools, www.cps.k12.il.us

SENIORS

- **Aging Assistance Information and Referral**, 312-744-4016
- **American Association of Retired Persons** (**AARP**), 312-458-3600
- **Elder Abuse Hotline**, 800-252-8966 (Illinois only)
- **National Council on Aging**, 202-479-1200
- **Senior Citizen Counseling**, 312-744-4016

- **Social Security and Medicare Eligibility Information**, 800-772-1213, www.ssa.gov

SHIPPING SERVICES

- **Airborne Express**, 800-247-2676, www.airborne.com
- **DHL Worldwide Express**, 800-225-5345, www.dhl-usa.com
- **FedEx**, 800-463-3339, www.fedex.com (for ground, express or air freight information)
- **Mail-Sort**, (Northbrook), 847-291-4900
- **Packaging Store**, 312-751-1640, 773-313-1640, 847-350-0500, www.gonavis.com
- **Pitney Bowes**, 800-811-1920
- **United Parcel Service** (**UPS**), 800-742-5877, www.ups.com
- **US Postal Service Express Mail**, www.usps.com

SPORTS

See **Sports and Recreation** chapter for full coverage of area teams.
- **Chicago Bears**, 847-615-2327, www.chicagobears.com
- **Chicago Blackhawks**, 312-455-7000, www.chicagoblackhawks.com
- **Chicago Bulls**, 312-455-4000, www.nba.com/bulls, www.bulls.com
- **Chicago Cubs**, 773-404-CUBS, http://chicago.cubs.mlb.com
- **Chicago White Sox**, 312-674-1000, http://chicago.whitesox.mlb.com
- **Professional/college teams** general information at www.ci.chi.il.us/Tourism
- **Schedules and Scores**: www.geocities.com/colosseum/bleachers/7965/sportslinkCHI
- **United Center**, 312-455-4000, www.unitedcenter.com

STREET MAINTENANCE

- **Commissioner's Office**, 311
- **Department of Transportation**, 312-744-3600
- **Inspection Offices**: check for the Ward Superintendent in your community at www.ci.chi.il.us/StreetsAndSan/Sanitation/WardOffices
- **Street cleaning and snow removal**, 312-745-1230
- **Traffic signals**, **sign repair**, etc., 311

TAXES

FEDERAL
- **Internal Revenue Service**, 312-566-4912, www.irs.gov

STATE OF ILLINOIS
- **State Department of Revenue**, 800-732-8866, www.revenue.state.il.us
- **State Franchise Tax Board**, 800-732-8866

COOK COUNTY
- **Cook County Assessor**, 312-443-7550, www.cookcountyassessor.com
- **Property/Real Estate Tax**, 312-603-5649

CITY OF CHICAGO
- **Chicago**: **City Comptroller's Office**, 312-744-7100, www.city-ofchicago.org
- **Department of Revenue**, 312-747-4747, www.cityofchicago.org

TOURISM AND TRAVEL

- **City Visitor Information Hotline**, 877-CHICAGO, TTY 866-710-0294, www.ci.chi.il.us/Tourism
- **Chicago Convention and Tourism Bureau**, 877-244-2246, www.chicago.il.org
- **Cook County Forest Preserve**, 800-870-3666, www.fpdcc.com
- **Illinois State Travel Information Line**, 800-2-CONNECT
- **Indiana Department of Tourism**, 888-Enjoy-IN, www.in.gov/enjoyindiana
- **International Assoc. for Medical Assistance to Travelers**, 716-754-4883
- **Michigan Department of Tourism**, 888-784-7328, www.michigan.org
- **Southwest Michigan Tourist Council**, 269-925-6301, www.swmichigan.org
- **US National Park Service Information**, Midwest Regional Office, 402-221-3471, www.nps.gov
- **Wisconsin Department of Tourism**, 800-432-8747, www.travel-wisconsin.com

TRANSPORTATION

AIRPORTS
- **O'Hare International Airport**, 800-832-6352, www.ohare.com
- **Midway Airport**, 773-838-0600, www.ohare.com/midway
- **Gary/Chicago Airport**, 219-949-9722
- **Palwaukee Municipal Airport** in Wheeling, 847-537-2580, www.palwaukee.org (non-commercial)
- **Schaumburg Regional Airport**, 847-895-0315 (non-commercial)

CITY OF CHICAGO PUBLIC TRANSPORTATION
- **CTA**, 888-YOUR-CTA, www.chicagotranist.com
- **RTA**, 312-836-7000, www.rtachicago.com

NATIONAL/REGIONAL TRAIN AND BUS SERVICE
- **Amtrak**, 800-USA-RAIL, www.amtrak.com
- **Greyhound Bus**, Chicago stations: 630 West Harrison, 312-408-5800; 14 West 95th Street, 312-408-5999; CTA Transit Building, 5800 Cumberland Avenue, 773-693-2474, www.greyhound.com
- **I-GO**, 773-278-4800 ext. 227, www.i-go-cars.org
- **Metropolitan Rail (Metra)**: Union Station, 312-322-4269; Union Pacific Station, 312-496-4777; Metra Electric (Randolph Street Station), 312-322-7819; South Shore Line, 312-782-0676
- **PACE Suburban Bus Service**, 847-364-7223, www.pacebus.com
- **Regional Transportation Authority (RTA)**, 312-836-7000, www.rtachicago.com

WATER TAXI SERVICE
- **Shoreline Taxis**, 312-222-9328
- **Wendella Riverbus**, 312-337-1446, www.wendellaboats.com

UTILITY EMERGENCIES

- **ComEd Electric**—wires down or other electrical emergencies, 800-334-7661
- **Gas leaks**, NICOR, 888-642-6748, www.nicor.com
- **Sewers/water main leaks**, 311
- **Telephone repair service**, SBC, 800-244-4444 (in state); 800-432-0015 (to report repairs out of state)

VITAL RECORDS

- **Office of the Cook County Clerk**, Division of Vital Records, www.cookctyclerk.com: 118 **North Clark** (lower concourse), Chicago, 312-603-6623; 312-603-7799 to order and pay for records by credit card
- **Rolling Meadows Courthouse**, 2121 Euclid Avenue, Rolling Meadows, 847-818-2850
- **State Department of Vital Records** (Illinois Department of Public Health), www.idph.state.il.us, 217-782-4977, TTY 800-547-0466

WEATHER

- **National Weather Service**, www.nws.noaa.gov
- **The Weather Channel**, www.weather.com
- **Weather Underground**: www.wunderground.com/US/IL/ Chicago.html; this link is connected to the State of Illinois page, www.illinois.gov.
- **Weatherpages**: www.weatherpages.com

ZIP CODE INFORMATION

- **USPS Zip Code information**, 800-275-8777, www.usps.com

READER RESPONSE FORM

We would appreciate your comments regarding this fourth edition of the *Newcomer's Handbook®* for *Moving to and Living in Chicago*. If you've found any mistakes or omissions or if you would just like to express your opinion about the guide, please let us know. We will consider any suggestions for possible inclusion in our next edition, and if we use your comments, we'll send you a *free* copy of our next edition. Please send this response form to:

Reader Response Department
First Books
6750 SW Franklin, Suite A
Portland, OR 97223 USA

Comments:

_____

_____

_____

_____

_____

_____

_____

Name: _____

Address _____

_____

Telephone (_____) _____

E-mail _____

6750 SW Franklin, Suite A
Portland, OR 97223
503-968-6777
www.firstbooks.com

FIRST BOOKS®

NEWCOMER'S HANDBOOK

ORDER FORM

THE ORIGINAL, ALWAYS UPDATED, ABSOLUTELY INVALUABLE GUIDES FOR PEOPLE MOVING TO A CITY!

Find out about neigborhoods, apartment and house hunting, money matters, deposits/leases, getting settled, helpful services, shopping for the home, places of worship, cultural life, sports/recreation, volunteering, green space, schools and education, transportation, temporary lodgings and useful telephone numbers!

	# COPIES	TOTAL
Newcomer's Handbook® for Atlanta	_____ x $17.95	$_____
Newcomer's Handbook® for Boston	_____ x $21.95	$_____
Newcomer's Handbook® for Chicago	_____ x $21.95	$_____
Newcomer's Handbook® for London	_____ x $20.95	$_____
Newcomer's Handbook® for Los Angeles	_____ x $17.95	$_____
Newcomer's Handbook® for Minneapolis-St. Paul	_____ x $20.95	$_____
Newcomer's Handbook® for New York City	_____ x $20.95	$_____
Newcomer's Handbook® for San Francisco	_____ x $20.95	$_____
Newcomer's Handbook® for Seattle	_____ x $21.95	$_____
Newcomer's Handbook® for Washington D.C.	_____ x $21.95	$_____
	SUBTOTAL	$_____
POSTAGE & HANDLING (*$7.00 first book, $1.00 each add'l.*)		$_____
	TOTAL	$_____

SHIP TO:

Name _____

Title _____

Company _____

Address _____

City _____ State _____ Zip _____

Phone Number (_____) _____

E-mail _____

FIRST BOOKS®

Send this order form and a check or money order payable to:
First Books

First Books, Mail Order Department
6750 SW Franklin, Suite A, Portland, OR 97223
Allow 1-2 weeks for delivery

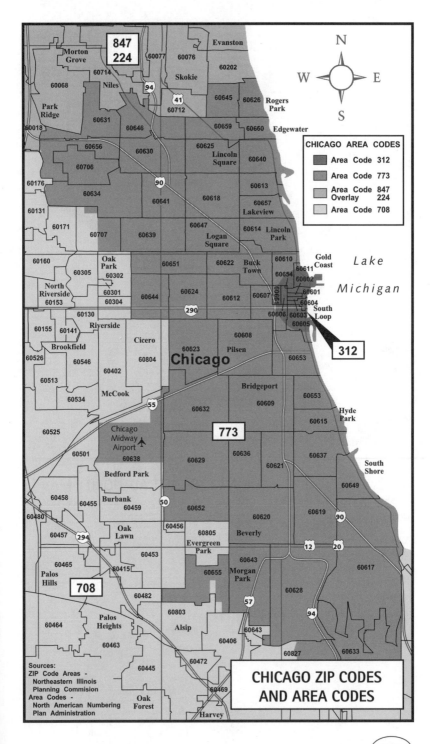

CHICAGO ZIP CODES
AND AREA CODES

CHICAGO AREA CODES

- Area Code 312
- Area Code 773
- Area Code 847 Overlay 224
- Area Code 708

Sources:
ZIP Code Areas -
Northeastern Illinois
Planning Commsion
Area Codes -
North American Numbering
Plan Administration

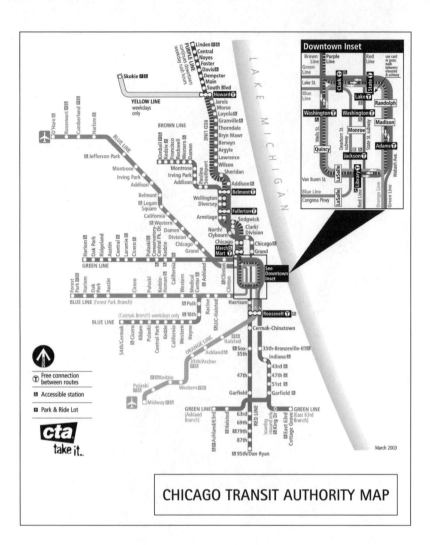

CHICAGO TRANSIT AUTHORITY MAP